Ben Forta

Sue Hove

SAMS
Teach Yourself

ColdFusion™
Express
in 24 Hours

SAMS

201 West 103rd St., Indianapolis, Indiana, 46290 USA

Sams Teach Yourself ColdFusion™ Express in 24 Hours

Copyright © 2001 by Sams Publishing

International Standard Book Number: 0-672-31662-5

Library of Congress Catalog Card Number: 99-61498

Printed in the United States of America

First Printing: December 2000

02 01 00   4   3   2   1

Trademarks

All terms mentioned in this book that are known to be trademarks or service marks have been appropriately capitalized. Sams Publishing cannot attest to the accuracy of this information. Use of a term in this book should not be regarded as affecting the validity of any trademark or service mark.

ColdFusion and HomeSite are U.S. Registered trademarks of Allaire Corporation.

Warning and Disclaimer

ACQUISITIONS EDITOR
Sharon Cox

EXECUTIVE EDITOR
Rosemarie Graham

DEVELOPMENT EDITOR
Kevin Howard

MANAGING EDITOR
Charlotte Clapp

PROJECT EDITOR
Elizabeth Roberts

COPY EDITOR
Rhonda Tinch-Mize

INDEXER
Deborah Hittel
Sheila Schroeder

PROOFREADERS
Jill Mazurczyk
Katherin Bidwell

TECHNICAL EDITORS
Emily Kim
Jo Stafford
Brian Brames

TEAM COORDINATOR
Meggo Barthlow
Pamalee Nelson

MEDIA DEVELOPER
Todd Pfeffer

INTERIOR DESIGNER
Gary Adair

COVER DESIGNER
Aren Howell

COPYWRITER
Eric Borgert

Contents at a Glance

Contents

About the Authors

BEN FORTA is Allaire Corporation's Product Evangelist for the ColdFusion product line. He has more than 15 years of experience in the computer industry in product development, support, training, and product marketing. Ben is the author of the best-selling *ColdFusion Web Application Construction Kit* (now in its third edition), and its sequel *Advanced ColdFusion 4 Development* (both published by Que), as well as *Sams Teach Yourself HomeSite 4 in 24 Hours*, *Sams Teach Yourself SQL in 10 Minutes*, and *Allaire Spectra E-Business Construction Kit*. He recently released books on WAP and JSP, and is now working on a study guide for the Allaire Certified ColdFusion Developer program. Ben coauthored the official Allaire ColdFusion training courses, writes regular columns on ColdFusion and Internet development, and now spends a considerable amount of time lecturing and speaking on ColdFusion and Internet application development worldwide. Born in London, England, and educated in London, New York, and Los Angeles, Ben now lives in Oak Park, Michigan with his wife Marcy and their six children. Ben welcomes your email at ben@forta.com, and invites you to visit his Web site at http://www.forta.com.

SUE HOVE is Allaire Corporation's Instructor Readiness Manager for the Training department. She has more than 15 years of experience in the computer industry in application design and programming, relational databases and training, and has applied her applications development and training expertise for software vendors such as Informix, Powersoft/Sybase, and Allaire. Sue is a highly qualified and much sought after instructor, and for the last three years has been shaping Allaire's ColdFusion curriculum by writing and delivering their training course offerings and certifying other instructors to teach their courses worldwide. Sue now lives in Cambridge, Massachusetts, and welcomes your email at shove@allaire.com.

Acknowledgements

First of all, I must thank all of you who have been clamoring for an entry-level ColdFusion book. I hope this is what you were looking for.

Thanks to my coauthor, Sue Hove, who split the writing of this book with me. I could never have done it myself, and being able to rely on an author as professional and as thorough as Sue makes coauthoring a pleasure. I look forward to our next collaboration, Sue.

Thanks to everyone at Macmillan who helped out on this book. And a very special thank you to my Acquisitions Editor, Sharon Cox, for putting up with me and my usually impossible schedule. Next time will be easier Sharon, I promise.

Thanks to my Technical Editors (and occasional critics), Emily Kim and Jo Norman, for keeping us authors on our toes.

And finally, thank you to my wonderful wife Marcy for the motivation to keep pushing myself on to new projects. I would not be where I am today without her.

—Ben

I'd like to thank Maria Morrissey for being a mentor in life and work, and Shawn Morrissey for being an inspiration. Special thanks goes to Carolyn Lightner for letting me stretch, and Robert Crooks for stretching, painfully, with me. Sharon, Elf, and Kevin were always there to answer my newbie-writer questions, and I thank them for that. This whole thing was possible through a kosher Chinese restaurant and the grace of Ben Forta.

—Sue

Tell Us What You Think!

As the reader of this book, *you* are our most important critic and commentator. We value your opinion and want to know what we're doing right, what we could do better, what areas you'd like to see us publish in, and any other words of wisdom you're willing to pass our way.

As an Executive Editor for Sams, I welcome your comments. You can fax, email, or write me directly to let me know what you did or didn't like about this book—as well as what we can do to make our books stronger.

Please note that I cannot help you with technical problems related to the topic of this book, and that due to the high volume of mail I receive, I might not be able to reply to every message.

When you write, please be sure to include this book's title and author as well as your name and phone or fax number. I will carefully review your comments and share them with the author and editors who worked on the book.

Fax: 317-581-4770
Email: rosemarie.graham@samspublishing.com
Mail: Rosemarie Graham
         Executive Editor
         Sams Publishing
         201 West 103rd Street
         Indianapolis, IN 46290 USA

Introduction

The World Wide Web is an exciting place, and everyone wants to be a part of it. Whether you are about to launch your corporate presence on the Web, or are creating a personal family site, you are becoming part of an ever growing family of developers, all dedicated to the growth of the phenomenon called the Internet.

Fortunately, creating Web sites is easy. Unfortunately, Web sites are also rather unexciting. Web sites can display all sorts of information, but that's about it. The real power of the Web is not in Web sites but in Web applications. Want to create an online store? What to allow users to search for information? Want to personalize your Web site? Want to create guestbooks, surveys, and other interactive pages? If you want to do all this, and more, you need to write Web applications.

And you can, with ColdFusion Express.

What Is ColdFusion Express?

ColdFusion Express is a scaled down version of Allaire Corporation's award-winning ColdFusion Application Server. Since its release in 1995, ColdFusion has proven itself to be a fast, efficient, secure, and highly scalable platform on which to build Web applications. And indeed, tens of thousands of organizations and hundreds of thousands of developers worldwide use ColdFusion every day to help shape the future of the Web.

ColdFusion is a commercial product and comes in two flavors: ColdFusion Professional and ColdFusion Enterprise. These products support all the features and technologies needed by application developers.

Despite all that power, ColdFusion's claim to fame has always been ease of use. ColdFusion is so easy to learn that most users are up and running by writing code in hours, not in days, weeks, or months. With each successive version, ColdFusion becomes even more powerful, and even easier to use.

ColdFusion Express is ColdFusion's little brother, a simplified version of the ColdFusion server that is made available to developers at no cost whatsoever. Although not as powerful or flexible as ColdFusion, ColdFusion Express does feature the basic technologies you need to start building Web applications. Using ColdFusion Express, you can

- Build dynamic Web pages using databases, conditional processing, and all sorts of data manipulation functions
- Create shopping carts, guestbooks, and many other applications
- Create secure applications, complete with access control

- Implement basic personalization to provide visitors with a more pleasant and rewarding online experience
- And much much more

And all at a price that can't be beat.

Who Should Use This Book?

This book is for anyone who wants to learn ColdFusion Express (or the full-blown ColdFusion). Whether you are building an online business, or enhancing your personal Web site, this book teaches you all you need to know to be productive quickly and efficiently.

To use ColdFusion Express you'll need one of the following:

- A computer running Windows 95, Windows 98, Windows NT, or Windows 2000
- A computer running RedHat Linux 6 or later

To run HomeSite, you need a computer running Windows 95, Windows 98, Windows NT, or Windows 2000.

There are other requirements too, but as long as you are running the operating systems previously listed, you'll be all set.

> This book teaches ColdFusion Express, not the full commercial versions of ColdFusion. However, as ColdFusion Express is a subset of ColdFusion, everything taught in this book applies to ColdFusion as well. As such, beginning ColdFusion developers will find this book useful too.

> To write ColdFusion code, you need to know HTML. If you need help with HTML, I'd recommend that you grab a copy of *Sams Teach Yourself HTML 4 in 24 Hours* (ISBN: 0672317249).
>
> Using databases with ColdFusion Express requires a working knowledge of SQL. Although basic SQL is covered in this book, if you need help brushing up on your SQL, grab a copy of my book, *Sams Teach Yourself SQL in 10 Minutes* (ISBN: 0672316641).
>
> And finally, this book just scratches the surface of what you can do with ColdFusion. When you are ready to migrate to the full commercial versions of ColdFusion, make sure that you arm yourself with my ColdFusion books, *The ColdFusion Web Application Construction Kit* (ISBN: 078971809X) and its sequel, *Advanced ColdFusion 4 Development* (ISBN: 0789718103).

What's on the CD-ROM?

The CD-ROM contains the following:

- ColdFusion Express for Windows
- ColdFusion Express for Linux
- A non-expiring version of HomeSite
- Evaluation versions of the full commercial editions of ColdFusion
- Evaluation version of ColdFusion Studio
- All the code and examples in this book

How to Use This Book

This book is designed to teach you topics in a series of lessons, each of which should take an hour (or less) to learn. All the books in the *Sams Teach Yourself* series enable you to start working and become productive with the product as quickly as possible. This book will do that for you too.

Each lesson starts with an overview of the topic to be taught. The overview helps you determine the nature of the lesson and whether the lesson is relevant to your needs.

Each lesson concludes with a set of questions and answers, and a quiz just to make sure that you were paying attention. (The answers can be found in Appendix A, just in case you need them.)

Interspersed in each lesson are special elements that provide additional information.

Conventions Used in This Book

This book uses different typefaces to differentiate between code and regular English, and also to help you identify important concepts.

Text that you type and text that should appear on your screen is presented in `monospace` type.

```
It will look like this to mimic the way text looks on your screen.
```

Placeholders for variables and expressions appear in `monospace italic` font. You should replace the placeholder with the specific value it represents.

This arrow (➥) at the beginning of a line of code means that a single line of code is too long to fit on the printed page. Continue typing all characters after the ➥ as though they were part of the preceding line.

A Note presents interesting pieces of information related to the surrounding discussion.

A Tip offers advice or teaches an easier way to do something.

A Caution advises you about potential problems and helps you steer clear of disaster.

Do/Don't boxes offer advice on what to do or not to do in certain situations. They look like this:

Do	Don't
DO brush after every meal.	**DON'T** take candy from strangers.

HOUR 1

Understanding ColdFusion Express

Unless you have made a conscious decision not to, by now you must have heard of the Internet, the Web, and those funny looking addresses that usually contain lots of w's and periods in them. The Internet truly has become the next revolution in computing, and the amazing rate of growth shows no sign of slowing any time soon. And now you, using ColdFusion Express, can join the revolution.

In this hour, you'll learn the following:

- What the Internet is, and what intranets and extranets really are
- How Web servers and Web browsers work their magic
- What ColdFusion Express is, and what it'll do for you

Understanding the Internet

ColdFusion Express is used to create Web-based applications—applications that run on top of the Internet (as well as intranets and extranets). As such, a solid understanding of what the Web and Internet are is a prerequisite to writing ColdFusion Express applications. So for starters, let's take a moment to review some Internet and Web fundamentals.

Much ambiguity and confusion surrounds the Internet, so we'll start with a definition. Simply put, the Internet is the world's largest network.

The networks found in most offices today are local area networks (LANs), comprised of a group of computers in relatively close proximity to each other and linked by special hardware and cabling (see Figure 1.1). Some computers are clients (more commonly known as *workstations*), whereas others are servers (also known as *file servers*). All these computers can communicate with each other to share information.

FIGURE 1.1

A LAN is a group of computers in close proximity linked by special cabling.

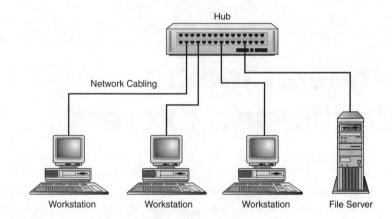

Now imagine a bigger network, one that spans multiple geographical locations. Larger companies, with offices in multiple locations, typically use this kind of network. Each location has its own LAN that links the local computers together. All these LANs are, in turn, linked to each other via some communications medium. The linking can be anything from a dial-up modem to high-speed T1 connections and fiber-optic links. The complete group of interconnected LANs (see Figure 1.2) is called a WAN, or wide area network. WANs are used to link multiple locations within a single organization.

Suppose that you need to create a massive network that links every computer everywhere. How would you do this? You'd start by running high-speed backbones, connections capable of moving large amounts of data at once between strategic locations—perhaps large cities or different countries. These backbones would be like high-speed, multilane, interstate highways connecting various locations. You'd build in fault tolerance to make these backbones fully redundant so that if any connection broke, at least one other way to reach a specific destination would be available.

FIGURE 1.2

A WAN is made up of multiple intercon-nected LANs.

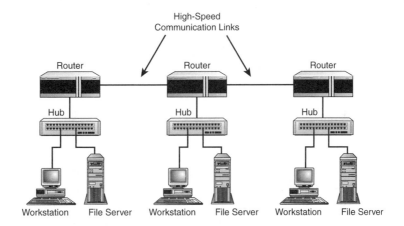

Next, you'd create thousands of local links that would connect every city to the back-bones over slower connections—like state highways or city streets. You'd allow corpo-rate WANs, LANs, and even individual users with dial-up modems to connect to these local access points. Some would stay connected at all times, whereas others would con-nect as needed.

You'd create a common communications language, so every computer connected to this network could communicate with every other computer.

Finally, you'd devise a scheme to uniquely identify every computer connected to the net-work. This would ensure that information sent to a given computer actually reaches the correct destination.

Congratulations, you've just created the Internet!

Okay, so I'll admit that this is something of an oversimplification, but the truth is this is exactly how the Internet works.

The high-speed backbones do exist. Most are owned and operated by the large telecom-munications companies.

The local access points, more commonly known as POPs (Points of Presence), are run by phone companies, cable television providers, online services, and local Internet service providers (also known as ISPs).

NEW TERM The common language is IP, the Internet Protocol, except that the term *language* is a misnomer. A *protocol* is a set of rules governing behavior in certain situations. Foreign diplomats learn local protocol to ensure that they behave correctly in another country. Protocols ensure that there are no communication breakdowns or serious misunderstandings. Computers need protocols, too, to ensure that they can communicate with each other correctly and to be sure that data is exchanged correctly. IP is the protocol used to communicate across the Internet, so every computer connected to the Internet must be running a copy of IP. (All modern operating systems—including Windows, Windows NT, Mac OS, and UNIX—come with a built-in copy of the IP software.)

NEW TERM In the IP world, you don't connect to computers, rather, you connect to *hosts*. But for the most part, a *host* is a computer, so when you see *host*, think computer.

The unique identifiers are IP addresses. Every host connected to the Internet has a unique IP address. These addresses are made up of four sets of numbers separated by periods—for example, 208.193.16.250. Some hosts have fixed (or *static*) IP addresses; others have dynamically assigned addresses. Regardless of how an IP address is obtained, no two hosts connected to the Internet may be using the same IP address at any given time. That would be like two homes having the same phone number or street address. Information would end up in the wrong place all the time.

Every time you request a Web page (or perform any other Internet-based transaction), data is being sent back and forth between your host (your computer) and the remote host (the computer you're requesting the data from). The data being sent back and forth passes through computers, hubs, routers, and other equipment.

If you want to see just how you're connected to the remote host, you can use the TRACERT program that comes with Windows and Windows NT. To use TRACERT (short for Trace Route), go to a DOS command prompt, and type **TRACERT** *HOST*, replacing the word *HOST* with the host name or IP address of the host you want to trace to (for example, TRACERT www.forta.com). You'll be amazed at where your data actually travels to get to you.

Internet Applications

The Internet itself is simply a massive communications network which in and of itself is not that exciting. During its early days that network was primarily used to transmit textual based information using far from intuitive tools like Telnet and Gopher. This is why it took 20 years for the Internet to become the phenomenon it is today.

The Internet has been dubbed the Information Superhighway, and that analogy is quite accurate. Highways themselves aren't nearly as exciting as the places you can get to by traveling them—and the same is true of the Internet. What makes the Internet so exciting are the applications that run over it and what you can accomplish with them.

The most popular application now is the World Wide Web, which single-handedly transformed the Internet into a household word. In fact, many people mistakenly think that the World Wide Web *is* the Internet. This is definitely not the case. Table 1.1 lists some of the more popular Internet-based applications.

TABLE 1.1 Popular Internet-Based Applications

Application	Description
Email	SMTP (Simple Mail Transfer Protocol) is the most popular email delivery mechanism; POP (Post Office Protocol) is one of the most popular protocols used to retrieve email.
FTP	File Transfer Protocol transfers files between hosts.
Gopher	This menu-driven, document-retrieval system was popular before the creation of the World Wide Web.
IRC	Internet Relay Chat allows real-time, text-based conferencing over the Internet.
NFS	Network File System is used to share files among different hosts.
Newsgroups	These threaded discussion lists (of which there are thousands) are built on the Network News Transfer Protocol (NNTP) .
Telnet	Telnet logs in to a host from a remote location allowing you to control that host remotely.
WWW	The World Wide Web (built on top of the HTTP protocol) has become almost synonymous with the Internet itself.

NEW TERM All these different applications, and many others, use IP to communicate across the Internet. The information transmitted by these applications is broken into *packets*, or small blocks of data, and sent to a destination IP address. The application at the receiving end processes the incoming information.

Displaying IP Connections

Depending on what programs you're running, your computer could be connected to multiple hosts at any given time.

You can display a list of all active IP connections by using the NETSTAT program. Go to a DOS or command prompt and type **NETSTAT -A** to display a list of all connections, the protocol being used, the ports that the connection is on, and the status of the connection.

So, don't confuse the Internet with the Web. The Internet is simply a massive network, and the Web is one type of application and data that runs on that network.

Intranets and Extranets

Intranets and extranets are now two of the industry's favorite buzzwords. Not too long ago, most people thought "intranet" was a typo; in a very short period of time, however, intranets and extranets have become recognized as legitimate and powerful new business tools.

NEW TERM | An *intranet* is nothing more than a private Internet. In other words, it's a private network, usually a LAN or WAN, that enables the use of Internet-based applications in a secure and private environment. As on the public Internet, intranets can host Web servers, FTP servers, and any other IP-based services.

Companies have been using private networks for years to share information. Traditionally, office networks haven't been information-friendly. Old private networks didn't have consistent interfaces, standard ways to publish information, or client applications that could access diverse data stores. The popularity in the public Internet has spawned a whole new generation of inexpensive and easy-to-use client applications. These applications are now making their way back into the private networks. Intranets are gathering so much attention now because they are a new and cost-effective solution to an old problem.

NEW TERM | Extranets take this new communication mechanism one step further. *Extranets* are intranet-style networks that link multiple sites or organizations by using intranet-related technologies. Many extranets actually use the public Internet as their backbone and employ encryption techniques to ensure the security of the data being moved over the network.

The two things that distinguish intranets and extranets from the Internet are who can access them and from where they can be accessed. Don't be confused by hype surrounding applications that claim to be "intranet-ready." If an application can be used over the public Internet, it will work on private intranets and extranets too.

DNS, the Domain Name Service

IP addresses are the only way to uniquely specify a host. When you want to communicate with a host—for example, a Web server—you need to specify the IP address of the Web server you're trying to contact. Similarly, when you connect to an FTP server, or specify the SMTP and POP servers in your mail client, you must specify the name of the host you want to connect to.

As you know from browsing the Web, you rarely specify IP addresses directly. You do, however, specify a host name, such as `www.forta.com`. If hosts are identified by IP address, how does your browser know which Web server to contact if you specify a host-name?

The answer is theDomain Name Service (DNS), a mechanism that maps host names to IP addresses. When you specify the destination address of `www.forta.com`, your browser sends an address resolution request to a DNS server asking for the IP address of that host. The DNS server returns an actual IP address—in this case, `208.193.16.250`. Your browser can then use this address to communicate with the host directly.

If you've ever mistyped a host name, you've seen error messages telling you that the host couldn't be found, or no DNS entry was found for the specified host. These error messages simply mean that the DNS server couldn't resolve the specified host name. Some browsers go a step further and attempt to explain why a page cannot be retrieved, as seen in Figure 1.3.

FIGURE 1.3

DNS resolution errors usually are the result of a mistyped URL.

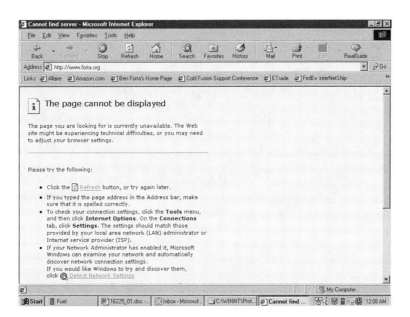

DNS is never required. Users can always specify the name of a destination host by its IP address to connect to the host. There are, however, some very good reasons not to use the IP address:

- IP addresses are hard to remember and easy to mistype. Users are more likely to remember and correctly type www.forta.com than they are 208.193.16.250.

- IP addresses are subject to change. For example, if you switch service providers, you might be forced to use a new set of IP addresses for your hosts. If users identified your site only by its IP address, they never could reach your host if the IP address changed. Your DNS name stays the same, even if your IP address switches. You need to change only the mapping so that the host name maps to the new correct IP address.

- Multiple hosts, each with unique IP addresses, can all have the same DNS name. This allows load balancing between servers, as well as the establishment of redundant servers.

- A single host, with a single IP address, can have multiple DNS names. This enables you to create aliases if needed. For example, ftp.forta.com and www.forta.com might point to the same IP address, and thus the same server.

DNS servers are special software programs. Often your ISP will host your DNS entries so that you don't need to install and maintain your own DNS server software.

You can host your own DNS server and gain more control over the domain mappings, but you inherit the responsibility of maintaining the server. If your DNS server is down, there's no way of resolving the host name to an IP address, and no one will be able to find your site.

Understanding the World Wide Web

As mentioned earlier, the most commonly used Internet-based application is now the World Wide Web. The recent growth of interest in the Internet is the result of the growth of interest in the World Wide Web—or simply, the Web.

The Web is built on the Hypertext Transfer Protocol (HTTP). HTTP is designed to be a small, fast protocol that is well suited for distributed multimedia information systems and hypertext jumps between sites.

1

Information on the Web is stored in pages. A page can contain any of the following:

Text	Tables
Headers	Forms
Lists	Graphics
Menus	Multimedia

Each Web page is an actual file saved on a host. When a Web page is requested, the file containing the Web page is read and its contents are sent to the host that asked for it.

NEW TERM A *Web site* is simply a collection of Web pages along with any supporting files (such as GIF or JPEG graphics). Creating a Web site thus involves creating one or more Web pages and linking them. The Web site is then saved on a Web server.

Web Servers

The Web consists of pages of information stored on hosts running Web server software. The host is often referred to as the *Web server*, which is technically inaccurate. The Web server is actually software and not the computer itself. Versions of Web server software can run on almost all computers, and although most Web server applications do have minimum hardware requirements, there is no special computer needed to host a Web server.

Originally, Web development was all performed under different flavors of UNIX. Most Web servers still run on UNIX boxes, but this is changing. There are now Web server versions for almost every major operating system. Web servers hosted on high-performance operating systems, such as Windows NT, are becoming more and more popular because UNIX is still more expensive to run than Windows NT and is also more difficult to use for the average user. Windows NT has proven itself to be an efficient, reliable, and cost-effective platform for hosting Web servers. As a result, Windows NT's slice in the Web server operating system pie is growing dramatically.

So, what exactly is a Web server? It's a program that serves up Web pages upon request. Web servers typically don't know or care what they're serving up. When a user at a specific IP address requests a specific file (a Web page), the Web server tries to retrieve that file and send it back to the user. The requested file might be the HTML source code for a Web page, a GIF image, VRML worlds, .AVI files, and so on. The Web browser determines what should be requested, not the Web server. All the server does is process that request, as shown in Figure 1.4.

FIGURE 1.4

Web servers process requests made by Web browsers.

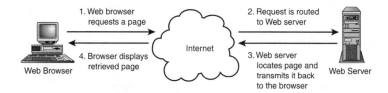

Pages on a Web server are stored in different directories. When requesting a Web page, a user might provide a full path (directory and filename) to specify a particular document.

Pages are stored on the Web server beneath the Web root—a directory or folder designated to contain all the files that make up the Web site. When a request is made for a specific page within a specific directory, that page is retrieved from the appropriate directory beneath the Web root.

Web servers allow administrators to specify a default Web page, a page that is sent back to the user when only a directory is specified, with a Web server. These default pages are often called index.html or default.htm. If no default Web page exists in a particular directory, it either returns an error message or a list of all available files, depending on how the server is set up.

Web Browsers

Web browsers are the programs used to view Web pages. The Web browser has the job of processing received Web pages, parsing (reading and interpreting) the HTML code, and displaying the page to users. The browser attempts to display graphics, tables, forms, formatted text, or whatever the page contains. The most popular Web browsers now in use are Netscape Navigator (see Figure 1.5) and Microsoft Internet Explorer (see Figure 1.6).

Web page designers must pay close attention to the differences between browsers because Web browsers behave in their own unique ways. Web pages are created using HTML (a language that we'll look at in a few moments). Unfortunately, not one single browser supports every feature of the HTML language. Furthermore, the same Web page often looks different on two separate browsers because every browser renders and displays Web page objects differently.

For this reason, most Web page designers use multiple Web browsers and test their pages in every one to ensure that the final output appears as intended. Without this testing, some Web site visitors can't see the pages you published correctly.

Most Web browsers also provide users with tools to manage a list of favorite sites (usually called *bookmarks* or *favorites*), as well as the capability to print pages and save shortcuts to specific Web pages.

FIGURE 1.5

Netscape Navigator runs on more platforms (operating systems) than any other browser.

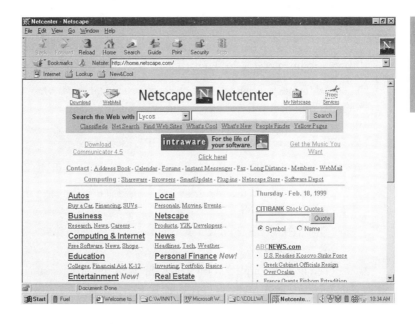

FIGURE 1.6

Microsoft Internet Explorer is the most popular browser among users of Windows and Windows NT.

To request a Web page, the browser user must specify the address of the page. The address is known as a URL.

URLs

Every Web page on the World Wide Web has an address. This is what you type into your browser to instruct it to load a particular Web page.

These addresses are called Uniform Resource Locators (URLs). URLs aren't just used to identify Web pages. Every single object within a Web site has a unique URL—an address that points to it and nothing else. And URLs are used by other applications too. Files on an FTP server, for example, also have URL identifiers.

As seen in Figure 1.7, World Wide Web URLs can be comprised of up to five parts:

- The protocol to use to retrieve the object. This is always `http` for objects on the World Wide Web.

- The Web server from which to retrieve the object. This is specified as a DNS name or an IP address.

- The host machine port on which the Web server is running. If omitted, the specified protocol's default port is used; for Web servers, this is port `80`.

- The file to retrieve or the script to execute. The filename often includes a complete file path.

- Optional script parameters, also known as the *query string*.

FIGURE 1.7
URLs are made up of multiple parts, the minimum of which is the host name.

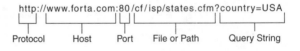

To understand how URLs work, look at a few examples:

- **http://www.forta.com** points to a Web page on the host www.forta.com. As no document or path was specified, the default document in the Web root directory is served. It is important to note that this URL retrieves the same thing as http://www.forta.com/, the extra / here explicitly requests a file from the Web root directory, which is the default directory if no path is specified.

- **http://www.forta.com/cf/books/** also points to a Web page on the host www.forta.com, but this time the directory /cf/books/ is specified. Because no page name was provided, the default page in the /cf/books/ directory is served.

- **http://208.193.16.250/cf/books/** points to the same file as the previous example, but this time the IP address is used instead of the DNS name.

- `http://www.forta.com:80/cf/books/` points to the same file as the previous two examples, but this time an explicit IP port was specified. Here a port of `80` was specified, which is the default port for http, but any other port value could be specified (assuming that the Web server running on the remote host was connected to that port).

- `http://www.forta.com/cf/books/news.cfm` again points to a Web page on the `www.forta.com` host. Both a directory and a filename are specified this time. This retrieves the file `news.cfm` from the `/cf/books/` directory, instead of the default file.

- `http://www.forta.com/cf/isp/states.cfm?country=USA` points to a script, rather than a Web page. `states.cfm` is a ColdFusion page that is executed when requested. Anything after the `?` are parameters that are passed to the script. In this example, a single parameter called `country` is being passed with a value of `USA`.

There are generally two ways to go to specific URLs. The first is by typing the URL in the Web browser's address field (or selecting it from a saved bookmark or favorite). The second is by clicking on a link within a Web page—links are simply references to other URLs. When a user clicks a link, the browser requests whatever URL it references.

Understanding HTML

Web pages are plain text files constructed with HTML, the Hypertext Markup Language. HTML is implemented as a series of easy-to-learn *tags*, or instructions. Web page authors use these tags to mark up a page of text. Browsers then use these tags to render and display the information for viewing.

HTML is very easy to learn. As long as you understand tags and attributes, you're all set. And as you'll soon see, the programming language used by ColdFusion Express is modeled on HTML, making it just as easy to learn.

HTML tags are always placed in between < and >. For example, to force a paragraph break, you would specify <P>.

Many tags are part of tag pairs that surround content. For example, to display the word *hello* in boldfaced text, you would specify the following code:

```
<B>hello</B>
```

Here the <B> tag turns bold on, and </B> turns it off again. End tags are always named with the same name as the start tag, preceded by a / character.

Some tags take one or more parameters in the form of attributes. Attributes are used to specify optional or additional information to a tag. For example, the <BODY> tag defines the body content of a Web page. <BODY> takes an optional attribute called BGCOLOR that specifies the page background color. So to create a page with a blue background, you could use the following code:

```
<BODY BGCOLOR="blue">
```

Some tags have no attributes, some have many. Attributes are almost always optional and can be specified in any order you want. Attributes must be separated from each other by a space, and attribute values should ideally be enclosed within double quotation marks.

HTML is constantly being enhanced with new features and added tags. To ensure backward compatibility, browsers must ignore tags they don't understand. For example, if you were to use the <MARQUEE> tag to create a scrolling text marquee, browsers that don't support this tag will still display the marquee text, but it won't scroll.

Web pages also can contain hypertext jumps, which are links to other pages or Web sites. Users can click links to jump within a page or to jump to other pages on the same Web site or any page on any site.

The word *Web* in World Wide Web refers to the way pages are all linked and cross-linked (kind of like a spider's web). This facilitates the ability to jump to any Web page on any Web server, and back again.

Introducing ColdFusion Express

Now that you know all about the Internet, the Web, and what makes them tick, it's time to look at ColdFusion Express.

 ColdFusion Express is a *Web Application Server*—a special type of software product that is used to create applications that run on top of the Web.

Understanding Web Applications

As I explained earlier, Web servers do just that: they serve. Web browsers make requests and Web servers fulfill those requests—they serve back the requested information to the browser. These are usually HTML files as well as the other file types previously discussed.

And that's really all Web servers do. In the grand scheme of things, Web servers are actually pretty simple applications—they sit and wait for requests that they attempt to fulfill as soon as they arrive. Web servers do not let you interact with a database; they do not let you personalize Web pages; they do not let you process the results of a user's form submission; they do none of that. All they do is serve pages.

So how do you extend your Web server to do all of the things I just listed? That's where Web Application Servers come into play. A *Web Application Server* is a piece of software which extends the Web server allowing it to do things that it could not do by itself—kind of like teaching an old dog new tricks.

Here's how it all works. When a Web server receives a request from a Web browser, it looks at that request to determine if it is a simple Web page or a page that needs processing by a Web Application Server. It does this by looking at the MIME type (or file extension). If the MIME type indicates that the file is a simple Web page (for example, it has an HTM extension), the Web server will fulfill the request and send the file to the requesting browser as is. But if the MIME type indicates that the requested file is a page that needs processing by a Web Application Server (for example, it has a CFM extension), the Web server passes it to the appropriate Web Application Server and returns the results it receives rather than the actual page itself. Figure 1.8 illustrates this concept.

FIGURE 1.8

Web servers pass requests to Web Application Servers, which in turn pass results back to the Web server for transmission to the requesting browser.

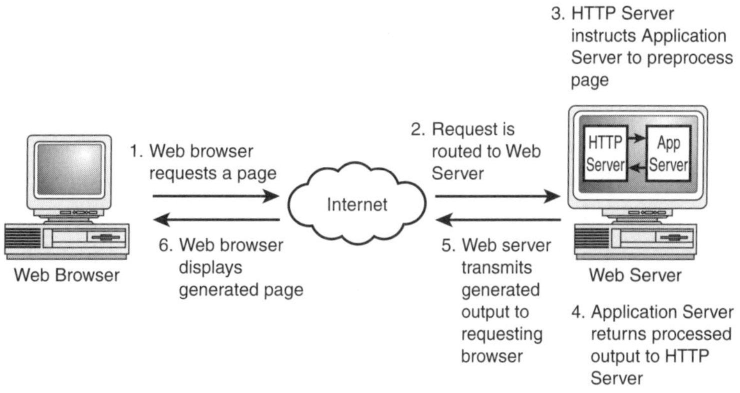

In other words, Web Application Servers are page preprocessors. They process the requested page before it is sent back to the client (the browser), and in doing so they open the door for developers to do all sorts of interesting things on the server such as the following:

- Creating guest books
- Conducting surveys
- Changing your pages on-the-fly based on date, time, first visit, and whatever else you can think of
- Personalizing pages for your visitors
- ...and much more

What Is ColdFusion Express?

ColdFusion is the name of Allaire Corporation's award-winning family of Web Application Servers. It is worthwhile to note that ColdFusion helped define what Web Application Servers are: after all, ColdFusion was the very first Web Application Server commercially available back in 1995. What this means is that the technology you are about to learn is proven and reliable, one that hundreds of thousands of developers have already built their own applications on.

Why is ColdFusion so popular? There are quite a few answers to this question, but the most important answer is that it is incredibly easy to learn. I've already explained HTML and its syntax, and ColdFusion uses the exact same language elements—tags and attributes. So if you are comfortable writing HTML, you already have all the skills you need to start writing CFML—ColdFusion Markup Language. That's not something that can be said about any other programming language out there.

Oh, and before I forget, don't let the simplicity and ease of use give you the wrong impression—CFML is a complete and powerful language as you'll soon see.

There are actually three different ColdFusion servers available:

- **ColdFusion Express** is the freely available version of ColdFusion (the version you have). It supports a basic set of functionality and runs on computers running Windows or Linux.

- **ColdFusion Professional** is a commercial version of ColdFusion that runs on computers running Windows or Linux. In addition to all the features offered by ColdFusion Express, ColdFusion Professional features integration with email and LDAP servers, support for all sorts of extensions, and the ability to write your own language extensions.

- **ColdFusion Enterprise** is a commercial version of ColdFusion that runs on computers running Windows, Linux, Solaris, or HP/UX. In addition to all the features offered by ColdFusion Professional, ColdFusion Enterprise also features high-end scalability and security options to ensure 100% uptime.

The good news is that what you are about to learn applies to all versions of ColdFusion. So when you are ready to migrate to the commercial product, you'll have all the basic skills you need under your belt.

Introducing HomeSite

ColdFusion pages, like HTML pages, are simple text files. As such, you can create and edit your Web pages in any text editor or word processor.

NEW TERM But that is definitely the masochistic way to create pages and applications. There now are dozens of products designed to simplify Web page and application development. These tools are often referred to as *page editors* or *authoring tools*, and the two aren't alike at all.

Web page authoring tools are built around the premise that you, the page developer, don't want to learn or know HTML. As such, authoring tools provide fancy graphical based interfaces that let you interactively create your Web site. Under the hood, these tools are actually generating HTML code for you, but the authoring tool attempts to hide this fact. To provide this level of abstraction and isolation, authoring tools have to cut corners and support a subset of HTML's capabilities. Not all of HTML can be graphically represented within a GUI environment.

Authoring tools have their place in the market. (Some, like Microsoft FrontPage, sell very well, so someone must be using them.) However, professional Web developers generally shy away from these tools for a simple reason—you can't do some things in HTML within an authoring environment. If you want total control over your Web pages, you can't and shouldn't ignore the underlying HTML. Manual fine-tuning of the tags and the attributes is often the only way to achieve specific results. Professional developers therefore use editors rather than authoring tools. Editors are programs used to manually create and manipulate HTML: They don't hide the HTML, they present it to you directly for you to edit.

So why use an editor if you have to edit the HTML manually anyway? Well, good Web page editors empower you with an array of tools that greatly simplify the Web site development process without compromising flexibility. In other words, you get the best of both worlds. You can edit the code manually so that you have all the power and flexibility you need, and you can also use tools and features that do lots of the grunt work for you.

And this is even more significant when you are developing a Web application as opposed to a Web site. Web application development requires that you edit and manipulate code directly, and you can't do that easily using an authoring tool.

This is why you'll be using HomeSite throughout this book. (Hour 3, "Using HomeSite," introduces you to the program.) HomeSite *isn't* an authoring tool. HomeSite *is* a Web page editor.

HomeSite is designed specifically for users who understand that you can't be scared of HTML if you want to develop professional Web pages and applications. But HomeSite is also the most powerful and flexible Web page editor on the market. And by using HomeSite, you can create Web sites and applications that are powerful, sophisticated, and professional, and you can do it all very easily. And because HomeSite is made by

Allaire Corporation, the same folks who brought you ColdFusion and ColdFusion Express, you can be sure that the two products are designed to complement each other.

ColdFusion Studio

In addition to HomeSite, Allaire offers another development environment called ColdFusion Studio. This is actually HomeSite's big brother; a more powerful and sophisticated version of HomeSite designed specifically for ColdFusion developers.

So why are we not using it in this book? Well, most of the more important features in ColdFusion Studio (things like a SQL Query Builder and a Remote Debugger) are only supported by ColdFusion Professional and ColdFusion Enterprise. These features are not supported by ColdFusion Express.

But, when you are ready to upgrade to the full-blown commercial versions of ColdFusion, you'll definitely want to grab a copy of ColdFusion Studio as well. If you know HomeSite, you'll feel right at home with Studio, and you'll have access to all the extra power and flexibility you'll need.

And with that, welcome to ColdFusion Express and the wonderful world of Web programming.

Summary

During this first hour, you were introduced to some important Internet fundamentals. Understanding how the Internet does what it does is an important part of developing Web applications, and so the basics of Web servers, Web browsers, URLs, DNS, and HTML were explained. You also learned exactly what ColdFusion and HomeSite are.

Before you can start experimenting with ColdFusion Express, the product needs to be installed. Hour 2, "Getting Started," walks you through the installation process.

Q&A

Q Why do some domains end with .com, whereas others end with .net, or .org?

A The text after the final period in a host name is called the top level domain. .com is used for commercial domain (most domains fall into this category), .org is reserved for non-profit organizations, .net is used by Internet service providers (ISPs), .edu is used by universities or colleges that grant four-year degrees, .gov is used by the U.S. Government, and .mil is used by the U.S. military. Other countries have domains that end with a two-letter country designator.

Q I see you have a domain named `forta.com`. How can I get my own domain?

A The basic rule is that if a domain name isn't currently taken, you can have it. Network Solutions is the organization responsible for assigning domains that end with `.com`, `.org`, `.net`, and `.edu`. Network Solutions charges a $35 annual fee for assigning your domain name. To obtain a domain name, simply fill in forms at Network Solutions' Web site at `http://www.networksolutions.com`. However, obtaining a domain name isn't enough. To actually use your domain name, it needs to be hosted on a DNS server. You can set up your own DNS servers (you must have at least two of them) if you have your own permanent Internet connection; otherwise, you'll need to have your ISP host it for you.

Q Most of the Web sites I visit have host names that begin with `www`. Is this required?

A Actually, you can name a host anything you'd like. Before the Web ever existed, the Internet was already being used to share information. Protocols such as FTP and Gopher were used to access data on other hosts. As single organizations would often offer multiple forms of data access, they named the machines by the service they offered (such as `ftp.forta.com`). This practice carried over into the Web, and it is still prevalent.

Q Where can I find a list of Web sites developed in ColdFusion?

A There are lots of lists out there, but you might want to start with one that I host at `http://www.forta.com/cf`. That is the largest user provided list available, and it can be browsed or searched as needed.

Workshop

The Workshop contains quiz questions and activities to help reinforce what you've learned in this hour. If you get stuck, the answers to the quiz questions can be found in Appendix A, "Answers to Quiz."

Quiz

1. What's the difference between the Internet, intranets, and extranets?
2. *True or false*: Every page on the Internet has a unique address.
3. *True or false*: Every host connected to the Internet has a unique DNS name.
4. Where does ColdFusion Express run: on the host running the Web server or on the host running the Web browser?
5. Why is HomeSite the editor of choice for ColdFusion Express development?

Exercises

1. Try and find sites on the Internet hosted by ColdFusion. How can you tell if ColdFusion is being used? Here's a hint: The MIME type is a dead giveaway. Look for URLs with a `.CFM` in them.

2. Want to find out more about a domain your visit regularly? The WHOIS utility returns information about registered domains. You can try this out at `http://www.networksolutions.com/cgi-bin/whois/whois`.

HOUR 2

Getting Started

Now that you know what ColdFusion Express is, you're undoubtedly anxious to start experimenting with it. But before you can do so, the product needs to be installed. You'll also be using HomeSite as your code editor, so that needs installing too.

In this hour, you'll learn the following:

- The steps required to prepare your computer for ColdFusion Express
- How to install ColdFusion Express and HomeSite
- How to access the ColdFusion Administrator and online documentation

Installing ColdFusion Express

As explained in the last hour, ColdFusion is a software program that runs on the same computer that runs the Web server software. And obviously, before you can write and execute ColdFusion code, you need to install the ColdFusion server software.

Preparing for Installation

Installing ColdFusion requires that your computer be correctly prepared before hand. At minimum, you must have a copy of IP installed, as well as a Web server and Web browser.

IP (the Internet Protocol)

As explained in Hour 1, "Understanding ColdFusion Express," IP is the underlying communication protocol used by all hosts connected to the Internet. As such, IP (the Internet Protocol) must be installed and running on any host before any Internet-related software can be used.

Of course, most computers now are running a copy of IP. If you use any Web or Internet based software (for example, a browser or a mail client), you are most likely running a copy of IP whether you know it or not.

Windows users can open the Network applet in the Windows Control Panel to display a list of installed protocols. If IP is not listed, it can be installed from this same applet.

One simple way to check that IP is installed and running is to do a self check using the `ping` utility that is supplied with almost every operating system. To use `ping` to check that a host is present, you tell `ping` which host to try to connect to (using an IP address or a hostname), and it'll try to connect to that host, reporting back whether this was successful. Techies refer to this process as *pinging a host*. You can use `ping` to check for the presence of any host, even your own machine. And as ridiculous as that sounds (obviously if you are executing `ping` from your own machine, it must be present), because `ping` requires that IP be installed and running, it provides a simple and effective way to verify that this is, in fact, the case.

`ping` is usually a command-line utility; to use it go to a command or MS-DOS Prompt (Windows users should click Start, and then select Command Prompt or MS-DOS Prompt from the Programs menu) and then type the following:

```
ping 127.0.0.1
```

You should see a series of success messages indicating that the `ping` succeeded. If not, you'll need to refer to your operating system documentation on installing and troubleshooting IP.

I said that `ping` required the IP address or hostname of the host to `ping`. So what was the address `127.0.0.1` that you just used in your `ping`?

The answer is actually an important one. Every host on the Internet has a unique IP address, but many hosts have dynamic IP addresses (as explained in the last hour). So how can you determine your own IP address? Well, there are utilities that can provide you with this information, but there is a simpler solution.

`127.0.0.1` is a special address, it *always* refers to your own host. No matter what the real IP address is, or whether it is static or dynamic, one thing is certain; address `127.0.0.1` will refer to the local host. And usually, there is a special hostname that you can use too, `localhost`. (You could have also used `ping localhost` to do the test.)

Throughout the rest of this book, we'll be using this technique when requesting pages from a Web server on your own machine.

Web Browser

Most computers have Web browsers installed. And although ColdFusion itself does not require a Web browser, downloading Web servers, accessing the ColdFusion Express Administrator, and reading the online docs all require that you are running a current Web browser. And of course, without a Web browser you'll not be able to test your applications.

Your best bet is to have the latest version of either Microsoft Internet Explorer or Netscape Navigator installed. And as explained in Hour 1, most developers find that they need both browsers (for compatibility testing).

To download Microsoft Internet Explorer, visit `http://www.microsoft.com/windows/ie/download/default.asp`.

To download Netscape Navigator, visit `http://home.netscape.com/computing/download`.

Web Server

Now you need a Web server. As explained in Hour 1, ColdFusion is not a Web server; it is an application server. ColdFusion Express requires that a supported Web server be installed and running.

Depending on the operating system you are using, you have a choice of several Web servers to choose from.

ColdFusion Express for Windows runs on

- Microsoft Personal Web Server (for Windows 95, Windows 98, and Windows NT Workstation)
- Microsoft Internet Information Server (for NT and Windows 2000)
- Netscape FastTrack Server (for Windows 95, Windows 98, and Windows NT)
- O'Reilly WebSite Pro (for Windows 95, Windows 98, and Windows NT)
- Apache (for Windows 95, Windows 98, and Windows NT)

ColdFusion Express for Linux runs on

- Netscape FastTrack Server
- Apache

Web server installation instructions obviously vary from one Web server to the next. Refer to your Web server documentation or online help for installation instructions if needed. Your Web server must be installed and functioning correctly before ColdFusion Express is installed.

To verify that your Web server is working, all you need to do is open your browser and request a page from it. Now that you know the localhost trick, the way to do this should be obvious. Open your browser and go to `http://127.0.0.1` or `http://localhost`. Your Web server's home page should be displayed. If you get a connection error, you either have no Web server, or it is not running. Check the installation, verify that the Web server is running, and then try again.

> Windows NT users should use the Service applet in the Control Panel to check that the Web server is running. (It'll show a status of `started` if it is running.) Windows 95 and 98 users should check the Windows task bar. Linux users should run `ps -ae` at a command prompt to verify that the installed Web server is running.

Installing on Windows

Now that your computer is set up correctly, the next step is to actually install ColdFusion Express. The software can be downloaded from the Allaire Web site (`http://www.allaire.com`) or accessed directly from the accompanying CD. To start the installation, execute the file (double-clicking on it in the Windows Explorer).

It is a good idea to close all open applications before starting the installation process. Windows NT and Windows 2000 users must be logged in with administrative privileges to perform the installation.

When the installer starts, you'll see a welcome screen like the one shown in Figure 2.1. Click the Next button to proceed.

FIGURE 2.1

The ColdFusion Express installer uses a set of wizard-type screens to walk you through the installation procedure.

You'll then be prompted to provide registration information (as seen in Figure 2.2). Fill in the fields as requested, and check the product update notification check box if desired. After you have completed the form, click Next.

If you opt to register, Allaire will be able to keep you notified of any product updates.

FIGURE 2.2

If you register with ColdFusion Express, Allaire will be able to keep you updated of important product enhancements or updates.

Next you need to specify the directory into which to install ColdFusion Express, as seen in Figure 2.3. The default is C:\CFUSION, and unless you have an important reason to do so (such as insufficient disk space on the C: drive), I'd highly recommend accepting the default value. When you are ready to proceed, click Next.

FIGURE 2.3

*The default
ColdFusion Express
installation directory
of C:\CFUSION
should be used if pos-
sible.*

The internal components and configuration options used by ColdFusion Express vary
greatly based on the Web server you are using. It is therefore very important that the
installer know exactly which Web server you'll be using with ColdFusion Express.

To simplify the process, the installation procedure attempts to identify the installed Web
server for you. As seen in Figure 2.4, the installer will present you with a list of detected
Web servers, and you'll be required to select one of them. When you have selected the
correct Web server, click Next.

FIGURE 2.4

*The installation pro-
gram attempts to auto-
matically detect the
Web server you are
using.*

The installation program displays an Other Server option that can be used if
your Web server was not correctly detected. You are strongly advised against
using this option. If you are using one of the servers listed above, it should
be correctly identified by the installer; and the fact that it was not is usually
indicative of some sort of problem. Rather than continuing the installation,
you are advised to click Cancel and make sure that the Web server is
installed and running properly; after which, you can retry the installation
again.

Next the installer needs to know where you'd like to install the pages that make up the
ColdFusion Express Administrator and the online documentation. By default these are
installed in directories beneath the Web server document root (see Hour 1 for an explanation of Web server root directories). The installer will attempt to detect the document

root automatically (just as it did with the Web server earlier), but you can provide an alternate path in the screen as shown in Figure 2.5. Unless you have a specific reason not to, accept the default path, and click Next to continue.

FIGURE 2.5

ColdFusion Express documentation and administrative pages are installed in directories beneath the Web server root.

Now that the installer knows where to install components, the next thing it needs to know is what to install. As seen in Figure 2.6, you can install the program files, the documentation, the examples, or any combination thereof.

Program files are required to actually run ColdFusion applications; you'd never uncheck this option unless you just wanted a copy of the documentation. The documentation and examples, however, are optional. Make your selections and click Next.

FIGURE 2.6

The ColdFusion Express program files must always be installed; documentation and examples are optional and should only be installed on development machines.

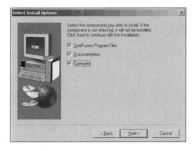

Documentation and examples should always be installed on the machine you do your development on, but generally should not be installed on production servers (the machines you run your finished application on, assuming that it is not the same as your development machine). The reason for this is security; the example applications are just that, examples. They are not highly-secure mission-critical code, nor were they designed as such. Although there is nothing inherently dangerous about them, best practices dictate that anything not needed on your Web should not be there. This will help secure your site in the event of the discovery of security holes in example applications.

ColdFusion Express features a Web-based administration utility that we'll look at briefly later this hour and in more detail in the next hour. Accessing this utility requires that a password be specified, and the installation program lets you select the password to use. As seen in Figure 2.7, you'll be asked to enter the password twice for verification purposes. After you have chosen and entered a password, click the Next button.

FIGURE 2.7

The ColdFusion Administrator is password protected using a password specified at install time.

ColdFusion Express stores the administrator password on the server. If you have previously installed ColdFusion Express, you might not be prompted for a password during subsequent installs; instead, the previously specified password will be used.

Incidentally, this is a security precaution designed to prevent someone from changing your password by simply reinstalling the software.

Don't like the password you picked at install time? Don't panic: You can change the password any time you'd like using the ColdFusion Administrator.

The final step before the installation is performed is the selection of the Windows program group name as seen in Figure 2.8. The default option should usually be accepted.

FIGURE 2.8

The installation program will create a Windows program group with shortcuts to the administrator, documentation, and other important choices.

When you have provided all the necessary information, the installer will do its thing—configuring and installing files and components as needed.

At this point, you might be prompted to restart your computer. If you are prompted, please do so.

That's all there is to it. ColdFusion Express for Windows is now installed and ready to use.

> How can you tell when ColdFusion is running? It depends on the operating system being used.
>
> Windows 95 and Windows 98 users will see little ColdFusion icons on the taskbar (next to the clock) when ColdFusion is running. Right-clicking on those icons will allow you to shut down ColdFusion Express. To restart ColdFusion, you'll need to load it from the ColdFusion program group.
>
> Windows NT and Windows 2000 users can use the Services applet in the Control Panel to see if the ColdFusion Services have been started. You can also click on the buttons there to stop and start ColdFusion Express.

Installing on Linux

ColdFusion Express for Linux runs on RedHat Linux 6.x or later. The recommended Web server is Apache 1.3.9 or later (1.3.12 or later is preferred).

> You must be logged in with root privileges to perform the installation.

> If you have a self-compiled version of Apache, make sure that it is compiled with DSO (dynamic shared object) support enabled.

ColdFusion Express for Linux is installed using a text-based installer that will walk you through the installation process. The install files are usually stored in a gz file for simplified (and quicker) distribution. So the first thing you must do is expand the gz file (using tar) as shown in Figure 2.9.

FIGURE 2.9

ColdFusion Express
for Linux must be
uncompressed before
you can proceed with
the installation.

After the files are uncompressed, you can launch the installer (file `cfinstall`) by typing the following command:

`./cfinstall`

A welcome message will be displayed, and you'll be prompted for the installation directory for ColdFusion Express as shown in Figure 2.10. You can press Enter to accept the default value.

The installer will then prompt you to identify the installed Web server and will even attempt to automatically detect it. Web servers must be correctly configured for use with ColdFusion Express, and the exact configuration varies based on the Web server being used. The installer can perform all this configuration for you if you so allow, as shown in Figure 2.11.

Next the installer needs to know where you want to install the pages that make up the ColdFusion Express Administrator and the online documentation. By default, these are installed in directories beneath the Web server document root (see Hour 1 for an explanation of Web server root directories). The installer will attempt to detect the document root automatically (just as it did the Web server earlier), but you can provide an alternate path in the screen as shown in Figure 2.12. Unless you have a specific reason not to, accept the default path.

FIGURE 2.10

The installation program will prompt you for an installation directory for the ColdFusion Express executables.

2

FIGURE 2.11

The installation program will attempt to automatically detect and configure the installed Web server.

FIGURE 2.12

ColdFusion Express documentation and administrative pages are installed in directories beneath the Web server root.

Installation of the ColdFusion Express documentation and example files are optional. The installer will prompt you to determine if you want these installed as shown in Figures 2.13 and 2.14.

FIGURE 2.13

Installation of the ColdFusion Express documentation files are optional, and should typically be installed.

Documentation and examples should always be installed on the machine you do your development on, but generally should not be installed on production servers (the machines you run your finished application on, assuming that it is not the same as your development machine). The reason for this is security; the example applications are just that, examples. They are not highly-secure, mission-critical code, nor were they designed as such. Although there is nothing inherently dangerous about them, best practices dictate that anything not needed on your Web should not be there. This will help secure your site in the event of the discovery of security holes in example applications.

2

FIGURE 2.14

Installation of the ColdFusion Express example files are optional and should only be installed on development machines.

ColdFusion Express features a Web-based administration utility that we'll look at briefly later this hour and in more detail in the next hour. Accessing this utility requires that a password be specified, and the installation program lets you select the password to use. As shown in Figure 2.15, you'll be asked to enter the password twice for verification purposes.

Don't like the password you picked at install time? Don't panic: You can change the password any time you want using the ColdFusion Administrator.

FIGURE 2.15
FIGURE 2.15

The ColdFusion Administrator is password protected using a password specified at install time.

Next you'll be asked for the account under which ColdFusion Express should run, as shown in Figure 2.16. You must specify the name of an existing account, and it should not be an account with root access.

FIGURE 2.16

The installer will prompt you for the account under which to run ColdFusion Express.

With that, the installer will copy all files and configure all settings for you. When complete, you'll see a confirmation screen like the one shown in Figure 2.17.

FIGURE 2.17

When finished, the installer will display a brief status report summarizing what was installed and notifying you of any problems (should they occur).

That's all there is to it. ColdFusion Express for Linux is now installed and ready to use.

> How can you tell when ColdFusion is running? Run ps -ae at a command prompt and look for the cfserver and cfexec processes.

Verifying the Installation

Now that ColdFusion is installed, it's a good idea to verify that the installation was successful. The best way to do this is to actually execute a ColdFusion application. This way you'll quickly know whether all is well.

Accessing the ColdFusion Administrator

As mentioned previously, ColdFusion Express comes with a Web based administrative tool—the ColdFusion Administrator. Being Web based, your ColdFusion Express can be managed from anywhere as long as you know the correct password.

The ColdFusion Express Administrator is written in ColdFusion, so ColdFusion must be working properly in order to access it. As such, accessing the Administrator makes for a great installation test.

> The ColdFusion Administrator might have been automatically launched upon completion of the installation process.

To start the ColdFusion Administrator, simply select the ColdFusion Administrator option from the ColdFusion Server program group. A Web browser will be opened, and you'll be prompted for the administrative password as seen in Figure 2.18. To access the administrator, simply enter the password. If the administrator screen, seen in Figure 2.19, is displayed, ColdFusion Express is installed and is working properly.

FIGURE 2.18

The ColdFusion Express Administrator will only be displayed if the correct password is specified.

The ColdFusion Administrator uses a framed interface. You select the screen you need from the navigation bar on the left to display it in the window on the right. There are six primary screens in the ColdFusion Express Administrator (and far more in the full commercial version).

The Server Settings Screen

The Server Settings screen, seen in Figure 2.20, is used to set systemwide settings. Use this screen to set the number of supported simultaneous connections, cache settings, and timeout options. Click the Apply button to save your changes.

We'll take a look at some of these options in Hour 22, "Improving Application Performance," and Hour 23, "Managing the ColdFusion Server."

FIGURE 2.19

*The ColdFusion
Express Administrator
also contains links to
tutorials, sample
applications, and all
sorts of supporting
documentation.*

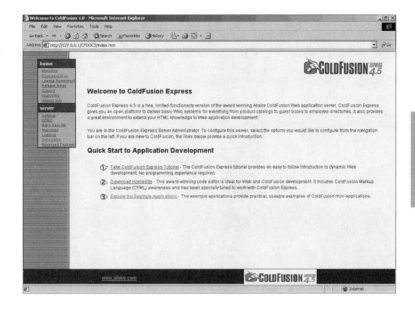

FIGURE 2.20

*The Server Settings
screen is used to set
systemwide settings.*

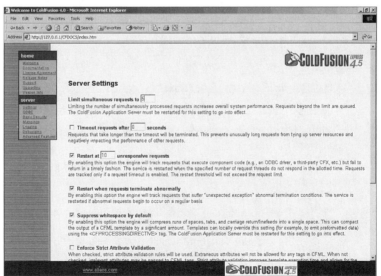

The ODBC Data Sources Available to ColdFusion Screen

The ODBC Data Sources Available to ColdFusion screen, seen in Figure 2.21, is used to
configure and manage ODBC data sources. ODBC and data sources (and how they are
used to connect to databases) are explained in Hour 11, "Connecting to a Database."

FIGURE 2.21
The ODBC Data Sources Available to ColdFusion screen is used to define and manage ODBC data sources.

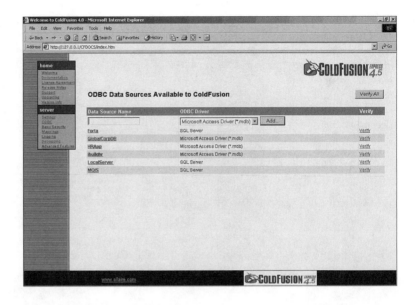

ColdFusion Express supports a limited set of ODBC data source types. Client server databases, like Microsoft SQL Server and Oracle, are not supported.

The Basic Server Security Screen

The Basic Server Security screen, seen in Figure 2.22, is used to manage the ColdFusion Administrator security—specifying whether a password is required, and changing that password as needed.

The term *Basic Server Security* implies that there are other security options, ones that are not so basic. And indeed, there are Advanced Security screens that provide sophisticated application security management, but those options are only available in ColdFusion Enterprise.

The Mapping Screen

The Add New Mapping screen, shown in Figure 2.23, is used to set ColdFusion level path mappings. We'll look at this in Hour 4, "Creating Your First ColdFusion Page."

FIGURE 2.22

The Basic Server Security screen is used to secure the ColdFusion Administrator.

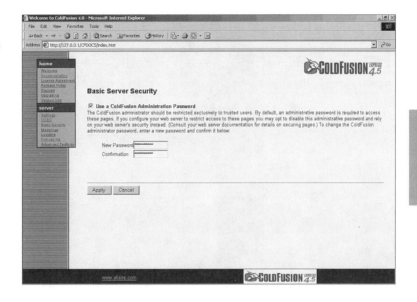

FIGURE 2.23

The Add New Mapping screen is used to set ColdFusion path mappings.

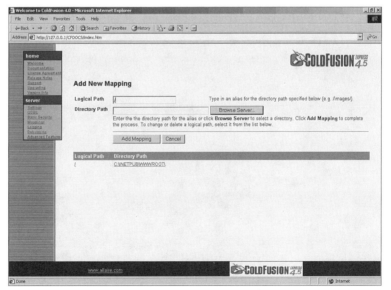

The General Error Logging Screen

The General Error Logging screen, seen in Figure 2.24, is used to set up logging and diagnostic settings. We'll review some of these in Hour 22.

FIGURE 2.24
*The General Error
Logging screen is used
to manage logging set-
tings.*

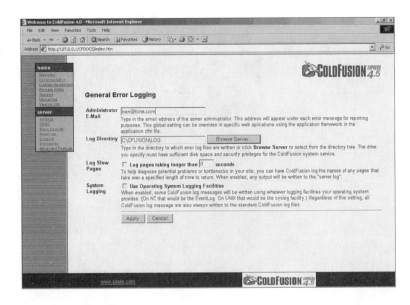

The Debug Settings Screen

The Debug Settings screen, seen in Figure 2.25, is used to enable and disable debugging
features and to manage client access to debugging information. We'll look at debugging
in Hour 21.

FIGURE 2.25
*The Debug Settings
screen is used to man-
age application debug-
ging options.*

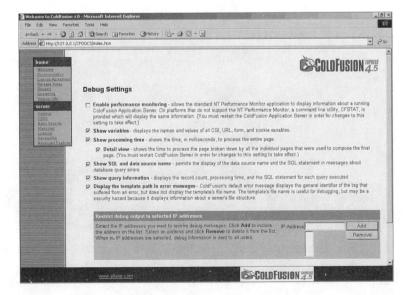

Accessing the Documentation and Examples

ColdFusion Express comes with a complete set of online documentation including a tutorial and language references. To access the documentation, simply select the ColdFusion Documentation option from the ColdFusion program group. A Web browser will be opened at the documentation home page and will be displayed as shown in Figure 2.26.

FIGURE 2.26

ColdFusion Express comes with extensive Web-based online documentation.

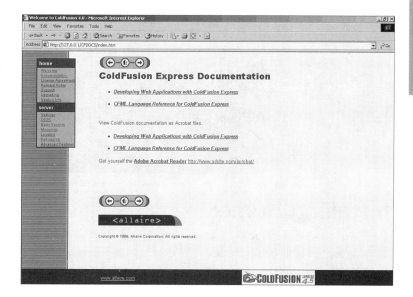

A complete sample application (shown in Figure 2.27) is also installed with ColdFusion Express (if you opted to install it). You can access this application from within the ColdFusion Administrator. (There is a link to it from the welcome page.)

Many developers find it useful to bookmark the online documentation right in their Web browsers so that it'll be immediately accessible whenever needed.

FIGURE 2.27

ColdFusion Express comes with a complete database-driven sample application that you can use for learning (as well as for borrowing ideas).

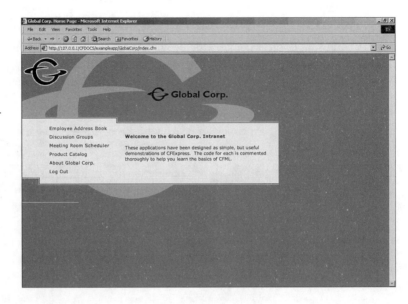

Installing HomeSite

We introduced HomeSite back in Hour 1, and we'll be using HomeSite extensively throughout this book. So, if you have not already done so, now would be a good time to install HomeSite.

There is no Linux version of HomeSite. For that matter, there is no version of HomeSite for any operating system other than Windows. Linux users who want to actually write code on their Linux machines will need to use a different text editor, and any text editor can be used.

It is important to note that although HomeSite will not run on Linux, it can be used to create applications that run ColdFusion on Linux.

The evaluation software can be downloaded from the Allaire Web site (http://www.allaire.com) or accessed directly from the accompanying CD. To start the installation, execute the file (double-clicking on it in the Windows Explorer).

When the installer starts, you'll see a welcome screen like the one shown in Figure 2.28. Click the Next button to proceed.

FIGURE 2.28

Like the ColdFusion Express installer, the HomeSite installer uses a set of wizard-type screens to walk you through the installation procedure.

Next you'll be asked for your name and company information as seen in Figure 2.29. If you are installing a registered version of HomeSite, you'll also be prompted for a serial number. If you are installing an evaluation version, the serial number will be the word `Evaluation`.

FIGURE 2.29

If you are using a registered version of HomeSite, you should enter the supplied serial number; if not, use the word `Evaluation`.

You'll then be prompted for installation directories for both HomeSite (see Figure 2.30) and TopStyle Lite (see Figure 2.31). The latter is a third-party cascading style sheet (CSS) editor that is fully integrated into HomeSite. Unless you have a compelling reason not to, I'd again recommend that you accept both default paths.

FIGURE 2.30

HomeSite can be installed on any drive or directory.

FIGURE 2.31

FIGURE 2.31

The TopStyle Lite style sheet editor is fully integrated into HomeSite.

The installer will then prompt you for the components to install as shown in Figure 2.32. The documentation only takes up about 5MB of disk space, so unless disk space is in short supply, you are better off installing everything.

FIGURE 2.32

You can choose the HomeSite components to install, although ideally you should install everything.

After you have verified the installation settings, the installer will complete the installation for you. You might be prompted to restart your computer. If you are prompted, please do so.

That's all there is to it. HomeSite is now installed and ready to use. We'll take a detailed tour of HomeSite in the next hour, and from that point on, you'll be using it in every hour in this book.

Summary

In this hour, you installed ColdFusion Express, and along the way learned a little more about IP, Web servers, and Web browsers. ColdFusion Express features extensive online documentation, and comes with Web-based administrative tools and examples, and you learned how to access all of this. You also installed HomeSite, and in the next hour, we'll take a detailed look at this important tool.

Q&A

Q **Isn't ColdFusion also supported on Solaris and HP-UX? You only mentioned Windows and Linux here.**

A ColdFusion Express is supported on Windows and Linux. Only the full commercial version of ColdFusion supports an additional two platforms—Solaris and HP-UX. These are not supported by ColdFusion Express.

Q **My computer is not a server; it isn't even usually connected to the Internet. Can I use it to develop ColdFusion applications?**

A As long as you have IP installed and have a running Web server, ColdFusion will work. The fact that you are not connected to the public Internet does not make a difference; you'll still be using the Internet Protocol even if it is just to communicate with services running on your own computer. However, it is worthwhile to note that if you use a dial-up connection to connect to the Internet, you might find your computer trying to connect to your ISP sporadically if not already connected.

Q **I have more than one Web server running on the same host. Can the same installation of ColdFusion Express be used with all my Web servers?**

A That depends on what you mean by "more than one Web server." If you have multiple sites hosted on your server, but all are hosted by the same Web server software, yes, ColdFusion Express will automatically support every site hosted by the same Web server. But if you have multiple Web server applications installed, you'll need to pick the one you want ColdFusion Express to use. You cannot select multiple Web servers during the install process, nor can you install multiple copies of ColdFusion Express (one for each Web server).

Q **If the ColdFusion documentation and Administrator are installed beneath the Web server root, they are going to be accessible to all my site visitors. Is this a security risk, and what should I do about it?**

A The documentation and Administrator must be installed where they can be accessed via the Web server. Whether they are in the document root or in any other directory is really irrelevant; either way they can be accessed from a Web browser. And yes, there are security considerations here, which is why I mentioned earlier that you really should not install documentation and example applications on production servers. The Administrator is a little different though because you have to install that on all servers or you won't be able to administer your server. Fortunately, the ColdFusion Administrator is password protected, and you can further protect it by moving it to a different directory (one that won't be as well-known as the default CFIDE directory) and by assigning a Web server or operating system level password as well.

2

Workshop

The Workshop contains quiz questions and exercises to help reinforce what you've learned in this hour. If you get stuck, the answers to the quiz questions can be found in Appendix A, "Answers to Quiz."

Quiz

1. What platforms are supported by ColdFusion Express?
2. What is it that allows ColdFusion Express to be administered from anywhere?
3. *True or false:* ColdFusion Express is a Web server.
4. How can you check that IP is installed and that your Web server is running?
5. *True or false:* The ColdFusion Administrator must be accessed from the local machine only.

Exercises

1. After you have verified that ColdFusion Express is working properly (meaning that IP and the Web server are working properly too), see what happens if the Web server is down. You can do this by shutting down the Web server and then trying to load the examples or the ColdFusion Administrator. It's useful to be familiar with the symptoms of a stopped Web server in case you ever run into this scenario.
2. Another useful scenario that you should be familiar with is in the case of the Web server running but ColdFusion Express not running. Try shutting down ColdFusion and then try to load the Administrator (see the notes at the end of the ColdFusion installation section above for information on now to do this). Notice the error that is returned; if you ever run into this error in the future (and you will), you'll now know what it means and what to do about it.

HOUR 3

Using HomeSite

As explained in Hour 1, "Understanding ColdFusion Express," Web application developers need access to professional development tools, and the professional editor we'll be using throughout this book is HomeSite 4.5.

In this lesson, you'll learn the following:

- How to navigate the HomeSite editor windows and panes
- How to use HomeSite's Resource Tab
- How to create and work with files

Getting to Know HomeSite

> HomeSite is a powerful and flexible editor, and there is no way I can explain all of its features in a single chapter. For full and detailed coverage of HomeSite, refer to my other book in this series, *Sams Teach Yourself Home-Site 4 in 24 Hours*, ISBN 0-672-31560-2. Although that book covers HomeSite 4 (and we're using version 4.5 here), most of the functionality is the same, so you should still find that book useful.

To start HomeSite, select the HomeSite 4.5 option from the HomeSite 4.5 Program menu beneath the Windows Start button. (If you don't have this Program menu on your computer, you'll need to install HomeSite; refer to Hour 2, "Getting Started," for details). A splash screen is displayed for a few seconds while the program loads, and then you see the HomeSite program window (see Figure 3.1).

FIGURE 3.1
The HomeSite program window is divided into several different panes and windows.

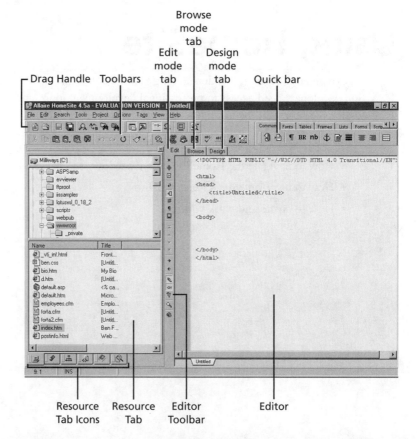

Now we will take a quick look at each major component of the HomeSite program window.

The Editor

As already explained, HomeSite is an editor. As such, the editor itself accounts for most of the HomeSite screen real estate. The editor window is where you write (and browse) your code.

HomeSite is an MDI (multiple document interface) editor, which means that you can have multiple documents open within it at any given time. Each file is represented by a tab at the bottom of the editor window. To switch between open files, click on the appropriate tab.

The file tabs at the bottom of the editor window are used primarily for document selection, but they also serve another important use. The document name within the tab changes color, indicating whether a file has been saved. If a file hasn't been saved, the filename is displayed in blue with a blue X in front of it. After a file is saved, the filename is displayed in black.

The HomeSite editor automatically color-codes your code. ColdFusion tags will appear in one color, text in another, HTML tables in another, and so on. This makes it easier to read your code, and also helps you find mismatched or misspelled tags (the colors will be wrong).

Along the left of the editor window is the Editor toolbar. Table 3.1 lists the buttons in this toolbar.

TABLE 3.1   Editor Toolbar Buttons

Button	Description
✖	Closes the currently active document.
⊕	Toggles split editor window.
▶	Shows a list of currently open files.

TABLE 3.1   continued

Button	Description
	Toggles word wrap on and off.
	Hides or shows gutter (the gray bar at the left of the editor window).
	Hides or shows line numbers in the gutter.
	Toggles display of hidden characters.
	Switches to full-screen mode.
	Goes to first open document.
	Goes to previous open document.
	Goes to next open document.
	Goes to last open document.
	Indents selected text.
	Unindents selected text.
	Toggles Tag Insight (a form of pop-up help).
	Toggles Tag Completion.
	Toggles Tag Validation.
	Hides or displays browser window beneath the editor (explained later).
	Launches Macromedia Dreamweaver. (This button will only be visible if Dreamweaver is installed, and integration has been enabled in the Settings dialog.)

Because you'll be spending most of your development time within the editor, we will take a look at some of HomeSite's more important editor features.

> HomeSite features all sorts of options that you can use to customize the behavior of the editor. You can access these options by selecting Settings from the Options menu.

Tag Chooser

Both HTML and CFML are tag-based languages. And although neither language is overly complex, remembering all the tags and what they are named can be difficult. To make life simpler, HomeSite features the Tag Chooser shown in Figure 3.2, which provides a tree-style control for tag selection. Tags listed in the Chooser are sorted into languages and categories to facilitate rapid location.

FIGURE 3.2

The Tag Chooser can greatly simplify the process of finding the exact tag you're looking for.

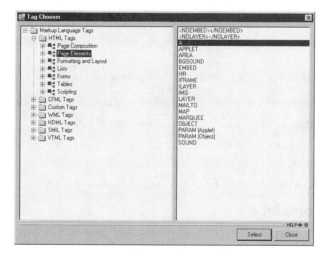

To use the Tag Chooser, do one of the following:

- Right-click in the editor window and select Insert Tag.
- Select Tag Chooser from the Tools menu.
- Press Ctrl+E.

Tag Editors

Tag Editors are pop-up dialogs that prompt you for the attributes for a specific tag. Using Tag Editors, as seen in Figure 3.3, prevents you from having to memorize all the possible attributes used by the tags.

FIGURE 3.3

HomeSite's Tag Editors are tag-specific dialogs that can be used to simplify tag attribute use.

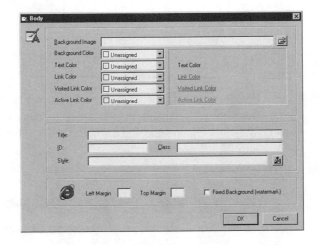

To display a Tag Editor, do one of the following:

- Right-click on any tag in the editor window and select Edit Tag.
- Select any tag in the editor window and press Ctrl+F4.
- Select any tag in the editor window and then select Edit Current Tag from the Tags menu.
- Select a tag from the Tag Chooser to insert a new tag.

Tag Completion

Many HTML and CFML tags are made up of tag pairs as explained in Hour 1. Mismatching tag pairs, or forgetting to close a tag with its appropriate end tag, is one of the most common beginner errors in both HTML and CFML development. To prevent this from occurring, HomeSite can automatically complete tag sets for you as you type them.

This option, called Tag Completion, is turned on by default. To turn if off (or to toggle it on and off as needed), click on the Tag Completion button in the Editor toolbar (refer to Table 3.1).

Tag Insight

Another form of help, one that will appeal to developers who favor the keyboard over the mouse, is Tag Insight. This feature, seen in Figure 3.4, allows HomeSite to detect when you need help and provide it automatically. Tag Insight is activated if you are typing the code for a tag and pause for more than a second or two. HomeSite will then pop up an inline list of context sensitive options from which you can select.

FIGURE 3.4

Tag Insight is the favorite help option of keyboard-oriented developers.

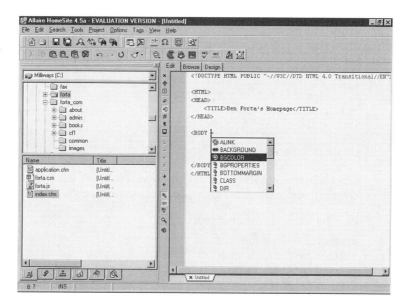

Tag Insight is turned on by default. To turn if off (or to toggle it on and off as needed), click on the Tag Insight button in the Editor toolbar (refer to Table 3.1).

Line Numbering

Line numbering, as its name suggests, is HomeSite's capability to display line numbers alongside your code. This feature is important when debugging applications, as ColdFusion reports code problems by telling you the line number at which problems occur.

The line number display can be toggled on and off by clicking the Show Line Numbers in Gutter button in the Editor toolbar (refer to Table 3.1).

Code Indentation

Take a look at the following code block :

```
<TABLE>
<TR>
<TD></TD>
<TD></TD>
<TD></TD>
</TR>
<TR>
<TD></TD>
<TD></TD>
<TD></TD>
</TR>
<TR>
<TD></TD>
<TD></TD>
<TD></TD>
</TR>
</TABLE>
```

The previous code creates an HTML table three rows high, each containing three columns. But you'd never know that without reading the code carefully.

Now look at this next code block :

```
<TABLE>
<TR>
        <TD></TD>
        <TD></TD>
        <TD></TD>
</TR>
<TR>
        <TD></TD>
        <TD></TD>
        <TD></TD>
</TR>
<TR>
        <TD></TD>
        <TD></TD>
        <TD></TD>
</TR>
</TABLE>
```

As you can see, the indented code is much cleaner and easier to read. And more important, it is also easier to debug. If there were a missing end tag or an incorrect level of tag nesting (tags within tags, as in the previous example), that would be blatantly obvious (you'd see that the code indentation wasn't lining up properly).

HomeSite has a feature called Auto Indent, which ensures that indentation is honored when you press the Enter key at the end of a line of code. This way if code is indented, the next line will automatically be indented too. (You'll have to unindent the line manually when you want to unindent the next line of code). You may turn off Auto Indent in the Editor screen in the Settings dialog (press F8 to access this dialog).

To indent or unindent specific lines or blocks of code, you can use the Indent and Unindent buttons in the Editor toolbar (refer to Table 3.1). Just click (or highlight) the lines to be indented or unindented, and click the appropriate button.

Buttons and Toolbars

Almost every feature in HomeSite can be accessed in more than one way. Standard Windows menus provide access to most functions. Toolbars and buttons provide shortcuts to menu operations. If you're more comfortable typing (as opposed to using the mouse), you can use shortcut key combinations or menu selections.

> Almost all HomeSite toolbars can be dragged, dropped, and anchored anywhere onscreen. If your screen doesn't look exactly like the ones in the figures, don't worry; it just means that elements were moved. If you can't find a particular screen element, you can always access it via the View menu.

The standard set of toolbars and their common buttons are listed in Table 3.2. In addition, one very important HomeSite feature is the Quick Bar, a tabbed set of toolbars that usually appears at the top right of the HomeSite screen. The Quick Bar contains multiple toolbars that you can select by clicking their tabs, and each tab contains one or more buttons.

TABLE 3.2   Toolbar Buttons

Button	Description
Standard Toolbar Buttons	
	Creates a new file by using the default template.
	Opens a file and displays the file selection dialog.

TABLE 3.2 continued

Button	Description
Standard Toolbar Buttons	
	Saves the currently selected (active) file.
	Saves all open files.
	Performs a search.
	Performs a search and replace operation.
	Performs a search using extended functionality.
	Performs a search and replace using extended functionality.
Edit Toolbar Buttons	
	Cuts the highlighted text
	Copies the highlighted text.
	Pastes Clipboard contents in current location.
	Shows the Clipboard contents.
	Pastes all Clipboard contents.
	Clears Clipboard contents.
	Undoes last steps.
	Redoes undone steps.

TABLE 3.2 continued

Button	Description

Edit Toolbar Buttons

Repeats last tag.

Activates the CodeSweeper.

View Toolbar Buttons

Toggles hiding and displaying the Resource Tab.

Toggles hiding and displaying the Results window.

Toggles hiding and displaying the Quick Bar.

Toggles hiding and displaying the Special Characters window.

Activates full-screen display.

Launches an external browser to display the currently selected page.

Tools Toolbar Buttons

Displays the Color Palette.

Verifies links in a page.

Validates the active document.

Displays the image thumbnail viewer.

Spell checks the active page.

Toggles the highlighting of misspelled words while you type.

TABLE 3.2   continued

Button	Description
Tools Toolbar Buttons	
	Launches the Stylesheet Editor.
	Launches the Image Map Editor.

 If there is a toolbar that you need frequent access to, you can undock it and make it float wherever you need it. To do this, just drag it by the double vertical line on its left.

The Integrated Browser

The only guaranteed way to preview what a Web page will look like in a browser is, well, to view it in a browser. Rather than require that you keep saving your changes and then view them in a separate browser, HomeSite integrates with Microsoft Internet Explorer (if you have it installed) to display the pages within a browser right within HomeSite.

Because the integrated browser is an actual Web browser (rather than a simulated preview), the page displayed within it is exactly what is displayed to visitors when your site is deployed. Furthermore, the browser is fully functional, and all HTML elements (images, tables, links, frames, and so forth) are displayed correctly within it.

This integrated browser is accessible in two different ways:

- To display a full-size browser window (complete with browser navigation buttons), click the Browse tab in the editor mode selector. The browser, seen in Figure 3.5, is displayed in place of the editor. To toggle back to the editor, click the Edit tab.

- The browser can also be displayed directly beneath the editor window (see Figure 3.6). In this mode, page changes are reflected in the browser as the code is changed in the editor window. To enable this browser, click the Show Browser Below Editor button on the Editor toolbar (refer to Table 3.1). To close the browser window, click the button a second time.

FIGURE 3.5

HomeSite is fully integrated with Microsoft Internet Explorer, allowing pages to be previewed directly within the editor.

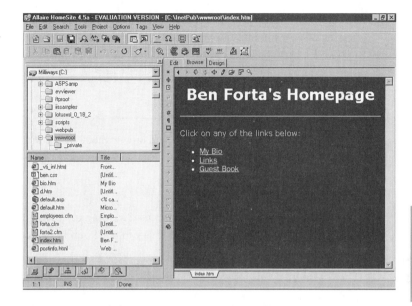

FIGURE 3.6

The integrated browser can be displayed beneath the editor window, so code changes can be seen as they are made.

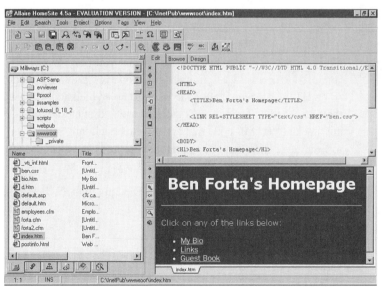

As I explained in Hour 1, various browsers often render the same HTML differently. For this reason, Web developers make it a point to preview their pages in as many different browsers as possible prior to deployment. To simplify this task, HomeSite supports the viewing of pages in multiple external browsers in addition to the integrated browser support. External browsers must be installed on your computer to use this feature, and after they are installed they must be registered with HomeSite using Configure External Browsers from the Options menu.

> To toggle between Edit and Browse modes, press the F12 key.

Design Mode

Even though HomeSite is an editor, not an authoring tool, HomeSite's creators understood that some HTML elements are tricky to code purely by hand. As such, HomeSite features a Design mode.

> ColdFusion developers find that Design mode is best used for initial page layout before any custom coding is introduced.

Design mode isn't a "what you see is what you get" (WYSIWYG) layout tool, nor is it supposed to be one. Design mode can, however, provide a graphical representation of some HTML elements, allowing them to be created and manipulated graphically rather than be coded by hand. The key difference is that Design mode is simply a way to generate blocks of HTML code that are inserted back into your page. When you switch back to Edit mode, you'll notice that HomeSite has generated and inserted clean and well-formatted HTML code into your page for you.

To use Design mode, simply click the Design tab in the Editor mode selector. You'll see a screen similar to the one shown in Figure 3.7.

> To toggle between Edit and Design modes, press Shift+F12.

FIGURE 3.7

*Design mode provides
a graphical interface
to some common
HTML layout tasks.*

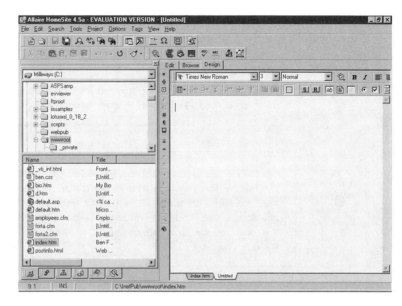

Using the Resource Tab

The Resource Tab is the large block usually on the left side of the HomeSite screen. The
Resource Tab is actually a collection of tabbed resources selected by clicking the tabs
beneath it. The Resource Tab has six tabs within it, as listed in Table 3.3.

TABLE 3.3   Resource Tab Icons

Tab	Description
	The Files tab
	The Projects tab
	The Site View tab
	The Snippets tab
	The Help tab
	The Tag Inspector tab

You'll be using the Resource Tab extensively throughout this book, so I'll take a moment to explain each of these tabs in more detail.

> To temporarily hide the Resource Tab (to increase the size of the Editor window), press the F9 key. Press F9 again to restore the Resource tab.

> Each tab in the Resource tab can be undocked and turned into a separate window by dragging it by its drag bar (the vertical bars on the left). In addition, the entire Resource tab (or specific tabs) can be moved and docked to any edge of the HomeSite window. To redock an undocked tab, either drag it back to the Resource Tab, or select Dock All from the View, Resource Windows menu.

The Files Tab

This tab provides an Explorer style tree control that you can use to browse and open files. Drives and folders (or directories) are displayed in one window, and files within the selected folder are displayed in a second window.

To open a file displayed in this tab, simply double-click it. You can also right-click any file to access other file manipulation operations.

> The Files tab can also be used with files on a network drive as long as you have rights to those files.

The Projects Tab

This tab is used to create and manage development projects. Projects are used to group all the files together that make up a Web site or application. We'll look at Projects in detail in Hour 24, "Deploying Your Applications."

The Site View Tab

This tab provides access to site management features. Here you can browse a hierarchical tree or chart view showing all files in your site and how they are linked.

To change the view style and options or to expand all links, right-click within the window and select the appropriate options. To expand a specific link, right-click that link.

 To prevent having to scroll to view the site tree, undock this tab to be able to resize it as large as necessary.

The Snippets Tab

This tab is used to save and access code snippets (little blocks of code saved for reuse). When code snippets have been saved, they can be inserted into pages as needed.

Code snippets are placed in folders. To create a folder, right-click the tab window and select Create Folder from the pop-up menu.

To create a snippet, right-click the tab windows and select Add Snippet to display the Snippet dialog box. You'll be prompted for a description (a title that you'll use to refer to the snippet) and the code.

After a snippet has been saved, it can be inserted into a document by double-clicking it, or by right-clicking it and selecting Insert into Document.

The Help Tab

This tab provides access to HomeSite's integrated help system. The help system is comprised of an extensive collection of Web pages that can be searched or browsed as needed. Access to the help system is facilitated via a set of buttons described in Table 3.4.

TABLE 3.4   Help Tab Buttons

Button	Description
	Displays the Search dialog.
	Switches to Help Reference tree view.
	Switches to Search Results view.
	Toggles the display location of help documents.
	Saves and manipulates help bookmarks.

If you need access to specific help pages, you can add bookmarks to them using the Bookmark button. This way, you can quickly return to the specific help pages by selecting the appropriate bookmarks. There is no limit to the number of bookmarks that you can add.

The Tag Inspector Tab

This tab provides a hierarchical tag-based view of the page being edited. The advantages of this view is that it allows you to see how and where tags are being used, and it provides rapid access to all tag attributes. This tab displays a window split into two panes. The upper pane displays a tree view of the tags being used and features a set of buttons described in Table 3.5. The lower pane displays the attributes for a selected tag and features a set of buttons described in Table 3.6.

TABLE 3.5 Tag Inspector Buttons and Controls

Button	Description
CFML and HTML Tags ▼	Select the tag profile.
	Configures and manages tag profiles.
	Collapses code in editor window according to the currently selected profile.
	Refreshes the tag list.

TABLE 3.6 Tag Inspector Attribute Buttons

Button	Description
	Edits tag definitions.
	Sorts attribute list by language version.
	Sorts attribute list by category.

TABLE 3.6 continued

Button	Description
	Sorts attribute list descending alphabetically.
	Sorts attribute list alphabetically.

> To filter the list of tags displayed by the Tag Inspector, select a profile from the drop-down list box at the top of the window (refer to Table 3.5).

> Tag attributes can be sorted or categorized by clicking the buttons above the tag attributes pane (refer to Table 3.6)

Creating and Working with Files

As explained in Hour 1, Web sites are simply collections of Web pages (and supporting graphics and other files). A Web page is simply a plain text file that usually contains embedded HTML code—the instructions used by the browser to correctly render the output. Similarly, ColdFusion application pages are simple HTML pages with additional CFML code in them.

There are basically three ways to create Web or Web application pages within HomeSite:

- Manually entering all the code by hand
- Using a template to start with a basic, predefined page
- Using a wizard to interactively create more complex pages

Using the Default Template

When HomeSite is launched, the Editor will display a simple Web page for you to start editing, as seen in Figure 3.8. The default template contains the shell of a basic page in which you can start writing your code. The default template is used every time you create a new file using the New button on the Standard toolbar.

FIGURE 3.8

*At startup, HomeSite
displays a page using
the default template.*

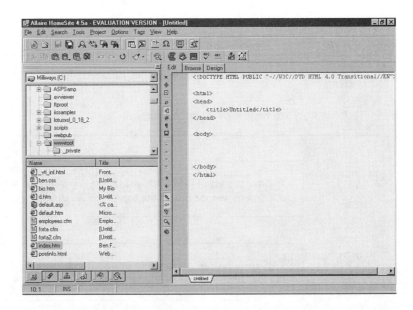

FIGURE 3.8

*At startup, HomeSite
displays a page using
the default template.*

HomeSite allows you to edit the default template, or even specify a template of your own to be used as the default template. To change the default template, select the Locations tab from the Settings window (press the F8 key).

Using Wizards and Templates

In addition to the default template just discussed, HomeSite ships with a set of additional templates and wizards that you can use when creating Web pages. To select a template or wizard, create a new file by selecting New from the File menu. This will display the New Document dialog shown in Figure 3.9.

Templates and wizards are both tools used to simplify the creation of new Web pages, but they are very different, as shown in the following:

- Templates—They are simply blocks of text that are dropped into any empty page. You can edit this text or use it as a starting block for your page. You can also create your own templates if you'd like.

- Wizards—They are sets of interactive screens that prompt you for information step by step so that a page (or set of pages) can be constructed for you. Creating your own wizards is possible, but this is an involved process, and is beyond the scope of this book.

FIGURE 3.9

FIGURE 3.9

The New Document dialog contains templates and wizards that you can use when creating new Web pages.

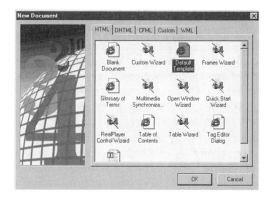

To use a template or wizard, simply double-click it (or select it and click the OK button).

Opening Existing Web Pages

Now you know how to create new pages in HomeSite. The next thing to look at is opening existing pages (for viewing or editing).

HomeSite can open files for viewing or editing in the following three ways:

- Any local files (or files accessed via the Network Neighborhood) can be opened using the Files tab explained previously, or using the Open option from the File Menu.

- HomeSite can read and write files on a remote server directly over an FTP connection. We'll look at this in detail in Hour 24.

- Any Web page that you can access (local, on the public Internet, and on intranets or extranets) can be opened directly by simply specifying its URL. To do this select File, Open From Web to display the Open from the Web dialog (shown in Figure 3.10), and then enter the desired URL.

FIGURE 3.10

The Open From Web dialog can be used to inspect the HTML code for any page on the Web.

One of the best ways to learn HTML is to see how other sites use it to create Web pages. This practice is legal, allowed, and highly recommended. The HTML code that makes up your Web page isn't secure or hidden. As a matter of fact, most Web browsers contain a View Source option that displays the underlying HTML in an integrated or external viewer. Of course, HomeSite makes viewing HTML source even easier, allowing you to open any URL within your Editor.

But don't expect to be able to view ColdFusion source using this technique. When you open a file to view its source, you'll be looking at the code that gets sent to the client's browser, not the original source code. We'll look at this concept in Hour 4, "Creating Your First ColdFusion Page."

Saving Local Pages

As explained previously, HomeSite displays a tab for each open file at the bottom of the editor window. Besides being used for switching between open files, this tab lets you know whether a page has been saved (it changes color if changes haven't been saved).

To save a Web page, do any of the following:

- Select Save from the File menu.
- Click on the Save button on the Standard toolbar.
- Press Ctrl+S.
- Right-click within the editor and select File, Save.

If the file has already been named, HomeSite will save the file without prompting you. If the file hasn't yet been named, you'll be prompted for the new filename.

By default, HomeSite will save files with an HTM extension. As you'll remember from Hour 1, ColdFusion files must be saved with a CFM extension. When saving files in HomeSite, you can explicitly specify the file extension, and HomeSite won't use the default values.

ColdFusion developers find it useful to change HomeSite's default extension from HTM to CFM. You can do this in the File Settings screen in the Settings dialog (press F8 to access the dialog).

If you don't save ColdFusion pages with the right extension, ColdFusion won't process and execute your code.

HomeSite lets you save your Web pages anywhere, in any directory, and on any server that you have access to. But not every directory is a suitable location for Web pages. If you are opening files within HomeSite (or even within your Web browser using its File Open option), any directory will probably work for you, except when you need to access the pages via a Web server.

As explained in Hour 1, Web pages are returned to visitors by Web servers. Web servers typically don't have access to entire servers or all directories. Rather, they have access to directories beneath a specified document root.

When you create pages for your Web site, they should be saved in a directory beneath the Web server's document root (or a sub-directory somewhere beneath it). This way you'll be able to access your pages via a Web server when you are ready to test them, and the underlying directory structure needed by the hosting Web server will already be in place. Even if you don't have a local Web server and are developing your site on a standalone machine, you should still use proper directory structures for your work.

Most Web site developers lay out their directory structure in a format similar to the following:

- A directory is created beneath the document root to contain the new Web site (this can be a directory directly beneath the document root, or in sub-directories anywhere beneath it). This new directory becomes the root directory for the Web site or application being developed.

- The entire Web site isn't saved in one mammoth directory, rather sub-directories are created for each subject or area. (Often these correspond directly to home page menu selections.)

- The Web site root contains just the home page (and any supporting files).

- Graphics (buttons, logos, toolbars, and so on) are stored in a IMAGES or GRAPHICS directory. (Keeping them grouped together makes reusing them simpler.)

After you have created your Web site and are ready to deploy it to a production Web server, the same directory structure (for your own site) should be used. This way any links and graphic references will work properly the first time. We'll look at deployment in detail in Hour 24.

Folders can be created within the HomeSite Resource Tab. To create a new directory, select the drive (or server) and directory in which you'd like the directory created, and then right-click the file window and select Create Folder.

Summary

This third hour introduced you to HomeSite by giving you a quick tour of its screen and windows. As you have undoubtedly discovered, HomeSite is a powerful and extensive application, and there is no way a single hour can provide the deserved coverage. You are strongly advised to experiment with HomeSite to learn its features. And if you'd like a book on HomeSite, take a look at my *Sams Teach Yourself HomeSite 4 in 24 Hours*, ISBN 0-672-31560-2.

Q&A

Q **HomeSite seems very code-centric. Will I have to write everything by hand?**

A HomeSite is code-centric, that is true. But no, you aren't forced to do everything by hand. HomeSite comes with menus, toolbars, tag selection features, wizards, and more to do much of the work for you.

Q **HomeSite looks incredibly feature rich. Will HomeSite do everything I need when creating Web sites, or will I need other tools and utilities too?**

A HomeSite is an editor—the best in its class. HomeSite provides you with all the editing features you require, but you will need other tools as well. Probably the most important tool you'll need is a graphics manipulation program—something you can use to create and manage graphics.

Q **I want to ensure that I am always running the latest and greatest version of HomeSite. How can I check to see if a new version is available?**

A The product can itself check to see if newer versions are available to ensure that you are always using the latest and greatest version of HomeSite. You can access this option by choosing Check for New Version from HomeSite's Help menu.

Q **I'd like to create my own HomeSite toolbars and add buttons to existing toolbars. Can I do this?**

A Yes, HomeSite's toolbars and buttons can be configured to embed tags, execute other applications and scripts, or perform other operations. Full coverage of these features is beyond the scope of this book, but feel free to experiment with these options by selecting Customize from the Options menu. And don't worry about making a mess of things; the Customize dialogs contain a button that will restore all toolbars back to their initial configurations.

Workshop

The Workshop contains quiz questions and exercises to help reinforce what you've learned in this hour. If you get stuck, the answers to the quiz questions can be found in Appendix A, "Answers to Quiz."

Quiz

1. Why does HomeSite feature an integrated Web browser and support for multiple external browsers as well?

2. *True or false:* HomeSite's Design mode is a full-featured WYSIWYG design tool.

3. Which HomeSite feature should be used to create and manage reusable blocks of code?

4. Which HomeSite feature should be used to manage sets of files that make up a Web site or Web application?

Exercises

1. HomeSite is chock-full of toolbars and buttons. If you hold your mouse over any of them, a text description of the button will pop up. Take a few moments to get to know which buttons are on which toolbar, and what they do.

2. One of the editor's most useful features is automatic color coding. Try opening any existing Web pages (using any of the techniques explained above) and see if you can determine why color coding is so invaluable.

3. The first time you conduct a search of the help system, HomeSite will ask you whether it should index the files for you. This can take a few minutes, but doing so will dramatically improve the speed of future help searches. Take a moment now to index the help files.

Hour 4

Creating Your First ColdFusion Page

This is it, the moment you've been waiting for. Having learned the basics of Web application servers, and having successfully installed and tested both ColdFusion Express and HomeSite, you are now ready to create your first ColdFusion page.

In this hour, you'll learn the following:

- How to create ColdFusion pages
- What makes a ColdFusion page a ColdFusion page
- How to create reusable code
- How and why to use path mappings

Building a Page

The best way to learn ColdFusion is to actually try it. We're going to start by creating a really simple static Web page (the kind you'd use on a traditional Web site), and then we'll turn it into a dynamic page using ColdFusion.

We'll be using HomeSite, so if you have not already done so, launch HomeSite by selecting it from the Start program menu.

> Hour 3, "Using HomeSite," introduced the HomeSite environment in detail. Refer back to that hour if needed.

Creating an Application Directory

The first thing we need to do is to create a working directory. As explained back in Hour 1, "Understanding ColdFusion Express," every Web server has a directory designated as the Web root. This is the top level directory from which requested files are retrieved.

For example, on my own Web site, www.forta.com, I have a directory named c:\inetpub\wwwroot, which is designated as the Web root. So if a user requests page www.forta.com/index.cfm, the index.cfm file will be retrieved from the c:\inetpub\wwwroot. If a user requests page www.forta.com/books, a file from the books subdirectory would be retrieved. www.forta.com/books maps to directory c:\inetpub\wwwroot\books. Similarly, URL www.forta.com/cf retrieves a file from c:\inetpub\wwwroot\cf, and so on. This relationship among files, directories, and URLs can be seen in Figure 4.1.

FIGURE 4.1

HomeSite can be used to create static HTML pages.

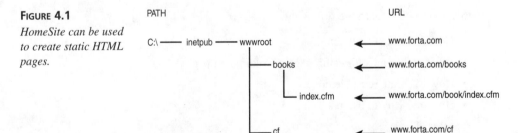

This type of directory structure is important when creating Web applications. You really don't want all your pages—as well as supporting images and any other files—sitting in the Web root. That would not be manageable at all. Instead, you typically create directories (or folders) beneath the Web root. Most developers create a new directory for each application they develop, and then create subdirectories within that new directory for different parts of the application.

> Don't know where your Web root is? The ColdFusion Express installer told you where root was when it prompted you for the path to install the online documentation and examples. If you don't remember the path, you'll have to open your Web server administration utility (not the ColdFusion Administrator) to find it.
>
> Here's a hint: If you are using a Microsoft Web server, the Web root will usually be c:\inetpub\wwwroot.

To Do: Create the Application Root Folder

▼ To Do

So to help organize your development, let's start by creating a directory for the lessons in this book. You can create folders using Windows Explorer, or any other file management utility, but we'll use HomeSite because you already have it open. Here are the steps to follow:

1. Open HomeSite (if it is not already open), and make sure that the Files tab in the Resource tab is selected.

2. Browse through the directory tree in the top pane to find the Web server root. It is important that you click on the Web server root to select it before proceeding (or you'll create the folder in the wrong place).

3. With the Web root selected, right-click in the file pane and select Create Folder to create a new folder in the Web root. A folder will be created in the directory pane (the top part of the tab), and you'll be able to name it. Specify `learncfe` as the folder name and press Enter to create the folder. Once created, the new folder will automatically be selected.

You now have a folder for your application. The URL to this folder will be `http://localhost/learncfe` (or `http://127 00 1/learncfe`). (Remember:
▲ `http://localhost` (which equates to IP address 127 0 0 1) points to your Web root.)

Creating a Work Folder

Now that you have a folder for your application, you need to create a folder within it for the work we'll do in this hour. I'll walk you through the process now, but, in future hours, you'll have to do this yourself.

To Do: Create the Application Root Folder

The individual folders for each hour are named hour4 for Hour 4, hour5 for Hour 5, and so on. Here are the steps to follow:

1. If it is not already selected, select the newly created learncfe folder in the top pane.

2. With the application root selected, right-click in the file pane and select Create Folder to create a new folder in the Web root. Once again, a folder will be created in the directory pane (the top part of the tab), and you'll be able to name it. Specify **hour4** as the folder name and press Enter to create the folder. Once created, the new folder will automatically be selected.

You now have a folder for this hour's work. The URL to this folder will be `http://localhost/learncfe/hour4`. learncfe is a folder beneath the Web root, and hour4 is a subfolder of learncfe.

> HomeSite is not required to create new folders. You can actually create folders using Windows Explorer or any other utility.
>
> But be careful. If you create a folder while HomeSite is running, that new folder might not show up in the Files tab on the Resource tab unless you refresh the file and directory list. To refresh the file list, right-click in the file pane and select Refresh, or press F5.

Static Pages

Let's start by creating a simple static page in HomeSite, similar to the one shown in Figure 4.2. This page uses basic HTML to display a welcome message.

FIGURE 4.2

HomeSite can be used to create static HTML pages.

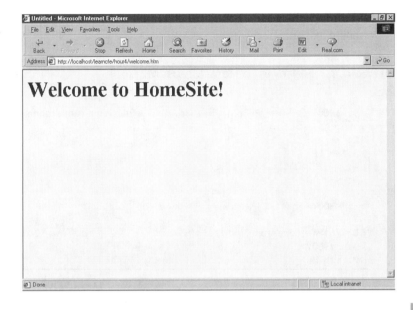

To Do: Create a Static Web Page

Here are the steps to follow to create this page. (I'll show you the complete code in a moment.)

1. If it is not already selected, select the newly created learncfe/hour4 folder in the top pane because that's where we want the new page to be created.

2. Click the New button to create a new page. (You can also select File, New and then double-click on Default Template.) The editor will now contain a basic page with head and body elements, but no content.

3. On a new line in between the <BODY> and </BODY> tags, type the following text:

   `Welcome to HomeSite!`

4. Highlight the text you just entered, select the Fonts tab from the HomeSite QuickBar, and click on the button marked H1. This will enclose your text with HTML <H1> tags.

5. Click the Save button to save your page (you can also select File, Save to do this) and you'll be prompted for the filename. The directory will automatically be correct because you were careful to select the hour4 folder in the Resource Tab beforehand. Enter `welcome.htm` as the file name, and click Save to save the file.

▼ The line numbers are for your reference and should not be typed in. The complete code should look like Listing 4.1.

LISTING 4.1   Welcome to HomeSite HTML Code

```
 1: !DOCTYPE HTML PUBLIC "-//W3C//DTD HTML 4.0 Transitional//EN">

 2: <HTML>
 3: <HEAD>
 4: <TITLE>Untitled</TITLE>
 5: </HEAD>

 6: <BODY>
 7:
 8: <H1>Welcome to HomeSite!</H1>
 9: </BODY>
10: </HTML>
```

To test the page, open your browser and go to `http://localhost/learncfe/hour4/welcome.htm`. You should see a page similar to the one shown in Figure 4.2.

> You might have noticed a Browse tab above the edit window in HomeSite. You can select this tab to browse the page you just created from within HomeSite, but that will only work for static pages, not for dynamic ones (like ColdFusion pages). More on that soon.

▲

Dynamic Pages

Now that you've created and tested a simple static Web page, you will create your first ColdFusion page, and you will start using the same page.

What distinguishes a ColdFusion page from a static Web page? The answer is the file extension. Static Web pages typically have an extension of HTM (or HTML), ColdFusion pages have an extension of CFM (or CFML).

To Do: Create a Dynamic Web Page

To Do

Here are the steps to follow to create the ColdFusion page:

▼ 1. Go to the line you typed (the welcome message) and replace the word HomeSite with **ColdFusion Express** so that the line now reads

   `<H1>Welcome to ColdFusion Express!</H1>`

▼ 2. Select Save As from the File menu and save this file as `welcome.cfm`.

3. To test the page, open your browser and go to
   `http://localhost/learncfe/hour4/welcome.cfm`.

And there you have it—your first ColdFusion Express page.

The Dreaded Error 403

Did you get an error (a 403 error, or an execution error) when you tried to open welcome.cfm? If so, your Web server is not configured to allow script execution. This is a very common problem among users of Microsoft Web servers as the default execution permissions on these servers is often set to none (which restricts scripts such as ColdFusion pages from being executed).

Fortunately this is a very simple problem to remedy. You'll need to open your Web server administrative utility (not the ColdFusion Administrator) and allow script execution. You may do this for your entire server by clicking on the Web root, and editing its properties to allow script execution. You can also enable scripts for specific directories only. If you opt to do this, turn on execution for the learncfe directory. (This will also allow execution in all subdirectories of learncfe). Figure 4.3 shows you the properties dialog as displayed on my computer, depending on what version of the Web server you are using yours may look a little different, but the end result is the same.

4

FIGURE 4.3

Web servers must allow script execution for ColdFusion pages to be processed.

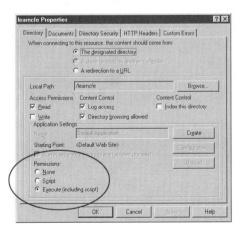

Okay, I agree that was rather anticlimactic, but realize what just happened. When you requested page welcome.htm, the Web server simply returned that page to your browser. But when you requested page welcome.cfm, the Web server submitted that page to the
▼ ColdFusion Express Application Server for processing and then returned the results back

▼ to you. Of course in this simple example, ColdFusion had nothing to do, so all you got
back is what you typed. Now that the page is being processed by ColdFusion, we can
▲ add server-side processing.

To Do: Use ColdFusion to Display the Date and Time

To show you what I mean, let's update the welcome.cfm page to show the current date
and time. Here are the steps to follow:

1. If it is not already open, open the welcome.cfm file.

2. Insert the following code on new lines after the welcome message (make sure to
   type it exactly as it appears here, complete with all the pound signs and parentheses):

```
<CFOUTPUT>
Today is #DateFormat(Now())#<BR>
It is #TimeFormat(Now())#
</CFOUTPUT>
```

3. Resave the updated file.

4. To test the page, open your browser and reload page
   `http://localhost/learncfe/hour4/welcome.cfm`. You should see a display similar to the one shown in Figure 4.4 (of course, your display will likely show a different date and time) .

FIGURE 4.4

ColdFusion pages can
display dynamic data,
for example, the cur-
rent date and time.

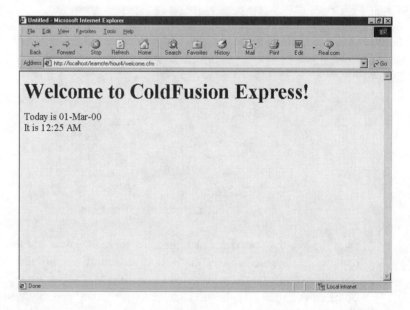

▼   If you ran into problems, check your code carefully. It should look like Listing 4.2.

LISTING 4.2   Welcome to ColdFusion Express CFM File

```
 1: <!DOCTYPE HTML PUBLIC "-//W3C//DTD HTML 4.0 Transitional//EN">
 2: <HTML>
 3: <HEAD>
 4: <TITLE>Untitled</TITLE>
 5: </HEAD>
 6:
 7: <BODY>
 8:
 9: <H1>Welcome to ColdFusion Express!</H1>
10: <CFOUTPUT>
11: Today is #DateFormat(Now())#<BR>
12: It is #TimeFormat(Now())#
13: </CFOUTPUT>
14:
15: </BODY>
16: </HTML>
```

And there you have it, your first ColdFusion Express page. Don't worry about the details
of the code you typed just yet; we'll cover this code in detail in Hour 5, "Working with
Variables and Expressions," and Hour 7, "Using Functions." For now it'll suffice to say
that <CFOUTPUT>, #DateFormat(Now())#, and other parts of what you typed are CFML—
ColdFusion Markup Language, the language used to create ColdFusion pages.

Dynamically generated pages cannot be browsed within HomeSite because
these pages must first be processed by ColdFusion before they can be displayed.

▲

Understanding CFML

As explained back in Hour 1, ColdFusion applications are written in a language called
CFML, or ColdFusion Markup Language. Unlike many other languages used for Web
application development, CFML was designed specifically for use on the Web, and is
thus modeled on the most successful markup language ever—HTML.

Just as HTML is made up of tags, so is CFML. There are tags used to interact with databases, tags used to display dynamic data, tags used for conditional processing, and many
more. The way you know that a tag is a CFML tag (as opposed to HTML or any other
markup language) is by the fact that **all** CFML tags begin with CF.

Only a subset of CFML is supported in ColdFusion Express. In order to use all of CFML, you'll need the commercial version of ColdFusion.

Some of the features supported only in the commercial versions of ColdFusion include sending and receiving email; writing language extensions (via your own tags, or through interfaces to COM, CORBA, C/C++, and Java); support for a greater selection of databases; interactive debugging; more sophisticated variable types; security systems; and integrated scalability and load-balancing technologies. Visit http://www.allaire.com to download an evaluation version of ColdFusion, or see the accompanying CD-ROM.

In addition to tags, CFML comes with a complete set of functions that you can use to convert, format, and manipulate data. We'll cover functions extensively in Hour 7, and you'll use many of them as you work through this book.

Even though you have yet to learn exactly what the code in page welcome.cfm did, you can clearly see that we used one tag, <CFOUTPUT>, and three functions, DateFormat(), TimeFormat(), and Now(). And everything you write in ColdFusion will be written in much the same way, using tags and functions.

The key to remember for now is that CFML is a set of instructions to the ColdFusion server. Let me demonstrate what I mean by that.

Using your Web browser, go back to page welcome.htm (the full URL was http://localhost/learncfe/hour4/welcome.htm). After the page has loaded, view the source in your browser (you'll find an option that you can use to view page source in your browser's menus). The source you see for the welcome.htm page is the same code that you typed into the welcome.htm file. In other words, the Web server returned that file to your browser as is; it did nothing to the page before it sent the page to you.

Now look at the source for the welcome.cfm file. (You'll need to go to http://localhost/learncfe/hour4/welcome.cfm.) The source you see will look something like this (with a different date and time, of course):

```
<!DOCTYPE HTML PUBLIC "-//W3C//DTD HTML 4.0 Transitional//EN">

<HTML>
<HEAD>
    <TITLE>Untitled</TITLE>
</HEAD>

<BODY>

<H1>Welcome to ColdFusion Express!</H1>
```

```
Today is 01-Mar-00<BR>
It is 12:25 AM


</BODY>
</HTML>
```

Take a look at this code. Where did the CFML tags and functions go? And how did that date and time end up there?

The answer is that CFML is a server-side language. All CFML tags and functions are instructions to the ColdFusion server, and ColdFusion processes them. CFML is never sent to the browser; it is always processed by ColdFusion. Instead of sending the CFML instructions back to the browser (where they'd be useless), ColdFusion processed them, striped them from the code, and then returned the results they generated back to the browser.

This is an important point to remember—CFML is executed on the server; it never gets sent to the client (the browser).

Now you'll understand why I said earlier that you can't browse dynamic pages using HomeSite's integrated browser. If you browsed the page that way, ColdFusion would never have the chance to process the code, the CFML would get sent straight to the browser, and, instead of the code being processed, you would find that parts of it would be displayed as code.

Incidentally, this is also why you must always open ColdFusion pages using a URL starting with http and not using your browser's File Open option. Like the integrated browser, that option will open the file without letting ColdFusion process it first.

Using Includes

The best way to learn how to use CFML tags is to actually use them, so let's take a look at one very useful tag, useful even independent of dynamic page creation.

I am creating two pages for my Web site. (These are static pages for now, just good old HTML.) The code (albeit incomplete) for the first one, books.cfm, is shown in Listing 4.3.

LISTING 4.3   books.cfm Code

```
 1: <HTML>
 2: <HEAD>
 3: <TITLE></TITLE>
 4: </HEAD>
 5:
 6: <BODY BGCOLOR="Blue" TEXT="Yellow" LINK="White" VLINK="White" ALINK="White">
 7:
 8: <TABLE WIDTH="100%" BGCOLOR="Maroon">
 9: <TR>
10: <TD>
11: <FONT FACE="Verdana" SIZE="+2" COLOR="Yellow">
12: <I><B>Forta.com</B></I>
13: </FONT>
14: </TD>
15: </TR>
16: </TABLE>
17:
18: <FONT FACE="Verdana">
19:
20: <H1>My Books</H1>
21: Information about my books goes here
22:
23: </FONT>
24:
25: </BODY>
26: </HTML>
```

Figure 4.4 shows the page displayed when this code is requested by my browser.

Now let's look at another block of code (also incomplete). Listing 4.4 shows page aboutme.cfm, and its output is shown in Figure 4.5.

LISTING 4.4   aboutme.cfm Code

```
 1: <HTML>
 2: <HEAD>
 3: <TITLE></TITLE>
 4: </HEAD>
 5:
 6: <BODY BGCOLOR="Blue" TEXT="Yellow" LINK="White" VLINK="White" ALINK="White">
 7:
 8: <TABLE WIDTH="100%" BGCOLOR="Maroon">
 9: <TR>
10: <TD>
```

```
11: <FONT FACE="Verdana" SIZE="+2" COLOR="Yellow">
12: <I><B>Forta.com</B></I>
13: </FONT>
14: </TD>
15: </TR>
16: </TABLE>
17:
18: <FONT FACE="Verdana">
19:
20: <H1>About Me</H1>
21: My bio goes here
22:
23: </FONT>
24:
25: </BODY>
26: </HTML>
```

FIGURE 4.5

Web pages typically have consistent menus, headers, and color schemes, which must often be repeated when creating Web pages.

As you can see (by looking at both the code and the figure), these pages have much in common. In fact, most of the code in these two pages is identical.

Code Reuse

Having that much repeated code in files books.cfm and aboutus.cfm is not a good thing. Developers go to great lengths to reuse as much code as possible. Here are some of the more common reasons for this:

- Being able to reuse existing code saves development time.
- If code is shared, changes need only be made in one place as opposed to many.
- When bugs are fixed in shared code, all files using that shared code benefit from the fix.

So how could we reuse common code using ColdFusion? Look at the code in listings books.cfm and aboutme.cfm, and you'll see that the top and bottom of the code blocks are the same—the page header (which includes the title bar) and the page footer. By extracting the header and footer code into their own files, that code can easily be shared. So I'd create two new files; I'll call them header.cfm and footer.cfm.

The header.cfm file would look like Listing 4.5.

LISTING 4.5   header.cfm Code

```
 1: <HTML>
 2: <HEAD>
 3: <TITLE></TITLE>
 4: </HEAD>
 5:
 6: <BODY BGCOLOR="Blue" TEXT="Yellow" LINK="White" VLINK="White" ALINK="White">
 7:
 8: <TABLE WIDTH="100%" BGCOLOR="Maroon">
 9: <TR>
10: <TD>
11: <FONT FACE="Verdana" SIZE="+2" COLOR="Yellow">
12: <I><B>Forta.com</B></I>
13: </FONT>
14: </TD>
15: </TR>
16: </TABLE>
17:
18: <FONT FACE="Verdana">
```

The footer.cfm would look like Listing 4.6.

LISTING 4.6   footer.cfm Code

```
1: </FONT>
2:
3: </BODY>
4: </HTML>
```

To include these two new files in my books.cfm and aboutme.cfm pages, I can use a ColdFusion tag called <CFINCLUDE>. As its name suggests, <CFINCLUDE> is used to add the contents of a file into another file. <CFINCLUDE> takes a single attribute, the name of the file to include, as seen in this revised books.cfm file:

```
<CFINCLUDE TEMPLATE="header.cfm">

<H1>My Books</H1>
Information about my books goes here

<CFINCLUDE TEMPLATE="footer.cfm">
```

When ColdFusion processes this code, it'll include the contents of the header.cfm and footer.cfm files at the locations of the <CFINCLUDE> tags, and doing so will generate the same output as shown in Figure 4.4.

The advantages to this are obvious. If I wanted to change my title bar colors, if I wanted to use columns in my page, if I wanted to include a graphic logo, or if I wanted to make any changes at all, the only thing I'd need to do is change the header and footer files, and any files that include the header and footer would be updated automatically.

Using Path Mappings

While on the subject of includes, it is important to briefly discuss path mappings.

As I explained earlier, paths in a URL refer to directories off the Web server root. So www.forta.com/books points to c:\inetpub\wwwroot\books. Although this is true of that folder in my Web site, not all URLs point to subdirectories that way.

Most Web servers allow you to define path mappings (also known as *aliases*). A *mapping* is a virtual name for a directory, kind of like a nickname that can be used instead of the real name.

- **To shorten and simplify URLs**. If a directory is buried beneath lots of other directories, the full URL to get to it will likely be long and difficult to remember. A path mapping could be used so that users could specify a shorter (and easier to remember and type) URL, and they wouldn't have to know the actual directory from which the files were retrieved.

- **To access files and folders outside the Web root.** URLs are relative to the Web root as explained previously. But what if you needed to retrieve files from outside the Web root (perhaps from another hard drive if you were running out of space on your main drive)? A path mapping could be used to map a virtual path to an alternate physical path. So whereas www.forta.com points to c:\inetpub\wwwroot, www.forta.com/books could in fact point to d:\ben\books, or c:\inetpub\wwwroot\ forta\ben\books, or just about any other path.

- **To hide true paths.** As you can see from the previous two bullets, mappings hide the true path and expose a virtual path to the user instead. Some Web site administrators use this as a security measure based on the assumption that the fewer outsiders who know about the structure of your file system, the better.

ColdFusion Path Mappings

All this talk of path mappings concerns how they relate to your Web server. If you use Web server mappings, there is nothing special you have to do in ColdFusion. Web server mappings are automatically supported.

The exception to this occurs when including files using <CFINCLUDE>. Although ColdFusion honors Web server mappings, it is not actually aware of them. This means that if you have a Web server map set up to provide an alias to a directory, you won't be able to use that alias to specify the location of the file to include when using <CFINCLUDE> unless you also create the same mapping in ColdFusion.

ColdFusion mappings are defined in the ColdFusion Administrator, as seen in Figure 4.6. To define a mapping, you must specify the logical path (the alias) and the directory path (the actual path). Once defined, you'll be able to use the mapping in your <CFINCLUDE> tags.

FIGURE 4.6

ColdFusion level mappings are used only by CFML tags.

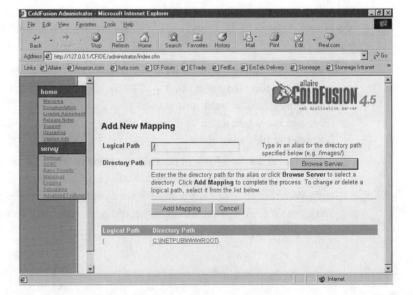

Logical pathnames must not include spaces or special characters.

Summary

Congratulations! You've successfully created your first ColdFusion page. In this hour, you learned about static and dynamic pages, and what it is that distinguishes them from each other. You also saw the way ColdFusion processes CFML on the server (never on the client), and you learned how to use <CFINCLUDE> to reuse and share common code. In the next hour, we'll start looking at variables and expressions.

Q&A

Q My ColdFusion programs are going to be hosted by my ISP. Is there a way for me to develop and test my ColdFusion code without having ColdFusion on my development computer?

A The full commercial version of ColdFusion (and not ColdFusion Express), in conjunction with its development tool ColdFusion Studio, does indeed support remote development. However, most developers find that development is far simpler and quicker when a locally installed ColdFusion server is used.

Q I understand the benefits of breaking up my code into smaller, reusable chunks, but I fear that the more files I have to work with, the less manageable my code will be. Is this a valid concern, and if yes, what are my options?

A Yes, it is a very valid concern. The more files you have to think about, the more likely it is that some will break, go missing, or be overlooked. For this reason, HomeSite includes project management features. We'll look at these briefly in Hour 24, "Deploying Your Applications." You can also refer to my book *Sams Teach Yourself HomeSite 4 in 24 Hours*, which has an entire chapter dedicated to working with projects in HomeSite.

Q Why would I want to use <CFINCLUDE> instead of my Web server's own server-side include feature?

A Some Web servers feature their own server-side include mechanisms that do the same thing as <CFINCLUDE>, but there is one big difference. Web server includes cannot include dynamic content (such as ColdFusion code); they can be used only to include static content. As such, you are almost always better off using <CFINCLUDE>.

4

Workshop

The Workshop contains quiz questions and exercises to help reinforce what you've learned in this hour. If you get stuck, the answers to the quiz questions can be found in Appendix A, "Answers to Quiz."

Quiz

1. How does a Web server know that a page is to be processed by ColdFusion?
2. *True or false:* CFML is made up only of tags.
3. Why can't ColdFusion pages be viewed with HomeSite's integrated browser?
4. How can aliases (path mappings) be used with <CFINCLUDE>?

Exercises

1. Create two files with the exact same contents, one an HTM file and one a CFM file. Which takes longer to execute? And why do you think that is the case?
2. Visit your favorite portal or e-commerce site and browse around. Which page components do you think are being reused?

HOUR 5

Working with Variables and Expressions

As explained in Hour 1, "Understanding ColdFusion Express," dynamic Web sites are created on-the-fly as needed. Creating dynamic Web sites usually involves extensive data manipulation, and much of this is performed using variables and expressions.

In this lesson, you'll learn the following:

- What variables are
- What expressions are
- How to create and manipulate variables and expressions in ColdFusion Express
- How to print out values of variables within your HTML code

What Are Variables?

Variables are containers that hold bits of information that are needed to make your programs run. You can use variables to temporarily store information that is needed to perform calculations.

NEW TERM Think of a variable as a box that holds a value. To remember what is stored in each box, you'll need to label the box with a name. The data you store in variables doesn't have to change, but often you'll need to change the value during the execution of the program. Variable contents change (which is why they are called *variables*), but the name of the variable (the label) doesn't. Figure 5.1 illustrates this concept.

FIGURE 5.1
Variables can be thought of as named boxes that can store values.

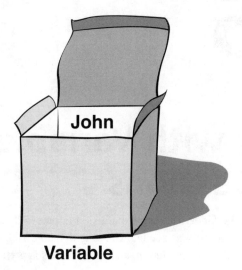

John

Variable

Creating Variables

Variables are created in CFML using the <CFSET> tag. Here is the syntax for the <CFSET> tag:

```
<CFSET Variable_Name="Value">
```

The following example creates a variable named FirstName and stores the value Sue in it:

```
<CFSET FirstName="Sue">
```

ColdFusion variable naming is important, and you need to follow the rules to prevent errors from occurring. The naming rules for variable names are as follows:

- It must begin with a letter (A–Z).
- It must contain only letters, numbers, and the underscore character (_); spaces should never be used.

> Your CFML code produces errors if you try to use spaces or special characters. For example, the following variable names are **not** valid:
> - My variable
> - $Value
> - #ofUsers
> - 1stItem

Naming conventions of variables are important for maintaining code. Programs are usually passed from developer to developer for maintenance, and it makes it easier for the next developer to read the code when the variables are descriptively named. There are many different opinions and conventions, but the most important thing is to be consistent. You want to name variables so that you can recall later what you meant to store in them. For instance, a variable named X doesn't conjure up the meaning of the data you want to store the same way that FirstName does.

> Some recommended conventions for naming variables are
> - All lowercase: myvariable
> - Mixed case: MyVariable
> - Use underscores in place of spaces: My_Variable

5

▲ To Do

To Do: Creating Page Variables

To create variables using CFML within your HTML documents, perform these steps:

1. Launch HomeSite.
2. Create a new page using the default template.
3. Change the text between the <TITLE> and </TITLE> tags to "Using Variables".
4. Position your cursor between the <BODY> and </BODY> tags.

▼ 5. Type **<CFSET FirstName="*Your Name*">** (of course, you should use your own first name).

6. Select Save from the File menu and save the file under the /learncfe/hour5 directory under the Web root as cfset.cfm.

7. Surf to the page in a browser to view the output.

What output do you see? You shouldn't see any. We have declared a variable, but we haven't done anything to print out the value to the page. For that, we'll need another
▲ CFML tag—<CFOUTPUT>.

Displaying Variable Values

<CFSET> allows you to create and manipulate variables, but it won't cause any output to be returned to the user. In order to print out the values of variables, you will need to use the <CFOUTPUT> tag.

<CFOUTPUT> tells ColdFusion Express that something is going to be generated and returned in the browser to the user for viewing. Like HTML tags, the <CFOUTPUT> tag has both an opening and a closing tag:

```
<CFOUTPUT>
    things to be shown to the user
</CFOUTPUT>
```

This tag only tells ColdFusion that there *might* be variables that need to be evaluated and printed out to the page, but it doesn't say what words inside the opening and closing tags are variables. In other words, the presence of a <CFOUTPUT> tag pair instructs ColdFusion Express to start looking for variables that need to be processed.

In order to indicate that you want to print out the value of a variable, you must surround the variable with pound signs (#):

```
<CFSET Age="29">
<CFOUTPUT>
    #Age#
</CFOUTPUT>
```

ColdFusion will scan the contents between the <CFOUTPUT> tags, find the pound signs, and know that it needs to evaluate the variable and print out the value. In this case, only the value of 29 is printed to the browser. Figure 5.2 shows the output generated by this code.

FIGURE 5.2

ColdFusion has evaluated the variable and printed out the value of 29.

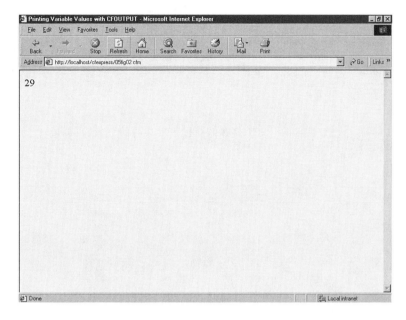

If you forget to put the pound signs around the variables, you will get the name of the variable printed out to the browser. For the following variable, you get the output shown in Figure 5.3:

```
<CFSET Age="29">
<CFOUTPUT>
    Age
</CFOUTPUT>
```

To Do: Printing Out Variable Values

Print out the value of the variable you created by performing the following steps:

1. Return to HomeSite and the cfset.cfm file.
2. After the `<CFSET>` tag, type the following:

   `<CFOUTPUT>#FirstName#</CFOUTPUT>`
3. Choose Save from the File menu to save the file.
4. Return to the browser and reload/refresh the page.

Notice that you will now see the value of the `FirstName` variable, which is your name. You might want to experiment by removing the pound signs and the `<CFOUTPUT>` tags to see what will happen if you make a mistake.

FIGURE 5.3

If you forget the pound signs, you'll see the variable name instead of the value.

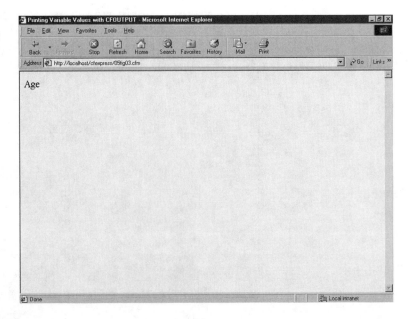

Variable Scope

NEW TERM   How long variables exist and where you can access them are known as the *variable scope*. The variables you have created thus far are only available to the page as it is processing. After the page is finished processing, the variables are destroyed and cannot be used on any other pages without recreating them.

Variable Families

NEW TERM   ColdFusion Express supports many different variable types, each with different purposes. The only type of variable that you have learned about so far is the simple page variable. But ColdFusion Express has many different types of variables, some of which are created by the Web server and Web browser, others are created by user input, and some variables allow you to send information from page to page using the URL. Think about each of these types of variables as a *family* of variables.

You will be learning about many different types of variables in CFML. Here's a list of the variables we'll be covering in this book in later hours:

- Page
- Query
- Form

- URL
- Cookie
- CGI
- Session
- Client
- Application

The variable type you have learned so far is just a simple page variable. It is possible, however, to have two or more variables of differing types with the same name. To help ColdFusion Express determine which variable you are referring to, it is recommended that you use the page variable's full name. This will make it clear what type of variable you are using.

Just as in a family in which the father and son have the same name, it is confusing when trying to ask for them by name. Often people use suffixes, such as Jr. or Sr. to specify the exact person they are referring to.

For CFML page variables, you can uniquely identify the variable and type using the VARIABLES prefix. So when you are printing out the value of a page variable, you can use this prefix to be more explicit:

```
<CFSET Age="29">
<CFOUTPUT>
    #VARIABLES.Age#
</CFOUTPUT>
```

> You don't need to uppercase the VARIABLES prefix. However, some developers prefer to do so because it makes that part of the variable stand out. As with all conventions, you should find the one that works for you and stick with it throughout your code.

You aren't required to specify the prefix. ColdFusion Express will look through all defined variables and will find the first variable of any type that matches the name. Unfortunately, it might not be the one that you were counting on. If you were to call for John, who is the father, but don't specify Sr., you might end up talking to the son instead.

5

Besides ensuring that you are referencing the correct type of variable, there is another benefit to using variable prefixes in your code. ColdFusion Express actually performs better if you explicitly prefix the variable when you use it. This is because it doesn't have to search through all defined variables to find the first one, but it goes directly to the variable requested.

Prefixing your variables might result in extra work for you, but the payoff will be reflected in easier maintenance of your code later on.

To Do: Prefixing Your Page Variable

You can refer to the page variable you created explicitly by performing the following steps:

1. Return to HomeSite and the `cfset.cfm` page you were working on.
2. Put the `VARIABLES.` prefix before the FirstName variable in the `<CFOUTPUT>` tag.

   You won't notice a difference in the output.

Using Expressions

NEW TERM   When you create a `ColdFusion` variable, you don't need to specify a data type explicitly. A *data type* describes the information stored in variables. The primary reason for different data types is because you might want to perform different operations on the data that makes it special.

For instance, you might want to be sure that a value entered as a date is truly a date in our calendar. You might want to add 10 days to a date to show when it will be shipped. Dates are another form of data type because there are special rules when working with them. There is a numeric data type because numbers need to be added, subtracted, and worked with in arithmetic calculations. Each data type has a set of rules for working with them.

NEW TERM   Because you aren't required to specify the type of data that will be stored, CFML is considered a *typeless language*.

The `<CFSET>` tag will take the value after the equal sign and assign it to the variable name specified. You can specify a numeric value using double quotes and still be able to use it in arithmetic operations:

```
<CFSET Age="29">
```

Some programming languages require that you specify the type of data that will go into the variable. These are known as *typed languages*. The following example using another language will create a variable called Age and assign it an integer value of 29. ColdFusion Express doesn't require that you specify variable data types.

```
Int Age=29;
```

NEW TERM When you assign a value to a variable that doesn't need to be evaluated, it is considered a *literal value*. Literal values can be text strings, numbers, special characters, or a combination of them all. To be consistent, surround all literal values with double quotes, as shown in the following:

```
<CFSET Age="29">
<CFSET FirstName="John">
<CFSET LastName="Doe">
<CFSET NumberOfPets="3">
```

ColdFusion will *cast*, or convert, variables from one data type to another on-the-fly, based on how you use it in your CFML code. This brings up the discussion of using expressions in <CFSET> tags.

Thus far, we have only assigned simple values to our variables. These simple variables are all literal values that don't require evaluation. The <CFSET> tag can be expanded to include expressions:

```
<CFSET Variable_Name=Expression>
```

Using expressions, CFML will construct the value of a variable by performing some type of operation, such as arithmetic or string manipulation. The following example will assign a literal value of 29 to the Age variable first, and then it will take that value, add 10 to it, and insert the result into the TrueAge variable:

```
<CFSET Age="29">
<CFSET TrueAge=Variables.Age+"10">
<CFOUTPUT>#Variables.TrueAge#</CFOUTPUT>
```

Figure 5.4 shows the output generated by the code.

A few things can be learned from this example. First, notice that Age is created before it is used. To use variables, they must first be created.

5

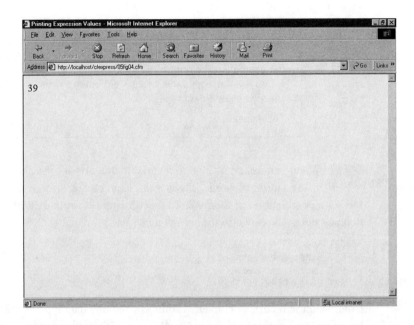

ColdFusion processes statements in order from the top of the page to the bottom:
Therefore, this type of processing is known as *top-down processing.*

Second, you cannot write code that depends on a variable that doesn't exist yet without
getting an error. The following code is an example of trying to use a variable before it is
actually defined. Note that the variable TrueAge tries to evaluate the variable Age, but Age
isn't created until the next line.

```
<CFSET TrueAge=Age+"10">
<CFSET Age="29">
```

If you try to use a variable in an expression that doesn't exist yet, you will receive the
error: "Error resolving parameter". If you see this error, check your typing. More
often that not, a misspelled variable name will be the cause of the error. Figure 5.5 shows
the error message you might receive.

Let's get back to the example: Next notice that Age doesn't have double quotes around it
in the assignment of TrueAge:

```
<CFSET Age="29">
<CFSET TrueAge=Age+"10">
```

FIGURE 5.5

Referring to variables that don't exist generates an error message.

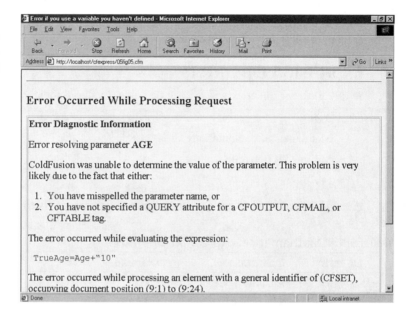

When you don't use double quotes for items in the expression, CFML assumes that you are referring to another variable. It doesn't attempt to take the string `"A-G-E"` and add 10 to it. This wouldn't make sense anyway because you don't want to take string values and use them in arithmetic operations. If you mistakenly put double quotes around a variable in an arithmetic expression, you would receive an error.

If you attempt to run the following code:

```
<CFSET Age="29">
<CFSET TrueAge="Age" + "10">
```

you would receive the error `"Cannot convert Age to number"`. See the next section for the reason for this error.

Data Types in Expressions

Here's where we need to think about data types again. ColdFusion Express is typeless in that it doesn't require you to tell it what type of data is being stored. But that doesn't excuse you from having to know your data.

It only matters what data type is stored when you try to perform an operation on it that requires a typed value.

You can use CFML functions to test what type of data is stored in variables. We'll look at them in Hour 7, "Using Functions."

Expression Operators

A variable assignment expression can be a literal value, another variable, or any of the following:

- Mathematical computations
- String concatenation
- Functions

Each mathematical operator and an example of its usage is listed in Table 5.1.

TABLE 5.1 Mathematical Expression Operators

Operator	Operation	Example	X Equals
+	Addition	`<CFSET X=1+2>`	3
-	Subtraction	`<CFSET X=1-1>`	0
*	Multiplication	`<CFSET X=1*2>`	2
/	Integer Division	`<CFSET X=4/2>`	2
\	Real Division	`<CFSET X=5\2>`	2
MOD	Modulo	`<CFSET X=10 MOD 3>`	1

NEW TERM You also have the ability to take two string values and put them together into one. The process of putting two strings together is known as *concatenation*. In CFML, the ampersand (&) is the concatenation character. The following example appends 'World!' to the end of the 'Hello ' string so that the end result of the Welcome variable is the full string 'Hello World!':

```
<CFSET Welcome="Hello " & "World!">
<CFOUTPUT>#Welcome#</CFOUTPUT>
```

The following code accomplishes the same thing, but demonstrates the use of multiple concatenations operators in a single expression:

```
<CFSET Welcome="Hello" & " " & "World!">
<CFOUTPUT>#Welcome#</CFOUTPUT>
```

As seen in Figure 5.6, the text is printed out as one string.

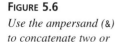

FIGURE 5.6

Use the ampersand (&) to concatenate two or more strings into one.

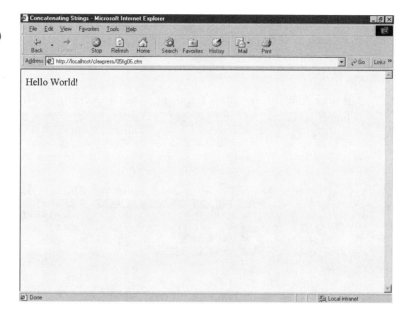

To Do: Concatenating Two Strings

You can concatenate two variables together using the ampersand (&) by performing the following steps. You will create separate variables to store your first and last names, and then concatenate them together into one variable called FullName.

1. Return to HomeSite and open the cfset.cfm page that you were working on.
2. Position your cursor after <CFSET FirstName="Your First Name">.
3. Type **<CFSET LastName="*Your Last Name*">**, (again, use your own name here).
4. Type **<CFSET FullName=Variables.FirstName & " " & Variables.LastName>**.
5. Type **<CFOUTPUT>#FullName#</CFOUTPUT>**.
6. Choose Save from the File menu to save the file.
7. Return to the browser and reload/refresh the page.

▲ You should see your full name printed in the browser.

Sprucing Up the Output

The rules for printing out variable values are as follows:

- Surround the variable with pound signs (#)
- Surround the output with the <CFOUTPUT> tag
- Prefix the variable with its type

The first rule tells ColdFusion Express that you want to print out the value of the variable and not literal text. The <CFOUTPUT> and </CFOUTPUT> tags tell ColdFusion to evaluate any variables between the tags. In order to say explicitly which variable you are referring to, use the prefix of the variable type.

The most common mistake is forgetting to use the <CFOUTPUT> tag. So if you start seeing pound signs in your browser (as seen in Figure 5.7), you forgot to use the <CFOUTPUT> tag around the output.

```
<CFSET Age="29">
#Age#
```

FIGURE 5.7

When you see pound signs in output, you've forgotten to use the <CFOUTPUT> *tag.*

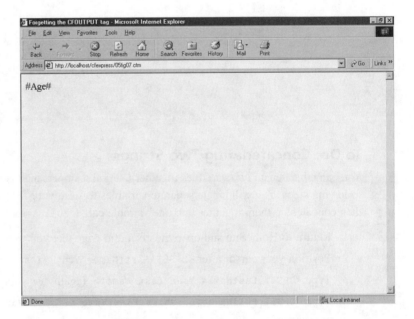

Now you can really make your page interesting by including text and any other HTML formatting you want. ColdFusion Express will not interpret any plain text or HTML formatting tags, so use them to spruce up the output. A simple page might include the HTML code found in Listing 5.1.

LISTING 5.1   Formatting CFML Pages

```
1:<!DOCTYPE HTML PUBLIC "-//W3C//DTD HTML 4.0 Transitional//EN">
2:
3:<HTML>
4:<HEAD>
```

LISTING 5.1   continued

```
 5:    <TITLE>My Page</TITLE>
 6:</HEAD>
 7:
 8:<BODY>
 9:
10:<CFSET FirstName="John">
11:<CFOUTPUT>
12:    My name is #Variables.FirstName#
13:</CFOUTPUT>
14:
15:</BODY>
16:</HTML>
```

Notice that the HTML tags and plain text are intermixed freely with the CFML code. In this example, the string 'My name is' doesn't have pound signs to indicate it is a variable, and thus it is left alone by ColdFusion Express. These plain text strings are returned as literal strings to the browser. As a matter of fact, because the text isn't contained within CFML tags or CFML pound signs, ColdFusion Express totally ignores it and sends it to the browser exactly as is. If you move the text 'My name is' outside of the <CFOUTPUT> tag, the page will behave in the same way. An example of this is shown in Listing 5.2.

LISTING 5.2   Placement of Plain Text

```
 1:<!DOCTYPE HTML PUBLIC "-//W3C//DTD HTML 4.0 Transitional//EN">
 2:
 3:<HTML>
 4:<HEAD>
 5:    <TITLE>My Page</TITLE>
 6:</HEAD>
 7:
 8:<BODY>
 9:
10:<CFSET FirstName="John">
11:My name is
12:<CFOUTPUT>
13:    #Variables.FirstName#
14:</CFOUTPUT>
15:
16:</BODY>
17:</HTML>
```

5

Which way do you think is better? In this case, it really doesn't matter which way you write your code. This is because ColdFusion Express will ignore anything that is not CFML code. Because the string `'My name is'` is just plain text and not a variable, it will be ignored by ColdFusion Express.

`<CFOUTPUT>` Placement

Some cases require a little more finesse with `<CFOUTPUT>` placement. Imagine that you are generating a form letter using ColdFusion Express. The text might be similar to the following, where variables would be used to fill in the unknown information:

```
Dear {addressee},

My name is Jane Doe and I have 3 pets in my family.
I am a great lover of pets and would like to get more
information on your pet store, {PetStoreName}. Please send
more information to jdoe@getmail.com.

Sincerely,

Jane Doe
```

If you use CFML variables to fill in the form items, your code might resemble Listing 5.3.

LISTING 5.3 Form Letter

```
1:<!DOCTYPE HTML PUBLIC "-//W3C//DTD HTML 4.0 Transitional//EN">
2:
3:<HTML>
4:<HEAD>
5:    <TITLE>Form Response</TITLE>
6:</HEAD>
7:
8:<BODY>
9:<CFSET Addressee="Sir or Madam">
10:<CFSET PetStoreName="Pets Galore">
11:
12:<p>
13:Dear <CFOUTPUT>#Variables.Addressee#</CFOUTPUT>,
14:</p>
15:<p>
16:My name is Jane Doe and I have 3 pets in my family.
17:I am a great lover of pets and would like to get more
18:information on your pet store, <CFOUTPUT>#Variables.PetStoreName#</CFOUTPUT>.
19:Please send more information to jdoe@getmail.com.
20:</p>
```

LISTING 5.3 continued

```
21:<p>
22:Sincerely,
23:</p>
24:<p>
25:Jane Doe
26:</p>
27:</BODY>
28:</HTML>
```

As shown in the output in Figure 5.8, this is valid and working code.

FIGURE 5.8

Having many
<CFOUTPUT> tags clut-
ters the code.

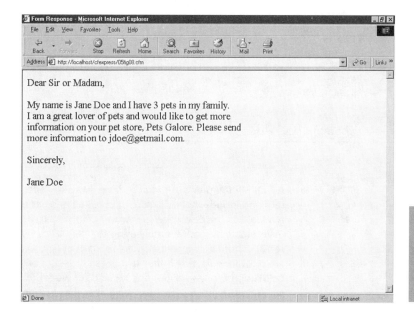

However, there is a better way to write this code. If you surround the entire text with one <CFOUTPUT> tag, the code becomes less cluttered and more maintainable, as shown in Listing 5.4.

LISTING 5.4 Use Less <CFOUTPUT> Tags

```
1:<HTML>
2:<HEAD>
3:    <TITLE>Form Response</TITLE>
4:</HEAD>
5:
6:<BODY>
```

LISTING 5.4   continued

```
 7:<CFSET Addressee="Sir or Madam">
 8:<CFSET PetStoreName="Pets Galore">
 9:
10:<CFOUTPUT>
11:<p>
12:Dear #Variables.Addressee#,
13:</p>
14:<p>
15:My name is Jane Doe and I have 3 pets in my family.
16:I am a great lover of pets and would like to get more
17:information on your pet store, #Variables.PetStoreName#. Please send
18:more information to jdoe@getmail.com.
19:</p>
20:</CFOUTPUT>
21:<p>
22:Sincerely,
23:</p>
24:<p>
25:Jane Doe
26:</p>
27:</BODY>
28:</HTML>
```

As seen in the previous example, it might be easier to use less <CFOUTPUT> tags and include more inside each one. This ensures that your code is more readable to the next developer who works with it. Besides just ensuring maintainability, appropriately using the <CFOUTPUT> tag also performs better. But this is a delicate balance—you don't want to put <CFOUTPUT> around too much text if that text doesn't need to be evaluated, or ColdFusion Express wastes time looking for work that needs to be done when none exists for it to do. Remember that text not enclosed within CFML tags is always processed quicker than within tags.

The following code is invalid and will generate an error message from ColdFusion Express:

```
<CFOUTPUT>
My name is #Variables.FirstName#
<CFOUTPUT>#Variables.LastName#</CFOUTPUT>
</CFOUTPUT>
```

You cannot nest <CFOUTPUT> tags except for a special use for grouping database data.

As you've previously learned, you can intermix freely your HTML and CFML tags. Therefore, you can apply all HTML formatting to any CFML-generated output. The code in Listing 5.5 places bold formatting on the name value in the browser output.

LISTING 5.5 Intermixing HTML and CFML

```
1:<!DOCTYPE HTML PUBLIC "-//W3C//DTD HTML 4.0 Transitional//EN">
2:
3:<HTML>
4:<HEAD>
5:    <TITLE>My Page</TITLE>
6:</HEAD>
7:
8:<BODY>
9:
10:<CFSET FirstName="John">
11:My name is
12:<CFOUTPUT>
13:    <B>#Variables.FirstName#</B>
14:</CFOUTPUT>
15:
16:</BODY>
17:</HTML>
```

The output is shown in Figure 5.9.

FIGURE 5.9

HTML formatting can be embedded into the CFML code.

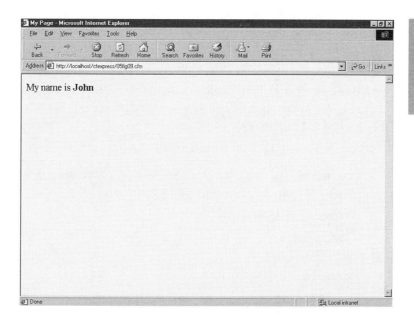

5

To Do: Sprucing Up Your Output

You can add some formatting to your page by performing the following steps:

1. Return to HomeSite and the cfset.cfm page you were working on.
2. Add bold formatting to the printout of your name.

   ```
   <CFOUTPUT><B>#Variables.FullName#</B></CFOUTPUT>
   ```

3. Surf to this page in the browser to view output.

▲ If you want, change the size and font face of the text.

Creating Variables with CFPARAM

There is another way to create page variables by using the <CFPARAM> tag. This tag is slightly different from <CFSET> in that it actually *might* or *might not* create the variable.

The syntax for the <CFPARAM> tag takes two attributes: a NAME attribute specifies the name of the variable and the DEFAULT attribute holds the default value of the variable if it's created:

```
<CFPARAM NAME="VariableName" DEFAULT="DefaultValue">
```

Actually, the <CFPARAM> tag is like a little program unto itself. It tests to see if the variable indicated already exists, and, if not, the <CFPARAM> tag then creates it.

If you had already created the Age variable with the <CFSET> tag, the <CFPARAM> tag does nothing. After these two statements, the value of Age is still 29.

```
<CFSET Age="29">
<CFPARAM NAME="Age" DEFAULT="39">
```

However, if the variable doesn't exist, the <CFPARAM> tag will create the page variable and set it to the value specified in the DEFAULT attribute. In this case, the Age variable is created and given a value of 39:

```
<CFPARAM NAME="Age" DEFAULT="39">
```

You print out page variables the same, no matter how they are created, using the <CFOUTPUT> tag and pound signs around the variables:

```
<CFPARAM NAME="Age" DEFAULT="39">
<CFOUTPUT>
    #VARIABLES.Age#
</CFOUTPUT>
```

The <CFPARAM> tag is used mostly in cases in which your page is expecting information to be passed into it. The page returns an error if you expect a variable to exist, but it was omitted erroneously. <CFPARAM> is used to create variables if they don't exist, so the program doesn't terminate abnormally. Or it is used to set a default value if none were supplied.

Summary

In this hour, you learned how to combine the use of variables and expressions to perform complex programming. This was made easy by the use of ColdFusion Express functions and expressions. This is the first step in making your Web applications dynamic. In the next hour, you'll learn how to combine conditional logic to make your pages even more dynamic.

Q&A

Q I've seen simple variable values, such as numbers and strings, but what about more complex data types such as a list of values?

A Yes, ColdFusion Express allows you to create more complex data types such as lists, arrays and structures. You'll learn more about these data types in Hour 18, "Using Advanced Variable Types."

Q What if I wanted to save some information in a variable and use it throughout my site? Can I do that?

A This is possible, but not with the page variables discussed in this hour. You'll need to learn more about variables that give you a scope for the browser session or the application. We'll cover these variable types in Hour 19, "Personalizing Your Web Site."

Q I am trying to use colors within `<CFOUTPUT>` tags, and I keep getting error about variables not being defined. Am I unable to use HTML colors in ColdFusion Express?

A You can definitely use colors: As a matter of fact, you can use any client technology—not just HTML. The problem you are running into is an interesting one. HTML has two ways to refer to colors: by name (for example, `red` or `green`), or by RGB value (for example, `#FF0000` or `#00FF00`). The RGB value format is more powerful—it supports a far greater range of colors and far more browsers. But it uses the `#` character, and as you already know, that character has special significance to ColdFusion Express. The reason you are getting an error message is because ColdFusion Express thinks that the `#` is the start of a variable, there is no closing `#`, and a variable of that name probably doesn't exist. The solution is to *escape* the pound sign by using double pound signs. So, to use an RGB value of `#FF00FF`, specify `##FF00FF`. ColdFusion Express will see the double pound sign and will know that what you really want is a single pound sign sent to the browser.

5

Q I've seen an example of a form letter in this hour. Can I use ColdFusion Express to generate emails for me with dynamic information?

A No. ColdFusion Express doesn't support the generation and delivery of Simple Mail Transfer Protocol (SMTP) email. Only the full versions of ColdFusion Professional and ColdFusion Enterprise support this feature. However, any code you write in ColdFusion Express is upwards compatible with the commercial versions of ColdFusion, so you can easily add that functionality later.

Workshop

The Workshop contains quiz questions and activities to help reinforce what you've learned in this hour. If you get stuck, the answers to the quiz questions can be found in Appendix A, "Answers to Quiz."

Quiz

1. What prefix would you use to designate a variable as a page variable?

2. *True or false*: CFML variables don't need to be initialized before they are used.

3. How would you describe a literal value?

4. *True or false*: The `<CFPARAM>` tag will always create a variable and assign it a default value.

Exercise

1. Create a page with variables that hold information about you, such as your name, phone number and email address. Print out these values with labels next to the variables.

   Experiment with formatting the data you printed out by changing fonts and colors. Put the output into an HTML table to see how CFML and HTML intermingle. (Look at the Q&A questions for important information about color use within ColdFusion Express pages.)

HOUR 6

Implementing Conditional Processing

Two basic and fundamental programming concepts are conditional processing and looping. These language features can help you dynamically generate
your Web page content.

In this lesson, you'll learn the following:

- How to code simple conditional statements
- Programmatically selecting one of a set of conditions
- How to make ColdFusion Express perform an action repeatedly in
  a loop
- How to build pages that use conditional processing to alter the output
  returned to the browser

Decision Making

Having your programs make decisions, called *conditional processing*, is one
of the basic building blocks of any programming language. With conditional

processing, the program might take different paths and return different output based on some evaluated condition.

You perform conditional processing every day. You make many decisions based on conditional factors in your life. For instance, you might say "If it's raining out, I'll drive. Otherwise, I'll walk to work." If your life were a program, you could depict this decision as in Figure 6.1.

FIGURE 6.1

You can decide how to get to work based on the weather.

It's not important to really understand the actual symbols and structure of the flow diagram itself, but you can easily see that you are making a decision based on the condition of the weather forecast. This decision can lead you to either drive or walk to work.

Using the <CFIF> Tag

In programming, you can make a program take different paths or yield different output based on a condition. In CFML, the <CFIF> tag is used for this purpose. The <CFIF> tag is a container tag that has both a start and end tag:

```
<CFIF Expression IS "TRUE">
    Do something if the expression is true
</CFIF>
```

The <CFIF> tag works by evaluating an expression and concluding either a TRUE or a FALSE condition. Therefore, all expressions in the <CFIF> tag must return a TRUE or FALSE result. In this example, the variable WeatherForecast is either equal to "GoingToRain" or not, thus returning a TRUE or FALSE value:

```
<CFIF WeatherForecast IS "GoingToRain">
    Drive to work!
</CFIF>
```

Before we reach the decision to walk to work, I need to show you the types of conditions that can be evaluated. Each of these decisions must yield a TRUE or FALSE value.

A value that is either TRUE or FALSE is also known as a Boolean value.

Several comparison operators allow you to return a TRUE or FALSE value to the <CFIF> tag. Each comparison operator, and an example, is listed in Table 6.1. Assume that the variable X has a value of 10 and FirstName has the value of Sue.

TABLE 6.1   Comparison Operators

Operator	Operation	Example	Yields
IS	Equality	<CFIF X IS 5>	FALSE
IS NOT	Inequality	<CFIF X IS NOT 5>	TRUE
GREATER THAN	Greater Than	<CFIF X GREATER THAN 5>	TRUE
LESS THAN	Less Than	<CFIF X LESS THAN 5>	FALSE
GREATER THAN OR EQUAL TO	Greater than or equal to	<CFIF X GREATER THAN OR EQUAL TO 5>	TRUE
LESS THAN OR EQUAL TO	Less than or equal to	<CFIF X LESS THAN OR EQUAL TO 5>	FALSE
CONTAINS	String comparison	<CFIF FirstName CONTAINS "Su">	TRUE
DOES NOT CONTAIN	String comparison	<CFIF FirstName DOES NOT CONTAIN "Bu">	TRUE

You could alter the conditional statement to drive to work only if it will rain more than two hours in a day:

```
<CFIF RainDurationHours GREATER THAN "2">
    Drive to work!
</CFIF>
```

As you can see by the table, these operators can get lengthy. If you are typing challenged, you might want to use the shorthand notation for some operators, as shown in Table 6.2.

TABLE 6.2   Shorthand Notation

Operator	Alternative Operator
IS	EQUAL, EQ
IS NOT	NOT EQUAL, NEQ
GREATER THAN	GT
LESS THAN	LT

6

TABLE 6.2   continued

Operator	Alternative Operator
GREATER THAN OR EQUAL TO	GTE, GE
LESS THAN OR EQUAL TO	LTE, LE

 The CONTAINS operator doesn't have a shorthand notation.

Another way to formulate the condition for driving if it rains less than two hours would be

```
<CFIF RainDurationHours GT "2">
    Drive to work!
</CFIF>
```

That'll save typing, but it is still understandable.

I'm sure you're wondering "Why can't I just use the operators I'm familiar with, such as the greater than symbol '>'?" There's a simple answer to this one—tag syntax.

If CFML allowed you to use the usual conditional operators, ColdFusion Express would be pretty confused trying to figure out where the tag ends:

```
<CFIF RainDurationHours > "2">
    Drive to work!
</CFIF>
```

In the previous example, ColdFusion Express would see the greater than symbol (>) and think the tag was being closed. Then it would get really confused trying to figure out what to do with the rest of the line, and a syntax error would occur.

For this reason, CFML doesn't allow the usual operators (=, <, >, <=, >=) in conditional expressions. This is one of the most common CFML programming mistakes, so keep your eye out for it.

The Fallback Decision

In CFML, there's a way to make a decision if all other conditions fail. This fallback decision is created using the <CFELSE> tag

Returning to the example of when to walk or drive to work, you are only deciding when to drive to work:

```
<CFIF WeatherForecast IS "GoingToRain">
    Drive to work!
</CFIF>
```

What happens if it is **not** going to rain? In this example, nothing. If we wanted the condition to perform another action when the <CFIF> statement is FALSE, we could use the <CFELSE> tag.

```
<CFIF WeatherForecast IS "GoingToRain">
    Drive to work!
<CFELSE>
    Walk to work!
</CFIF>
```

The <CFELSE> tag allows you to say what to do if the <CFIF> condition is FALSE. In this case, if WeatherForecast isn't GoingToRain, the program will suggest that you walk to work.

To Do: Creating <CFIF> Statements

▲ To Do

Try writing a conditional statement by performing the following steps:

1. Launch HomeSite.

2. Create a new page using the default template.

3. Change the <TITLE> value to "Deciding the Commute".

4. Save the page in the /learncfe/hour4 directory under the Web root as cfif.cfm.

5. Between the opening and closing <BODY> tags, type **<CFSET WeatherForecast="MostlySunny">**.

6. Write a conditional statement that will check the WeatherForecast variable and print a message to walk if it will be mostly sunny, and drive otherwise. The code should look like the following:

   ```
   <CFSET WeatherForecast="MostlySunny">
   <CFIF WeatherForecast IS "MostlySunny">
       Walk to work!
   <CFELSE>
       Drive to work!
   </CFIF>
   ```

7. Save the page and then browse the file to see what happens.

8. Now go back to HomeSite and change the <CFSET> tag so that it sets the weather to "Raining".

9. Save the page and refresh your browser to see the change in output.

6

Making a Decision from Multiple Choices

So far, we have only checked if WeatherForecast is "MostlySunny" and will drive as long as it isn't. What if you wanted to create multiple conditions and decide amongst them? You can take many different paths based on separate conditions in your life, and so can a ColdFusion Express program.

In order to create a conditional statement that would decide amongst more than one decision, you will need to use the <CFELSEIF> tag. This tag allows you to make any number of decisions to determine which one is true:

```
<CFIF WeatherForecast IS "GoingToRain">
    Drive to work!
<CFELSEIF WeatherForecast IS "MostlySunny">
    Walk to work!
<CFELSE>
    I'm not sure what to do, since I don't know what the weather is!
</CFIF>
```

Most developers indent their code, as seen in the previous example. This will greatly enhance the readability and maintainability of your code. You will also need to use indenting to separate <CFIF> statements that are nested inside one another, so get into the habit of using this convention.

In this example, you are making strict decisions based on the value of WeatherForecast. If both the <CFIF> and all the related <CFELSEIF> tags are FALSE, it will fall through and get processed by the <CFELSE> tag.

It is important to know that ColdFusion Express will only evaluate the <CFIF> statement until it finds *the first true condition*. Once found, the instructions in that condition will be executed and then ColdFusion Express will jump out of the <CFIF> statement.

Figure 6.2 depicts where processing is resumed after a true condition is evaluated.

FIGURE 6.2

After evaluation, ColdFusion Express resumes processing following the </CFIF> tag.

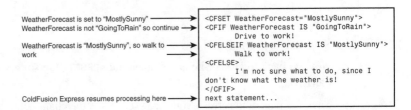

Nesting Decisions?

You not only make decisions every day, but also you make decisions based on other decisions that were already made. In the programming world, this is known as *nesting decisions*, or nested conditional processing.

Think, for example, that you might decide to walk to work in the rain if you have your galoshes at home. You might make the decision as depicted in Figure 6.3.

FIGURE 6.3

You might decide to walk to work in the rain if you have your galoshes.

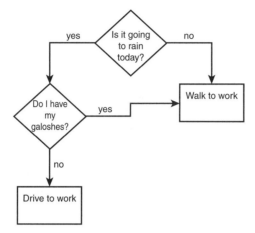

The decision of whether it is going to rain determines if you make the next decision of walking to work if you have your galoshes. So the rules are as follows:

```
If it's going to rain
    If you have your galoshes
        You'll walk to work
    If you don't have your galoshes
        You'll drive to work
If it's not going to rain
        You'll walk to work.
```

You can start writing this code by making the outermost decision first—the one that you need to make before any others can be made:

```
<CFIF WeatherForecast IS "GoingToRain">
    …
<CFELSEIF WeatherForecast IS "MostlySunny">
    Walk to work!
<CFELSE>
    I'm not sure what to do, since I don't know what the weather is!
</CFIF>
```

Now you can fill in the decision of whether you have your galoshes:

```
<CFIF WeatherForecast IS "GoingToRain">
    <CFIF Galoshes IS "Yes">
        Walk to work!
    <CFELSE>
        Drive to work!
```

```
    </CFIF>
<CFELSEIF WeatherForecast IS "MostlySunny">
    Walk to work!
<CFELSE>
    I'm not sure what to do, since I don't know what the weather is!
</CFIF>
```

Once again, notice the indention of the code. This makes it very easy to read and decipher later on.

You can nest as many <CFIF> statements as you need to make the decision.

> ColdFusion Express will support as many levels of nested conditional statements as you'd like. But be careful when doing so. It is very easy to introduce bugs when writing complex nested statements. In addition, the more you nest the harder you make ColdFusion Express work, and that could harm the performance of your application.

Compound Conditions

You can also make a decision that is a result of a few conditions being true within the same <CFIF> tag. This compound condition can be implemented using a logical operator. *Logical operators* allow you to combine two or more comparisons into a single decision.

The logical operators are AND, OR, and NOT. With these three operators, you can make a decision based on multiple conditions. Logical operators and examples are shown in Table 6.3. Assume that X=1 and Y=5.

TABLE 6.3 Logical Operators

Operator	Description	Use	Yields
AND	Produces TRUE if both sides are TRUE.	<CFIF X IS 1 AND Y IS 2>	FALSE
OR	Produces TRUE if either side is TRUE.	<CFIF X IS 1 OR Y IS 2>	TRUE
NOT	Produces the opposite TRUE or FALSE results.	<CFIF NOT(X IS 1)>	FALSE

If you will walk to work when it is sunny or you have your galoshes with you, you could write the <CFIF> tag as such:

```
<CFIF WeatherForecast IS "MostlySunny" OR Galoshes IS "Yes">
    Walk to work!
<CFELSEIF WeatherForecast IS "GoingToRain">
    Drive to work!
<CFELSE>
    I'm not sure what to do, since I don't know what the weather is!
</CFIF>
```

As in the previous code, most times nested <CFIF> logic can be replaced with the correct logical operator.

> In this case, the order of the <CFIF> and <CFELSEIF> conditions is very important. If you were to reverse the conditions as in the following code, in rainy weather you would drive to work regardless of whether you had your galoshes:
>
> ```
> <CFIF WeatherForecast IS "GoingToRain" >
>     Drive to work!
> <CFELSEIF WeatherForecast IS "MostlySunny" OR Galoshes IS "Yes">
>     Walk to work!
> <CFELSE>
>     I'm not sure what to do, since I don't know what the weather
> is!
> </CFIF>
> ```

TRUE and FALSE Values

Up to this point, I've told you and shown you that the <CFIF> tag only can accept values of TRUE and FALSE. That is correct, but what I haven't told you is that there are other values that are equivalent to TRUE and FALSE. Examine the following code:

```
<CFSET X="5">
<CFIF X>
    X is true!
<CFELSE>
    X is false!
</CFIF>
```

Because the variable X is set to "5", you might think that the output will be "X is false!". In fact, the result is that X is TRUE. What could account for this?

In CFML, as well as other programming languages, the value TRUE is equivalent to a non-zero value—as long as the value is non-zero it will evaluate to TRUE. The number

6

can even be a negative number and it will evaluate to TRUE. Table 6.4 shows the equivalent values for TRUE and FALSE.

TABLE 6.4   TRUE/FALSE Equivalent Values

TRUE/FALSE	Equivalent
TRUE	Any non-zero number, YES
FALSE	Zero, NO

As seen in this table, the string YES is also equivalent to TRUE, and NO is equivalent to FALSE.

We will take a look at an example of a function called IsNumeric(). You will look at functions in depth in Hour 7, "Using Functions," but suffice it to say that this function will take a variable value and return an indicator if the value is a number. In this example, we are testing the value of a variable X and storing the result of the test into the Result variable:

```
<CFSET X="5">
<CFSET Result=IsNumeric(X)>
<CFOUTPUT>Result = #Result#</CFOUTPUT>
```

> Notice that the IsNumeric(X) function doesn't require double quotes around it in the <CFSET> tag. This is because it is not a literal value but instead needs to be evaluated by ColdFusion Express.

The output is depicted in Figure 6.4.

As you can see by the output, the IsNumeric() function returns a YES if the variable is a number (and NO otherwise). Because this function returns a value that <CFIF> can directly evaluate, you can use this function inside the tag:

```
<CFSET X="5">
<CFIF IsNumeric(X)>
    X is a number!
<CFELSE>
    X is not a number!
</CFIF>
```

FIGURE 6.4

The IsNumeric() *function returns a* YES *or* NO.

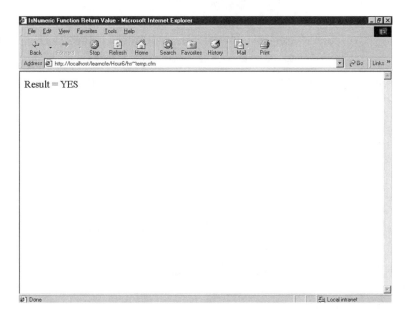

You could put the full evaluation into the <CFIF> tag:

```
<CFSET X="5">
<CFIF IsNumeric(X) IS "TRUE">
    X is a number!
<CFELSE>
    X is not a number!
</CFIF>
```

Using this syntax ColdFusion Express will have to do extra work to get the result, which is YES, and convert it to the value TRUE. For this reason, just using the function performs better.

SWITCHing Gears

There is another <CFML> tag that you can use to make a decision ba

sed on the outcome of a comparison—the <CFSWITCH> tag. This tag allows you to make a decision about one condition and perform a task based on its value.

The <CFSWITCH> tag is a container with opening and closing tags:

```
<CFSWITCH EXPRESSION="expression">
    cases for each value of expression…
</CFSWITCH>
```

6

The biggest difference between the <CFIF> construct and the <CFSWITCH> tag is that <CFSWITCH> can only evaluate one expression at a time. The expression is set in the Expression attribute and all cases compare to that value.

If you wanted to evaluate the value of the WeatherForecast variable, you could code the tag in this way:

```
<CFSET WeatherForecast="MostlySunny">
<CFSWITCH EXPRESSION="#WeatherForecast#">
    cases for each value of expression…
</CFSWITCH>
```

Notice that the Expression attribute value has pound signs around the variable #WeatherForecast#. This is a quirk about the <CFSWITCH> tag. You must tell it to take the value of the variable instead of assuming that it will do so on its own. This is a very common error that affects both new and seasoned CFML programmers alike, so beware!

In order to decide what to do for each value of the expression (in this case, the value of the WeatherForecast variable), you would use the <CFCASE> tag. The format of this tag is

```
<CFCASE VALUE="ValueToCompare">
    What to do if Expression=ValueToCompare
</CFCASE>
```

If you wanted to decide what to do for each value of WeatherForecast, you could code the full <CFSWITCH> tag as follows:

```
<CFSET WeatherForecast="MostlySunny">
<CFSWITCH EXPRESSION="#WeatherForecast#">
        <CFCASE VALUE="MostlySunny">
            Walk to work!
        </CFCASE>
        <CFCASE VALUE="GoingToRain">
            Drive to work!
        </CFCASE>
</CFSWITCH>
```

If you wanted to walk to work if you had your galoshes, you couldn't use the <CFSWITCH> tag because it only allows one expression to be evaluated.

The <CFSWITCH> tag performs better than the <CFIF> tag. So use it whenever you have one expression that needs to be evaluated.

In order to determine what to do if all <CFCASE> values aren't matching the expression, you can use the <CFDEFAULTCASE> tag. This tag will be the fallback decision if all other decisions are FALSE:

```
<CFSET WeatherForecast="MostlySunny">
<CFSWITCH EXPRESSION="#WeatherForecast#">
<CFCASE VALUE="MostlySunny">
    Walk to work!
</CFCASE>
<CFCASE VALUE="GoingToRain">
    Drive to work!
</CFCASE>
<CFDEFAULTCASE>
    I'm not sure what to do, since I don't know what the weather is!
</CFDEFAULTCASE>
</CFSWITCH>
```

Looping

If you were an assembly line worker, your job might be to repeat a set of steps over and over again throughout the day. If you installed the rearview mirror on the windshield, you would perform the same steps for installing each one. You would perform these steps until your shift ended and then you'd go home for the day. This process might contain the following steps:

Step 1 Car arrives to your station

Step 2 Take rearview mirror from its packing

Step 3 Measure windshield to determine middle of width

Step 4 Affix rearview mirror with adhesive

Step 5 Test that the mirror is working properly

You would repeat each of these steps for every car that comes to your station until your shift was over.

The <CFLOOP> Tag

Looping in the programming world is similar because it allows you to repeat a set of instructions or display output over and over until one or more conditions are met. The <CFLOOP> tag allows you to create programming loops in CFML. This tag has an opening and closing tag, with the instructions you want to perform multiple times enclosed within the tags:

```
<CFLOOP ..>
HTML or CFML code to loop over ...
</CFLOOP>
```

6

`<CFLOOP>` supports five different types of loops:

- Looping over a list
- Index loops
- Condition loops
- Looping over a query
- Looping over a structure

The type of loop is determined by the attributes of the `<CFLOOP>` tag. You won't understand the last two types of loops (query and structure) until you learn about those concepts.

> You will be learning about structure loops in Hour 18, "Using Advanced Variable Types."

Looping over a List

As an example of a loop list, you can take a list of colors and display them in table cells:

```
<TABLE BORDER="1">
    <TR>
    <CFLOOP INDEX="MyColor"
            LIST="red,blue,silver"
            DELIMITERS=",">
        <CFOUTPUT>
        <TD BGCOLOR="#MyColor#">
            <B>#MyColor#</B>
        </TD>
        </CFOUTPUT>
    </CFLOOP>
    </TR>
</TABLE>
```

Figure 6.5 depicts the output of this code.

Wrapping Code

Notice my `<CFLOOP>` tag and its attributes are each on separate lines and nicely aligned. I was able to get HomeSite to do that for me through the Tag Dialog for `<CFLOOP>`. To do this yourself, position yourself on top of the `<CFLOOP>` tag and choose Edit Tag. The dialog has a checkbox at the bottom that enables you to turn off the Output on a single line option. This helps your code be more readable.

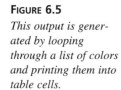

FIGURE 6.5

This output is generated by looping through a list of colors and printing them into table cells.

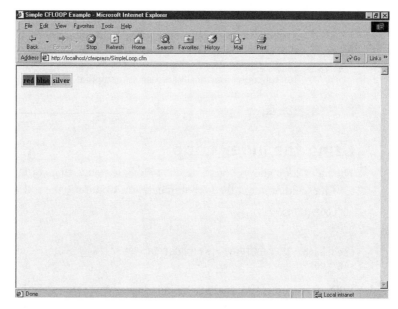

We will now dissect this code. Inside the `<TR>` tag, you see a `<CFLOOP>` tag. This tag has a few attributes:

- `INDEX`—This attribute holds the value of each item in the list as the loop steps through the list.
- `LIST`—A comma-separated list of values; in this case, `"Red,Blue,Silver"`.
- `DELIMITERS`—Specifies the character that separates each list value; in this case, the comma (`,`).

For each value in the list, it will execute the following code:

```
<CFOUTPUT>
<TD BGCOLOR="#MyColor#">
    <B>#MyColor#</B>
</TD>
</CFOUTPUT>
```

This will take each color value and use it for the background color of the `<TD>` tag as well as print out the name of the color. The `<CFOUTPUT>` tag specifies that the variables need to be resolved to their values. This yields a three-column table with one row because there are three values in the list.

This loop, known as a list loop is used to execute code a number of times equal to the number of values in the list.

6

Lists are extremely important to ColdFusion Express developers because the
comma delimited list format is used by HTML (for form submissions) and SQL
(in IN operators). As such, ColdFusion Express provides a whole family of
functions specifically for use in manipulating lists. We'll look at lists in detail
in Hour 18.

Using the Index Loop

The index loop allows you to iterate code based on a series of numeric values. To loop
ten times and print out the loop number, you would use the following code:

```
<CFLOOP INDEX="i"
FROM="1"
TO="10" >
Loop number: <CFOUTPUT>#i#</CFOUTPUT><BR>
</CFLOOP>
```

When this loop is first started, the index variable i (INDEX attribute) is set to the initial
value of 1 (FROM attribute). It will go through the following process:

1. Executes the code inside the <CFLOOP> tag to print out the string
   "Loop number: 1".

2. Returns to the opening <CFLOOP> tag and increments INDEX to 2.

3. Executes the code inside the <CFLOOP> tag to print out "Loop number: 2".

This process is repeated until it goes through the loop for the last time with a value of 10.
The output is as shown in Figure 6.6.

The full syntax of the <CFLOOP> tag for an index loop is shown as follows:

```
<CFLOOP INDEX="IndexVariable"
FROM="StartValue"
TO="EndValue"
STEP="Increment">

</CFLOOP>
```

Notice that there is a STEP attribute to this tag. The default is to increment by 1 from the
FROM value to the TO value. You can change the increment value by using the STEP
attribute. For instance, you can increment by 2:

```
<CFLOOP INDEX="i"
FROM="1"
TO="10"
STEP="2">
The loop index is <CFOUTPUT>#i#</CFOUTPUT><BR>
</CFLOOP>
```

*This index loop will
iterate 10 times.*

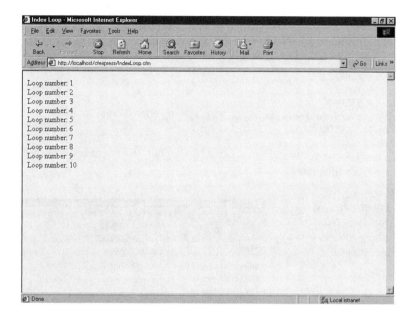

This loop will only execute five times, as the output in Figure 6.7 illustrates.

*This index loop will
iterate five times, step-
ping by 2.*

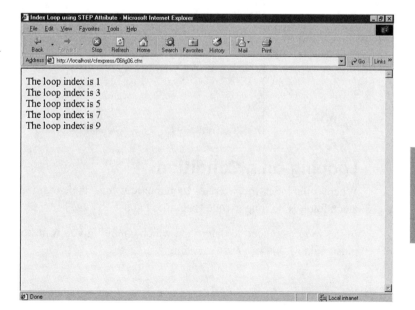

6

The STEP attribute can also take a negative value, if you want to count backwards. For instance, you can decrement by 1:

```
<CFLOOP INDEX="i"
FROM="10"
TO="1"
STEP="-1">
The loop index is <CFOUTPUT>#i#</CFOUTPUT><BR>
</CFLOOP>
```

This loop will only execute 10 times, but will count backwards as the output in Figure 6.8 illustrates.

FIGURE 6.8

This index loop will iterate 10 times counting backwards.

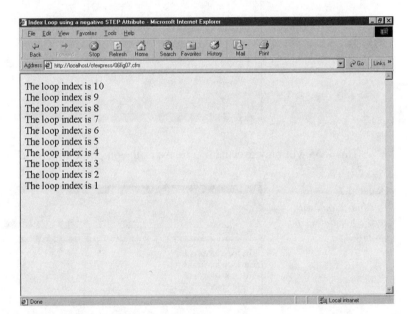

Looping on a Condition

Whereas the index loop iterates by numeric values, the conditional loop will iterate until a condition is no longer TRUE (becomes FALSE).

In this loop, you need to determine which condition you want to test, and that condition must yield a TRUE or FALSE outcome.

In the following code example, you will begin by initializing a CountVar variable to 0, and you will test and increment that variable until it exceeds a value of 10:

```
<!--- Set the variable ConditionVariable to 0 --->
<CFSET ConditionVariable=0>

<!--- Loop until ConditionVariable = 10 --->
<CFLOOP CONDITION="ConditionVariable LESS THAN OR EQUAL TO 10">
<CFSET ConditionVariable=ConditionVariable + 1>
The ConditionVariable is <CFOUTPUT>#ConditionVariable#</CFOUTPUT>.<BR>
</CFLOOP>
```

Notice in this example that the loop will run 11 times, as Figure 6.9 shows. This loop executes 11 times because it is counting from 0 to 10, inclusive, which is 11 times.

FIGURE 6.9

This conditional loop will iterate 11 times.

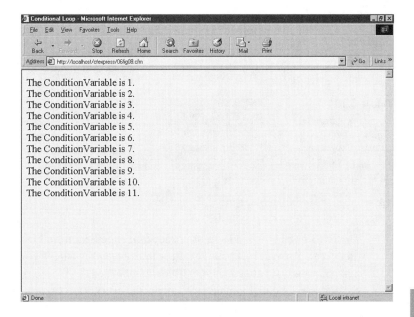

Does the logical operator—LESS THAN OR EQUAL TO—look familiar? It should. All the same operators that apply to the <CFIF> tag also apply to the conditional loop.

6

 Don't forget that all loops must come to an end. If you incorrectly form your condition, it might never reach a FALSE result and therefore will never end. If this happens, it's called an *endless loop*. Kinda like the directions on the shampoo bottle—lather, rinse, repeat—it never tells you when to stop.

Using <CFLOOP> to Create a Color Palette

We will look at an application of using the <CFLOOP> tag. To set this up, you must understand the colors available to the Web.

HTML has two ways to refer to colors, by name (for example, red or green), or by RGB value (for example, #FF0000 and #00FF00). The RGB value format is more powerful—it supports a far greater range of colors and far more browsers. This color palette is known as the Browser Safety Palette, which should be supported by most browsers.

To Do: Looping to Create the Browser Safety Palette

View the Browser Safety Palette in HomeSite by performing the following steps:

1. Launch HomeSite

2. On the main toolbar, choose the Palette option.

3. You will see the Browser Safety Palette as shown in Figure 6.10. Move the mouse over the colors, and you will see the hexadecimal value for each.

FIGURE 6.10

HomeSite's Browser Safety Palette can be displayed by choosing the palette toolbar item on the main toolbar.

▲

The RGB number is made up of hexadecimal numbers from black (#000000) to white (#FFFFFF). You can build all the colors in between by using a combination of hexadecimal pairs—00,33,66,99,cc,ff. If you combine each of these pairs with the others into six-digit hexadecimal numbers, you will find every RGB color available.

For instance, you can concatenate three pairs in this order:

```
00 & 00 & 00 = 000000
00 & 00 & 33 = 000033
00 & 00 & 66 = 000066
00 & 00 & 99 = 000099
00 & 00 & cc = 0000cc
00 & 00 & ff = 0000ff
00 & 33 & 00 = 003300
00 & 33 & 33 = 003333
```

If you were to continue and combine each pair with the other, all colors in the palette would be created. To do this, you can create three nested loops:

```
<CFSET hex="00,33,66,99,cc,ff">
<CFLOOP INDEX="Red" LIST="#hex#">
    <CFLOOP INDEX="Green" LIST="#hex#">
        <CFLOOP INDEX="Blue" LIST="#hex#">
            <CFSET RGB=Red & Green & Blue>
            <CFOUTPUT>#RGB#</CFOUTPUT><BR>
        </CFLOOP>
    </CFLOOP>
</CFLOOP>
```

Each of the three pairs of digits are concatenated together using the ampersand (&) into one RGB variable. Figure 6.11 shows some of the output for this code.

FIGURE 6.11

Nested loops can be used to construct strings.

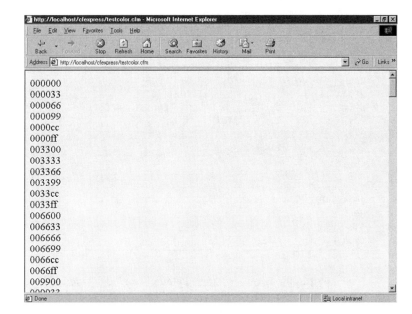

Next we will use the generated RGB number as the background color of a table cell; one for each RGB number generated as shown in Listing 6.1.

Listing 6.1   Using CFLOOP to Produce the Browser Safety Palette

```
1:<!DOCTYPE HTML PUBLIC "-//W3C//DTD HTML 3.2 Final//EN">
2:
3:<HTML>
4:<HEAD>
5:    <TITLE>Using CFLOOP to produce the Browser Safety Palette</TITLE>
6:</HEAD>
7:
8:<BODY>
9:
10:<!--- set hex pairs --->
11:<CFSET hex="00,33,66,99,cc,ff">
12:
13:<!--- loop through each list of hex pairs--->
14:<TABLE>
15:<CFLOOP INDEX="Red" LIST="#hex#">
16:    <CFLOOP INDEX="Green" LIST="#hex#">
17:        <TR>
18:        <CFLOOP INDEX="Blue" LIST="#hex#">
19:        <CFSET RGB= Red & Green & Blue>
20:        <CFOUTPUT><TD BGCOLOR="#RGB#"
21:                        WIDTH="100"
22:                        ALIGN="center">#RGB#
23:                </TD>
24:        </CFOUTPUT>
25:        </CFLOOP>
26:        </TR>
27:    </CFLOOP>
28:</CFLOOP>
29:</TABLE>
30:
31:</BODY>
32:</HTML>
```

Each color in the Browser Safety Palette is now displayed in a table, as shown in Figure 6.12.

This is just one of the many reasons to use the <CFLOOP> tag.

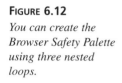

FIGURE 6.12

You can create the Browser Safety Palette using three nested loops.

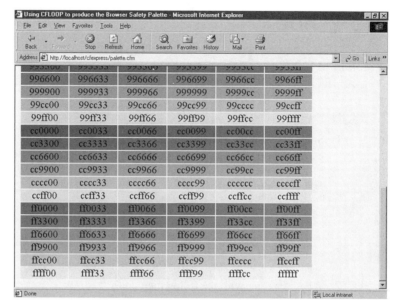

Summary

You've spent this hour learning some of the basics in programming, and in ColdFusion Express. These programming concepts can help you write as complex logic as you need in your ColdFusion Express applications. Conditional logic and looping will be used throughout this book to effect the processing and appearance of your pages.

Q&A

Q **You have warned me to avoid nesting too many layers of `<CFIF>` statements. What's an alternative?**

A There is actually a ColdFusion Express function that performs better than the `<CFIF>` tag—`IIF`. You will learn more about functions in Hour 7, "Using Functions."

Q **Some of the examples of index loops were rather contrived. What would be real reasons to use these loops?**

A You are right: They were rather contrived. But real uses of them require knowledge we haven't given you yet. Index loops are used for manipulating data that is stored in an array. You will learn about arrays in Hour 18. You can use them to create a visual calendar for your users, but that requires some date functions you haven't learned yet, but will in Hour 7. So make sure that you remember these loops because you'll be needing them.

6

Workshop

The Workshop contains quiz questions and activities to help reinforce what you've learned in this hour. If you get stuck, the answers to the quiz questions can be found in Appendix A, "Answers to Quiz."

Quiz

1. Study the following code:

```
<CFIF WeatherForecast IS "GoingToRain">
    Drive to work!
</CFIF>
Walk to work!
```

   A. What message will you see if WeatherForecast is "GoingToRain"?

   B. What message will you see if WeatherForecast is **not** "GoingToRain"?

   C. How would you change this code to work properly?

2. What is wrong with the following code?

```
<CFIF Name = "Sue">
```

Exercise

1. Try recreating the browser safety palette yourself, to learn how <CFLOOP> works. You can refer to the code in this hour if you need guidance, but try doing it yourself first.

HOUR 7

Using Functions

Almost every computer language supports the use of functions. Functions are tools used to return or manipulate data, and ColdFusion Express features a rich set of functions that you can use within your applications.

In this hour, you'll learn the following:

- What functions are
- How ColdFusion Express functions are used
- How to combine tag and function usage
- How to nest ColdFusion Express functions

Understanding Functions

The English definition of the word *function* (well, one of the definitions) is "an assigned task", and that's exactly what functions in computer languages are. Functions are special commands that perform tasks.

Consider the following tasks:

- Obtain the current date or time
- Convert text to uppercase

- Find the length of a string of text
- Check for the existence of a file
- Determine if a year is a leap year

These are all examples of calculations or tasks to be performed, and all are performed using functions.

All functions share one common characteristic: They return data to you. Some functions require that you pass data to them, others require no passed data at all, and yet others allow you to pass optional data to them (assuming default values where appropriate). But regardless of data passed to functions (usually called *parameters*), functions *always* return data back to you.

Understanding Functions in ColdFusion Express

ColdFusion Express features over 200 functions that you can use in your applications. These functions are often divided into categories to make it easier to locate the ones you are looking for.

Although it is impossible to provide detailed usage instructions for all of ColdFusion Express' functions, we'll spend most of this hour looking at usage rules and examples for some of them.

ColdFusion Express has far too many functions to list here in this book. Although many functions are used here, you'll need to consult the ColdFusion Express documentation for the complete authoritative function list (along with syntax and examples for each).

Need help finding a function? HomeSite has a built in list of all of them, with help on each. To access the function list, right-click in your code at the location to insert the function, and then select Insert Expression to display the HomeSite Expression Builder. Under Express Elements you'll find a tree branch called Functions that you can click on (or expand) to locate the function you need.

If you do know the function you need, but can't remember the syntax, just type the function name in your editor and press F1 for immediate function specific help.

Function Syntax

Just like variables (introduced in Hour 5, "Working with Variables and Expressions"), functions can be used within any ColdFusion code block. In addition, just like variables, functions cannot be used in text that is not enclosed within ColdFusion tags.

As a matter of fact, all the rules of variable usage apply to functions as well, including the use of pound signs (the # character). The only way to distinguish between variables and functions is that functions have parentheses after their names (for example, the Now() function that returns the system date and time). Those parentheses tell ColdFusion that what you are using is a function, not a variable.

And those parentheses have another purpose. If the function you are using takes parameters, these must be specified in between the parentheses. For example, the LCase() function is used to convert a string to lowercase, and obviously a string must be provided to this function or you'll generate an error (after all, you can't convert nothing). To convert the name BEN to lowercase, you could do the following:

```
LCase("BEN")
```

When multiple parameters are passed, each parameter must be separated by a comma. For example, the RandRange() function is used to generate a random number within a specified range. To generate a random number between 1 and 10, you'd do the following:

```
RandRange(1, 10)
```

> Notice that string parameters are enclosed within quotes; numeric parameters are not.

Nesting Functions

There's one last important thing to know about functions—they can be nested. This means that a function can be passed as a parameter to another function. To demonstrate this, let's look at an example:

```
DateFormat(Now())
```

The DateFormat() function is used to format a date so that it is in a clean readable format (we'll look at this function again later this hour). DateFormat() requires that a date be passed to it as a parameter: This is the date that it'll format. The Now() function returns the current system date and time. To format the current system date and time for display, Now() can be passed directly to DateFormat(). This is called *nesting*, and there is no limit to how far you can nest your functions.

7

Using ColdFusion Express Functions

Now that you know the rules and syntax of function usage, let's look at some examples. I encourage you to try each of these examples for yourself: The best way to learn function usage is to use them.

String Functions

The string functions are probably the most used of all of ColdFusion Express' function library. These functions are used to manipulate strings of text. Common uses for string functions are

- Converting string case
- Trimming or padding text
- Finding out the length of a string
- Extracting substrings (parts of a string)

To Do: String Function Example Number 1

Let's look at an example of string function usage. Here are the steps so that you can follow along:

1. Open HomeSite (if it isn't already open), and make sure that the learncfe directory is the current directory in the Resource Tab. Create a new directory beneath learncfe, name it **hour7**, and make it the current directory.

2. Create a new file by clicking on the New button (or by selecting New from the File menu and select the Default Template).

3. Type the following code between the BODY tags in your page (of course, you can use your own name, you don't have to use mine).

```
<CFOUTPUT>
My name is Ben<BR>
My name in lowercase is #LCase("Ben")#<BR>
My name in uppercase is #UCase("Ben")#<BR>
My name backwards is #Reverse("Ben")#<BR>
My name is #Len("Ben")# characters long<BR>
</CFOUTPUT>
```

4. Save the file as **funcs_string.cfm** in the learncfe directory.

5. To browse the file, open your browser and go to http://localhost/learncfe/hour7/funcs_string.cfm. The display should look like the one shown in Figure 7.1 (of course, if you used your own name, it'll be displayed instead of mine).

FIGURE 7.1
String functions are used to manipulate text.

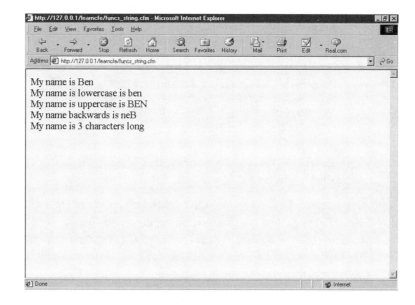

As you can see, the previous code used four different string functions:

- The LCase() function converts a string to lowercase.
- The UCase() function converts a string to uppercase.
- The Reverse() function reverses the contents of a string (okay, so it isn't a function you'll use that often, I know; but it makes for fun demos).
- The Len() function returns the length of a string.

To Do: String Function Example Number 2

In the previous example, we used functions to manipulate strings. But the use of functions is not limited to static strings. In fact, functions are just as useful (perhaps more useful) for manipulating the contents of variables.

To demonstrate this, let's update the previous code listing. Instead of hard-coding my name five times, we'll use a variable containing the name.

1. Go back to HomeSite and open the funcs_string.cfm file (if it isn't already opened).

7

▼ 2. Update the code so that it looks like the following (you are adding one `<CFSET>` statement, and then replacing all the hard-coded names with a variable named name):

```
<CFSET name="Ben">
<CFOUTPUT>
My name is #name#<BR>
My name in lowercase is #LCase(name)#<BR>
My name in uppercase is #UCase(name)#<BR>
My name backwards is #Reverse(name)#<BR>
My name is #Len(name)# characters long<BR>
</CFOUTPUT>
```

3. Resave the file, and then browse it once again. The output should be identical to what it was before.

One interesting thing to note is that when you converted the functions to use variables instead of static text, you had to remove the quotes from around the text; for example, `#LCase("Ben")#` became `#LCase(name)#` and not `#LCase("name")#`. Had the quotes been left there, ColdFusion would have converted the text name as opposed to the evaluated contents of the variable named name.

Three very useful string manipulation functions, especially when working with data retrieved from a database (as you'll see in later hours), are the trim functions. These functions are `Trim()`, which trims leading and trailing spaces from a string; `RTrim()`, which trims trailing spaces; and `LTrim()`, which trims leading spaces.

▲ There you have it: That's how you use functions.

Date Functions

If string functions are the most used, date functions are a close second. You use date functions to manipulate dates and times. Common uses for date functions are

- Obtaining the system date and time
- Extracting date or time parts (for example, just the year, or just the hour)
- Adding or subtracting days, weeks, months, or years to a date
- Checking the difference between dates

To Do: Date Function Example

Let's take a look at some example code that uses date functions. Here are the steps so that you can follow along:

1. Open HomeSite (if it isn't already open), and make sure that the hour7 directory is the current directory in the Resource Tab.

2. Create a new file by clicking on the New button (or by selecting New from the File menu).

3. Type the following code in your page between the BODY tags.

```
<CFOUTPUT>
Today is #DateFormat(Now())#<BR>
Tomorrow is #DateFormat(DateAdd("d", 1, Now()))#<BR>
It is #DayOfWeekAsString(DayOfWeek(Now()))#<BR>
The year is #Year(Now())#<BR>
It is day #DayOfYear(Now())# of year #DatePart("yyyy", Now())#<BR>
</CFOUTPUT>
```

4. Save the file as funcs_date.cfm in the learncfe directory.

5. To browse the file, open your browser and go to http://localhost/learncfe/hour7/funcs_date.cfm. The display should look like the one shown in Figure 7.2.

FIGURE 7.2

ColdFusion Express features a complete set of date manipulation functions.

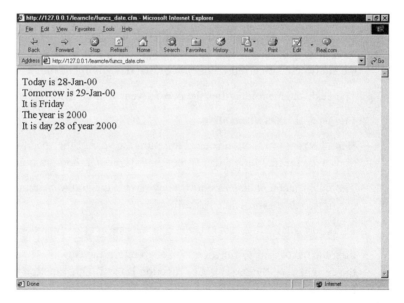

7

▼ This example is a bit more complex than the string example, so let's look at each state-ment one at a time.

```
Today is #DateFormat(Now())#
```

This first statement simply displays the current date by passing Now() to the DateFormat() function. This is the same example discussed earlier in this hour.

The next statement displays tomorrow's date. This is a bit more complex because there is no function that returns tomorrow's date. Instead, we have to use Now() to get today's date and then use DateAdd() to add a day to it to get tomorrow's date. The code looks like this:

```
Tomorrow is #DateFormat(DateAdd("d", 1, Now()))#
```

DateAdd() can be used to add days, weeks, months, and other date parts. The first para-meter passed to DateAdd() specifies what is to be added; here we specified "d", meaning days. The second attribute is the number of parts to add; we specified 1, so one day would be added to the specified date. DateAdd() adds a day to today's date, and then returns it to DateFormat() for displaying.

The next statement displays the day of week (Sunday, Monday, and so on). This involves the use of three functions as follows:

```
It is #DayOfWeekAsString(DayOfWeek(Now()))#
```

The Now() function should be familiar. DayOfWeek() returns the day number within a week for a specified date; so for Sunday, it'll return 1, for Monday 2, and so on. The DayOfWeekAsString() function takes a day of week number (1, 2, and so on) and returns the equivalent string representation of that day, giving us the result we want.

The next statement identifies the current year. The code looks like this:

```
The year is #Year(Now())#
```

Here the Year() function is used to return the year of the specified date. Similar func-tions exist for returning a date's month, day, quarter, hour, minute, and second.

The final statement displays how many days it is into the current year. This involves the use of two date expressions, as follows:

```
It is day #DayOfYear(Now())# of year #DatePart("yyyy", Now())#
```

First the DayOfYear() function is used to return the current day of year. Then, to display the current year, the DatePart() function is used. This function takes a specifier as the first parameter, which indicates what part of the date is to be returned. Of course, in this
▼ particular example, we could just have easily used the Year() function.

DateFormat() takes an optional mask parameter that can be used to specify how a date is presented (with or without the day of week, month as a number or string, two or four digit year, and so on). Refer to the documentation for help using this parameter.

The Now() function is also used for time operations because Now() returns both the current date and time. There are time equivalents for all date functions; for example, to format time values, you can use TimeFormat().

Decision Making Functions

Another interesting set of functions are the decision making functions. These all return TRUE or FALSE states (called *Boolean values*), allowing you to perform conditional processing based on the results of these functions. Common uses for these functions include

- Checking for the existence of a variable
- Checking to see if a value is a number or a date
- Checking to see if a date is valid

To Do: Decision Function Example

Let's take a look at some example code that uses a decision making function. Here are the steps so that you can follow along:

1. Open HomeSite (if it isn't already open), and make sure that the hour7 directory is the current directory in the Resource Tab.

2. Create a new file by clicking on the New button (or by selecting New from the File menu).

3. Type the following code in your page between the BODY tags.

```
<CFOUTPUT>
<B>Leap years</B><BR>
1900: #YesNoFormat(IsLeapYear(1900))#<BR>
2000: #YesNoFormat(IsLeapYear(2000))#<BR>
2100: #YesNoFormat(IsLeapYear(2100))#<BR>
</CFOUTPUT>
```

4. Save the file as **funcs_decision.cfm** in the learncfe directory.

5. To browse the file, open your browser and go to http://localhost/learncfe/hour7/funcs_decision.cfm. The display should look like the one shown in Figure 7.3.

7

FIGURE 7.3

*Decision functions are
used to return* TRUE *or*
FALSE *based on a con-
dition being met
or not.*

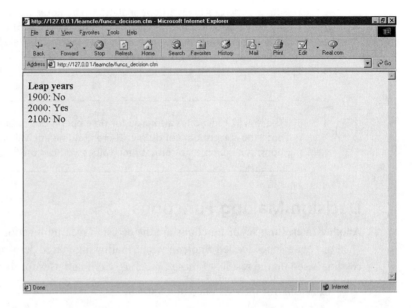

IsLeapYear() is a decision making function. It checks to see whether a specified year is
a leap year, returns TRUE (or 1) if yes, and FALSE (or 0) if not. Because 1900 and 2100 are
not leap years, those two IsLeapYear() statements will return FALSE. 2000 is a leap year,
so IsLeapYear(2000) will return TRUE.

Displaying TRUE or FALSE is not very intuitive. Here the result returned by each
IsLeapYear() function is passed to the YesNoFormat() function. This special function
takes Boolean values and return the text Yes or No accordingly.

Using Functions in Tags

So far, all the functions we have used have been within a <CFOUTPUT> block. This was
done only to simplify the examples, and functions can be used with *any* ColdFusion
Express tag.

For example, in Hour 5, you learned how to use the <CFPARAM> tag to create default values for variables. The syntax for <CFPARAM> usually looks like this:

```
<CFPARAM NAME="quantity" DEFAULT="1">
```

To use a function to assign a default value, you could do something like this:

```
<CFPARAM NAME="date" DEFAULT="#Now()#">
```

To Do: Decision Function Example

Let's look at another example of function usage within a tag, this time within a `<CFIF>` statement. (`<CFIF>` statements were introduced in Hour 6, "Implementing Conditional Processing.") This code example will wish Good morning, Good afternoon, Good evening, or Good night depending on the time of day. Here are the steps so that you can follow along:

1. Open HomeSite (if it isn't already open), and make sure that the hour7 directory is the current directory in the Resource Tab.

2. Create a new file by clicking on the New button (or by selecting New from the File menu).

3. Type the following code in your page between the BODY tags.

```
<CFIF Hour(Now()) LESS THAN 12>
   Good morning
<CFELSEIF Hour(Now()) LESS THAN 18>
   Good afternoon
<CFELSEIF Hour(Now()) LESS THAN 21>
   Good evening
<CFELSE>
   Good night
</CFIF>
```

4. Save the file as **tag_funcs.cfm** in the learncfe directory.

5. To browse the file, open your browser and go to `http://localhost/learncfe/hour7/tag_funcs.cfm`.

Here Hour(Now()) (which returns the current hour of day) is used as the condition in a `<CFIF>` statement. If the function returns a value less than 12, a Good morning greeting is displayed; if the function returns a value greater than 12 and less than 18 (6 p.m.), a Good afternoon greeting is displayed; and so on.

As you can see, functions can be used wherever expressions are used.

Saving Function Results

It is important to remember that functions do not convert or manipulate data; rather, they return converted or manipulated data. The difference is subtle. Look at the following code (part of an earlier example):

```
#LCase(name)#
```

7

This code converts the contents of the variable name to lowercase; rather, it returns the converted text. The contents of name are left intact. In our example, the converted text is never saved; it is just displayed when converted. To save the converted text, you would use <CFSET> to save the results into a variable.

This following code snippet saves a lowercase version of name into a variable named lname:

```
<CFSET lname=LCase(name)>
```

By saving the converted text to a new variable, both the converted and unconverted texts exists, each in a different variable.

Of course, if you want to convert text (as opposed to returning converted text), you can do that too. All you have to do is use <CFSET> to set the same variable, like this:

```
<CFSET name=LCase(name)>
```

Here the original variable will be overwritten with the converted text because the same variable name was used.

> If you ever find yourself using the same function over and over against the same data within a single page, you might want to use <CFSET> to save a single copy of the function output into a variable, and then use that variable throughout the page. This will eliminate unnecessary function processing, which can improve processing time.

Summary

ColdFusion Express features an extensive selection of functions that you can use within your applications. In this hour, you learned what functions are and how to use them. You also created several detailed examples to help learn the various forms of functions usage along with nesting and parameter passing. And finally, you learned how to use functions with ColdFusion Express tags. You'll be using many more functions as you work through this book, including specialized functions used for database and advanced data type processing.

Q&A

Q The Expression Builder is a great tool for helping determine which functions I need. But my problem is not the function itself, but the parameters. With over 200 functions, what help is available so that I don't have to memorize all those functions and parameters?

A I agree, there are a lot of functions. With each new version of ColdFusion, the number of functions seems to grow. The good news is that a new feature in HomeSite 4.5 (and ColdFusion Studio 4.5) called Function Insight can help you here. To use Function Insight, type the name of a function in the editor window followed by the open parentheses character, and then wait a couple of seconds. HomeSite will pop up a context-sensitive inline list of attributes for the function you are typing.

Q You explained how to add dates using the `DateAdd()` function. But I can't find an equivalent function to subtract dates. How can I find out yesterday's date without that function?

A The `DateAdd()` function is actually used to both add and subtract dates. To subtract, all you need to do is pass a negative value as the amount to add. So adding `-1` days to `Now()` will return yesterday's date.

Q Are ColdFusion Express' date functions all Y2K compliant?

A Yes, ColdFusion Express (and indeed all current versions of ColdFusion) are fully Y2K compliant. Details of compliance are listed on the Allaire web site at `http://www.allaire.com/`.

Q How can I create my own functions?

A Unfortunately you can't; at least, not yet. Future versions of ColdFusion will allow custom function creation, but that feature likely will be available only in the full commercial versions of ColdFusion and not ColdFusion Express. In the meantime, however, you should find that by using different combinations of nested functions, you can usually accomplish whatever task you need.

Workshop

The Workshop contains quiz questions and exercises to help reinforce what you've learned in this hour. If you get stuck, the answers to the quiz questions can be found in Appendix A, "Answers to Quiz."

7

Quiz

1. What tells ColdFusion that an expression is a function and not a variable?

2. *True or false:* Every function returns a value.

3. *True or false:* Functions must always be enclosed within pound signs.

4. Why is HomeSite the editor of choice for ColdFusion Express development?

Exercises

1. Look through the ColdFusion Express function list. What function would you use to check if a variable contained a date? What function would you use to check if a variable contained a number?

2. In the last hour, you learned how to use the <CFLOOP> tag. Create a page that loops through from 1000 to 2000 displaying each loop count as a cleanly formatted number. Hint: Look at the NumberFormat() function.

3. Adapt the previous date example so that it displays information about the day you were born instead of the current day. To do this, you could simply replace all occurrences of Now() with your date of birth. But that's not the ideal way to do this. Hint: Look at the revised string example.

HOUR 8

Working with Links

If you've ever browsed a Web page, you'll know what links are. Technically called *anchors*, links connect pages together, turning a collection of pages into a site or application. Links contain references to files—the files to be linked to. These references are specified as URLs (or parts of URLs). As explained in Hour 1, "Understanding ColdFusion Express," URLs are used to identify objects on the Web. URLs are most commonly used to refer to Web pages, but actually all objects, even specific elements within a Web page, have unique addresses—URLs.

In this hour, you'll learn the following:

- What links are and how they are used
- How to programmatically create links
- How ColdFusion Express provides access to URL parameters
- How to gracefully handle missing URL parameters
- How to safely pass data in URL parameters

Understanding Links

Links are integral to the Web. They are the glue that holds Web pages together allowing visitors to travel from page to page. Links can be textual or graphical, and can point to servers, directories, pages, and even specific locations within pages.

There are actually only two ways to connect pages, and of the two, links is the more commonly used method. The other method is via the use of forms, which we'll discuss in the next hour.

Links are created using the HTML `<A>` (anchor) tag. `<A>` takes an attribute named `HREF`, which contains the URL to link to. For example, the following code displays the text `Ben Forta's Homepage` and takes the user to `http://www.forta.com` if that text is clicked on. The clickable text is not specified as an attribute; instead it is placed between the `<A>` and `</A>` tags.

```
<A HREF="http://www.forta.com">Ben Forta's Homepage</A>
```

Graphical links are created the same way, but instead of specifying clickable text between `<A>` and `</A>`, an image is specified using the `<IMG>` tag, like this:

```
<A HREF="http://www.forta.com"><IMG SRC="/images/forta.gif"></A>
```

In this example, two URLs are used, the site to be linked is specified as a complete URL in the `<A>` tag, and the image to display is passed as a local URL (absolute on the same server) in the `<IMG>` tag.

Links to external sites must always be specified as complete URLs, starting with `http://`. Links to pages on your own site can be partial URLs (either absolute or relative).

Every `<A>` tag must have a matching `</A>` tag. If you omit the `</A>`, the browser will assume that you want all text until the end of the page clickable.

Creating Links

You can create links to any files, not just HTML pages. Links can point to images, spreadsheet files, downloadable ZIP files, and more. Any URL that can be typed in the address line in the browser can also be specified in the <A> tags HREF attribute.

Of course, you can also link to ColdFusion Express files. To do so, all you need do is specify the URL to that file as the HREF value.

> Most Web servers allow you to specify ColdFusion Express pages as the default page. This allows you to link to a ColdFusion Express page using server or directory URLs (without having to specify the exact file). You should use this feature if it is supported by your Web server.

Linking to ColdFusion Express Pages

As explained earlier, links are created using the <A> tag. This isn't a difficult tag to use manually as you are about to see. In addition, HomeSite provides several shortcuts to further simplify link creation.

To Do: Create the Files to Be Linked

To Do ▼

Before you can experiment with linking files you'll need to create those files (a file to link from, and a file to link to). Here are the steps to follow:

1. Open HomeSite (if it isn't already open), and make sure that the learncfe\hour8 directory is the current directory in the Resource Tab. If the hour8 directory doesn't exist, select the learncfe directory, and then right-click in the file pane and select Create Folder to create a new folder, specify hour8 as the folder name, and press Enter to create the folder. When created, the new folder will automatically be selected.

2. Select New from the File menu and select Blank Document from the New Document dialog box's HTML tab to create a new blank document.

3. Type the code from Listing 8.1 into the new page.

LISTING 8.1   index.cfm

```
<HTML>
<HEAD>
<TITLE>Working with Links</TITLE>
</HEAD>
```
▼

LISTING 8.1 continued

```
<BODY>
</BODY>
</HTML>
```

4. Select Save from the File menu to save this file as **index.cfm** in the hour8 directory.

5. Create a second file (same procedure as in step 2) and type the HTML code used in step 3 into it. Save this file as **link.cfm** (also in the hour8 directory).

6. Verify that you have created two files. They should both appear in the file pane in the HomeSite Resource Tab, and both files should be open. (You should see two file tabs beneath the editor window, which you can click on to switch between files.)

7. Verify that both files have been created properly. You can do this by opening the files in a Web browser. The first can be called as http://localhost/learncfe/ hour8/index.cfm and the second as http://localhost/learncfe/hour8/ link.cfm. (If you have index.cfm established as a default document, you'll be able to use the URL http://localhost/learncfe/hour8 for the first file.)

▲ Now that you have created the two files, let's look at how you could link them.

To Do: Create a Link Manually

Before we take a look at HomeSite's shortcuts, we will first have a go at creating the link manually. Here are the steps to follow:

1. Select the index.cfm file for editing. If it is open, you can simply click on its tab beneath the editor window. If it isn't open, double-click on the file in the hour8 directory.

2. Insert a blank line between the <BODY> and </BODY> tags, and type the following in it:

   <A HREF="link.cfm">Click Me</A>

3. Save the updated index.cfm file.

4. To test the link, open your browser and go to http://localhost/learncfe/hour8/index.cfm. The display should look like the one shown in Figure 8.1, and you should be able to click on the link to go to the link.cfm page (which is basically empty at this point).

FIGURE 8.1

It is a good idea to test links in a browser as you create them.

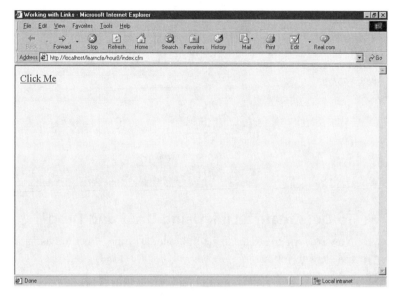

To Do: Create a Link Using HomeSite's Tag Editors

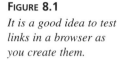

Now we will create the same link; this time using Tag Editors. Here are the steps to follow:

1. Select the index.cfm file for editing. If it is open, you can simply click on its tab beneath the editor window. If it isn't open, double-click on the file in the hour8 directory.

2. Delete the entire <A> tag line you just entered and save the file.

3. Click on the Anchor button in the Common toolbar to display the Anchor Tag Editor (seen in Figure 8.2).

4. In the HREF field, type **link.cfm**, or click on the folder button to the right of the field and select that file.

5. In the Description field, type **Click Me**.

6. Click the OK button, and then save the updated file.

7. To test the link, open your browser and go to http://localhost/learncfe/hour8/index.cfm. It should look and behave just as it did before.

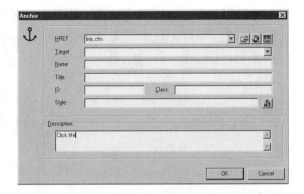

FIGURE 8.2

*The Anchor Tag Editor
provides a simple
interactive interface to
link creation.*

To Do: Create a Link Using Drag and Drop

Now we will create the same link one last time; this time using drag and drop. Here are
the steps to follow:

1. Select the index.cfm file for editing. If it is open, you can simply click on its tab
   beneath the editor window. If it isn't open, double-click on the file in the hour8
   directory.

2. Delete the entire <A> tag line you just entered and save the file.

3. Select the link.cfm file from the file pane and drag it onto the blank line in your
   editor (between the <BODY> and </BODY> tags).

4. When using drag and drop, the link text defaults to the linked file title (in this case,
   Working with Links). Edit the link text so that it reads Click Me.

5. Save the updated file.

6. To test the link, open your browser and go to
   http://localhost/learncfe/hour8/index.cfm. It should look and behave just as
   it did before.

> Drag and drop link creation can only be used if the files being linked (both
> files) have already been saved. If the file has not been saved yet, HomeSite
> will prompt you to save it.

Passing URL Parameters

Now that you know how to link files, it's time to move into to a more advanced link
topic—URL parameter passing. To understand this concept, consider this example.

Suppose that you wanted to display a list of your favorite movies on your Web site. You could create one page that lists all the movie titles, and another page for each movie you want to list. That second page would contain all the movie details, and would be linked back to the first page allowing visitors to click on any movie title to see movie details.

 Incidentally, this type of interface—known as *data drill down*—is very common on the Web because it allows users to efficiently and gradually work their way through lists of data to find what they are looking for.

So, if you listed five movies, you'd create six pages—one with the list of titles, and one for each movie. If you listed 30 movies you'd have to create 31 pages, and so on.

You can imagine that as the number of movies listed increases, so does the complexity in managing that many pages. Instead of a page per movie, what you'd really like is a single page that could display information on any movie. That's where URL parameters come into play.

In our example scenario, you could create two files. The first file—we'll name it movies.cfm—lists all the movie titles and links each of them to the second file, which we'll name details.cfm. So how does details.cfm know which movie title was clicked? The answer is that the movie is passed as a URL parameter.

Look at the following code snippet:

```
<UL>
<LI><A HREF="details.cfm?movie=100">E.T.</A></LI>
<LI><A HREF="details.cfm?movie=101">A Fish Called Wanda</A></LI>
<LI><A HREF="details.cfm?movie=102">Dangerous Liaisons</A></LI>
</UL>
```

The previous code lists three movies in a list; all linked to details.cfm. The only difference between the links is in what comes after the question mark (the ? character). This part of a URL is called the *query string,* and it is used to pass data to a URL. The passed data are parameters in the form of name=value. In this example, a parameter named movie is passed to details.cfm, and each time movie has a different value, first 100, then 101, and then 102. Those numbers would be used to identify the movie that was selected. The code in the details.cfm file could look at the movie parameter, and then display different content based on its value.

To Do: Pass a URL Parameter

Because URL parameter passing is an extremely important part of building Web based applications, we will give it a try together. Here are the steps to follow:

1. Select the index.cfm file for editing. If it is open, you can simply click on its tab beneath the editor window. If it isn't open, double-click on the file in the hour8 directory.

2. Go to the line of code containing the link, and edit it so that it looks like this:

   ```
   <A HREF="link.cfm?option=1">Option 1</A>
   ```

3. Save the updated file.

4. To test the link, open your browser and go to `http://localhost/learncfe/hour8/index.cfm`. The link text should now read `Option 1`, but clicking on it will display the same page as before because we haven't modified the link.cfm page.

> To check that your link is working, click on it and look at the URL displayed in the browser's address field. It should show the complete URL, with the new query string.

Passing Multiple URL Parameters

Thus far you have seen how to pass a single parameter to a URL. Passing multiple URL parameters is just as easy. You still start with a ? after the URL itself (to separate the URL from the query string). But individual parameters must be separated from each other too, and you do this using an ampersand (the & character) .

To pass parameters `firstname` and `lastname`, you could do the following:

```
<A HREF="lookup.cfm?firstname=Ben&lastname=Forta">Ben Forta</A>
```

In this example, two parameters are passed. `firstname` has a value of `Ben` and `lastname` has a value of `Forta`. Both are passed to a file named lookup.cfm, which can use these parameters as needed.

> As a rule, you should pass the least amount of data possible via URL parameters. Different browsers have different maximum length restrictions, and if you create long URLs, you could end up losing data.

You must specify URL query strings correctly or they won't work. A ? must be used to separate the query string from the actual URL, and an & must be used to separate parameters (if more than one is specified) .

Dynamic URL Creation

Like any other page component, links within a page can be dynamically created using ColdFusion Express. Common uses for this include

- Displaying links that change based on user login or other criteria.
- Displaying a list of links driven by a database lookup (more on that in Hours 13, "Creating Data Driven Pages," and 15, "Displaying Dynamic Pages").
- Building sites that are completely dynamic.

Creating lists dynamically is no more complicated than dynamically creating any other output. You use the same tags and techniques that you've learned in the past seven hours. To show you just how easy it really is, we'll look at an example together.

To Do: Create a Dynamically Populated List

This example displays a bulleted list of options created using a simple loop. Here are the steps to follow:

1. Select the index.cfm file for editing. If it is open, you can simply click on its tab beneath the editor window. If it isn't open, double-click on the file in the hour8 directory.

2. Remove any code that you have in between the <BODY> and </BODY> tags, and replace it with the following:

```
<UL>
<CFLOOP INDEX="option" FROM="1" TO="10">
<CFOUTPUT>
<LI><A HREF="link.cfm?option=#option#">Option #option#</A>
</CFOUTPUT>
</CFLOOP>
</UL>
```

3. Save the updated index.cfm file.

4. To test the link, open your browser and go to http://localhost/learncfe/hour8/index.cfm. The display should look like the one shown in Figure 8.3.

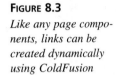

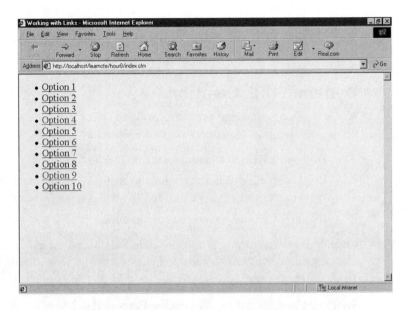

Before we go any further, let's look at the code we just inserted. Bulleted lists are created using the HTML unordered list tags <UL> and </UL>, so to display the list of options in a bulleted list, the entire code block is enclosed within those tags.

Then comes the loop itself. This <CFLOOP> tag uses a simple index loop (see Hour 6, "Implementing Conditional Processing," if you need a reminder on how <CFLOOP> is used). This particular loop is set to repeat 10 times (from 1 to 10), and, each time, the current iteration number is returned in the variable option. (You are more than welcome to experiment with a different range of numbers; you might want to use a TO value of 20, or 50, or 1000.)

Within the loop block, a link is created (within <CFOUTPUT> tags of course). The link itself uses the option variable twice, once for the link and once for the display. On the fourth iteration through the loop (when option is 4), the following code

```
<LI><A HREF="link.cfm?option=#option#">Option #option#</A>
```

generates the following output:

```
<LI><A HREF="link.cfm?option=4">Option 4</A>
```

8

▼ Looping through the output 10 times thus generates the following list (as seen previously in Figure 8.3):

```
<UL>
<LI><A HREF="link.cfm?option=1">Option 1</A>
<LI><A HREF="link.cfm?option=2">Option 2</A>
<LI><A HREF="link.cfm?option=3">Option 3</A>
<LI><A HREF="link.cfm?option=4">Option 4</A>
<LI><A HREF="link.cfm?option=5">Option 5</A>
<LI><A HREF="link.cfm?option=6">Option 6</A>
<LI><A HREF="link.cfm?option=7">Option 7</A>
<LI><A HREF="link.cfm?option=8">Option 8</A>
<LI><A HREF="link.cfm?option=9">Option 9</A>
<LI><A HREF="link.cfm?option=10">Option 10</A>
</UL>
```

The key point to note here is that the same link.cfm page is being linked to in every sin-
▲ gle link. The only thing that differs is the option value in the query string.

Using URL Parameters

As you can see, creating links, even highly dynamic links, is very simple in ColdFusion Express. And the good news is that using the passed parameters is just as easy.

In Hour 5, "Working with Variables and Expressions," you learned how to use <CFOUTPUT> to display the contents of variables. You learned how to display local variables created with <CFSET> or <CFPARAM>, and those same techniques can be used to display URL parameters. Even though internally a URL parameter is very different from a local variable, ColdFusion Express does you the favor of hiding those differences from you. You can simply use URL parameters (and other variable types as you'll see in later hours) like simple variables.

To use the option URL parameter created in the last example within your code, you can simply refer to it as #option# or #URL.option#. The URL prefix is optional, and if used specifies that you only want the URL parameter option and not any other variable named option (for example, a local variable or a form field).

To Do: Display a URL Parameter

To demonstrate the use of passed URL parameters, we'll update the link.cfm page to display the selected option. Here are the steps to follow:

1. Select the link.cfm file for editing. If it is open, you can simply click on its tab beneath the editor window. If it isn't open, double-click on the file in the hour8 directory.

▼ To Do

▼   2. Insert the following code in between the `<BODY>` and `</BODY>` tags:
```
<CFOUTPUT>
You selected option #URL.option#
</CFOUTPUT>
```

   3. Save the updated link.cfm file.

   4. To test the link, open your browser, go to `http://localhost/learncfe/hour8/index.cfm`, and click on any option. Pay close attention to the URL that is displayed in the browser address field when the link.cfm file is displayed. The display should look like the one shown in Figure 8.4. (Of course if you select an option other than option 4, the one I selected, your display will reflect that.)

FIGURE 8.4

URL parameters can be used and displayed like any other variables.

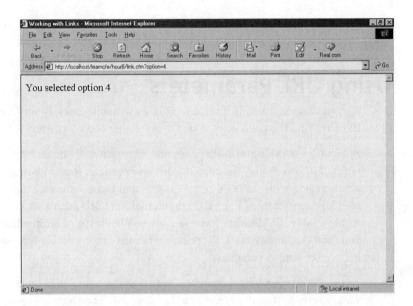

As you can see, using URL parameters in your code is very simple indeed. And although this example simply displayed the passed parameter, you could just as easily have used it ▲ in conditional processing or any other code.

Handling Missing Parameters

Before you run off to use URL parameters, there's one last important topic to cover—the handling of missing parameters.

To demonstrate what I mean, open your browser and go to `http://localhost/ learncfe/hour8/link.cfm`. You should see an error message similar to the one shown in Figure 8.5.

FIGURE 8.5

Referring to a nonexistent URL parameter will generate a ColdFusion error.

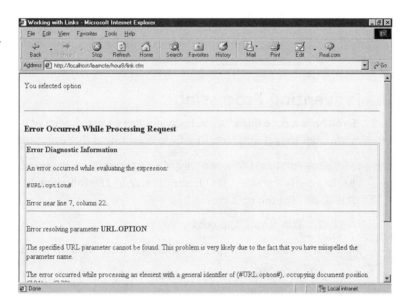

Why is this happening? It is happening because your code is referring to a nonexistent variable. You are attempting to display `#URL.option#`, and no URL parameter named `option` was provided.

Obviously generating this kind of error isn't a good thing. Your code therefore must be able to handle missing URL parameters, and there are several different ways to do this depending on what you want to occur. Basically there are three possible actions you might want to perform if an expected URL parameter isn't present:

- Prevent processing of the page
- Continue processing using a default value
- Process the page differently

We'll now look at each of these options.

Don't ever assume that a page is safe just because the only way to get to it is by clicking on a link that you create. Although your own links might be safe, there is no guarantee that all future links will be; plus, users could type the URL of linked pages directly (bypassing your links). You should always write your code to be able to handle missing parameters, even if you are convinced that this will never happen to you.

Preventing Processing

If you have a page that absolutely cannot be processed without a passed parameter, you might want to prevent processing from occurring if that parameter is missing.

Doing this requires determining whether a parameter was passed, and this can be checked easily with the IsDefined() function. The following line statement will return TRUE if URL.option isn't present:

```
<CFIF NOT IsDefined("URL.option")>
```

Now that you know URL.option wasn't specified, what do you do?

One option is to display an error message and prevent further processing. This can be done easily as follows:

```
<!--- Stop if URL.option not present --->
<CFIF NOT IsDefined("URL.option")>
 <H1>ERROR! URL parameter option is required</H1>
 <CFABORT>
</CFIF>
```

This code snippet, which would typically go at the very top of the linked page, checks to see whether URL.option exists. If it doesn't, it displays an error message (formatted as <H1> in this example), and then prevents any further processing by calling the <CFABORT> tag. This tag is used to abort further processing, effectively terminating the page at that point.

To Do: Handle Missing Parameters by Aborting Processing

If you'd like to try this technique for yourself, here are the steps to follow:

1. Select the link.cfm file for editing. If it is open, you can simply click on its tab beneath the editor window. If it isn't open, double-click on the file in the hour8 directory.

▼ To Do

▼   2. Insert the following code at the very top of the page:

```
<!--- Stop if URL.option not present --->
<CFIF NOT IsDefined("URL.option")>
 <H1>ERROR! URL parameter option is required</H1>
 <CFABORT>
</CFIF>
```

      3. Save the updated file.

      4. To test the code, open your browser and go to
         `http://localhost/learncfe/hour8/link.cfm` (making sure not to pass any URL
         parameters). You should see an error message displayed.

      5. Now make sure that this code change didn't break anything. Go to
         `http://localhost/learncfe/hour8/index.cfm` and click on a link to verify that
         the original processing still works correctly.

Displaying error messages is an effective solution to the problem. But it isn't a very user-
friendly solution. The truth is, if users aren't supposed to get to this page (if the option
parameter expected that users got to this page supposedly by clicking on a link elsewhere), a better alternative would be to redirect the user to where he really should have
been. Take a look at this code snippet:

```
<!--- Redirect if URL.option not present --->
<CFIF NOT IsDefined("URL.option")>
 <CFLOCATION URL="index.cfm">
</CFIF>
```

Here a `<CFIF>` statement is once again used to check that `URL.option` exists. If it
doesn't, a `<CFLOCATION>` tag is used to redirect the user to another page; in this case the
index.cfm page. This way if the user mistakenly ends up at link.cfm, he'd automatically
be redirected to where he should have been. Obviously this is a more user-friendly inter-
▲   face.

To Do: Handle Missing Parameters by Redirection

If you'd like to try this technique for yourself, here are the steps to follow:

      1. Select the link.cfm file for editing. If it is open, you can simply click on its tab
         beneath the editor window. If it isn't open, double-click on the file in the hour8
         directory.

      2. Insert the following code at the very top of the page (removing any previously
         inserted error checking code beforehand):

```
<!--- Redirect if URL.option not present --->
<CFIF NOT IsDefined("URL.option")>
 <CFLOCATION URL="index.cfm">
</CFIF>
```

▼ 3. Save the updated file.

4. To test the code, open your browser and go to
   `http://localhost/learncfe/hour8/link.cfm` (making sure not to pass any URL
   parameters). You should be redirected to the page containing the list of options.

5. Now make sure that this code change didn't break anything. Go to
   `http://localhost/learncfe/hour8/index.cfm` and click on a link to verify that
▲ the original processing still works correctly.

Providing Defaults

Often URL parameters are passed as optional values to pages. For example, perhaps your
page allows custom colors to be passed at runtime; in which case, you'd want to use the
supplied colors if provided and default values if not.

You can specify default values using the <CFPARAM> tag (<CFPARAM> was introduced in
Hour 5). Look at the following line of code:

```
<CFPARAM NAME="URL.color" DEFAULT="red">
```

In this example, a default value for URL.color is specified. What this means is that if no
URL parameter named color is present, ColdFusion Express will create one automatically and assign the default value to it. Of course, if URL.color was present, the
<CFPARAM> tag would do nothing at all.

The key point is that one way or another, after that <CFPARAM> tag is processed, a variable named URL.color would exist. Your code can now safely refer to the variable and
will never know (or care) whether it was actually passed with the URL or not.

To Do: Handle Missing Parameters by Redirection

If you'd like to try this technique for yourself, here are the steps to follow:

1. Select the link.cfm file for editing. If it is open, you can simply click on its tab
   beneath the editor window. If it isn't open, double-click on the file in the hour8
   directory.

2. Insert the following code at the very top of the page (removing any previously
   inserted error checking code beforehand):
   ```
   <!--- Default URL.option to "" --->
   <CFPARAM NAME="URL.option" DEFAULT="">
   ```

▼ 3. Save the updated file.

4. To test the code, open your browser and go to
   `http://localhost/learncfe/hour8/link.cfm` (making sure not to pass any URL
   parameters). You should see the page displayed but with no option specified.

5. Now make sure that this code change didn't break anything. Go to
   `http://localhost/learncfe/hour8/index.cfm` and click on a link to verify that
   the original processing still works correctly.

Conditional Processing

You'll often find that you need to handle missing parameters by continuing with conditional processing. In other words, you'd process the page but do something differently if the expected URL parameter wasn't specified.

The key to performing conditional processing is detecting whether a parameter is present, and as I showed you earlier, you can perform this detection using the `IsDefined()` function.

Look at the following code snippet. It first checks to see if `URL.option` exists. If it does, the selected option is displayed. If it doesn't exist, a notification saying `No option specified` is displayed instead.

```
<!--- Check it option specified --->
<CFIF IsDefined("URL.option")>
 <!--- Yes, display it --->
 <CFOUTPUT>
 You selected option #URL.option#
 </CFOUTPUT>
<CFELSE>
 <!--- No, display notification --->
 No option specified.
</CFIF>
```

To Do: Handle Missing Parameters by Conditional Processing

If you'd like to try this technique for yourself, here are the steps to follow:

1. Select the link.cfm file for editing. If it is open, you can simply click on its tab beneath the editor window. If it isn't open, double-click on the file in the hour8 directory.

2. Insert the following code at the very top of the page (removing any previously inserted error checking code and output code beforehand):

```
<!--- Check it option specified --->
<CFIF IsDefined("URL.option")>
 <!--- Yes, display it --->
 <CFOUTPUT>
```

```
You selected option #URL.option#
</CFOUTPUT>
<CFELSE>
<!--- No, display notification --->
No option specified.
</CFIF>
```

3. Save the updated file.

4. To test the code, open your browser and go to `http://localhost/learncfe/hour8/link.cfm` (making sure not to pass any URL parameters). You should see the page displayed with the `No option specified` notice.

5. Now make sure that this code change didn't break anything. Go to `http://localhost/learncfe/hour8/index.cfm` and click on a link to verify that the original processing still works correctly.

Summary

URL parameter passing is a fundamental component of any Web-based application. In this hour, you learned how to create URL with and without query string parameters, as well as how to create parameters dynamically. You also learned how to detect missing parameters, and how to gracefully handle this kind of error condition.

Q&A

Q Sometimes I see extraneous text, even whole lines of code, in my URLs. What causes this?

A The most common culprit is mismatched (or missing) double quotes around the HREF value in your <A> tag. As a rule, the value passed to HREF should always be enclosed within double quotes.

Q If ? is used to separate the URL from the query string, and & is used to separate parameters, does that mean I cannot use those characters in my parameter names and values?

A Absolutely. And to make it worse, spaces, periods, commas, pound signs, equal signs, and many other characters cannot be used within URLs. If your URL parameter names or values contain those characters, you'll find yourself with missing, misnamed, and truncated parameters, or worse, links that won't work at all. Although there isn't much you can do about parameter names (other than to make sure they don't contain invalid characters), parameter values are a different story. To allow the use of these characters, a special format is used, which allows you to

8

specify a special code that represents the character being used, and there are hundreds of these codes. Before you panic, no, there is no need for you to remember all the codes. Instead, you can just use the ColdFusion `URLEncodedFormat()` function, which will take any string and return a URL safe version of it. So, if you need to embed the variable `#firstname#` in your URL, it is far safer to embed `#URLEncodedFormat(firstname)#` instead. This way if there are any problematic characters, they'll be converted automatically to codes that are safe to use. Even better still, when you use the passed URL parameters, ColdFusion Express will *automatically* decode them back to their normal text.

Q **Are there any restrictions to the number of parameters that may be passed in a query string?**

A No, there is no maximum number of allowed parameters. But as mentioned earlier, different browsers allow different maximum number of characters. Although there are no hard and fast rules for what is acceptable, for the most part a few hundred characters seems to work in all major browsers.

Workshop

The Workshop contains quiz questions and exercises to help reinforce what you've learned in this hour. If you get stuck, the answers to the quiz questions can be found in Appendix A, "Answers to Quiz."

Quiz

1. What is the name of the text that appears after a ? in a URL?
2. *True or false:* Every URL parameter must be separated by a ?.
3. Why is missing parameter handling so important when using URL parameters?

Exercises

1. Visit your favorite major Web site. Look at the URLs that are used as you browse or search through the site, and try to work out what URL parameters are being passed and what their values are.
2. I briefly mentioned absolute and relative URLs. What do these terms mean, and why would you use one form of URL over another?
3. Visit the Allaire Web site at `http://www.allaire.com`. Can you see how URL parameters are being passed so that a single ColdFusion file serves different content for different pages? Hint: Look at the URL parameters as you browse through the site.

HOUR 9

Using Forms

You've learned a lot of CFML tags and techniques in the last eight hours, but so far you have been unable to accept information from users of your Web sites. In this hour, you'll learn how to interact with your users using forms. HTML enables you to create forms, which are the interface screens used to collect information from users.

In this lesson, you'll learn the following:

- What forms are and how to collect data from users
- What types of information you can capture with a form
- How to use form controls, and how not to
- How to use form information within your applications

Creating Forms

You've probably used forms many times on the Web, perhaps to perform one of the following:

- Sign a site guest book
- Search for information
- Place orders for books or products

Each of these activities requires that you use HTML forms. Anytime you want to collect data from your visitors, you do so using forms.

Using the <FORM> Tag

In order to create a form, begin by using the <FORM> tag. This tag defines the interface the user will see. The <FORM> tag has several attributes, but we're going to concentrate on two of them for now:

```
<FORM ACTION="URL" METHOD="POST">
. . .
</FORM>
```

The ACTION attribute specifies the CFML page that you want all form data to be passed to for processing. The METHOD attribute should always be set to POST for CFML to work properly.

To Do: Create a Form

Follow along with me as I teach you how to create an HTML form. Start by creating a new page using the default template in HomeSite and name it guestbook.cfm. Save this file with the files created in the previous hours in the learncfe directory under the Web server's root directory.

1. Change the <TITLE> of the page to **"My Guest Book"**.
2. Place your cursor in between the page's <BODY> and </BODY> tags.
3. Select the Quick Bar Forms toolbar, and click the Form button (the first one on the left) to display the <FORM> Tag Editor (see Figure 9.1).
4. You must specify the form action in the ACTION field—type **insert_guest.cfm**. (That file hasn't been created yet; we'll get to that in a few moments.)
5. Select POST as the form METHOD. (ColdFusion forms should always use the POST method.)
6. Leave all the other fields with their default settings, and click the Apply button to generate the form code.

Figure 9.1

The <FORM> Tag Editor prompts for the form action, method, and other attributes.

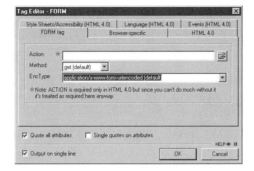

9

Form Controls

The interface elements in HTML forms are referred to as *form controls*. There is a limited set of form controls, but they should cover most of your interface needs. All form controls are defined inside the <FORM> tag.

To demonstrate the use of these controls, we will examine a Guest Book form as shown in Figure 9.2.

Figure 9.2

HTML supports different control types for use within forms.

Using the Text Field

If you've ever filled out your name or email address on a Web site, you've used a text field. This is an interface element that allows user input and echoes to the screen what the user types.

Text fields scroll text automatically if more text is entered than can be displayed. You can modify the behavior of the text field by adding attributes to the <INPUT> tag.

To create a text field, use the HTML <INPUT> tag. This tag is a multi-use tag that allows you to create many types of interface elements, which you will use later in this hour.

> HTML offers another interface element, called a *password field,* that is similar to a text field. Password fields behave just like text fields except the text that you type isn't displayed as regular text, but rather as asterisks (*). In this way, you can safely type your password without worrying that it might be revealed to a casual observer.

The input tag shown in the following snippet will create a text field with a visual size of 10 characters that allows a maximum of 20 characters to be entered as it scrolls. The NAME attribute specifies the name of the form control. This name will be used to reference the information entered into the control. Each form element should be labeled so that the user will know what information is being requested. Here we are using the label "Name".

```
Name: <INPUT TYPE="text"
       NAME="GuestName"
       SIZE="10"
       MAXLENGTH="20">
```

> Don't confuse the name of a form control with the text label before it. The NAME attribute will become a form variable name, whereas the text label of "Name:" is merely to tell the user what is expected of them to enter into the form control.
>
> Also, be sure to set the NAME attribute to a valid name for a ColdFusion variable. See variable naming conventions in Hour 5, "Working with Variables and Expressions."

To Do: Prompt for Name and Email

Return to guestbook.cfm to create input text fields, which will capture the guest's name and email address.

1. Place your cursor in between the page's <FORM> and </FORM> tags and press Enter to add white space to work within.

2. Type the text **Name:** on a new line between the <FORM> and </FORM> tags. (This will be the field label.)

3. Click the Text button in the Quick Bar Forms toolbar (the one with the bolded "ab" in it) to display the <INPUT> Tag Editor (shown in Figure 9.3).

FIGURE 9.3

The <INPUT> Tag Editor is a tabbed dialog that is used for all field types other than text area boxes and list boxes.

4. Specify the name of this control in the Name field of the dialog box. Because this field will contain your visitor's name, we'll call it GuestName.

5. Set the Size attribute to 20 (the actual size of the control on the window) and the Maxlength attribute to 30 (the number of characters that will be accepted).

6. Leave all the other options as they are and then click the Apply button to write the INPUT code into your editor.

7. Create another text control with a label of Email, a NAME of Email, a SIZE of 20 and a MAXLENGTH of 30.

8. Save the page and open a browser to surf to this page. It should look like Figure 9.4.

FIGURE 9.4

It is a good idea to test your forms incrementally as you create them. Each time you add a control, check to see that the form looks as it should.

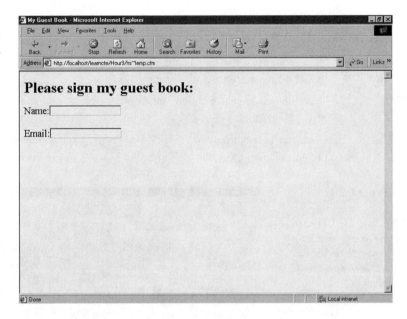

Use a label of "`Email:`" and name the control `Email`. Insert HTML `<BR>` breaks in between the controls or they'll end up on one line.

All form controls *must* be placed between the `<FORM>` and `</FORM>` tags. Without the form tags, the controls might not show up, or worse; they'll show up but won't work.

Using Check Boxes

Check boxes are used for on/off fields (also known as *flags* or *true/false fields*). They only have two possible values: `ON` and `OFF`.

Check boxes are created using the `<INPUT>` tag with a `TYPE` of `checkbox`. The following code shows how to create a check box:

```
Is this your first site visit?
<INPUT TYPE="checkbox"
       NAME="FirstVisit">
```

Check boxes can only be ON or OFF. However, you can use many check boxes on a page to indicate multiple selections. For instance, you might have a set of check boxes on a survey, where you ask the user to check all choices that apply to the question. So check boxes aren't just for single inputs if you use them in groups.

9

My Guest Book uses a check box to ask users whether this is their first visit.

To Do: Prompt for First Visit—Yes or No

▼ To Do

Now we'll create the check box field:

1. Type the text **Is this your first site visit?** on a new line. (This will be the field label).

2. Click the check box button in the Quick Bar Forms toolbar (the one with the picture of a check box in it) to display the <INPUT> Tag Editor with the Check box tab selected.

3. Specify FirstVisit as the control Name.

4. Specify the Value attribute as Yes. In this way, when the user checks the check box, the form control will be given a value of Yes.

5. Click the Apply button to write the <INPUT> code into your editor.

6. Add a <BR> tag to the end of the line for spacing.

▲   Again, remember to test your form each time you add a control.

Using Radio Buttons

Radio buttons allow a user to select one of a set of mutually exclusive options. My Guest Book uses radio buttons to ask the user what he thinks of my site.

Although I probably could have used a text field and allowed users to specify whatever they want, collecting structured data is usually preferable if I am planning on running statistics or reports on the collected data.

These controls are a little more complicated than the <INPUT> we have created thus far because each radio button requires its own <INPUT> tag. To create a set of three radio buttons to rate a site, use three separate <INPUT> tags, one for each radio button:

```
How would you rate my site?<BR>
   Great!<INPUT TYPE="radio"
```

```
                NAME="Rating"
                VALUE="3"
                CHECKED><BR>
      Mediocre<INPUT TYPE="radio"
                NAME="Rating"
                VALUE="2"><BR>
     It stinks!<INPUT TYPE="radio"
                NAME="Rating"
                VALUE="1">
```

Each radio button is labeled, and each is given a value. In this case, I've allowed the user to rate the site from Great!, which I've assigned a value of 3, down to It stinks!, which has a value of 1. When I process the user selection, I will know that 3 is the best rating and 1 is the worst. These values are arbitrary and only have the meaning that you assign to them. Later, you check for the value you assign in your processing of the data. Notice that the first radio button uses the CHECKED attribute, which means that it is the default when the user first gets the form.

How does the browser know to treat these fields as one set? The answer is the control name. A set of radio buttons must all have the same name; they differ not by name but by value. This way the browser treats them as a set (when one is selected, the others are automatically deselected), and when the form is submitted, the value of the selected radio button is submitted.

To Do: Prompt for Site Rating

Here are the steps to add the radio buttons to our Guest Book:

1. Type the text **How would you rate my site?** on a new line. (This will be the field label.)

2. Click the radio button in the Quick Bar Forms toolbar (the one with the picture of a radio button in it) to display the <INPUT> Tag Editor with the Radio tab selected.

3. Specify Rating as the control Name.

4. Specify great as the Value.

5. Click the Apply button to write the <INPUT> code into your editor.

6. Each radio button needs a label, text that describes what it represents, so provide a label by typing **Great!** before the generated <INPUT> code.

▼ 7. Repeat steps 2 through 6 to add the next button: make sure that the name is `Rating` (so that the fields are grouped) and specify a value of `mediocre` and a label of `Mediocre`.

▲ 8. Repeat steps 2 through 6 to add the final button: make sure that the name is Rating and specify a value of `stinks` and a label of `It stinks!`.

When you are done, test your form. Make sure that the radio buttons are displayed correctly and that selecting one radio buttons deselects the others.

> When you look at your form, are the controls on the same line? Be sure to use the <BR> tag anywhere you want to space out the controls on different lines. If you need to, go back now and add <BR> tags.

Using List Boxes

List boxes (or *drop-down list boxes*) are similar to radio buttons in that they usually allow for the selection of one or more of a set of options. But there are two key differences between list boxes and radio buttons:

- Radio buttons are all displayed on the screen, allowing visitors to see all options before making a selection. List boxes usually display a single selection and the visitor must click the down arrow to display the other options. As such, radio buttons take up more screen space, and are not well suited for long lists of options. It is best to keep the list short, for a maximum of five options.

- Radio buttons only allow the selection of a single option. List boxes can be constructed to allow the selection of multiple options if desired.

My Guest Book uses a list box to prompt the visitor for information on how they ended up at my site. I want to know where my users are coming from and how they got to my site in the first place.

List boxes aren't created using the <INPUT> tag. Instead, you need to use two new tags. The <SELECT> tag is used to create a list box (HTML calls these *select controls*), and the <OPTION> tag is used to populate the list box with options, as shown here:

```
How did you get here?
    <SELECT NAME="GotHere"
            SIZE="1">
            <OPTION VALUE="Unknown">Don't know</OPTION>
            <OPTION VALUE="Search">Searched for it</OPTION>
            <OPTION VALUE="Stumbled">Stumbled on it</OPTION>
    </SELECT>
```

When you can select at most one value from the drop-down list, set the SIZE attribute to 1.

As with radio buttons, the values I've assigned are arbitrary—I will know when I process the form that the only possible values are Unknown, Searched, and Stumbled and will process it accordingly.

> The <SELECT> control allows you to indicate that the user can select multiple values using Shift+Click or Control+Click. This is done by using the MULITPLE keyword inside the opening <SELECT> tag.
>
> Be aware of your audience. Do your users know they can select multiple selections by using Shift+Click and Control+Click? This type of control can be rather unfriendly to a new user. You might consider multiple check boxes if there aren't too many options.

To Do: Prompt for Referral to Site

As you'd expect, HomeSite simplifies creating list boxes as follows:

1. Type the text **How did you get here?** on a new line. (This will be the field label.)
2. Click the select button in the Quick Bar Forms toolbar (the one on the far right) to display the <SELECT> Tag Editor (as seen in Figure 9.5).

FIGURE 9.5

The <SELECT> Tag Editor is a tabbed dialog that can also create <OPTION> tags if desired.

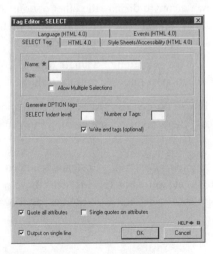

3. Set the field name to GotHere.
4. Set the SIZE field to 1.

▼   5. Type the number **3** into the `SIZE` field to have HomeSite create three option tags for you. (You can add and remove options later if needed.)

       6. Click the Apply button to write the `<SELECT>` and `<OPTION>` tags into your editor.

       7. Now populate the options. Each option needs a `VALUE` (what gets returned when the user selects the option), and the display text (what the user actually sees on the screen). HomeSite sets each `VALUE` attribute to an incremental number, so you'll need to change that value to what you want. The display text is specified in between the `<OPTION>` and `</OPTION>` tags, so use `<OPTION VALUE="Unknown">Don't know</OPTION>` for the `Don't know` option. For the second option, use `<OPTION VALUE="Search">Searched for it</OPTION>`. And for the third option, use `<OPTION VALUE="Stumbled">Stumbled on it</OPTION>`.

▲   After you have specified the options, save and test your page.

Using Text Area Boxes

Text area fields are used to collect multiline freeform text. Unlike text fields, text area fields allow users to enter as much text as they want on as many lines as they want. You can control the size of the text area box, but not the number of lines or characters that can be entered.

> By default, text area boxes don't wrap text. This means that the entire box will scroll to the right when the end of a line is reached. Most browsers, however, support optional text area box wrapping. Because this makes for a far more pleasant user interface, as a rule you should always use this option in your own forms. To wrap the text, use the `WRAP` attribute, which takes one of three values:
>
> - **off**—Don't wrap the text (default for Netscape browsers).
> - **soft**—Wrap the text to fit the size of the text area field (default for Microsoft Internet Explorer browsers).
> - **hard**—for each line break, insert a line break character.

> HTML enables you to control the size of the text area box. The width of a text area box is specified in columns, the number of columns of text that can be displayed. Unfortunately, different browsers have different ways of interpreting *columns*. As such, your text area box will be one size in Netscape Navigator and a different size in Microsoft Internet Explorer. There isn't much you can do about this, but at minimum you should check your forms in multiple browsers to ensure that the controls look right in all of them.

Text area fields are created using the <TEXTAREA> tag. This tag allows you to set the number of rows and columns the user will see, and allows you to put in default text, such as "Put comments here". In the following code snippet, note that the number of columns is 30 and the number of rows is 3.

```
Comments:<BR>
     <TEXTAREA COLS=30
          ROWS=3
          NAME="Comments">Put comments here</TEXTAREA>
```

> Because you're a good developer, you want to clean up your code and use proper indentation. Unfortunately, putting the <TEXTAREA> and </TEXTAREA> tags on separate lines (using the Enter key) will cause unwanted behavior later on. The Enter key (really, the associated control character for it) will be put into the text area field. If you are using this control to update a long text field in the database, you will get an extra Enter in your column each time you update anything in that record. So be sure to keep the tags on the same line.

My Guest Book uses a text area field for the comments field, which allows visitors to enter any text they'd like. In the next task, I'll show you how to prompt your users for comments that you can collect to learn more about the people visiting your site.

To Do: Prompt for Comments

The last field we need is the comments field, a text area box. Perform the following steps to add this field:

1. Type the text **Comments:** on a new line (this will be the field prompt) followed by a line break (the <BR> tag).

2. Click the text area button in the Quick Bar Forms toolbar (the one with a picture of a folded over page) to display the <TEXTAREA> Tag Editor (see Figure 9.6).

3. Use Comments as the field name.

4. Set the control size; I used 30 for the columns and 3 for the rows.

5. On the Browser-Specific tab, set wrapping to SOFT. (This option will make the control behave like most Windows text area boxes.)

6. Click the Apply button to write the <TEXTAREA> code into your editor.

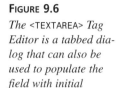

Figure 9.6

The <TEXTAREA> Tag Editor is a tabbed dialog that can also be used to populate the field with initial content.

9

Using Buttons

Several different types of buttons are available, but we will only look at the Submit and Reset buttons. All buttons are clickable and perform some action on the form.

The Submit button is used to submit the form after data entry is complete. Every form is associated with an ACTION. This is usually a page to which the collected data is sent. When the submit button is clicked, the collected data is sent to the ACTION page, which processes the data and takes the user along in the interface.

The Reset button does just that—it resets the form. If the user clicks on this button, the data entered will be cleared out. The user can then re-enter data.

> Many Web developers avoid using Reset buttons as visitors often click them by mistake when trying to click the submit button. Understandably, users are not going to like retyping all their text, and omitting the Reset button can prevent this from occurring. But if you want to include it, be sure to put it on the left-hand size of the Submit button. Users like the final action to be performed at the bottom right-hand side of the window.

To create both the Submit and Reset buttons, you will use the <INPUT> tag. The Submit button doesn't need to be named usually, but it should always be labeled using the VALUE attribute as shown here:

```
<INPUT TYPE="submit" VALUE="All Done">
```

The Reset button syntax is very similar to the Submit button:

```
<INPUT TYPE="Reset" VALUE="Start Over">
```

> If you don't specify button text, Reset buttons will use the default caption of Reset and Submit buttons will use Submit Query. Rather than use these default (and not very intuitive) values, always specify your own captions in the button's VALUE attribute.

To Do: Submit or Reset the Form

All we need now are the two buttons, the Reset and Submit buttons. Here are the steps to follow:

1. Place your cursor at the beginning of a new line after your text area but before the closing </FORM> tag.
2. Click the Reset button on the Quick Bar Forms toolbar (the one with a button with an R on it).
3. Button text is specified in the Value attribute, so change it to Start Over.
4. Click Apply to write the button code to the editor.
5. Place your cursor at the beginning of a new line.
6. Click the Submit button on the Quick Bar Forms toolbar (the one with a button with an S on it).
7. Once again, leave the name field empty, but specify a caption of All Done.
8. Click Apply to write the button code to the editor.

Now save your form, and test it. It should look similar to Figure 9.2, which is shown at the beginning of this hour.

The Completed Form

Your Guest Book form is now complete. What follows is my own Guest Book code, which you can refer to if yours doesn't look as you expected.

LISTING 9.1   Guest Book Form

```
 1:<!DOCTYPE HTML PUBLIC "-//W3C//DTD HTML 4.0 Transitional//EN">
 2:
 3:<HTML>
 4:<HEAD>
 5:    <TITLE>Guest Book</TITLE>
 6:</HEAD>
 7:
 8:<BODY>
 9:
10:<H2>Please sign my guest book:</H2>
11:
12:<FORM ACTION="insert_guest.cfm"
13:      METHOD="post">
14:
15:Name:<INPUT TYPE="text" NAME="GuestName"
16:      SIZE="20" MAXLENGTH="30">
17:<BR><BR>
18:Email:<INPUT TYPE="text" NAME="Email"
19:      SIZE="20" MAXLENGTH="30">
20:<BR><BR>
21:Is this your first site visit?
22:    <INPUT TYPE="checkbox"
23:      NAME="FirstVisit"
24:      VALUE="Yes">
25:<BR><BR>
26:How would you rate my site?<BR>
27:    Great!<INPUT TYPE="radio"
28:      NAME="Rating"
29:      VALUE="Great"
30:      CHECKED>
31:    Mediocre<INPUT TYPE="radio"
32:      NAME="Rating"
33:      VALUE="Mediocre">
34:    It stinks!<INPUT TYPE="radio"
35:      NAME="Rating"
36:      VALUE="Stinks">
37:<BR><BR>
38:How did you get here?
39:    <SELECT NAME="GotHere"
40:            SIZE="1">
41:            <OPTION VALUE="Unknown">Don't know</OPTION>
42:            <OPTION VALUE="Search">Searched for it</OPTION>
43:            <OPTION VALUE="Stumbled">Stumbled on it</OPTION>
44:    </SELECT>
45:<BR><BR>
46:Comments:<BR>
47:    <TEXTAREA COLS=30
48:        ROWS=3
```

9

LISTING 9.1   continued

```
49:        WRAP="soft"
50:        NAME="Comments">Put comments here</TEXTAREA>
51:<BR><BR>
52:  <INPUT TYPE="Reset" VALUE="Start Over">
53:  <INPUT TYPE="submit" VALUE="All Done">
54:
55:</FORM>
56:</BODY>
57:</HTML>
```

Remember that the form is only half the story—you need to code the action page to process the data that is submitted.

Understanding Action Pages

Creating a visual form is only half the story. Prompting the users for information is useless unless you intend to do something with that information—register them, email them, allow them access to your site, or some other operation. You need two pages to collect and process the data:

- HTML Form page
- Action page

Figure 9.7 illustrates the relationship between the form and an action page.

FIGURE 9.7

Every HTML form page must have an associated action page in order to process collected information from the user.

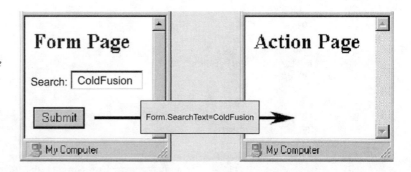

Each value the user inputs gets sent to the action page for processing. Because HTML isn't a programming language, it cannot process the data alone. The action page associated with the form page uses CFML tags to process the data. The following section explains how action pages work with form data.

Working with Form Data

Each HTML control creates a variable to hold the value the user selects or types. It is confusing at first because, thus far, you have created your variables explicitly using the <CFSET> tag. HTML takes care of creating the form variables for you when the form is submitted by the user to the action page. If a user surfs to a Web page with an HTML form and submits it, HTTP actually takes each form control, creates a variable to hold the user's input, and sends those variable/value pairs to the action page. The action page can do anything with the variables. Your only job is to create the form page with controls, and to process the resulting form fields in the action page.

To see what information users put into the form controls, we will start with a simple action of printing out the values. To do this, use the <CFOUTPUT> tag and surround the variables with pound signs. You learned all this in Hour 5. The difference is that these variables aren't page variables, they are form variables. This means that they require the FORM prefix to designate them as coming from a form:

```
<CFOUTPUT>
    The user entered a name of: #Form.GuestName#
</CFOUTPUT>
```

In the next exercise, take the form variables that were created by the form and print out the user input in the action page.

To Do: Print Out Form Variable Values

Using <CFOUTPUT>, print out all form variable values in the action page. Here are the steps:

1. Create a new page using the default template.

2. Change the <TITLE> value to "Processing Guest Book Information".

3. Save the file in the /learncfe/hour9 directory as insert_guest.cfm.

4. Put your cursor between the <BODY> and </BODY> tags.

5. Using the CFML Quick Bar toolbar, click the Out button to get the <CFOUTPUT> dialog and click Apply without specifying any of the attributes.

6. Inside the <CFOUTPUT> tags, print out each of the form's variable values. For instance, if you want to print out the value the user typed for the guest name, use #FORM.GuestName# to refer to the text control for name. Refer to the form to remember what you named each form control, so you will use the correct name of the form variable. Don't forget to use pound signs. Put each on a separate line using the <BR> tag.

7. Browse to the form, fill it out, and then select the All Done button to view the results.

Did you receive an error when you submitted the form? You might have because there's a quirk with HTML that you need to code around. Figure 9.8 shows how I filled out the form, and the error I received when I submitted it.

FIGURE 9.8

When I fill out the form as shown, I receive an error message that Form.FirstVisit doesn't exist.

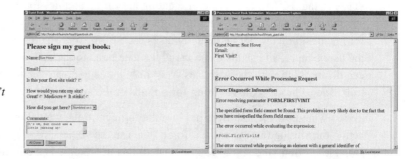

If you notice by my input, I didn't fill out the Email field or designate that this was my first visit by selecting the check box. The problem we're experiencing is that HTML doesn't create check box form variables if the user doesn't check them. This is the same for some of the controls, but not all of them.

The following list shows the form controls for which no associated form variable is created when not selected, checked, or given a value.

- check box
- multiple select control without a defaulted value
- set of radio buttons without one being selected
- buttons that are not clicked

You will need to code around this issue by creating a form variable if it doesn't exist. Do you remember what tag can create a variable if it doesn't exist? As seen in Hour 5, we can use the <CFPARAM> tag. Create a form variable using the FORM prefix and make a default value for it:

```
<CFPARAM Name="FORM.FirstVisit" Default="No">
```

Code this at the top of the action page. This way, no matter what goes wrong, the page won't produce an error if a form variable doesn't exist. This also alleviates the problem if a user attempts to go directly to the action page without going to the form first.

To Do: Create Default Form Variables

Using `<CFPARAM>`, set default values for all form variable values in the action page. Here are the steps to follow:

1. Return to HomeSite and the insert_guest.cfm page.
2. Right after the opening `<BODY>` tag, create a `<CFPARAM>` tag for each one of the form controls you have printed out.
3. Save the file and then return to the browser.
4. Browse the form, fill it out as you want, and then submit it. You shouldn't see an error this time.

9

> A common mistake for those new to forms is that they attempt to browse directly to the action page while testing. Action pages process data submitted by a form, so you should remember to always browse to the form page first and submit it to see your action page results.

After you have successfully created your form and the action page, the action page output should show you the information the user entered into the form, as shown in Figure 9.9.

FIGURE **9.9**

When I fill out the form and submit it, I should see all user input information.

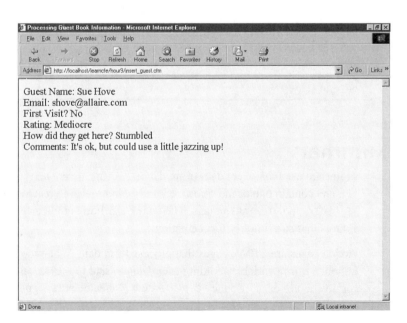

The Completed Action Page

Your completed action page, which includes default settings using the tag and the print-out of each variable, should resemble the following code in Listing 9.2.

LISTING 9.2   Completed Action Page

```
 1:<!DOCTYPE HTML PUBLIC "-//W3C//DTD HTML 4.0 Transitional//EN">
 2:<html>
 3:<head>
 4:    <title>Processing Guest Book Information</title>
 5:</head>
 6:
 7:<body>
 8:<CFPARAM NAME="Form.GuestName" DEFAULT="">
 9:<CFPARAM NAME="Form.Email" DEFAULT="">
10:<CFPARAM NAME="Form.FirstVisit" DEFAULT="No">
11:<CFPARAM NAME="Form.Rating" DEFAULT="">
12:<CFPARAM NAME="Form.GotHere" DEFAULT="">
13:<CFPARAM NAME="Form.Comments" DEFAULT="">
14:
15:<CFOUTPUT>
16:    Guest Name: #Form.GuestName#<BR>
17:    Email:  #Form.Email#<BR>
18:    First Visit? #Form.FirstVisit#<BR>
19:    Rating: #Form.Rating#<BR>
20:    How did they get here? #Form.GotHere#<BR>
21:    Comments: #Form.Comments#<BR>
22:
23:</CFOUTPUT>
24:
25:</body>
26:</html>
```

Summary

Forms are used to collect data from visitors. Forms are created using the HTML <FORM> tag, and contain one or more form controls. Controls are created using the <INPUT>, <SELECT>, and <TEXTAREA> tags. The Quick Bar Forms toolbar provides access to Tag Editors that can simplify form creation.

Action pages are CFML pages that process form data. When the user clicks the Submit button, all form variables holding user data are sent to the action page. To be sure that all form variables exist, use the <CFPARAM> tag to create and assign defaults.

Q&A

Q **The form we created this hour is rather messy. Is there a better way to organize the placement of form controls?**

A The best way to organize form controls is to use HTML tables. You could create a table with a row for each form control. You could put the label and the form control itself in separate table cells to be sure that all form controls are aligned properly as shown in this code example:

```
<FORM ACTION="insert_guest.cfm"
    METHOD="post">
<TABLE>
<TR>
    <TD>Name:</TD>
    <TD><INPUT TYPE="text"
    NAME="GuestName"
    SIZE="20"
    MAXLENGTH="30"></TD>
</TR>
...
</TABLE>
</FORM>
```

Q **Is there a simple way to send form data to an email address without using CFML processing?**

A Yes, you can use a `mailto` attribute for the form `ACTION`. For example, specifying `<FORM ACTION="mailto:username@company.com">` will send the form fields to shove@allaire.com via email. But this technique will work *only* if the visitor has an email client installed on her computer. When you upgrade to the full commercial version of ColdFusion, you'll be able to use a special tag called `<CFMAIL>`, which can send email directly from the server.

Q **In the code samples in this hour, you instructed me to use a `METHOD` of `POST`. What is the significance of `METHOD`, and what are `GET` and `POST`?**

A `GET` and `POST` are different ways in which the browser can submit form data. The `GET` method appends form information to the end of the `ACTION` URL, and the `POST` method send form fields separately. When using backend processing, it is preferable to use the `POST` method because `POST` can support a greater number of fields (and larger values) than `GET`. But `POST` requires a backend script to process the page; `GET` doesn't. Because we were submitting the form to an HTML page (and not a script), we had to use a `METHOD` of `POST`.

Workshop

The Workshop contains quiz questions and exercises to help reinforce what you've learned in this hour. If you get stuck, the answers to the quiz questions can be found in Appendix A, "Answers to Quiz."

Quiz

1. *True or false*: Form controls must be used in between <FORM> and </FORM> tags.
2. What is the difference between check boxes and radio buttons?
3. What field type would you use to ask an applicant their gender?
4. *True or false*: Check boxes don't generate form variables if they are not checked.

Exercise

1. Take a look at forms on search engine or e-commerce sites. What controls do they use? Try to determine why they chose the controls they did.

   From a purely functional perspective, radio buttons and drop-down lists accomplish the same thing. So when would you use one over another? Here's a hint—try creating a form with a large number of options using both control types.

HOUR 10

Validating Form Fields

In the last hour, you learned how to create HTML forms that are used to obtain information from your users.

In this lesson, you'll learn the following:

- What form validation is
- What are the different ways you can validate data
- Methods for using CFML to validate data

Understanding Form Validation

If you've ever filled out a form on the Web, you have probably encountered form validation. Perhaps you didn't fill in a required form field; thus, you generated an error when placing an order and received an error message. Or perhaps you entered an invalid date in a Date Of Birth field. Checking for valid form data is known as *form field validation*.

As annoying as it is to a user, it's necessary if the data is important to your business. You might have heard the computer-world saying: garbage in, garbage out. This means that if you can't get the correct data input, you certainly won't get the correct data output either.

> Users don't like to take the time to fill out lengthy forms, and they are often afraid that you'll spam them (send them unsolicited email) or sell their information to other companies for marketing purposes. You should always explain to the users why you need the information, tell them what you're going to do with it, and reassure them that you will respect their privacy.

In the guest book you created last hour, you prompted the user for several pieces of information as shown in Figure 10.1.

FIGURE **10.1**

This guest book form prompts the user for information, but doesn't perform validation.

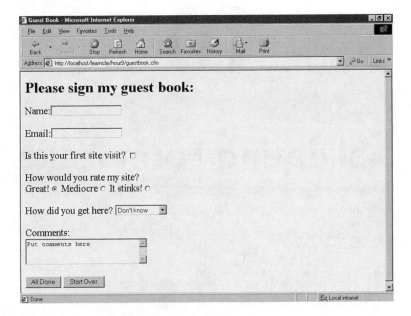

In HTML text fields, you can't control the input that users enter; actually, you can't even require them to enter it. If you want to require that information be entered, you have to use form validation. Several reasons exist for using form field validation, and they usually involve being able to require input or a particular type of input. When a user doesn't enter the correct information your application needs, a message stating that something is wrong should be returned to the user, and it should give the user details about how to fix the problem.

Form Validation Types

Three ways to perform form field validation are as follows:

- Server-side validation using CFML
- Custom server-side validation using CFML
- Client-side scripting validation (using JavaScript, for example)

The designation of server-side and client-side tells you where the validation takes place. Server-side validation is performed by CFML using ColdFusion Express on the server. Client-side validation is performed by the browser using a scripting language such as JavaScript. In this hour, we will explore how to implement form validation in both ways for standard and custom validation.

You might want to validate form data for

- Ensuring that users enter data where it is required
- Ensuring that users input valid data, such as a valid calendar date
- Ensuring that the input matches the type of data you are storing, such as inputting exactly nine digits for a social security number input

You must determine, based on what you are trying to capture, which validation rules must be implemented to get the correct data to be input by the users.

CFML Server-Side Validation

ColdFusion Express will handle form validation for you if you add a hidden HTML form control. Hidden form controls are exactly that—they are hidden from the user's view. However, HTML still creates a form variable that corresponds to the hidden field and passes the value to the action page. A hidden field specifies the form field name and the value to be passed:

```
<INPUT TYPE="hidden" NAME="HiddenField" VALUE="HiddenValue">
```

Hidden fields have several uses, but for now we're just going to explore them in relation to server-side validation.

Begin by determining the type of validation you need to perform on the form fields. ColdFusion Express offers several types of CFML validation, as shown in Table 10.1.

TABLE 10.1   CFML Form Validation

Validation Type	Description
Required	Requiresf a value in the form field.
Integer	Requires the input value to be an integer. Will round any input floating point numbers.
Float	Requires the input value to be a floating point number.
Range	Requires a numeric value between specified boundaries.
Date	Requires a date value. Will accept most common date forms: for example, 9/1/98 or September 9, 1998.
Time	Requires a time value. Will accept time values down to a second: for example 12:01:04 p.m.
European Date	Requires a date in the European Format (Day, Month, Year) .

For each form field you want to validate, you will create a matching hidden form field with the appropriate validation type.

Remember that you must always define the action page and be sure that it is created. If you try to test validation and the action page doesn't exist, you will receive the HTML 404 error that the page was not found. This happens prior to any validation checks.

Required Validation

To require a user to input information into a form control, use a hidden field and designate the form field as required. Each required form field will have a hidden field with the same name using the `_required` suffix (don't forget the underscore separating the field name from the `required` rule) .

```
Name: <INPUT TYPE="text"
      NAME="GuestName">
<INPUT TYPE="hidden"
      NAME="GuestName_required"
      VALUE="Please input your name.">
```

This tells ColdFusion Express that the form field is required and automatically generates an error message and sends it to the user. You do not need to programmatically test the value on the action page because ColdFusion Express will do it for you using the hidden control. The `VALUE` attribute specifies the error message displayed to the user. Figure 10.2

shows the error message that's generated if the user tries to submit the form without specifying a value for the field.

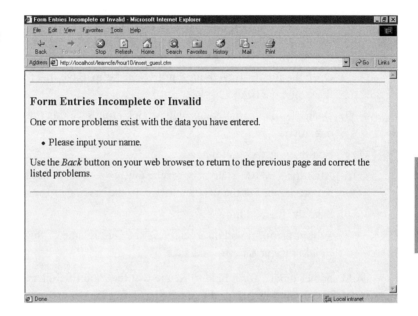

10

Because ColdFusion Express generates this error message, you don't have control over the layout or format of this page. The only thing you can control is the bulleted error message that is displayed.

The user will be required to select the browser's Back button to return to the form, correct any mistakes, and resubmit the form.

Remember that because you're using a hidden form control, all CFML server-side validations must be defined inside the <FORM> and </FORM> tags. They don't need to be in any particular order (the validation can be specified before or after the associated field), but most developers prefer to group all validation code at the beginning of the form.

To Do: Require the Guest's Name and Email Address

▲ To Do

Apply CFML validation to the name and email form fields using server-side validation. Follow these steps to apply validation:

1. Return to HomeSite and make sure that the Local Files tab is pointing to the /learncfe/hour10 directory.

2. Open the file /learncfe/hour9/insert_guest.cfm. Save this file in the /learncfe/hour10 directory.

3. Open the file /learncfe/hour9/guestbook.cfm. Save this file in the /learncfe/hour10 directory.

4. Edit the guestbook.cfm page.

5. After the <INPUT> statement for the GuestName form field, add a hidden field to require input. Set the VALUE attribute to the message Please input your name.

6. Save the file and browse.

7. Submit the form without specifying the GuestName or the Email address. You should receive an error message.

Add another hidden form field to ensure that the Email field has a value upon submission. Try submitting the form without specifying the GuestName and Email values. You should receive the error page as shown in Figure 10.3.

FIGURE 10.3

If the user doesn't fill in the name and email fields, she receives errors for both at the same time.

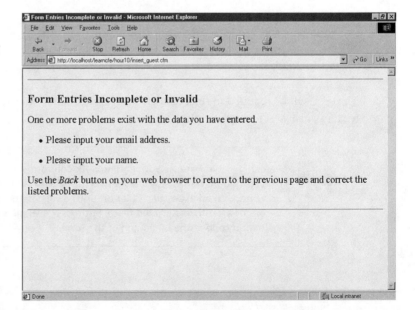

▼

> ColdFusion Express will go through all form fields looking for validation rules. This way, it can display all errors in the form to the user at once, instead of requiring the user to keep changing and resubmitting the form.

Numeric Validation

Thus far, we haven't done anything with the form data that requires specific types of information. But whenever you start prompting for numeric values, you'll want to be sure that the user doesn't enter other characters and mess up your program. This is especially true when you start trying to store the form values into a database table.

> Checking for a data type doesn't make it a required field. It only requires that *if* the user inputs a value, it must be of the correct type. If the user doesn't input a value, no error message is generated. You can, of course, add another validation for requiring input by adding another hidden form field.

Two ways to validate numeric values exist—using validation for integer values or floating-point numbers. Integer values are whole numbers that can be signed as a positive or negative number, as in 9 or –1. Floating-point numbers are numbers with digits to the right of the decimal point, such as 1.2 and 3.038.

If you require a user to input a numeric value, such as her age, you can implement CFML server-side validation using a hidden form field. This form field name must match the form control you want to validate, with an _integer prefix (again, don't forget the underscore):

```
Name: <INPUT TYPE="text"
        NAME="Age">
<INPUT TYPE="hidden"
        NAME="Age_integer"
        VALUE="Please input a valid age.">
```

To Do: Make Sure that the Guest's Age Is Numeric

Create a text field to prompt for the guest's age, and apply CFML validation to make sure that it's numeric. Follow these steps to apply validation:

1. Return to HomeSite and the guestbook.cfm page.
2. After the Email field, create a text field to prompt for the user's age. Name the field Age, and set the SIZE to 4 and the MAXLENGTH to 4. Make a field label of Age:. Your form will look as shown in Figure 10.4.

FIGURE 10.4

The completed guest book now prompts for the user's age.

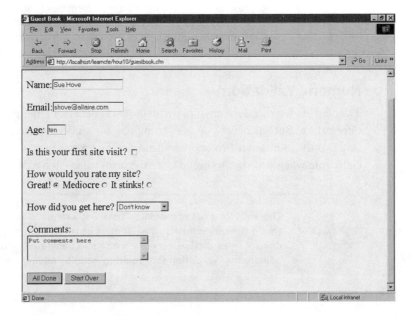

3. Use a `<BR>` tag to put the Age control on its own line.

4. Add a hidden form field to make sure that the value input in the Age column is numeric. Set the VALUE attribute to `Please input a valid age`.

5. Browse to the page and try to input a non-numeric value into Age to see the displayed error text. The error message generated is shown in Figure 10.5.

Float validation is similar to integer validation, but it is used for form fields that use decimal numbers. An example would be if a form prompted the user for a dollar value.

Date Validation

Dates are always tricky to work with because so many different formats are used. Some ways to specify the same date are

- September 8, 2000
- 9/8/2000
- 9/8/2000
- 08-Sept-2000

All these values represent the same date, but it would be tough to figure that out if users mistyped or misspelled what they input. For this reason, you need to use some type of validation to get meaningful date values from users.

FIGURE **10.5**

If you attempt to input a non-numeric value, ColdFusion Express returns an error page to you.

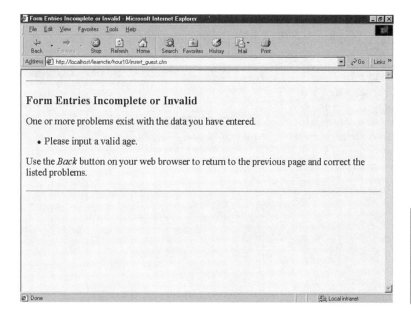

10

Take an example of a form, shown in Figure 10.6, which prompts for a person's name and date of birth.

FIGURE **10.6**

This form prompts for the user's name and date of birth. The date of birth must be validated to ensure that it's a valid date.

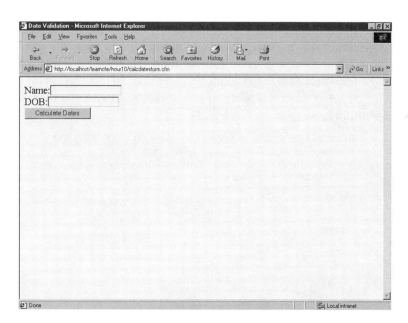

The form uses the date of birth to return the day of the week she was born on (Sunday thru Saturday) and the number of days she has been alive, as shown in Figure 10.7.

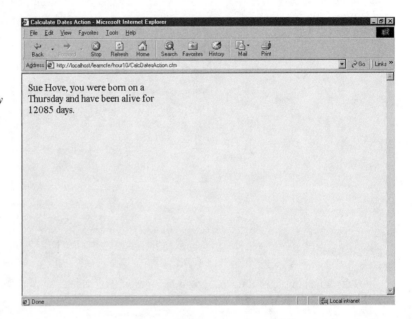

Because this action requires that a valid date be entered, validation must be added to the form to test to be sure that the format is correct. To do this, you can use CFML server-side validation for dates. Take the form field for the date and create a matching hidden form field with a _date suffix. ColdFusion Express handles the rest for you and displays the error message Please Input A Valid Date Of Birth if the date was incorrectly formatted:

```
<FORM ACTION="calc_dates_action.cfm" METHOD="post">
    Name:<INPUT TYPE="Text" NAME="Name"><BR>
    DOB:<INPUT TYPE="Text" NAME="DOB"><BR>
    <INPUT TYPE="Hidden"
            NAME="DOB_date"
            VALUE="Please input a valid date of birth">
    <INPUT TYPE="submit" VALUE="Calculate Dates">
</FORM>
```

I have shown you how to use the <CFPARAM> tag to assign default values to FORM variables if they aren't given a value. But in this case, the program doesn't make any sense if a date of birth isn't input. So you should include both a required validation and a date validation on this form field. You can do this by creating two hidden fields: each one with the appropriate validation suffix and error message.

To Do: Create the Date Calculation Form

Create The form seen in Figure 10.6 and apply date validation to the date of birth form field. Follow these steps to apply validation:

1. Create a new page using the default template.
2. Rename the <TITLE> to **Date Calculation Form**.
3. Save the page under the /learncfe/hour10 directory as calc_date_form.cfm.
4. Inside the <BODY> and </BODY> tags, create a <FORM> tag with an ACTION of calc_date_action.cfm and a METHOD of post.
5. Inside the <FORM> and </FORM> tags, put a label of Name: and create a text field control called Name.
6. Create another text field control called DOB with a label of DOB.
7. Don't forget to space out the controls using <BR> tags.
8. Anywhere inside the <FORM> and </FORM> tags, create a hidden field with a NAME of DOB_date and a VALUE of Please input a valid date of birth (example: mm-dd-yyyy).
9. Create another hidden form field named DOB_required with a VALUE of The DOB field is required.
10. Save the file.
11. Create a new page using the default template.
12. Rename the <TITLE> to **Date Calculation Action**.
13. Save the page under the /learncfe/hour10 directory as **calc_date_action.cfm**.

Leave the action page empty for now because you want to test the validation piece. Browse to the form and submit it with a bad date, such as Sep-8-0000. You should see an error message as shown in Figure 10.8.

FIGURE 10.8

If you submit an invalid date, ColdFusion Express generates an error message for you.

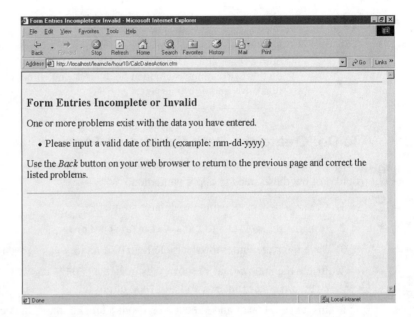

> It is helpful to put the required format for input either on the form itself or in the validation error message. This keeps the user from guessing the format you are looking for.

Now you can do the fun part—use date functions to calculate the day of birth and the number of days alive. This would not be fun if you had to do these calculations yourselves. Instead, you can rely on ColdFusion Express to give you all the functionality you need in simple functions.

I will begin by taking the user input value, stored in `FORM.DOB`, and use the `DayofWeek()` function to find the numeric representation for the day of the week:

```
<CFSET DayofBirth=DayofWeek(FORM.DOB)>
```

This will return a number from 1 through 7 to represent the day of the week from Sunday through Saturday. The number isn't very interesting, so we will use the `DayofWeekAsString()` function:

```
<CFSET DayofBirth=DayofWeekAsString(DayofWeek(FORM.DOB))>
```

To figure out the number of days the user has been alive, you can use the `DateDiff()` function and the `Now()` function:

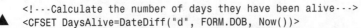

```
<!---Calculate the number of days they have been alive--->
<CFSET DaysAlive=DateDiff("d", FORM.DOB, Now())>
```

For a full syntax for any of these functions, refer to Hour 7, "Using Functions," and the ColdFusion Express Language Reference Guide.

To Do: Create the Date Calculation Action Page

To Do ▼

Follow these steps to calculate the day of birth and the number of days the user has been alive:

1. Return to HomeSite and the calc_date_action.cfm page.

2. Use the `DayofWeek()` and `DayofWeekAsString()` functions to take the user input and calculate the day the user was born.

3. Use the `Now()` and `DateDiff()` functions to calculate the number of days the user has been alive.

4. Print out the information to the user as in: `{username}, you were born on a {day of week born} and have been alive for {number of days alive}` days. Use the form fields and the function results to display the username, day of week born, and the number of days alive.

5. Save the file and browse to the calc_date_form.cfm page. Submit a valid date in the format of `mm-dd-yyyy` to see the result, as shown in Figure 10.7.

The European date validation works similarly to regular date validation, except it requires that date values be input in the European format. This format requires the day to come before the month, as in `dd-mm-yyyy`. The validation suffix for the hidden form field should be set to `_eurodate`.

Time Validation

Time validation can be used for applications in which users input a time value, such as a scheduling or time tracking system. To enforce time validation, create a hidden form field with a suffix of `_time` in the name:

```
<FORM ACTION="schedule_action.cfm" METHOD="post">
    Name:<INPUT TYPE="Text" NAME="Name"><BR>
    Time:<INPUT TYPE="Text" NAME="ScheduledTime"><BR>
        <INPUT TYPE="hidden" NAME="ScheduledTime_time"
            VALUE="Please input a valid time value (example: 10:24pm)">
        <INPUT TYPE="submit" VALUE="Schedule">
</FORM>
```

Time values can also include a date portion, as in 09/08/1999 10:24pm. Combining dates and times is a valid operation. However, users might have a problem with formatting it correctly, so it's best to prompt for each part, date and time, individually on a form.

When you print out time values in an action page using CFML validation, they will show up in military time. Military time is based on the 24 hour clock, which begins counting at 0:01 just after midnight and continues to 24:00 at midnight. Instead of 1 p.m., it is 13:00 in military time. For example, if the user were to input 10:24pm into a form, printing out the value as in the following code will look like the output in Figure 10.9:

```
<CFOUTPUT>
Name:   #FORM.name#<BR>
Input time: #FORM.ScheduledTime#
</CFOUTPUT>
```

FIGURE 10.9

If you submit a time of 10:24pm, the output is in military time of {t '22:24:00'}.

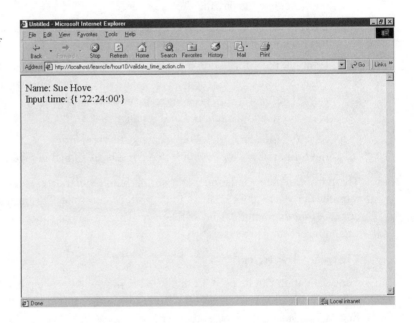

The funky output with the curly braces {} and the t is actually the ODBC syntax to represent date and time values. You will learn more about the ODBC syntax in Hour 12, "Collecting Data." At this point, it is enough to say that this syntax is accepted by all ColdFusion Express' date and time functions and makes dates easier to work with because they all represent the same format. Functions that can be used with time values include Hour(), Minute(), and Second(), which parse out just those portions of time values should you care to use them.

You can also specify a time value in fractions of seconds. For instance, you can specify a time of 10:24:33pm, which represents 10:24 p.m. and 33 seconds of time.

Range Validation

Range validation takes a numeric input value and makes sure that it is between two values in a range, inclusive of those two values. For instance, a time tracking system might require a manager's authorization for accepting working hours over 40 per week. CFML validation can be used to require the user's input at 40 hours per week:

```
<FORM ACTION="validate_range_action.cfm" METHOD="post">
Name:<INPUT TYPE="Text" NAME="Name"><BR>
Hours worked:<INPUT TYPE="Text" NAME="WorkingHours"><BR>
    <INPUT TYPE="hidden" NAME="WorkingHours_range" VALUE="MIN=1 MAX=40">
    <INPUT TYPE="submit" VALUE="Enter Time">
</FORM>
```

Using this type of validation is a little different from the others. With range validation, you must specify the lower and upper limit of acceptable values. To do so, you specify a MIN and MAX in the VALUE attribute, as shown in the preceding code example. These values are separated by a space. You don't specify the error message that is displayed, but instead get an error message similar to the one shown in Figure 10.10.

10

FIGURE 10.10

If you submit a value outside the range of the MIN and MAX, you will receive an error message similar to the one shown.

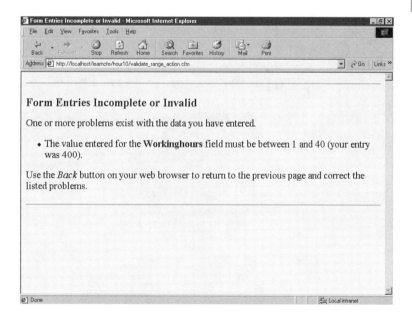

CFML Custom Validation

CFML server-side validation is easy and efficient for providing error handling for required and data types and ranges. However, if you wanted to control the look and feel of error pages or perform special types of validation, you might want to use your own custom validation written in CFML.

If you want to perform other validations, such as validation for the length and format of a social security form field, you have to write your own validation. Using CFML, this is fairly easy.

To validate a social security form field, you can take the value the user input and test to be sure that it has the correct number of characters, which is 11: xxx-xx-xxxx.

To do so, you can use the Len() function in a conditional statement, which returns the number of characters in a string:

```
<CFIF Len(FORM.SSN) IS NOT "11">
    <p>
    Input error: SSN does not have the correct format (xx-xxx-xxxx)
    </p>
    <p>
    Please hit the BACK button in your browser, correct the mistake, and
    resubmit the form
    </p>
    <CFABORT>
</CFIF>
```

If the length of the input value doesn't match exactly 11 characters, you want to generate an error to the user and allow him to fix his input. In order to stop processing after the error message is displayed, use the <CFABORT> tag. This displays the error message, but halts all other page processing and passes the error back to the user. Do not pass go, do not collect $200—straight back to the browser as shown in Figure 10.11.

FIGURE 10.11

Using custom CFML validation, users can receive error pages that are formatted as you want them to be.

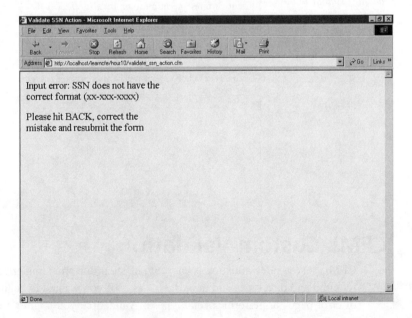

You could even forgo implementing CFML server-side validation using hidden form fields and apply your own custom validation to control the output. For instance, if you want to validate that the Age form field receives only numeric values, you can write your own validation using conditional logic and the `IsNumeric()` function:

```
<CFIF NOT IsNumeric(FORM.Age)>
    Input error: Age needs to be a valid number
<p>
    Please hit BACK, correct the mistake and resubmit the form
    <CFABORT>
</CFIF>
```

 For more information on functions, see Hour 7, "Using Functions."

Client-Side Validation

All validation discussed up to this point has been performed on the server. This is a powerful way to protect your application and database data, but isn't too pleasant for the user. The need to submit the form, wait to receive errors, and then select Back to fix things is rather clunky from a user's point of view.

A way to validate data even before it gets back to the server is through the use of a client-side scripting language, such as JavaScript. Scripting languages can be included in pages to manipulate page contents in response to user events, and they can perform form field validation.

JavaScript is easy to download because it is only code text that is interpreted by the browser. It performs well in most newer browsers (Netscape 2.0+ and Internet Explorer 3.0+) and doesn't introduce security risks.

 The biggest problem with JavaScript is that it is implemented differently in various browsers and, in some cases, different releases of the same browser. Microsoft's implementation is known as JScript, which was spun off from Netscape's original JavaScript language. Scripts need to be tested on all target browsers to ensure proper functioning.

To require the input of a form field, use the `<SCRIPT>` tag, which is usually found in the `<HEAD>` tag. Inside the `<SCRIPT>`, you'll find JavaScript functions. The functions listed in the following example are used for form field validation. In this case, they require that the `GuestName` field is filled in, or an error appears as illustrated in Listing 10.1.

10

LISTING 10.1   JavaScript Validation

```
 1:<HTML>
 2:<HEAD>
 3:<TITLE>JavaScript Validation Example</TITLE>
 4:    <SCRIPT LANGUAGE="JavaScript">
 5:    <!--
 6:    // to require a text field
 7:    function checktext() {
 8:        if (document.GuestForm.GuestName.value == "") {
 9:        alert("The Guest Name is required!");
10:        return false;
11:        }
12:        else {
13:        return true;
14:        }
15:    }
16:    // overall validation function
17:    function formValidate() {
18:        if (checktext()) {
19:        return true;
20:        }
21:        else {
22:        return false;
23:        }
24:    }
25:    //-->
26:    </SCRIPT>
27:
28:</HEAD>
29:    <BODY>
30:    <FORM ACTION="insert_guest.cfm"
31:        NAME="GuestForm"
32:        onSubmit="return formValidate();">
33:
34:        Guest Name: <INPUT TYPE="Text" NAME="GuestName">
35:        <BR><BR>
36:        <INPUT TYPE="Submit" VALUE="Add Guest">
37:    </FORM>
38:</BODY>
39:</HTML>
```

In this example, the <FORM> tag has an added attribute, onSubmit. This takes the name of a JavaScript function that will be executed on the browser before the form is submitted. That function must return either TRUE or FALSE. If TRUE is returned, the form will be submitted; if FALSE is returned, the form won't be submitted. This allows you to write validation code in your JavaScript function and then control form submission programmatically.

In this example, if the user tries to submit the form without specifying a value for the name, he will receive the JavaScript alert as shown in Figure 10.12.

FIGURE 10.12
The JavaScript alert pops up when the user submits invalid data. This alert is generated by the client (browser) without going back to the server.

10

A good way to learn what JavaScript can do is to go out on the Web and find examples of JavaScript in pages. Because JavaScript is interpreted by the browser, it gets sent along with the HTML text to be rendered. You can view the source of the page in the browser to learn how the page author implemented the JavaScript functionality.

JavaScript is a popular way to enhance the user experience, but it's not for the faint at heart. If you're interested in JavaScript, look at another book in this series, *Sams Teach Yourself JavaScript 1.3 in 24 Hours* (ISBN: 0-672-31407-X).

Comparing Validation Types

Now that you've seen three ways to validate form data—CFML server-side validation, CFML custom validation, and client-side validation—we can discuss the optimal solution for handling form input. There are pros and cons to each solution, so the reality is most Web developers end up using a combination of all three methods. The reasons for this include

- Server-side processing is clunky and users get annoyed by going back and forth to fix errors.

- Client-side processing is better for both the user and the server. Users get to see errors right away instead of waiting for a round trip to the Web server, and the Web server is saved some processing load.

- If a browser doesn't support JavaScript, having server-side validation can be a second level of defense against getting bad data into your application and database tables.

- Server-side validation is easier to learn and to implement for most HTML developers.
- Server-side validation will work with any browser; client-side validation is very client specific.
- You might need to perform custom validation for things that need extra information to validate, such as information out of a database.

The bottom line is that you need to protect your application from bad data. Two things to consider as you plan your application pages are

- Target audience—Who is your target audience? Can you reliably say they will support JavaScript in their browser? If so, you will need to test your pages in all browsers you expect to support.
- Development Staff—Who is on your development staff? Will they be able to program in a more complex language such as JavaScript?

The combination of validation methods can fully secure your applications and make for a better user experience. If you do opt for client-side validation, for added security, seriously consider using server-side validation as well. This way, if the client-validation fails (because of JavaScript problems or browser compatibility issues), the server-side validation will catch the errors upon submission. And if the client-side validation does indeed work, the server-side validation won't do anything at all.

Summary

To ensure that your applications are collecting the correct data, use form field validation in your ColdFusion Express applications. These applications can employ the use of server- or client-side validation, or a combination of both. Data validation becomes more important when you start to insert information into database tables, which I will cover in the next hour.

Q&A

Q Using CFML server-side or custom validation both require a separate page to be displayed, and the user needs to select Back, fix the data, and return. Is there a way they can receive the form page with the errors to fix listed on it?

A Yes, you can use custom validation (that you write) for all errors. You can put the error message into a variable and pass it in the URL back to the form (see Hour 8, "Working with Links," for a refresher). After the form validation takes place in the action page, use the <CFINCLUDE> tag (as you've learned in Hour 4, "Creating Your First ColdFusion page") to include the form and print out the error message at the top. So the pseudocode for the action page would be

- Perform all custom error checking

- Put any errors encountered into a variable

- If, after all validations, errors have occurred, print out the cumulative messages

- After the message, perform a <CFINCLUDE> on the form

- After the <CFINCLUDE>, perform a <CFABORT> to stop any more action page processing

Q Are ColdFusion's built-in date validation options Y2K compliant?

A Yes, you'll be relieved to know that ColdFusion is fully Y2K compliant. If you need documentation to this effect visit the Allaire Web site at http://www.allaire.com.

Q Is there any easier way to use JavaScript in my pages?

A Full ColdFusion Professional and Enterprise versions include a <CFINPUT> tag, which extends the <INPUT> tag and automatically generates JavaScript for you. Unfortunately, these are not included in ColdFusion Express, so you will have to create the JavaScript manually for yourself.

10

Workshop

The Workshop contains quiz questions and exercises to help reinforce what you've learned in this hour. If you get stuck, the answers to the quiz questions can be found in Appendix A, "Answers to Quiz."

Quiz

1. *True or false*: To validate a social security number, you can use a hidden form field.

2. What is the difference between the _date and _eurodate validation types?

3. *True or false*: Using _float will require the input number to have decimal places in the number.

4. What is the difference between client-side and server-side validation?

Exercise

1. Surf the Web to find a site that uses an HTML form. (You can find one anywhere you try to perform online ordering.) Try to submit the form without specifying any data and see if you receive an error. If so, can you try to figure out how they programmed it? Was it JavaScript (which puts up a dialog alert) or server-side validation?

HOUR 11

Connecting to a Database

In the last 10 hours, you have been creating Web applications without need of a database. However, databases are the backbone of Web applications, and ColdFusion Express is no exception. Here we will introduce the concepts behind connecting to a database.

In this lesson, you'll learn the following:

- What databases are
- Why you would want to use a database on the Web
- How to communicate with databases using SQL
- Which databases ColdFusion Express can connect to
- How ColdFusion Express connects to databases

Databases

A database is an organized collection of data, kind of like a filing cabinet, that stores information in an orderly fashion. However, in the case of databases, the information is stored electronically and not in paper form. Databases exist solely to manage data.

If you've ever been to a doctor's or a dentist's office, you've seen the complicated way they label and organize their patient files. The need for paper trails in this case is crucial, and there are some things that cannot be stored electronically, such as x-rays.

If they didn't store information electronically as well, they would take a lot of time sorting through all the charts to find what they need. Say that they wanted to see which patients are in need of their checkups, or check on accounts in arrears. To go through all the files for this information as well as countless other requests for data would be a time consuming operation. Or they'd have to maintain a bunch of separate lists for each type of reporting they wanted to perform.

Databases have evolved out of the need to store information in an orderly fashion, and to get the information out in any way possible immediately, if not sooner.

The way information is stored electronically has evolved over the past 20 years. A result of the efforts of countless minds and hours is the ordering of data into a relational database.

Database Types

There are several different types of databases available; however, by far, the relational database outnumbers any other kind of database. In this book when we refer to a database, we mean a relational database.

Enter the Relational Database

Even before electronic storage of data was available, humans were able to logically group information and sort it into the most meaningful form for practical use. The evolution of that thought process was fully realized by the relational database, which is optimized for electronic storage.

You might have heard of an RDBMS, or DBMS. *RDBMS* stands for the relational database management system. The *relational database* is really only a concept, and RDBMS is the software that allows you to create and manage physical databases.

The theory is that data can be organized into groupings of related information. These groupings become database *tables*, which all reside inside a database. The key to understanding how to group information is to decide what the information refers to.

For instance, when storing information about dental records, you can define all the information about a patient into one table. This table could contain

- Patient name
- Patient address
- Patient phone number
- Patient insurance carrier

Notice that all pieces of data describe one type of object, here a patient. You can group this information into a table and store many records, as depicted in Figure 11.1.

FIGURE 11.1

A table contains a set of related information about one type of object. This table stores all information pertaining to a patient, and stores as many patient records as necessary.

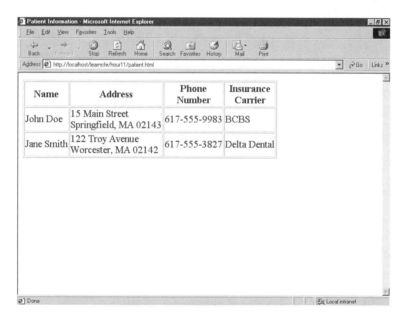

Related data is the detail about each patient's visit to the doctor's office. Information about each visit might include

- Date of visit
- Reason for visit
- Visit outcome

Again, all information about a visit can be stored in a Visit table, with a record for each patient visit to the dentist over time, as depicted in Figure 11.2.

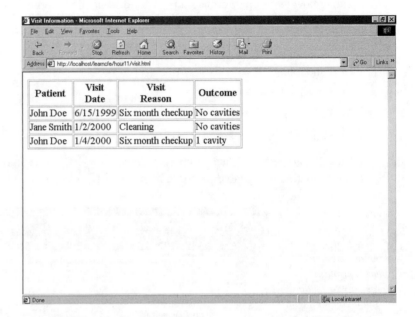

In order to understand databases, you'll need to understand the basic building blocks: tables, columns, and rows.

Tables

As you've just learned, tables are groupings of information about one particular object. This object can be a person, place, thing, event, or idea.

In the previous example, you've seen two tables; one for patient information and one for information about each patient visit. A table can be represented by a box as depicted in Figures 11.3 and 11.4.

Figure 11.4

A visit, which can be described by a date, a reason, and an outcome, can be stored in the Visit table.

Visit
Name
VisitDate
Reason
Outcome

Columns

Each descriptive piece of information about a patient—such as the name, address, phone number, and insurance carrier—is stored in a separate column in the table. But there's more to a column than just descriptive information. A column, by design, must only contain one piece of information. In the Patient table, the address can contain many bits of information, such as the following:

- Address line 1
- Address line 2
- City
- State
- ZIP code

Therefore, having all the previous information in a single column is not considered good design for a database column. You will need to separate out each bit of information into a separate column, as depicted in Figure 11.5.

Figure 11.5

Each piece of information should be separated into different columns in the table.

Patient
Name
Address1
Address2
City
State
ZipCode
Phone
Insurance_Carrier

11

Breaking Up Data

The reason you should separate information into individual pieces is for retrieval of that information later. For instance, you might want to retrieve all patients in one city, or in a particular state. If this information was all stored in one column, retrieving the individual pieces would be very difficult, if not impossible.

Each column has an associated datatype. A *datatype* defines what type of data the column can contain. For example, you would want to make sure that the visit date was actually a valid date and not just any value. You can restrict the type of data by specifying the correct datatype.

There are different data types for different DBMSs, but the primary ones are textual values, numbers, dates, currency, and automatically-generated numbers. Check the documentation for your DBMS to find out what datatypes are supported.

Rows

Each column in the table holds a piece of information that describes the entity. For instance, all columns in the Patient table describe the patient; one column could contain the patient's name, another the date of birth, and so on. Collecting all information about a particular patient and putting it into the columns creates table *rows*, as you saw in Figure 11.1. Notice that each row contains information for a particular record; in this case, a patient.

A row in this case represents all information about a particular patient. There can be many patients, and there is a row for each patient the doctor sees.

Relationships

When we describe a visit to the dentist, it is always a patient's visit. You cannot describe a visit to the dentist without the person doing the visiting. That implies that there is a relationship between a patient and her visits to the office.

Relational databases are called relational for a reason. It infers that each table in the database refers to at least one other table. In our example, the relationship between a patient and his visit to the office can be described as

- A patient can go to the doctor's office many times
- When recording information about a visit, including the reason and outcome for the visit, that information refers to one patient

Now we need to create a relationship between these two tables. Both tables have the patient name in them, but that isn't going to work if there is more than one patient with the same name. Consider the sample data in both tables, as shown in Figure 11.6.

This is where we need to somehow link together these two tables. In order to understand relationships, you need to understand primary and foreign keys.

FIGURE **11.6**

We need to relate the patient information with the visit information. The name won't work because it isn't unique.

Name	Address	Phone Number	Insurance Carrier
John Doe	15 Main Street Springfield, MA 02143	617-555-9983	BCBS

Patient	Visit Date	Visit Return	Outcome
John Doe	6/15/1999	Six month checkup	No cavities
Jane Smith	1/2/2000	Cleaning	No cavities
John Doe	1/4/2000	Six month checkup	1 cavity

Uniquely Identifying Rows of Data

What purpose do you think our social security numbers serve? The IRS can bill us, and we can receive those checks when we retire. But it is used for many things. In some states, the social security number (from this point forward, it is referred to as SSN) is used as the driver's license number. Your employer uses your SSN to track your information, such as salary and benefits. Why is this number used so often?

The answer is that it is a means to uniquely identify people. You cannot uniquely identify people by their first and last names, their address, or any other combination of information. If the IRS couldn't uniquely identify you, they wouldn't be able keep track of all U.S. citizens' tax records. (Hmmm…Would this be a bad thing?)

Taking our example, there is a need to uniquely identify a patient, so his records are kept together and he is billed accordingly. At this point, we have no way of uniquely identifying a patient for this purpose. This is where the concept of primary key enters the picture.

A *primary key* is nothing more than a unique identifier for a table row. It can be one column that's unique within the table (for each row), or it can be a combination of columns that make it unique.

> ## Always Define Primary Keys
>
> Not every table has another table related to it. However, you should get into the habit of creating a primary key for each table. It is better for design, and also for possibly adding related tables in the future. Furthermore, without guaranteed unique keys, there is no way to safely update or delete individual rows without affecting others.

11

Because the patient doesn't naturally have a unique identifier, we can let the database assign one for us.

> **Autonumbers**
>
> Every database has the capability to create a number that automatically gets incremented for each row that is input into the table. Using Microsoft Access, this is known as an *autonumber* data type. SQL Server uses the term *identity field*. Other databases have other terms for this type of field.

Using this unique number, we'll now have a primary key for each of our tables, as seen in Figure 11.7.

FIGURE 11.7
The Patient_ID column will uniquely identify a Patient, and Visit_ID will uniquely identify a Visit.

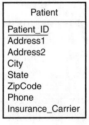

There are rules that should always be followed for each table with regards to primary keys:

- Each row must have a unique primary key value, and it cannot be unspecified.
- The column or columns containing the primary key values should never be updated.
- Primary key values can never be reused. (If a row is deleted, that primary key value can never be reused.)

The Missing Link

The next step in creating a relationship between two tables is to determine the type of relationship that exists. As we've discussed, the relationship can be described as

- A patient can go to the doctor's office many times
- When recording information about a visit, including the reason and outcome for the visit, that information refers to one patient

A patient can have many visits, but a visit must refer to one patient. This is known as a *one-to-many* relationship. For these types of relationships, the primary key column of the one table is put into the many table as a link between the two. When a primary key is put into another table to create a relationship, this is known as a foreign key. A *foreign key* is a copy of the primary key value that creates the link.

For this example, the primary key of Patient is put into the Visit table as a foreign key. Figure 11.8 shows this relationship.

Figure 11.8

*The primary key of Patient (*Patient_ID*) is copied into the Visit table (here, as* Patient_ID*) as a foreign key to create the relationship.*

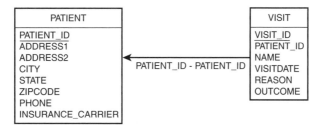

Name Your Foreign Keys the Same as the Primary Key When Possible

You are really creating a copy of the primary key value and putting it into the foreign table to create the link. The name of the columns for the primary and foreign keys do not need to match, but it does make it easier to see the relationship if it does.

11

Learning More

This book covers how to access and use databases, and not how to create them. But we are trying to give you an idea of why they exist, and how they might have been created. Good database design techniques are key to any successful application that's driven by database data.

Databases and the Web

There are many reasons to store information in a database for use in your Web applications. Such uses can be to

- Leverage an existing database of product information for your customers
- Store all employee information for an HR intranet site
- Store a list of menu options to dynamically generate a toolbar

- Store a list of valid login and password information to authenticate users when they log in
- Store information specific to each user who comes to your site for personalization

In any case, you are trying to leverage existing data for use on the Web to make your life easier, and your Web applications more robust.

Take an example of a Web site in which you display a list of products that you offer for sale. Without a database, you would need to code separate HTML pages for each product in your catalog. Then each time a product was added or changed, you'd find yourself manually coding each HTML page. This is a cumbersome process and only gets worse over time as you struggle to maintain many different pages.

The premise here is that each product has the same set of attributes about them, such as

- Product name
- Description
- Price
- Image of product

It is possible to get a superset of attributes about all your products. By taking this set of attributes, it's possible to create a standard layout for all product pages. Consider a layout as shown in Figure 11.9.

FIGURE 11.9

You can design a product page that can display any product in your catalog.

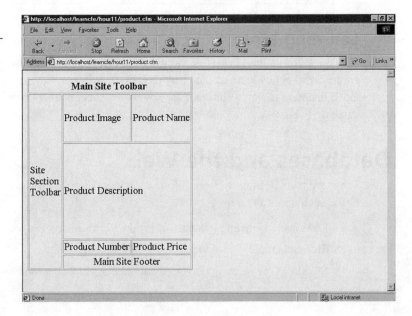

This makes a perfect case for storing product information in a database. You can use a template of an HTML page to pull out each product and dynamically create the HTML page as the user requests it. That's one template for all products versus an HTML page for each product. That's where the true strength of databases and ColdFusion Express emerges.

What Is SQL?

SQL, which stands for Structured Query Language, is a language designed specifically for communicating with databases. Standard SQL is governed by the ANSI standards committee, and thus called ANSI SQL.

SQL Extensions

All major DBMSs support SQL, but might have extensions to the language specifically for their database. The SQL syntax discussed in this book is considered ANSI standard SQL.

The SQL language is made up of three types of statements:

- Data definition—Allows you to create objects in a database, such as database tables.
- Data manipulation—Allows you to retrieve, insert, modify, and remove information from a table or set of tables.
- Data control—Allows you to set permissions for the database or for individual tables and columns.

In this book, we will only concentrate on data manipulation statements. Using these statements, you can maintain the data in your database using ColdFusion Express applications.

SQL Reference

For more information on using SQL, refer to *Sams Teach Yourself SQL in 10 Minutes* (ISBN 0-672-31664-1).

The four main data manipulation statements in SQL are as follows:

- INSERT—Used for inserting a row into a table
- SELECT—Used for retrieving a row or rows from a table or set of tables

11

- UPDATE—Used for updating a row or rows into a table
- DELETE—Used for deleting a row or rows from a table

You will learn about each of these types of statements in upcoming hours.

How ColdFusion Express Connects

ColdFusion Express connects to databases using Open Database Connectivity (ODBC) drivers. *ODBC* is a standard way to connect to virtually any database in a uniform way.

Open Database Connectivity

ODBC works like a translator to turn a standard database language, SQL, into the native language needed to talk to any of a vast array of databases. Figure 11.10 depicts how ColdFusion Express communicates with any of the databases using ODBC.

FIGURE **11.10**

ODBC works as a translator to take SQL and translate it into the native language of the target database.

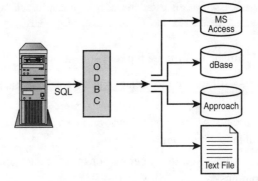

> ### ODBC As a Translator
>
> As an analogy to ODBC drivers, consider that you work in international sales, and have several other countries in your territory. You have a need to get out the same message to all countries, but aren't able to speak their native languages. You might call upon a translator to take your English and translate it into the local language. In this case, you are speaking the same language, but it is translated into many other languages to communicate with your customers. This is what ODBC does for databases.

ODBC Data Source

In order to connect to a database, you must first specify how to connect to it in an ODBC data source. This *data source*, often referred to as a DSN, or data source name, is a profile of connection information. Because ODBC connects to many types of databases, there is different information needed to connect to each. So ODBC has created a superset of connection information for all databases that it connects to. Connection information that might be required includes

- The path and file name of the database
- The username and password to connect with
- The server on which the database resides

Using the ColdFusion Express Administrator, you can define how to connect to the database you are trying to use. This definition is stored as an ODBC data source for reference in your CFML pages.

Data Sources Are Profiles

As an analogy to an ODBC data source, consider how you log into your Linux or Windows systems. You input your name and password, but you don't have to specify your home directory, or where your files are stored by default. When you log in, there is a profile of information that you can customize just for you. This profile is stored with your login information so that you can use it each time you log in. The same is true for the ODBC data source. You can specify the login information once, and then refer to the profile each time you want to connect to the database using CFML.

11

Supported Databases

ColdFusion Express allows you to connect to any of the following databases from the Windows platform:

- Microsoft Access
- Borland Paradox
- Borland dBase
- Microsoft FoxPro
- Microsoft Excel files
- Text files
- Lotus Approach

Scaling Your Database

If you want to connect to a larger scale database, such as Oracle or Sybase, you must purchase either ColdFusion Professional or ColdFusion Enterprise.

Creating the Data Source

In order to create the ODBC data source, you will use the ColdFusion Express
Administrator. When you have defined a data source, you can use it for all your CFML
pages.

To Do: Create an ODBC Data Source

Create the ODBC data source for the learncfe database, which comes on the CD that
accompanies this book. Use the administrator to create the connection information to this
Microsoft Access database:

1. Under the Start menu, choose Programs, ColdFusion Express 4.5, ColdFusion
   Express Administrator. This will bring up your browser and show you the administrative interface.

2. If it prompts for a password, enter the password you assigned while installing
   ColdFusion Express.

3. Under the server grouping, select the ODBC option.

4. Drop down the ODBC Driver select box to see the available databases that
   ColdFusion Express supports. Select Microsoft Access, which is the first option.

5. Put in a data source name of learncfe and click Add.

6. Put in the optional description so that you remember what it is later.

7. Next to the Database File text field, click Browse Server.

8. When this Java applet comes up, drill down under your Web root to find the
   learncfe directory. When selected, you will see the learncfe.mdb Microsoft Access
   database file. Highlight this file and click OK.

9. Your connection information to the learncfe data source should be similar to Figure
   11.11. This will depend on where your learncfe directory is installed.

10. Click Create to create the data source.

After you create a data source, ColdFusion Express automatically goes out and tries to
test the connection. It will show you either a Verified or Failed message, as seen in
Figure 11.12. If you receive a failed status, you should go back and fix it before
proceeding. Most likely, you haven't selected the correct database file.

FIGURE 11.11
*The ColdFusion
Express Administrator
allows you to create a
connection to a data-
base.*

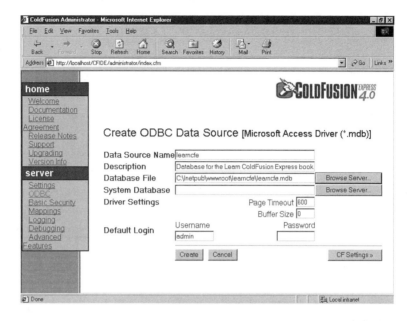

FIGURE 11.12
*After creating a data
source, ColdFusion
Express will test to be
sure that the connec-
tion was successful.*

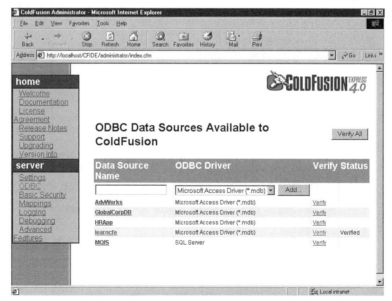

11

Table 11.1 describes the connection parameters required to connect to a Microsoft
Access database.

TABLE 11.1   Microsoft Access Connection Parameters

Parameter	Description
Data source name	Name of the data source that you will use in your applications. Must not contain spaces or special characters.
Description	Optional description of the data source.
Database File	The path and filename of the Access database (.mdb file)
Default Login	The default login information for Access. This value should be set to `admin`.
Password	The default login password. By default, this should be blank.

Other connection parameters exist, but they aren't required.

Q&A

Q Can I store images in my database and then display them in my pages?

A Most databases have a data type for this type of data, known as binary data. Access
has a data type for OLE objects, and enterprise databases consider them Binary
Large Objects, or BLOBs.

ColdFusion Express, however, doesn't give you the ability to retrieve this information from the database for use in your applications. You can always store the path
to the image in the database and then use the HTML <IMG> tag to include it in your
page.

**Q I've used the ODBC Administrator to connect to databases before. Can I use
this to set up my data source for ColdFusion Express?**

A As long as you create your data source as a System DSN, you can access it through
ColdFusion Express. However, ColdFusion Express' Web interface allows you to
maintain your data sources remotely, whereas the ODBC Administrator forces you
to be on the ColdFusion Express server to create them. There is also more information specific to ColdFusion Express about the data source that you can specify
using the ColdFusion Express Administrator.

Q **Does ColdFusion Express provide any tools for creating and managing databases?**

A ColdFusion Express doesn't have any tools that can help you with creating and managing your databases. Each database usually has a set of tools that can help you do this prior to setting up the data source and connecting using ColdFusion Express.

Workshop

The Workshop contains quiz questions and exercises to help reinforce what you've learned in this hour. If you get stuck, the answers to the quiz questions can be found in Appendix A, "Answers to Quiz."

Quiz

1. *True or false*: A foreign key is a column or set of columns that uniquely identifies each row in the table.

2. Why did the relational database emerge?

3. What is the difference between a relational database and a Relational Database Management System?

Exercises

1. If you have Microsoft Access or MySQL, open the learncfe database in your environment to see the tables and columns provided for your use throughout the class.

2. Check with your database documentation to see if there is a sample database installed on your system. If so, see if you can open it up in the DBMS. After you become familiar with the tables and columns, use it throughout this book to have another example of a database with data to look through.

11

Hour 12

Collecting Data

By combining your knowledge about creating HTML forms and connecting to databases, you'll now learn how to insert information into database tables.

In this lesson, you'll learn the following:

- How to insert data into a database table
- Interacting with the database using CFML
- How to create an insert form
- What statements to use to insert the data into the database

The Need for Data

There are many reasons that your Web applications might need to collect data. You can collect data to

- Authenticate users using entered logins and passwords
- Gather marketing information in surveys and preferences
- Offer online shopping through e-commerce by exposing your product list
- Personalize your site's contents to encourage users to keep returning

Collecting this information would be useless unless you stored it and used it later in some fashion. It is possible to store this information into flat files on your system. However, it is more useful to organize the data into a relational database. This information can then be leveraged for many different purposes.

Collection Methods

You can collect data in your site by tracking the links users click on, or by counting the number of hits to each page. However, there is also a need to allow users to fill in HTML forms and then store that data out to the database. This process requires an HTML form for requesting the data, and an action page for processing the data input, which you learned in Hour 9, "Using Forms." In this hour, the action page you create will contain a SQL statement that allows you to put the data into a database. This statement is the INSERT statement. I will begin by discussing the INSERT statement as it would be used in any database programming language; then incorporate it into your use of ColdFusion Express.

Inserting Data

With any application programming language, you insert data into database tables using the INSERT SQL statement. This statement allows you to insert one row of data at a time into a database table.

The INSERT statement has the following syntax:

```
INSERT INTO tablename (columnlist)
VALUES (valuelist);
```

The tablename value should say which table you want to insert information into. Specify each column you want to put a value into using columnlist, and a matching value for each one in valuelist.

Some databases are picky about the statements they will accept. For instance, some databases require a semicolon (;) at the end of each statement. It would be a good idea to get used to using this syntax as you begin.

As an example, assume that you have a database table called Guestbook that stores, among other things, the guest's name and email address. To insert a row of data into the Guestbook table for these values, you would use the following INSERT statement:

```
INSERT INTO Guestbook(GuestName, EmailAddress)
VALUES ('John Doe', 'jdoe@company.com');
```

Notice the single quotes around each of the values. Databases are very particular about the data that gets input into them, so you need to know how to correctly format the information you insert. The following rules apply to data types:

- Whenever you are inserting into text fields, you will need to surround the values in single quotes.
- You likewise cannot use single quotes around numeric values.
- Dates are generally tricky as well and require special handling, which could sometimes be differently by divergent databases.

You need to take care to match up each column in the INTO clause with its appropriate value in the VALUES clause. If you forget any of these rules, the database will remind you with an error message. You will learn how to use the correct formatting for these types in a later section.

Validating Data Input

The only check that the database can perform on insert is to make sure that the value you are trying to insert matches the type of data the column is designed to store. If you try to put in data that doesn't have the correct data type, you will receive an error message from the database. For instance, if you tried to insert a text value into a numeric column, the database wouldn't insert the data and would return an error message.

There are ways to make the database do other types of checks, so look through your DBMS documentation for more information.

> The only thing worse than getting an error message is not getting an error message when you have made a mistake. If you are inserting into two columns that are both text fields and you mix up the values, you will have garbage data in your table.
>
> ```
> INSERT INTO Guestbook(EmailAddress, GuestName)
> VALUES ('John Doe', 'jdoe@company.com')
> ```
>
> Because the data types are both text columns, this won't generate an error message. In this case, the email address and guest name are mistakenly switched and now the data will be wrong.

Understanding Null Values

If you insert data into a database table and do not supply a value for each column, all unspecified columns will be given a value of null. *Null* is not zero, is not an empty string, but is in fact the absence of a value. Databases treat these null values different from empty strings, so it's important to know the difference. You will learn more about nulls and getting information out of the database in later hours.

Inserting Nulls by Design

You can also tell the database to insert a null value for a column explicitly by using the NULL keyword. For instance, if you wanted to insert the name and use a null for the email address, you would use the following SQL statement:

```
INSERT INTO Guestbook (EmailAddress, GuestName)
VALUES (NULL, 'Doe');
```

Notice that NULL doesn't have quotes around it. It is not a string value, but a reserved SQL keyword.

SQL and ColdFusion Express

If you were using a DBMS program to input data into a database, you would do nothing more than write and execute the INSERT statement alone. However, we need to tell ColdFusion Express to send the INSERT statement on to the database instead of processing it. (ColdFusion Express doesn't understand SQL; the database does.)

In order to do this, we need to use a CFML tag <CFQUERY> to tell ColdFusion Express to take the SQL statement and pass it to the database for processing. Simply wrap any SQL statement within a <CFQUERY> tag.

```
<CFQUERY…>
    INSERT INTO Guestbook(GuestName, EmailAddress)
    VALUES ('John Doe', 'jdoe@company.com');
</CFQUERY>
```

The <CFQUERY> tag has many attributes, some of which we'll explore in later hours, but for now you only need to worry about two attributes:

```
<CFQUERY Datasource="learncfe" Name="InsGuestbook">
    INSERT INTO Guestbook(GuestName, EmailAddress)
    VALUES ('John Doe', 'jdoe@company.com');
</CFQUERY>
```

The Datasource attribute specifies the ODBC datasource you created during Hour 11, "Connecting to a Database" using the ColdFusion Administrator. It designates the database that you want to send the statement to.

> Don't let the name <CFQUERY> fool you. Although that tag can be used to
> query data, it is actually an all-purpose SQL tag, one that can be used for
> *any* valid SQL operations.

The Name attribute specifies the name of the statement. If the SQL statement returns data, this is the name with which you'll reference it later. If the statement doesn't return data, as with an INSERT, UPDATE, or DELETE statement, the Name attribute is not required.

Naming Conventions

Notice that I named this query with an "Ins" prefix. This designates the SQL inside the tag as an INSERT statement. If you follow a naming convention, such as "get" for data retrieval queries, "del" for deletes, and so on, it becomes easier to maintain later on.

Working with Dates

Because we are connecting to our databases in a uniform way via ODBC, we can always rely on our ColdFusion Express functions to help us out with dates. There are a few functions that you can use to format date values properly for a database to accept them. These functions include

- CreateODBCDate()
- CreateODBCDateTime()
- CreateODBCTime()

These functions take one argument, a date/time value in the period from 100 AD to 9999 AD. For instance, the following assignment will create a variable called FormattedDate using the CreateODBCDate() function:

```
<CFSET FormattedDate=CreateODBCDate("01/25/2000")>
<CFOUTPUT>#Variables.FormattedDate#</CFOUTPUT>
```

The output from ODBC date functions contains the ODBC syntax for dates. In this example, the output value looks like this:

```
{d '2000-01-25'}
```

The date is displayed in curly braces, with the d representing the code for date, followed by the date for January 25, 2000.

12

Inserting Variable Values

You have seen an INSERT statement that inserts values, but they have all been literal values. (Remember that you learned literal values in Hour 5, "Working with Variables and Expressions.") You can also insert values that are generated from variables or from user input. In this case, you want to use a ColdFusion Express variable within the INSERT statement.

You can do so by surrounding variable names with pound signs. In this example, a page variable contains a string for the guest name, which is then used inside the INSERT statement:

```
<CFSET GuestName = "Sue">
<CFQUERY NAME="InsGuest" DATASOURCE="learncfe">
    INSERT INTO Guestbook(GuestName, EmailAddress)
    VALUES ('#Variables.GuestName#', 'jdoe@company.com');
</CFQUERY>
```

Although it isn't often that you would call a page variable you just set, this example shows that you can use any type of variable in your SQL statement. Here we set the page variable GuestName to Sue, and then referenced GuestName in the INSERT statement.

> **Don't Forget to Quote**
>
> Even with ColdFusion Express variables, you must determine what type of data a column is expecting. In the case of the GuestName, it is expecting a string and thus the variable must be surrounded by single quotes. They cannot be double quotes.

Tracking Page Hits

As an example of storing data, you might want to keep track of users who visit your home page, and when they hit it to ascertain your peak times. In order to save this information for each user, you could store it in a database table. First, you will need a database table with a column that can store the time of day the user visited, as shown in Figure 12.1.

In your home page, you would then code an INSERT statement to put a row into the PageHits table for each request. This example will evaluate the current time using the Now() function and then use the CreateODBCDateTime() function to turn it into what the database can understand as a date:

```
<CFQUERY NAME="InsPageHits" DATASOURCE="learncfe">
    INSERT INTO PageHits (PageHit_Date)
    VALUES (#CreateODBCDateTime(Now())#);
</CFQUERY>
```

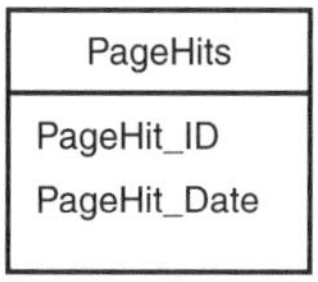

FIGURE 12.1

*The PageHits table
contains an automatic
primary key and the
time the user hit the
page.*

PageHits
PageHit_ID
PageHit_Date

ColdFusion Express will always make a pass through everything inside the <CFQUERY> tag to evaluate code or variables that need to be evaluated. After it has done that, it will send the resulting SQL statement to the database for processing. In order to tell it to replace any variables, you must specify the pound signs around the value.

To Do: Insert Page Hits into a Database Table

Perform the following steps to capture page hits and insert the time of the hit into the database table:

1. Return to HomeSite and make sure that you're working under the Web root in the /learncfe/hour12 directory.
2. Create a new page using the default template.
3. Change the <TITLE> value to **Adding Page Hits**.
4. Save the page in the /learncfe/hour12 directory as **pagehits.cfm**.
5. Between the <BODY> and </BODY> tag, write the <CFQUERY> tag with an INSERT statement to insert a row into the PageHits table. (Refer to the SQL statement previously discussed.)
6. Return to the browser and surf to the page. If it was successful, you won't receive any output. However, the row will be inserted into the table. If you have access to the database software on your machine, you can open the table and see for yourself.

If you use this in production, you'll want to clean out the table periodically. It could get fairly large if every request inserts a record, depending on your expected traffic over time.

Inserting User Data

In Hour 9, you created an HTML form to collect user data. At that time, you were only able to print the user values or perhaps email it to someone. Now that you've learned how to insert data into database tables, you can begin to use databases to store information that users input into HTML forms.

In order to insert user data into a database table, you will need two pages, as depicted in Figure 12.2.

- An HTML form with a control for each column you want to insert data into
- An action page that contains a statement to insert the row into the database table

FIGURE 12.2

Create an HTML form that prompts for information, and submit it to an action page that stores the data in a database table.

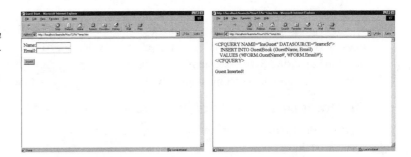

Creating an Insert Form

You have already created a form to collect guest information. The difference between the form you've created and an insert form is that you need to consider the database table you will be inserting information into. For instance, you must consider

- Creating a form control for each column you want to put data into. Be sure to name each control the same as the column name to make it easier to match up form values and columns.
- Assigning the proper HTML control for the type of data in the column.
- Defaulting data that is commonly input.
- Using validation to make sure that the correct data types are inserted into the columns.
- Using validation to require information that is also required by the database table.

Choosing Controls

Begin by analyzing the data in the target database table to see what types of controls you want to use. I've included Table 12.1 to summarize each form control type and the reason for its use.

TABLE 12.1 Use the Correct Form Controls for the Data

Control	Used for
Text field	Text, numeric, or date columns.
Password	Text, numeric, or date columns that are echoed to the user using asterisks.
Radio buttons	A column that represents one selection out of a group of options.
Checkbox	A column that represents a YES/NO or binary field. Can be grouped to form a list of selections.
Select list	A column that represents one or more selections out of a group of options. This data can be derived from another table in the database such as a lookup table.
Text area	A column that allows users to enter multiple lines of text, such as a long, text, or memo column.

Defaulting Data

To lessen typing, you should default any controls to values that the user would most likely input. For each type of control, the way you default values is different.

Text Controls

If you want to default a text control to a value the user would usually enter, use the VALUE attribute of the <INPUT> tag:

```
<INPUT Type="Text" Name="GuestName" VALUE="Put name here">
```

Using this value can help the user by telling him what is required in the text control.

Check Boxes

A check box is either checked or not (ON or OFF). In order to default a check box to checked, you would use the CHECKED attribute of the <INPUT> tag:

```
<INPUT TYPE="checkbox" NAME="SendEmail" CHECKED>
```

This attribute doesn't get a value; it is just present for checking the check box when the form loads.

Select Lists

You can default a select list item to be highlighted when the form loads by using the SELECTED attribute of the <OPTION> tag within the <SELECT> tag:

```
<SELECT NAME="GotHere" SIZE="1">
    <OPTION VALUE="Unknown">Don't know</OPTION>
    <OPTION VALUE="Search" SELECTED>Searched for it</OPTION>
    <OPTION VALUE="Stumbled">Stumbled on it</OPTION>
</SELECT>
```

12

In this example, the second option will be highlighted when the form loads. The user can change the option, but it will save him time if this is the one usually chosen.

Radio Buttons

Because each radio button has its own tag, you would use the CHECKED attribute to specify which radio button you want highlighted on page load.

```
<INPUT TYPE="radio"
    NAME="Rating"
    VALUE="Great"
    CHECKED>
```

If you try to default more than one radio button in a group, it picks the last one defined and defaults to that.

Text Areas

You have already defaulted a text area control when you first defined one in Hour 9. You need only put text in between the opening and closing <TEXTAREA> tags for it to show up when the form loads.

```
<TEXTAREA COLS=30 ROWS=3 NAME="Comments">Put comments here</TEXTAREA>
```

Remember not to put the ending </TEXTAREA> on another line, or there will be an extra line inserted into the value.

Validating Data Input

As we stated earlier, the database is very picky about the type of data it will accept in table columns. If the database doesn't like the type or format of the data, it will give back an ugly error message to the user. In order to keep those messages from getting back to the user (the errors are generally confusing and wouldn't help the user anyway), you want to make sure that the data you try to insert is correct before going to the database.

Things that you'll need to look out for and code around are

- The data must be of the correct type, such as numeric, character, date, and so on.
- The database might enforce that certain columns must have a value. You need to make sure that the user inserts all necessary data values.

In order to ensure that the data is correct prior to insertion into the database table, you can use code validation rules into your ColdFusion Express applications. Refer to Hour 10, "Validating Form Fields," to refresh your memory on how to validate input.

Creating an Insert Action Page

When you have a form that contains a control for each database column, you can create an action page to take the form values input by users and insert them into the database. There are two ways that you can insert data from a form into a database table:

- By using the <CFQUERY> tag and the SQL INSERT statement
- By using the <CFINSERT> tag

Using <CFQUERY> and INSERT

You've just learned the <CFQUERY> tag with the SQL INSERT statement. In this case, the current time is formatted and inserted into the database table PageHits:

```
<CFQUERY Name="InsPageHits" Datasource="learncfe">
    INSERT INTO PageHits (PageHit_Date)
    VALUES (#CreateODBCDateTime(Now())#)
</CFQUERY>
```

When you want to take form data and insert it into a database column, you reference the name of the form control inside the SQL statement. If you had an HTML form that collected a guest's name and email address destined for a database table, you might have the following HTML code:

```
Name:<INPUT TYPE="text" NAME="GuestName"
      SIZE="20" MAXLENGTH="30">
Email:<INPUT TYPE="text" NAME="Email"
      SIZE="20" MAXLENGTH="30">
```

Assuming that there is a Guestbook table that contains these two as columns, GuestName and EmailAddress, you would use the following SQL statement:

```
<CFQUERY Datasource="learncfe" Name="InsGuestbook">
    INSERT INTO Guestbook(GuestName, EmailAddress)
    VALUES ('#FORM.GuestName#', '#FORM.Email#')
</CFQUERY>
```

All unspecified columns will receive a null value. Because both of these columns are text fields, they must both be surrounded by single quotes. In this case, I've named my form control Email, whereas my database column is called EmailAddress. I've done this to stress the point that you must be careful to know the difference between the form and the database column in your INSERT statement. But it does help to name them the same and save the confusion.

12

To Do: Insert Guest Form Information into the Guestbook Table

Perform the following steps to use your Guest Book form created in Hour 9 and store the user input into a database table.

1. Return to HomeSite and make sure that you're working under the Web root in the /learncfe/hour12 directory.

2. Either copy /learncfe/hour9/guestbook.cfm form that you created in Hour 9 to the /learncfe/hour12 directory or refer to that unit to create it now.

3. Copy the /learncfe/hour9/insert_guest.cfm action page that you created in Hour 9 to the /learncfe/hour12 directory or create it as specified in that hour now.

4. After the code for printing out each form variable value, insert the following <CFQUERY> tag:

```
<CFQUERY DATASOURCE="learncfe"
    INSERT INTO Guestbook (GuestName, Email, FirstVisit, GotHere,
    Rating, Comments)
    VALUES ('#FORM.GuestName#', '#FORM.Email#', #FORM.FirstVisit#,
    '#FORM.GotHere#',
    '#FORM.Rating#', '#FORM.Comments#'>
```

5. After the insert, display a message "Row inserted!".

6. Return to your browser and surf to the page.

Did you receive an error message? You might, if the check box form control for First Visit in guestbook.cfm does not have the VALUE attribute set to Yes. In the database, the FirstVisit column is a data type of Yes/No. Therefore, if the user checks the box, FORM.FirstVisit will be set to Yes, and if he doesn't check the box, the variable will be set to No using the <CFPARAM> tag you created inside insert_guest.cfm. Check these if you receive an error.

▲ If you don't receive an error message, the insert was successful. If you have access to the database software, you can check the database to see that it was inserted correctly.

How to Debug Problems

The most common error you will receive when you have troubles in your SQL statement is "ODBC Error Code = 07001 (Wrong number of parameters)". If you receive this error, check that the

- Column names are correctly spelled
- Table name is correctly spelled
- Form variables are quoted if they are text columns
- Form variables are surrounded by pound signs
- The form variable you referenced exists in the form

Using `<CFINSERT>`

We've started at the harder way to insert form data, so this part should be easy. ColdFusion Express has given you a tag in the form of `<CFINSERT>` that does a lot of the work for you when inserting data.

Taking the same two form controls that collect guest data, you can specify the following `<CFINSERT>` tag instead of using `<CFQUERY>` and SQL INSERT:

```
<CFINSERT DATASOURCE="learncfe" TABLENAME="GuestName">
```

This tag does the following steps for you:

- Matches up form variables submitted from a form to related database columns by how they are named.
- Detects the data types of each column and puts single quotes around text form values and formats dates into ODBC format.
- Creates an INSERT statement and sends it to the database for processing.

This is an easy way to insert data quickly. But it does have limitations that you need to be aware of:

- Only data coming from a form can be used.
- Each form control must be named the same as the corresponding table column.
- If your form has any other controls that don't have corresponding table columns, you must use the FORMFIELDS attribute to exclude them or you'll receive an error message.

In order to explicitly state the form controls that should be used to insert, you can specify a comma-separated list of form variable names in the FORMFIELDS attribute:

```
<CFINSERT DATASOURCE="learncfe" TABLENAME="GuestName" FORMFIELDS="GuestName,
Email">
```

To Do: Using `<CFINSERT>`

Perform the following steps to use your Guest Book form created in Hour 9 and store the user input into a database table using `<CFINSERT>`.

1. Return to HomeSite and the insert_guest.cfm page.
2. Comment out the `<CFQUERY>` tag you created in the last To Do.

12

▼   3. Insert the following `<CFINSERT>` tag:

```
<CFINSERT DATASOURCE="learncfe"
    TABLENAME="GuestBook"
    FORMFIELDS="GuestName, Email, FirstVisit, GotHere, Rating,
    Comments">
```

   4. Return to your browser and browse the form page. Fill out some test data and submit the form. If you don't receive an error message, the insert was successful. If
▲   you have access to the database software, you can check the database to see that it
       was inserted correctly.

Summary

In this hour, you learned how to take data input, either literal strings or variables, and input them into a database table using the INSERT statement. I've shown you the two ways to insert the data using either `<CFQUERY>` tag with a SQL INSERT statement, or in the shortcut `<CFINSERT>` tag. You will learn how to allow users to update data inserted into the database in a later hour.

Q&A

Q You explained the difference between strings and numbers, but what about number like ZIP codes or telephone numbers; should those be strings or numbers?

A The answer is it depends on the way your database expects the data to be insert. When designing your database, you might consider storing numbers such as ZIP codes and phone numbers as text values. This is because you don't perform any arithmetic operations on these numbers and it's more efficient to store them as text values. Either way, you must match the data types as specified in your database table.

Q Is there a way to insert multiple rows at once?

A The only way you can insert more than one row into a table at one time (in one INSERT statement) is if you are inserting rows from one table into another. This is beyond the scope of this book, but refer to a SQL book for more information. As for user input, you can only insert one row at a time using the INSERT statement.

Q **Must the columns specified in the INSERT statement be in any specific order? And are they required?**

A You can specify the column list in any order you choose, so long as the VALUES list matches it exactly. If you don't include a column list in your INSERT statement, the database will expect that you have listed each value in the VALUES list in the same order as in the table, and have included a value for each column. Remember that you can also specify a NULL keyword for a placeholder to insert an undefined value into a column.

Q **If I use the auto number type field discussed in Hour 11, can I find out the value assigned to my newly inserted row?**

A Yes, and no. You can try to obtain the last (highest) inserted number using the SQL SELECT statement. (You'll learn this statement in a later hour.) However, there is no guarantee that another user hasn't already inserted another row into the database table in the meantime. Using ColdFusion Professional or ColdFusion Enterprise, you can lock down the record in a transaction to do so, but not with ColdFusion Express.

Workshop

The Workshop contains quiz questions and exercises to help reinforce what you've learned in this hour. If you get stuck, the answers to the quiz questions can be found in Appendix A, "Answers to Quiz."

Quiz

1. *True or false*: You cannot insert a row into more than one table with one INSERT statement.

2. *True or false*: The <CFINSERT> tag can be used to insert data, and you don't have the need to use <CFQUERY> and INSERT.

3. What are the rules about formatting text for insert into a database table column?

Exercise

1. Try creating a new table in the learncfe database to store information about your family members. (Be sure to back up the file, just in case.) You could start by creating columns to hold their name, email address, and date of birth. Create a auto-generated column and designate it as the primary key. Then create a form for this table to insert row. Experiment with different data types in the database to see how to format them for insert within your CFML pages.

HOUR 13

Creating Data Driven Pages

You've just learned how to get information into a database, so the next step is to get information out. This data can be used to create dynamic, data-driven Web pages.

In this lesson, you'll learn the following:

- How to query information from a database table
- Selecting from the database using CFML
- How to print out query resultsets
- Displaying data in simple lists or tables
- Finding record counts and row numbers
- Using aliases to rename columns in queries

Understanding Data-Driven Templates

Thus far you've been able to create an HTML form and prompt the user for data. That data has been inserted into a database table for safekeeping. Saving data into a database doesn't make much sense unless you intend to use it in some way. In order to "use" data in a database, you retrieve, or select, information out of the tables.

In Hour 12, "Collecting Data," you collected information from guests of your Web site and stored it into a Guestbook table. You might now want to retrieve that information back from the database to see who visited your site and what they thought of it. In this case, the data doesn't even exist until users input it. You will need to use ColdFusion Express to retrieve the guest information from the database and print it out for you.

There are many uses for retrieving data to generate dynamic, data-driven Web pages. Tables are useful to prompt for and capture information from users. But tables can also be created to store information about your Web site as well. You can generate your own tables and use them to

- Dynamically generate options in your toolbar to make it easy to add or remove options
- Use data that you already have in a database and publish it to your Web site
- Store user information in a database table and use it to let users log in and be authenticated

After you learn the basics of data retrieval and output, you'll find many uses for database data in your Web sites.

Selecting Data

In order to get information out of a database and onto your Web pages, you need to perform two steps:

1. Retrieve, or select, the information from the table.
2. Print out the results to your Web page.

In order to retrieve information from database tables, use the SQL SELECT statement. This statement allows you to select information from one table or many tables joined together.

The simplest form of the SELECT statement has the following syntax:

```
SELECT columnlist
FROM tablename;
```

The *columnlist* specifies which columns you want to get information from, and *tablename* specifies which table it belongs in. For instance, if you wanted to retrieve all Guests and their email addresses from the Guestbook table, you would use the following SELECT statement:

```
SELECT GuestName, Email
FROM Guestbook;
```

If you really wanted to be pristine with your SQL, you could also specify the table name as a prefix on the columns. This SELECT statement takes the table name and uses it to specify the table for the column:

```
SELECT Guestbook.GuestName, Guestbook.Email
FROM Guestbook;
```

This is not necessary because the database will always know which table the column is in when there's only one table used. But it becomes more important when you try to get information out of more than one table at a time. We'll get back to this later.

Returning All Columns

SQL gives you a shortcut for requesting all columns in a table. This shortcut comes in the form of a wildcard. A *wildcard* is a character that can be used as a placeholder to specify a variable list of things. When used within a SELECT statement, it means to return all columns:

```
SELECT *
FROM Guestbook;
```

In this example, all rows and all columns in the Guestbook table are returned.

Restrict Data Returned

Using the wildcard (*) returns all columns. Take care to resist the ease of using a wildcard. If you don't need all data, you will be returning more information than you need and could therefore be tying up valuable resources that other users could be sharing. The performance of your system is best served by only selecting what you need.

13

Ordering Data

Because you haven't specified otherwise, all guest rows will be returned, and the order will be determined by the database. If you wanted to sort the returned values by the GuestName column, add an ORDER BY clause to the statement as in the following:

```
SELECT GuestName, Email
FROM Guestbook
ORDER BY GuestName;
```

SQL Statements Are Not Case Sensitive

SQL statements are not case sensitive, which means you can use SELECT, select, or Select and it will still retrieve the same way. Most developers find it easier to read when the actual SQL words are capitalized, and the column lists and table names are mixed case.

Filtering Data

It isn't always practical or desirable to return all rows from a table. In order to reduce the rows returned in a query, you would create a filter in a WHERE clause. A *filter* is a clause that attempts to restrict the amount of data returned by making sure that the data meets some rules. For instance, you might only want to see information about a guest named John Doe. The SELECT statement necessary to limit the result to this row would be

```
SELECT GuestName, Email
FROM Guestbook
WHERE GuestName = 'John Doe';
```

This will save your pages a lot of time in returning unnecessary information when you only want specific information.

Use of Whitespace

All extra whitespace within a SQL statement is ignored when that statement is processed. SQL statements can be specified on one line or broken up over many lines. Breaking them up makes it much easier to read and maintain.

You can specify as many filters in your SELECT statement as you need. To do so, chain together the filter statements using the AND clause or the OR clause.

Learn More About SQL

We cannot do justice to the SELECT statement in this book. In order to learn more about this and other SQL statements, refer to *Sams Teach Yourself SQL in 10 Minutes* (ISBN: 0-672-31664-1).

SQL and ColdFusion Express

As with the INSERT statement, if you were working directly with the database in its native environment, the SELECT statement would be run and data would be displayed for your viewing pleasure. But just like the INSERT statement, you need to tell ColdFusion Express to send the SELECT statement to the database for processing.

To do this, use the all-purpose database tag—the <CFQUERY> tag. This will tell ColdFusion Express to take the SELECT statement from inside the tag and pass it to the database for processing. The following example takes the SELECT statement for guest information and sends it to the learncfe data source for processing:

```
<CFQUERY NAME="qGetGuest" DATASOURCE="learncfe">
    SELECT GuestName, Email
    FROM Guestbook
    ORDER BY GuestName;
</CFQUERY>
```

The NAME attribute specifies how you will reference the data in your pages later on.

Naming Conventions

I named my <CFQUERY> "qGetGuest" in this case. This indicates that it is a query and returns guest information. Following naming conventions makes it easier to maintain the code later on.

To Do: Retrieving Guest Information

Follow these steps to retrieve information from the GuestName table. Hopefully, you've already used your input form in Hour 12 to insert some rows. If not, go back and insert some so that you'll see them when we retrieve them.

1. Go into HomeSite and make sure that your Local Files tab is pointing to the /learncfe/hour13 directory under your Web root directory.

2. Create a new page using the default template.

3. Change the <TITLE> value to "Retrieving Guest Information".

4. Save the page as **select_guest.cfm**.

5. Between the opening and closing <BODY> tags, insert a <CFQUERY> tag as shown in the following:

```
<CFQUERY NAME="qGetGuest" DATASOURCE="learncfe">
    SELECT GuestName, Email
    FROM Guestbook
    ORDER BY GuestName;
</CFQUERY>
```

To Do

13

▼   6. Save the page.

    7. Browse to the page.

You won't see any output yet. That's because the <CFQUERY> tag requests the information from the database, but it doesn't print it out for you. You'll learn how to do that in Hour 21, "Debugging and Troubleshooting."

If you look at the debugging information at the bottom of the page, you'll see that the query has been executed, and that it has returned a number of rows to ColdFusion
▲ Express. Now you just need to learn how to print out those rows.

Accessing the Resultset

In order to print out the results of a query, you must first know how ColdFusion Express brings back and stores the query information from the database.

As an example, say that we executed the following query:

```
<CFQUERY NAME="qGetGuest" DATASOURCE="learncfe">
    SELECT GuestName, Email
    FROM Guestbook
    ORDER BY GuestName;
</CFQUERY>
```

Figure 13.1 shows you the process for returning a query resultset:

FIGURE 13.1

A request is made to the database for information, and that information is sent back to ColdFusion Express for processing.

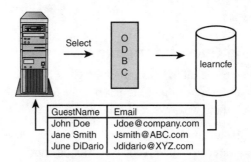

When ColdFusion Express receives the data back from the database, it stores the result-set in memory. This resultset is referenced by using the NAME attribute of the <CFQUERY> tag and is only available for the life of this page. After the query is executed, you can print out the resultset. After the page is executed, the resultset is cleaned up.

If you use the table name prefixes on the columns, they are stripped off by ColdFusion Express in the returned resultset. For instance, if the SQL SELECT statement you run looks like this example:

```
<CFQUERY NAME="qGetGuest" DATASOURCE="learncfe">
    SELECT Guestbook.GuestName, Guestbook.Email
    FROM Guestbook
    ORDER BY Guestbook.GuestName;
</CFQUERY>
```

The resultset would be returned with two columns, named GuestName and Email. The Guestbook. prefix will have been stripped off by ColdFusion Express. This becomes important when you want to print out the data.

Printing Out Query Results

The rules for printing out page variables from Hour 5, "Working with Variables and Expressions," are

1. Use the <CFOUTPUT> tag around any variables that must be resolved.

2. Surround each variable with pound signs (#).

3. Prefix your query variables.

Applying this to a ColdFusion Express resultset will almost get you there. Start by creating a <CFOUTPUT> tag and using the column names as the variables you want to print out. For the Guestbook query we've been using, you have the following code:

```
<CFQUERY NAME="qGetGuest" DATASOURCE="learncfe">
    SELECT GuestName, Email
    FROM Guestbook
    ORDER BY GuestName;
</CFQUERY>

<CFOUTPUT>
    #Variables.GuestName#
    #Variables.Email#<BR>
</CFOUTPUT>
```

13

This won't work because query resultsets aren't accessed using the Variables prefix. Query resultset variables are different from page variables, and need a different prefix. Because there can be many queries on one page, you need to uniquely identify each one. This is done by specifying the name of the query as set in the <CFQUERY> tag's NAME attribute. In the previous example, the name of the query has been set to `qGetGuest`. This is the prefix that you need to use to access the query results. The code now should read as follows:

```
<CFQUERY NAME="qGetGuest" DATASOURCE="learncfe">
    SELECT GuestName, Email
    FROM Guestbook
    ORDER BY GuestName;
</CFQUERY>

<CFOUTPUT>
    #qGetGuest.GuestName#
    #qGetGuest.Email#<BR>
</CFOUTPUT>
```

However, you still aren't there yet. We've used this to print out simple page variables, but we might have many rows in the resultset that we need to print out. Therefore, we need a mechanism to loop over the query resultset rows and print out each one. This is done by using the QUERY attribute of the <CFOUTPUT> tag. By using the QUERY attribute, you are telling ColdFusion Express to execute any code inside a <CFOUTPUT> block *for each row in the resultset*. This can be used to print out every row because it will execute once for each row. It's all done for you with ColdFusion Express. The full listing of the code, including the HTML, now looks as shown in Listing 13.1.

LISTING 13.1 Retrieving and Printing Database Data

```
 1:<!DOCTYPE HTML PUBLIC "-//W3C//DTD HTML 4.0 Transitional//EN">
 2:
 3:<html>
 4:<head>
 5:    <title>Retrieving Guest Information</title>
 6:</head>
 7:
 8:<body>
 9:<CFQUERY NAME="qGetGuest" DATASOURCE="learncfe">
10:    SELECT GuestName, Email
11:    FROM Guestbook
12:    ORDER BY GuestName;
13:</CFQUERY>
14:
15:<CFOUTPUT QUERY="qGetGuest">
16:    #qGetGuest.GuestName#
17:    #qGetGuest.Email#<BR>
18:</CFOUTPUT>
19:</body>
20:</html>
```

The output to the browser is displayed in Figure 13.2.

Just to drive home the point of how ColdFusion Express processes the queries and generates HTML for the browser, you can use the View Source browser option to view what HTML was generated and sent back. Figure 13.3 shows the HTML that was returned from this example.

Consider the following code. What do you think the output of this would be? In this case, I am using the <CFOUTPUT> tag with the QUERY attribute, but am not printing out any resultset columns.

```
<CFQUERY NAME="qGetGuest" DATASOURCE="learncfe">
    SELECT GuestName, Email
    FROM Guestbook
    ORDER BY GuestName;
</CFQUERY>

<CFOUTPUT QUERY="qGetGuest">
    Hello!<BR>
</CFOUTPUT>
```

Using the QUERY attribute only tells ColdFusion Express how many times to execute the <CFOUTPUT> tag. In this case, we will receive as many Hello! messages as there are rows in the table; which are four. This output is shown in Figure 13.4.

13

FIGURE 13.3

If you view the returned HTML for the page, each resultset row was resolved and printed to the browser.

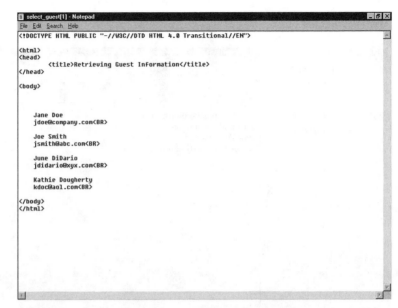

FIGURE 13.4

Using the <CFOUTPUT> tag and the QUERY attribute loops over any code inside the <CFOUTPUT> tag for the number of rows in the resultset.

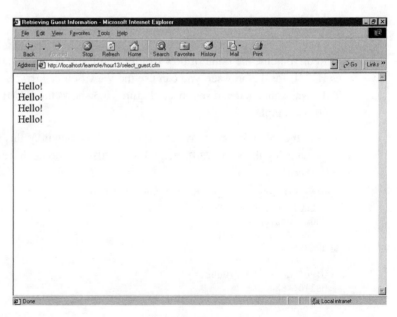

Now that you know this, I hope you realize that you have full control over what gets displayed inside a <CFOUTPUT> tag.

To Do: Displaying Guest Information

Follow these steps to display the retrieved information from the GuestName table.

1. Return to HomeSite and the select_guest.cfm page.

2. After the `<CFQUERY>` tag, use a `<CFOUTPUT>` tag to print out the Guestname and Email columns, as shown in the following:

```
<CFOUTPUT>
    #GuestName#
    #Email#<BR>
</CFOUTPUT>
```

3. Save the page.

4. Browse to the page. You will receive an error message because it doesn't know where these variables come from.

5. Now alter the output to use the query scope, as in the following code:

```
<CFOUTPUT>
    #qGetGuest.GuestName#
    #qGetGuest.Email#<BR>
</CFOUTPUT>
```

6. Save the page.

7. Browse to the page. You will only see one row of data returned.

8. Alter the output to use the QUERY attribute of the `<CFOUTPUT>` tag, as follows:

```
<CFOUTPUT QUERY="qGetGuest">
    #qGetGuest.GuestName#
    #qGetGuest.Email#<BR>
</CFOUTPUT>
```

9. Save the page.

10. Browse to the page. You now should see all rows in your Guestbook table.

▲ If you receive errors, make sure that your `<CFQUERY>` NAME attribute matches your `<CFOUTPUT>` QUERY attribute. Refer to the full code listing for additional help.

13

Formatting Display of Results

In the examples used thus far, the only formatting used for the output was the use of the `<BR>` tag to put each row of data on a separate line. You can now freely intermingle your HTML formatting code with your CFML variables to create more attractive output.

Creating a Dynamic List

HTML gives you the ability to format data into a list. Lists come in several formats, including an unordered list for bulleting, an ordered list for numbering, and a definition list for glossary-like output.

You can print out the data returned from a query formatted as an ordered list by using the <OL> and <LI> tags. A standard ordered list might have the following code:

```
<OL>
    <LI>List Item 1</LI>
    <LI>List Item 2</LI>
</OL>
```

The <OL> container tag surrounds each individual <LI> tag for each list item. Because ColdFusion Express will print out each row in the query using <CFOUTPUT QUERY="queryname">, we can surround the <CFOUTPUT> tag with the <OL> container and use a <LI> for the data, as in Listing 13.2.

LISTING 13.2 Formatting Using Lists

```
 1:<!DOCTYPE HTML PUBLIC "-//W3C//DTD HTML 4.0 Transitional//EN">
 2:
 3:<html>
 4:<head>
 5:    <title>Formatting Using Lists</title>
 6:</head>
 7:
 8:<body>
 9:<CFQUERY NAME="qGetGuest" DATASOURCE="learncfe">
10:    SELECT GuestName, Email
11:    FROM Guestbook
12:    ORDER BY GuestName;
13:</CFQUERY>
14:
15:<OL>
16:    <CFOUTPUT QUERY="qGetGuest">
17:        <LI>#qGetGuest.GuestName# #qGetGuest.Email#</LI>
18:    </CFOUTPUT>
19:</OL>
20:
21:</body>
22:</html>
```

This will print out the data from the query and format it into an ordered list as in Figure 13.5.

FIGURE **13.5**

Intermix your HTML with your CFML to create formatted documents, as in this ordered list.

You can use the same formatting for the unordered, or bulleted, list.

To Do: Displaying Guest Information as a List

Follow these steps to display the retrieved information from the GuestName table as a numbered (ordered) list.

1. Return to HomeSite and the select_guest.cfm page.

2. Select File, Save As and save it as select_guest_ol.cfm.

3. Change the `<CFOUTPUT>` tag to print out the Guestname and Email columns in a bulleted list, as shown in the following:

```
<OL>
    <CFOUTPUT QUERY="qGetGuest">
        <LI>#qGetGuest.GuestName# #qGetGuest.Email#</LI>
    </CFOUTPUT>
</OL>
```

4. Save the page.

5. Browse to the page. You now should see all rows in your Guestbook table formatted in a bulleted list.

Creating a Dynamic Table

You often want to format the data returned from a query resultset into an HTML table. HTML tables are used to format information logically and to make all columns line up

together to make it more readable. Tables lend themselves naturally to resultsets because
data is usually thought of in tabular format.

A simple HTML table includes a container <TABLE> tag, with embedded table row (<TR>)
and table data (<TD>) tags. A simple table with three rows, the first one being the table
header, and two columns of data is shown in the following:

```
<TABLE>
<TR>
    <TH>Name</TH>
    <TH>Email</TH>
</TR>
<TR>
    <TD>Cyndi Piehl</TD>
    <TD>cpiehl@mysite.com</TD>
</TR>
<TR>
    <TD>Jane Doe</TD>
    <TD> jdoe@company.com</TD>
</TR>
</TABLE>
```

This table is hard-coded with guest information. If we intermix our HTML table tags
with our CFML tags and variables, we can get ColdFusion Express to generate a table
out of a resultset for us.

You want all data to be put into a table, so start by surrounding the <CFOUTPUT> with a
<TABLE> tag. Each row in the result represents a table row, so all data will be put inside a
<TR> container tag. Finally, each data column should print out in it's own table cell, so
place them inside a <TD> tag. If you want column headers for the entire table, you can
specify a table row outside the <CFOUTPUT> tag with the header. The result is the following code:

```
<!DOCTYPE HTML PUBLIC "-//W3C//DTD HTML 4.0 Transitional//EN">

<html>
<head>
    <title>Retrieving Guest Information</title>
</head>

<body>
<CFQUERY NAME="qGetGuest" DATASOURCE="learncfe">
    SELECT GuestName, Email
    FROM Guestbook
    ORDER BY GuestName;
</CFQUERY>

<TABLE BORDER="1">
<TR>
```

```
        <TH>Name</TH>
        <TH>Email</TH>
    </TR>
    <CFOUTPUT QUERY="qGetGuest">
    <TR>
        <TD>#qGetGuest.GuestName#</TD>
        <TD>#qGetGuest.Email#</TD>
    </TR>
    </CFOUTPUT>
    </TABLE>
    </body>
    </html>
```

Incorrectly Nesting Tables

A common mistake for new developers is that they put the entire <TABLE> tag inside the <CFOUTPUT> tag. This would result in a table **for each** row in the resultset, which is not usually what you are trying to do.

The result is an HTML table with a border and two columns, one for Name and one for Email. Figure 13.6 shows the output of this template.

FIGURE 13.6

Create HTML tables easily by using the table tags intermixed with the ColdFusion Express resultset output.

13

To Do: Displaying Guest Information in a Table

Follow these steps to display the retrieved information from the GuestName table as a tabular format:

1. Return to HomeSite and the select_guest.cfm page.

2. Select File, Save As and save it as **select_guest_table.cfm**.

3. Change the <CFOUTPUT> tag to print out the Guestname and Email columns in a table, as shown in the following:

```
<TABLE BORDER="1">
<TR>
    <TH>Name</TH>
    <TH>Email</TH>
</TR>
<CFOUTPUT QUERY="qGetGuest">
<TR>
    <TD>#qGetGuest.GuestName#</TD>
    <TD>#qGetGuest.Email#</TD>
</TR>
</CFOUTPUT>
</TABLE>
```

4. Save the page.

5. Browse to the page. You now should see all rows in your Guestbook table formatted in a table.

▲

Extra Query Information

There is extra information received for each query you execute using ColdFusion Express. This information retrieved includes

- The total number of rows returned in the query

- A line number for each row in the query

- A variable that contains all columns returned in the query

- A variable that stores the amount of time it took to execute the query

RecordCount

For each query, a RecordCount variable is created that stores the total number of rows returned by the query. This information can be displayed in the output as #queryname.RecordCount#.

Because this value is the total number of rows, you wouldn't want to use it in the <CFOUTPUT QUERY="queryname"> block, or it would be printed out for each row returned.

Therefore, it is usually included at the top or bottom of the query printout. Listing 13.3 has the code with the RecordCount display bolded.

LISTING 13.3 Displaying the Record Count

```
1:<html>
2:<head>
3:    <title>Retrieving Guest Information</title>
4:</head>
5:
6:<body>
7:<CFQUERY NAME="qGetGuest" DATASOURCE="learncfe">
8:    SELECT GuestName, Email
9:    FROM Guestbook
10:    ORDER BY GuestName;
11:</CFQUERY>
12:
13:<TABLE BORDER="1">
14:<TR>
15:    <TH>Name</TH>
16:    <TH>Email</TH>
17:</TR>
18:<CFOUTPUT QUERY="qGetGuest">
19:<TR>
20:    <TD>#qGetGuest.GuestName#</TD>
21:    <TD>#qGetGuest.Email#</TD>
22:</TR>
23:</CFOUTPUT>
24:</TABLE>
25:<P>
26:Total number of Guests: <CFOUTPUT>#qGetGuest.RecordCount#</CFOUTPUT>
27:</P>
28:</body>
29:</html>
```

To Do: Displaying Record Count

▼ To Do

Follow these steps to display the retrieved information from the GuestName table as a tabular format.

1. Return to HomeSite and the select_guest_table.cfm page.

2. After the ending </TABLE> tag, insert the code to print out the total record count, as in the following code:

```
<P>
Total number of Guests: <CFOUTPUT>#qGetGuest.RecordCount#</CFOUTPUT>
</P>
```

3. Save the page.

▲ 4. Browse to the page. You now should see the count of rows returned after the table.

13

CurrentRow

Another variable that is created for each query is `queryname.CurrentRow`. This variable is stored for each row of the query, and refers to the number of the row. This value is useful for showing a line number next to each row. Because this value increments by each row, it should be printed out inside the `<CFOUTPUT QUERY="queryname">` tag. The following code listing will print out each row with the current row as the first column of the output. The code with the `CurrentRow` display is bolded in Listing 13.4.

LISTING 13.4   Displaying the Current Row

```
 1:<html>
 2:<head>
 3:    <title>Retrieving Guest Information</title>
 4:</head>
 5:
 6:<body>
 7:<CFQUERY NAME="qGetGuest" DATASOURCE="learncfe">
 8:    SELECT GuestName, Email
 9:    FROM Guestbook
10:    ORDER BY GuestName;
11:</CFQUERY>
12:
13:<TABLE BORDER="1">
14:<TR>
15:    <TH>Line<BR>No.</TH>
16:    <TH>Name</TH>
17:    <TH>Email</TH>
18:</TR>
19:<CFOUTPUT QUERY="qGetGuest">
20:<TR>
21:    <TD>#qGetGuest.CurrentRow#</TD>
22:    <TD>#qGetGuest.GuestName#</TD>
23:    <TD>#qGetGuest.Email#</TD>
24:</TR>
25:</CFOUTPUT>
26:</TABLE>
27:<P>
28:Total number of Guests: <CFOUTPUT>#qGetGuest.RecordCount#</CFOUTPUT>
29:</P>
30:</body>
31:</html>
```

To Do: Displaying the Current Row

Follow these steps to display the retrieved information from the GuestName table as a tabular format with each row numbered using CurrentRow.

1. Return to HomeSite and the select_guest_table.cfm page.

2. Change the table to include a header and data column for the line number, as in the following code:

```
<TABLE BORDER="1">
<TR>
    <TH>Line<BR>No.</TH>
    <TH>Name</TH>
    <TH>Email</TH>
</TR>
<CFOUTPUT QUERY="qGetGuest">
<TR>
    <TD>#qGetGuest.CurrentRow#</TD>
    <TD>#qGetGuest.GuestName#</TD>
    <TD>#qGetGuest.Email#</TD>
</TR>
</CFOUTPUT>
</TABLE>
```

3. Save the page.

4. Browse to the page. You now should see the line number of each row returned, as seen in Figure 13.7.

FIGURE 13.7

You have now printed out the total number of rows using RecordCount *and a line number for each row using* CurrentRow.

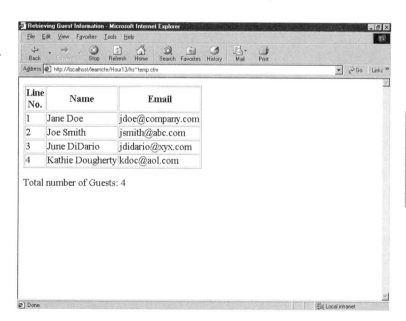

13

ColumnList

For each query executed, a variable is created called *queryname*.ColumnList. This variable is populated with a comma-separated list of columns returned. To print it out, just use a <CFOUTPUT> block and pound signs (#) as you do with any page variable:

```
<CFOUTPUT>#qGetGuest.ColumnList#</CFOUTPUT>
```

ExecutionTime

CFQUERY.ExecutionTime returns the amount of time it took to execute a query. This might be useful for debugging purposes.

```
<CFOUTPUT>#CFQUERY.ExecutionTime#</CFOUTPUT>
```

Notice that all other variables are prefixed with the query name. In the case of ExecutionTime, the prefix is CFQUERY instead. This variable is reset after each query with the time it took to execute that query.

Aliasing Query Columns

An alias is a SQL feature that allows you to rename a SQL element. It can be used to rename a column or a table within a SELECT statement. In the following example, I'm selecting from the Guestbook table but renaming it to G:

```
SELECT GuestName, Email
    FROM Guestbook G
    ORDER BY GuestName;
```

It doesn't make much sense in this query until you want to use the table name. If you remember from earlier in this hour, you learned that table names can be prefixed on the column name to fully qualify the column:

```
SELECT Guestbook.GuestName, Guestbook.Email
    FROM Guestbook
    ORDER BY GuestName;
```

In this case, it is extra typing to use the Guestbook table prefix on the columns. Using an alias, you rename the table for the life of the statement. In this case, using a table alias will save you typing because the table has been renamed to G for the life of the query:

```
SELECT G.GuestName, G.Email
    FROM Guestbook G
    ORDER BY GuestName;
```

This can save a lot of typing when you have many tables and columns to select from.

Aliases can also be used to rename columns as well. However, when you use an alias for a column, the syntax required usually uses the AS keyword, as in the following example:

```
SELECT G.GuestName AS GName, G.Email AS GEmail
    FROM Guestbook G
    ORDER BY GuestName;
```

This SELECT statement renames the GuestName and Email columns to GName and GEmail, respectively. This is where it impacts ColdFusion Express.

Because the columns have been renamed, ColdFusion Express actually gets these columns with the new names. Using the previous query, you would now need to refer to the query columns using the new, aliased column names:

```
<CFQUERY NAME="qGetGuest" DATASOURCE="learncfe">
    SELECT G.GuestName AS GName, G.Email AS GEmail
    FROM Guestbook G
    ORDER BY GuestName;
</CFQUERY>

<TABLE BORDER="1">
<TR>
    <TH>Line<BR>No.</TH>
    <TH>Name</TH>
    <TH>Email</TH>
</TR>
<CFOUTPUT QUERY="qGetGuest">
<TR>
    <TD>#qGetGuest.CurrentRow#</TD>
    <TD>#qGetGuest.GName#</TD>
    <TD>#qGetGuest.GEmail#</TD>
</TR>
</CFOUTPUT>
</TABLE>
```

Using aliases is necessary for several scenarios within your ColdFusion Express applications. These reasons include

- Spaces in Column Names
- Aggregate functions
- Two columns with the same name

Spaces in Column Names

ColdFusion Express doesn't like spaces in variable names. Therefore, if you have a database that allows spaces in column names and you have used them, you must use aliases

13

to rename the columns so that ColdFusion Express can access them later on. For instance, the following column name has a space, so I am using an alias to rename it:

```
<CFQUERY NAME="qGetGuest" DATASOURCE="learncfe">
    SELECT Guest Name AS Gname
    FROM Guestbook;
</CFQUERY>
```

Now your application can refer to the column as qGetGuest.Gname.

Aggregate Functions

Another reason you must use aliases is if you are using any SQL aggregate functions. An aggregate function is one that groups rows together to get information about that group. For instance, if you used the Count(*) function to return the number of rows, you would need to alias it. This is because ColdFusion Express cannot have either the parenthesis or the asterisk in a variable name. The following example will rename the result of the Count(*) column so that it can be used within the template:

```
<CFQUERY NAME="qGetGuest" DATASOURCE="learncfe">
    SELECT Count(*) AS GuestCount
    FROM Guestbook;
</CFQUERY>
```

Your template can now access qGetGuest.GuestCount as it would any other query column. This would also be used for the other aggregate functions, such as Sum(), Max(), Min(), and Avg().

To Do: Using Aliases in SELECTs

Follow these steps to alias columns and use them in your templates.

1. Return to HomeSite and the select_guest_table.cfm page.

2. Select File, Save As and save the file as **select_guest_alias.cfm**.

3. Add an alias to the GuestName and Email columns, as in the following code:
```
<CFQUERY NAME="qGetGuest" DATASOURCE="learncfe">
SELECT G.GuestName AS GName, G.Email AS GEmail
    FROM Guestbook G
    ORDER BY GuestName;
</CFQUERY>
```

4. Change the <CFOUTPUT> code to reference the new aliased column names, as in the following code:
```
<TABLE BORDER="1">
<TR>
    <TH>Line<BR>No.</TH>
    <TH>Name</TH>
```

```
          <TH>Email</TH>
      </TR>
      <CFOUTPUT QUERY="qGetGuest">
      <TR>
          <TD>#qGetGuest.CurrentRow#</TD>
          <TD>#qGetGuest.GName#</TD>
          <TD>#qGetGuest.GEmail#</TD>
      </TR>
      </CFOUTPUT>
      </TABLE>
```

5. Save the page.

6. Browse to the page. You should see the same output as before.

The final code listing for the aliased columns is shown in Listing 13.4.

LISTING 13.4   Using SQL Aliases

```
 1:<!DOCTYPE HTML PUBLIC "-//W3C//DTD HTML 4.0 Transitional//EN">
 2:
 3:<html>
 4:<head>
 5:    <title>Using Aliases in SELECTs</title>
 6:</head>
 7:
 8:<body>
 9:
10:<CFQUERY NAME="qGetGuest" DATASOURCE="learncfe">
11:SELECT G.GuestName AS GName, G.Email AS GEmail
12:    FROM Guestbook G
13:    ORDER BY GuestName;
14:</CFQUERY>
15:
16:<TABLE BORDER="1">
17:<TR>
18:    <TH>Line<BR>No.</TH>
19:    <TH>Name</TH>
20:    <TH>Email</TH>
21:</TR>
22:<CFOUTPUT QUERY="qGetGuest">
23:<TR>
24:    <TD>#qGetGuest.CurrentRow#</TD>
25:    <TD>#qGetGuest.GName#</TD>
26:    <TD>#qGetGuest.GEmail#</TD>
27:</TR>
28:</CFOUTPUT>
29:</TABLE>
30:</body>
31:</html>
```

13

Q&A

Q **What if I wanted to take a dump from an Microsoft Excel spreadsheet and upload it into a database table? Can ColdFusion Express do that for me?**

A ColdFusion Express doesn't have the capability to read information from a file. You would need to obtain either ColdFusion Professional or Enterprise to perform this functionality using the `<CFFILE>` tag.

Q **Is there any way to limit the number of rows that get displayed?**

A Yes, you can use the MAXROWS attribute of the `<CFOUTPUT>` tag to limit the number of rows displayed.

Workshop

The Workshop contains quiz questions and exercises to help reinforce what you've learned in this hour. If you get stuck, the answers to the quiz questions can be found in Appendix A, "Answers to Quiz."

Quiz

1. *True or false*: the `<CFQUERY>` tag returns data from the database and displays it on the page.

2. How can I print out all rows resulting from a `<CFQUERY>` tag?

3. What are some uses for aliasing?

Exercise

1. Alter the select_guest_table.cfm page to make every other data row shaded with a background color. To do so, you'll need to use the BGCOLOR attribute of the `<TR>` tag. In order to figure out every other row, find the even rows and shade them. This will require using conditional logic inside the `<TR>` tag around a BGCOLOR="grey" attribute. If the row is even (if there is no remainder), shade it. You will need to use the Mod() operator on the CurrentRow variable.

HOUR 14

Creating Dynamically-Generated Searches

In the last hour, you learned how to query a database for information and display it on your Web pages. You'll build on this knowledge to create dynamic queries to customize the data returned.

In this lesson, you'll learn the following:

- How to create dynamically-generated queries
- How to use the debugging options to view your dynamic queries
- How to use a URL parameter in your query

Understanding Dynamic Queries

In the query you learned about in the last hour, you retrieved information from the Guestbook table. This query returns the GuestName and Email columns from the table and returns all rows:

```
SELECT GuestName, Email
FROM Guestbook
ORDER BY GuestName;
```

All queries that you've written thus far have returned varying amounts of columns and rows from the table. However, once written these SQL statements will always retrieve the same information because the SELECT statement remains the same. What if you wanted to change the rows that were returned? With what you know, you'd have to change the SELECT statement and add a WHERE clause for a filter. This example returns only the rows in the Guestbook table where the GuestName is 'John Doe':

```
SELECT GuestName, Email
FROM Guestbook
WHERE GuestName = 'John Doe';
```

If you wanted to change the guest name you are looking for, you'd have to manually change the WHERE clause and then re-run it. This isn't a very flexible way to allow your applications to return data. You will want to build your applications to be flexible and usable without having to change the code each time. This is where dynamic queries come in.

A *dynamic query* is where the resulting SQL statement isn't known until the page executes. Some information will be supplied at runtime to complete the statement.

Take the following SELECT statement, which uses a placeholder for a name to be specified at runtime:

```
SELECT GuestName, Email
FROM Guestbook
WHERE GuestName = 'some name';
```

This unknown information could be supplied from different sources, including

- Information specified by a user in a form and used for a dynamic search
- Data passed from one page to another on the URL for use in the query

You will learn how to incorporate form data into a search interface in Hour 16, "Creating Rich Search Interfaces." Today, you will be using URL parameters in a SELECT statement to dynamically generate a page of data.

CFML in SQL

The first thing to understand in dynamic SQL is the use of CFML code inside the SQL statement. You can use any combination of the following to generate dynamic SQL:

- Use variables inside the SQL statement by specifying the variable surrounded by pound signs (for example, #VARIABLES.SearchValue#).
- Use conditional logic inside the <CFQUERY> to conditionally determine the resulting SQL.

Variables in Queries

In Hour 12, "Collecting Data," you learned to use ColdFusion Express variables inside the <CFQUERY> tag. This would require ColdFusion Express to process the information inside the <CFQUERY> tag before being sent to the database for insertion. Each form variable would be resolved to the value input by the user for inserting into the database.

With a simple example of using a variable inside a <CFQUERY> for retrieving information, a page variable could be created implementing the <CFSET> tag, and then that variable value can be used to generate the resulting SQL. In this example, a page variable called SearchName is set, and then referenced in the WHERE clause.

```
<CFSET SearchName = "John Doe">
<CFQUERY NAME="qGetGuests" DATASOURCE="learncfe">
    SELECT GuestName, Email
    FROM Guestbook
    WHERE GuestName = '#VARIABLES.SearchName#'
</CFQUERY>
```

Database Types

Remember that databases are picky about how you specify data in the SQL statements. Any text or character columns require the use of single quotes around values in the statement. Here, a set of single quotes are placed around the variable and will remain around the resulting value for submission to the database. Dates require special handling as well.

Before ColdFusion Express sends the SQL statement inside the <CFQUERY> to the database, it first scans through to see if any CFML code needs to be resolved. In this case, it sees the use of the pound signs around VARIABLES.SearchName and then resolves the value into the string 'John Doe'. This replacement for '#VARIABLES.SearchName#' into 'John Doe' occurs before it gets sent to the database for processing. This important function allows you to create dynamic SQL statements and rich interfaces.

To Do: Creating a Dynamic Query

Follow these steps to create a dynamic query using a variable. This query will return information from the Guestbook table, so be sure that you have input guest information in Hour 12.

1. Go into HomeSite and make sure that your Local Files tab is pointing to the /learncfe/Hour14 directory under your Web root directory.

2. Create a new page using the default template.

3. Change the <TITLE> text to "Creating a Dynamic Query".

14

▼ 4. Save the file as **dynamic_query.cfm**.

5. Between the <BODY> and </BODY> tags, create the following <CFQUERY> tag:

```
<CFQUERY NAME="qGetGuests" DATASOURCE="learncfe">
    SELECT GuestName, Email
    FROM Guestbook;
</CFQUERY>
```

6. After the <CFQUERY> tag, use a <CFOUTPUT> tag to print out the guest information.
    Refer to the following code for help:

```
<CFOUTPUT QUERY="qGetGuests">
    #qGetGuests.GuestName# #qGetGuests.Email#<BR>
</CFOUTPUT>
```

7. Save the file and browse to it. Remember one of the guest name values for use in
    later testing.

8. Return to HomeSite. Above the <CFQUERY> tag, create a page variable called
    SearchName and give it a value equal to a guest name in the table.

9. Add a WHERE clause to the SELECT statement that uses the page variable
    SearchName as shown:

```
<CFQUERY NAME="qGetGuests" DATASOURCE="learncfe">
    SELECT GuestName, Email
    FROM Guestbook
    WHERE GuestName = '#VARIABLES.SearchName#'
</CFQUERY>
```

10. Save the page and browse to it. You should now only see the row (or rows) of data
    that have a GuestName specified in the variable. The complete code is shown in
    Listing 14.1.

LISTING 14.1   Creating a Dynamic Query

```
 1: <!DOCTYPE HTML PUBLIC "-//W3C//DTD HTML 4.0 Transitional//EN">
 2:
 3: <html>
 4: <head>
 5:     <title>Creating a Dynamic Query</title>
 6: </head>
 7:
 8: <body>
 9: <!---Create a local variable to store the name to search for --->
10: <CFSET SearchName = "">
11:
12: <!---Retrieve the guest information for the search name --->
13: <CFQUERY NAME="qGetGuests" DATASOURCE="learncfe">
14:     SELECT GuestName, Email
15:     FROM Guestbook
16:     WHERE GuestName = '#Variables.SearchName#';
```

▼

LISTING 14.1   continued

```
17: </CFQUERY>
18: <!---Print out the results from the qGetGuests query --->
19: <CFOUTPUT QUERY="qGetGuests">
20:      #qGetGuests.GuestName# #qGetGuests.Email#<BR>
21: </CFOUTPUT>
22:
23: </body>
24: </html>
```

▲

Viewing Resulting SQL

The <CFQUERY> tag has an option, which enables you to view the resulting SQL that is generated and sent to the database. This is enabled by using the DEBUG attribute. This attribute isn't set to a value, but will display debug information if it is present in the tag. In the following code, the DEBUG option is set:

```
<CFQUERY NAME="qGetGuests" DATASOURCE="learncfe" DEBUG>
    SELECT GuestName, Email
    FROM Guestbook;
</CFQUERY>
```

The query debug information will be appended to the end of the page whenever the DEBUG attribute is specified. Figure 14.1 shows the output of this code execution.

FIGURE 14.1

The <CFQUERY> tag allows you to enable debugging information about the query to be displayed on your pages.

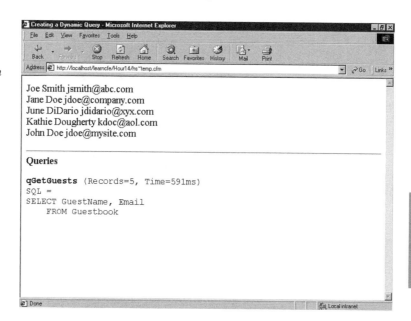

14

This attribute is especially useful when debugging dynamic SQL. Take the code in which the entire SQL statement is a variable:

```
<CFSET SQLStatement = "SELECT GuestName, Email FROM Guestbook ">

<CFQUERY NAME="qGetGuests" DATASOURCE="learncfe">
    #VARIABLES.SQLStatement#
</CFQUERY>
```

Using the DEBUG attribute can help you point out errors when you view the generated SQL, as seen in Figure 14.2. Without this option, you won't be able to see the data source and the resulting SQL statement of the error.

FIGURE 14.2

Debug information is useful when generating dynamic SQL to see if it is correctly formed.

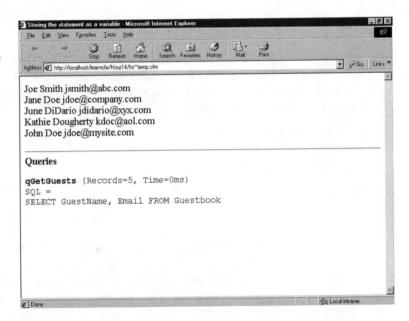

Don't Use DEBUG in Production

Because the DEBUG attribute displays sensitive information, such as your table and column names, you don't want to use this option on a production server. It is to be used only when you are writing and debugging your <CFQUERY> tags. After they are fully functional, they should be removed.

To Do: View Debugging Information

Follow these steps to view debug information about the query using the DEBUG attribute.

1. Return to HomeSite and make sure that the Local Files tab is pointing to the /learncfe/hour14 directory.

2. Re-open query_variable.cfm.

3. Enable debugging of the SQL statement by adding the DEBUG attribute to the <CFQUERY> tag, as shown in the following:

```
<CFQUERY NAME="qGetGuests" DATASOURCE="learncfe" DEBUG>
    #VARIABLES.SQLStatement#
</CFQUERY>
```

4. Save the file and browse to it. You should see all rows in the Guestbook table followed by debugging information about the query and the number of rows returned

Using Conditional Processing

It isn't a big leap of faith to understand that variables inside <CFQUERY> tags are resolved to their values, similar to inside a <CFOUTPUT> tag where values are printed out. However, incorporating conditional logic to generate dynamic queries might not seem so straightforward. In order to understand this concept, consider the following example:

```
<CFSET PrintText = "Yes">
<CFIF PrintText IS "Yes">
    Here I am printing some text!
</CFIF>
```

In the previous example, there is a simple page variable, PrintText, that is initialized using <CFSET>. This variable contains the string "Yes". This value is compared in the <CFIF> tag. If PrintText is equal to "Yes", the text Here I am printing some text! is printed out to the browser. But what gets printed out if PrintText is not equal to yes? Consider this code example:

```
<CFSET PrintText = "No">
<CFIF PrintText IS "Yes">
    Here I am printing some text!
</CFIF>
```

In this case nothing gets printed. That's because the <CFIF> tag is evaluated, and the contents between the opening <CFIF> and closing </CFIF> are only executed when the condition is true. Because the value PrintText was changed to something other than "Yes", there will be no printout at all.

14

The <CFIF> tag works similarly inside the <CFQUERY> tag. ColdFusion Express can evaluate a conditional block inside the tag to determine what the SQL statement will look like before it goes to the database. You can also use other CFML code inside a <CFQUERY> tag, as long as the final result is well-formed SQL.

In the guest book example, print out all rows if there is no value specified in the variable VARIABLES.SearchName. In the following code, the WHERE clause will always be appended to the SQL statement, even if VARIABLES.SearchName was empty.

```
<CFSET SearchName = "">
<CFQUERY NAME="qGetGuests" DATASOURCE="learncfe" DEBUG>
    SELECT GuestName, Email
    FROM Guestbook
    WHERE GuestName = '#VARIABLES.SearchName#'
</CFQUERY>
```

This would not work properly because it will look for all rows in which the GuestName column is the empty string. If you only wanted to include the WHERE clause if VARIABLES.SearchName has a value, you would want to use conditional processing. In this example, the <CFIF> tag is used around the WHERE clause.

```
<CFSET SearchName = "">
<CFQUERY NAME="qGetGuests" DATASOURCE="learncfe">
    SELECT GuestName, Email
    FROM Guestbook
    <CFIF Variables.SearchName IS NOT "">
        WHERE GuestName = '#VARIABLES.SearchName#'
    </CFIF>
</CFQUERY>
```

If VARIABLES.SearchName is not empty, use the WHERE clause. Otherwise, do not use a WHERE clause at all. This is difficult to see unless you have the ability to view the resulting SQL statement. You can do so by using the DEBUG option to view the resulting SQL.

Spaces in Values

Spaces are seen as true characters in SQL. Therefore, the string "John Doe" is not equivalent to " John Doe ". The extra spaces would be searched for. Therefore, it is always a good idea to use the Trim() function to trim off any leading or trailing spaces, as in the following:

```
<CFSET SearchName = "">
<CFQUERY NAME="qGetGuests" DATASOURCE="learncfe" DEBUG>
    SELECT GuestName, Email
    FROM Guestbook
    <CFIF VARIABLES.SearchName IS NOT "">
        WHERE GuestName = '#Trim(VARIABLES.SearchName)#'
    </CFIF>
</CFQUERY>
```

To Do: Using Conditional Logic in Queries

▼ To Do

Follow these steps to create a dynamic query using conditional processing inside the `<CFQUERY>` tag. This query will return information from the `Guestbook` table.

1. Return to HomeSite and the file /learncfe/Hour14/dynamic_query.cfm.

2. Inside the `<CFQUERY>` tag, surround the `WHERE` clause with a `<CFIF>` block. Test to be sure that the value of `VARIABLES.SearchName` is not the empty string. The code should look as follows:

```
<CFQUERY NAME="qGetGuests" DATASOURCE="learncfe" DEBUG>
    SELECT GuestName, Email
    FROM Guestbook
    <CFIF VARIABLES.SearchName IS NOT "">
        WHERE GuestName = '#Trim(VARIABLES.SearchName)#'
    </CFIF>
</CFQUERY>
```

3. Save the page and browse to it. You should see the row (or rows) of data, which has a `Guestname` that you specified in the variable.

4. Return to HomeSite and change the `<CFSET>` tag. Change the variable value to the empty string (`""`).

5. Save the page and browse to it. You should now see all rows displayed because the `WHERE` clause was not appended.

Compound Logic

In the following example, there is only one filter to the `SELECT` statement in the `WHERE` clause:

```
SELECT GuestName, Email
FROM Guestbook
WHERE GuestName = 'John Doe'
```

However, if you have multiple filters, you would add additional statements using the `AND` or `OR` clause. The first condition must always start with the `WHERE` clause, but there must only be one. If you wanted to find those guests who stumbled on your site and thought it was great, you would use the following compound `WHERE` clause using `AND`:

```
SELECT GuestName, Email
FROM Guestbook
WHERE GotHere = 'stumbled'
AND Rating = 'great'
```

14

When you dynamically build SELECT statements that have variable filters, you need to make sure that the first one uses the WHERE clause and the subsequent ones use AND or OR. Consider the following example:

```
<CFSET NavMethod = "stumbled">
<CFSET SiteRating = "great">

<CFQUERY NAME="qGetGuests" DATASOURCE="learncfe">
    SELECT GuestName, Email
    FROM Guestbook
    WHERE GotHere = '#VARIABLES.NavMethod#'
    AND Rating = '#VARIABLES.SiteRating#'
</CFQUERY>
```

If you wanted to only use these filters when the variables (NavMethod and SiteRating) were not empty, you would use conditional processing to conditionally append the WHERE and the AND clauses, as in the following:

```
<CFSET NavMethod = "stumbled">
<CFSET SiteRating = "great">

<CFQUERY NAME="qGetGuests" DATASOURCE="learncfe">
    SELECT GuestName, Email
    FROM Guestbook
    <CFIF VARIABLES.NavMethod IS NOT "">
        WHERE GotHere = '#VARIABLES.NavMethod#'
    </CFIF>
    <CFIF VARIABLES.NavMethod IS NOT "">
        AND Rating = '#VARIABLES.SiteRating#'
    </CFIF>
</CFQUERY>
```

This works fine if both the variables are either not empty or empty. However, consider if NavMethod was empty, but SiteRating was not:

```
<CFSET NavMethod = "">
<CFSET SiteRating = "great">

<CFQUERY NAME="qGetGuests" DATASOURCE="learncfe">
    SELECT GuestName, Email
    FROM Guestbook
    <CFIF VARIABLES.NavMethod IS NOT "">
        WHERE GotHere = '#VARIABLES.NavMethod#'
    </CFIF>
    <CFIF VARIABLES.SiteRating IS NOT "">
        AND Rating = '#VARIABLES.SiteRating#'
    </CFIF>
</CFQUERY>
```

The resulting SQL statement would have the AND clause, but not the WHERE clause, as in the following:

```
SELECT GuestName, Email
FROM Guestbook
AND Rating = 'great'
```

This is ill-formed SQL and will result in an error from the database. If you have the scenario in which the entire WHERE clause is a variable, you can perform a tricky shortcut to ensure that your SQL is well-formed. Because the first filter must be a WHERE clause, you can append a dummy clause on to it to ensure that it always exists. A dummy clause must always be true; therefore, it will never actually filter data. One such true statement is for a column to be equal to itself. Choosing the primary key column for the Guestbook table, the dummy WHERE clause might be

```
WHERE GuestBook_ID = GuestBook_ID
```

This statement will always be true, and will not affect that data returned. But it is a placeholder for the WHERE clause, and all other variable clauses can be appended using the AND or the OR clause without any special programming on your end. The resulting logic would be as follows:

```
<CFSET NavMethod = "">
<CFSET SiteRating = "great">

<CFQUERY NAME="qGetGuest" DATASOURCE="learncfe">
    SELECT GuestName, Email
    FROM Guestbook
    WHERE GuestBook_ID = GuestBook_ID
    <CFIF VARIABLES.NavMethod IS NOT "">
        AND GotHere = '#VARIABLES.NavMethod#'
    </CFIF>
    <CFIF VARIABLES.SiteRating IS NOT "">
        AND Rating = '#VARIABLES.SiteRating#'
    </CFIF>
</CFQUERY>
```

The static portion of the SELECT statement would always be valid and well-formed, and the rest of the clauses can be appended optionally.

As long as the statement is always evaluated to true, you can use it. For instance, you could also use "WHERE 0=0", which will always be evaluated to true and therefore will have the same effect.

14

> If you are using a series of OR clauses instead of AND clauses, you'll want the statement to be false instead of true. In those cases, use something like "WHERE 1=0".

Viewing SQL Debugging

As discussed in Hour 2, "Getting Started," ColdFusion Express contains a wealth of debugging information for helping you debug your pages. Two options are used specifically for debugging your SQL statements. These options are available in the ColdFusion Administrator server menu group under the debug settings, as shown in Figure 14.3.

FIGURE 14.3

The ColdFusion Administrator allows you to enable debugging information to be displayed on your pages.

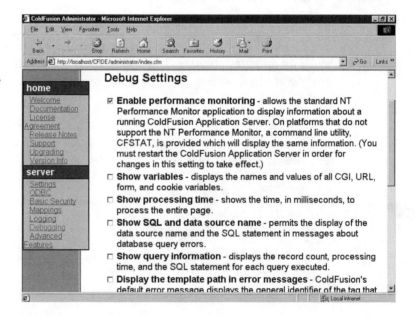

Two debugging options that will enable you to view information as you communicate with your data sources are as follows:

- Show SQL and data source name—This option permits the display of the data source name and the SQL statement in messages about database query errors.

- Show query information—This option displays the record count, processing time, and the SQL statement for each query executed.

The first option is useful for debugging errors because it will show the resulting SQL statement as it was sent to the database. The result will look similar to Figure 14.4.

FIGURE 14.4

Enabling the Show SQL *and* data source name *debug option displays the resulting SQL statement that caused an error.*

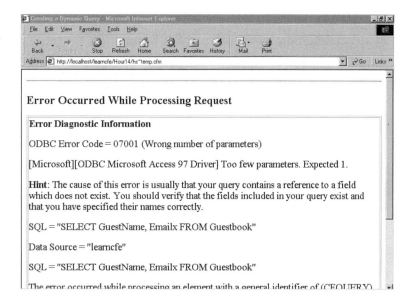

The second option shows query information about each successful query, including the resulting SQL. The debug output is similar to Figure 14.5.

FIGURE 14.5

Enabling the Show query information *debug option displays the resulting SQL statement and query information.*

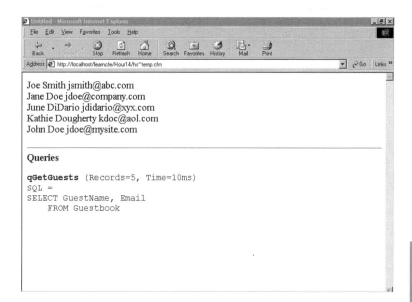

14

> **Debugging Information Is Not Secure**
>
> When you enable debugging, you open up your database information to anyone who browses to the page. Be sure to limit the output of debugging information to only those in development; don't use it at all on a production server.

To Do: Enable and View Debugging Information

Follow these steps to enable SQL debugging and view information about the query as you execute your page.

1. Launch the ColdFusion Administrator by selecting the Start Menu, and choosing Programs, ColdFusion Server 4.5, ColdFusion Administrator.

2. Choose the Debugging option under the Server group in the menu.

3. Be sure that the following two debugging options are checked: Show SQL and data source name and Show query information. Click Apply at the bottom of the page.

4. Return to HomeSite and the file /learncfe/Hour14/dynamic_query.cfm.

5. Browse to the file. Note the debugging information at the bottom of the page. Your SQL statement should not have a WHERE clause, but it should appear as follows:
```
SELECT GuestName, Email
    FROM Guestbook
```

6. Return to HomeSite and change the <CFSET> tag back to a valid guest name in your guestbook.

7. Save the page and browse to it. You should now see the resulting SQL statement with the WHERE clause appended.

Using URL Parameters in Queries

Thus far we have only used simple page variables for dynamic values in our SQL. This is still hardcoded and therefore less useful. A typical way to get dynamic input to generate dynamic SQL is using URL parameters or form input. You will learn to use form data in Hour 16.

You learned how to work with URLs and URL parameters in Hour 8, "Working with Links." Here, we will use URL parameters to describe the data we want displayed on the page. These URL parameters will be used within the <CFQUERY> tag as a filter for the SELECT statement.

Consider an example using the Guestbook table. Guests were asked to fill information about their site visit into the form. One such piece of information is how they got to the site. Figure 14.6 shows you the SELECT box dropped down with the three choices.

FIGURE 14.6

The Guest Book form prompts for how the user got to the site.

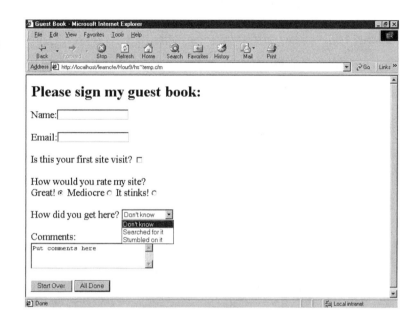

Three values to choose from are as follows:

- Don't know
- Searched for it
- Stumbled on it

These three options in the SELECT control were given values of unknown, search, or stumbled, respectively. These values are inserted into the database based on the user selection.

If you want to get a list of guests based on how they got to your site, you could create a page with these three categories as hyperlinks. Each of the hyperlinks could point to the same page, which will print out the guests who indicated that choice. Even though you are trying to create three separate reports, you only need to create two pages because the pages will be dynamic. These two pages are

- Navigation Options page— Allows them to choose which group of guests they would like to see.
- Navigation Report page—Contains a dynamic query that can accept any of the three options and generate a dynamic report.

14

Navigation Options Page

This page contains three hyperlinks, one for each of the three options you might want to see a report on. Listing 14.2 creates the three hyperlinks

LISTING 14.2   Navigation Options Page

```
 1: <!DOCTYPE HTML PUBLIC "-//W3C//DTD HTML 4.0 Transitional//EN">
 2: <html>
 3: <head>
 4:     <title>Navigation Options</title>
 5: </head>
 6: <body>
 7:     <H2>Generate Navigation Report</H2>
 8:     <A HREF="navigation_report.cfm">Don't Know</A><BR>
 9:     <A HREF="navigation_report.cfm">Searched for it</A><BR>
10:     <A HREF="navigation_report.cfm">Stumbled on it</A><BR>
11: </body>
12: </html>
```

Pass a URL parameter into the navigation_report.cfm page to generate the list of guests who came to the site using each method. This parameter, here called NavMethod, will take the value of unknown, search, or stumbled, depending on which hyperlink the user chooses. The code that has changed is highlighted in Listing 14.3.

LISTING 14.3   Navigation Options Page with URL Parameters

```
 1: <!DOCTYPE HTML PUBLIC "-//W3C//DTD HTML 4.0 Transitional//EN">
 2:
 3: <html>
 4: <head>
 5:     <title>Navigation Options</title>
 6: </head>
 7:
 8: <body>
 9:     <H2>Generate Navigation Report</H2>
10:     <A HREF="navigation_report.cfm?NavMethod=unknown">Don't Know</A><BR>
11:     <A HREF="navigation_report.cfm?NavMethod=search">Searched for it</A><BR>
12:     <A HREF="navigation_report.cfm?NavMethod=stumbled">Stumbled on
     ➥it</A><BR>
13: </body>
14: </html>
```

The output is a simple page with three hyperlinks, as shown in Figure 14.7.

FIGURE 14.7

The Navigation Options page will allow the user to choose which group of guests the user wants to see.

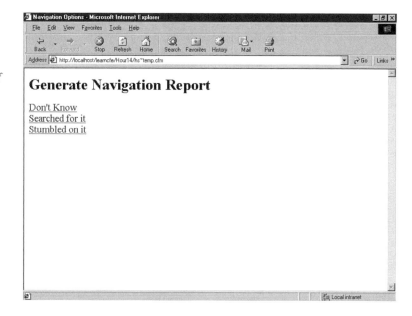

To Do: Creating a Hyperlink Page

Follow these steps to create a set of hyperlinks that pass information to a linked page for use in a dynamic query.

1. Return to HomeSite and make sure that the Local Files tab is pointing to the /learncfe/hour14 directory.

2. Create a new page using the default template.

3. Change the `<TITLE>` text to `"Generate Navigation Report"`.

4. Save the file as **navigation_options.cfm**.

5. Create a level 2 header for the page as "Generate Navigation Report".

6. Create three hyperlinks using the `<A>` tag that all point to the same page, navigation_report.cfm. Refer to the following code if you need to:

```
<A HREF="navigation_report.cfm">Don't Know</A><BR>
<A HREF="navigation_report.cfm">Searched for it</A><BR>
<A HREF="navigation_report.cfm">Stumbled on it</A><BR>
```

7. At the end of each `HREF` value, append a URL parameter called `NavMethod`, and set it equal to `unknown`, `search`, or `stumbled` based on the hyperlink text. The following code reflects this change:

```
<A HREF="navigation_report.cfm?NavMethod=unknown">Don't Know</A><BR>
<A HREF="navigation_report.cfm?NavMethod=search">Searched for it</A><BR>
<A HREF="navigation_report.cfm?NavMethod=stumbled">Stumbled on it</A><BR>
```

To Do

14

▼ You will receive an error if you try to run this page at this time because the linked
page doesn't yet exist. We'll do that in a minute. The complete code is shown in
Listing 14.4.

LISTING 14.4   Creating a Hyperlink Page with the Navigation Report

```
 1: <!DOCTYPE HTML PUBLIC "-//W3C//DTD HTML 4.0 Transitional//EN">
 2:
 3: <html>
 4: <head>
 5:     <title>Generate Navigation Report</title>
 6: </head>
 7:
 8: <body>
 9: <H2>Generate Navigation Report</H2>
10: <A HREF="navigation_report.cfm?NavMethod=unknown">Don't Know</A><BR>
11: <A HREF="navigation_report.cfm?NavMethod=search">Searched for it</A><BR>
12: <A HREF="navigation_report.cfm?NavMethod=stumbled">Stumbled on it</A><BR>
13:
14: </body>
15: </html>
```

▲

Navigation Report Page

The Navigation Report page will accept the URL parameter, NavMethod, that was passed
in and use it to generate the dynamic SELECT statement for the correct rows in the database. It will be used as a filter on the GotHere column:

```
<CFQUERY NAME="qGetNavigationReport" DATASOURCE="learncfe">
    SELECT GuestName, Email
    FROM Guestbook
    WHERE GotHere = '#Trim(URL.NavMethod)#';
</CFQUERY>
```

This will work, but only if the user always uses a hyperlink from the
navigation_options.cfm page. Therefore, you always want to safeguard your applications
from errors by performing some error handling to test for the existence of the URL parameters.

Assume that you would like to return all rows if the URL parameter is not specified. You
could use the <CFPARAM> tag to create the URL parameter if it doesn't exist and initialize
it to the empty string. Then, inside the <CFQUERY> tag, you could include the WHERE
clause only if the URL parameter is not empty. The code would be as follows:

```
<CFPARAM NAME="URL.NavMethod" DEFAULT="">
<CFQUERY NAME="qGetNavigationReport" DATASOURCE="learncfe">
```

```
      SELECT GuestName, Email
      FROM Guestbook
      <CFIF URL.NavMethod IS NOT "">
          WHERE GotHere = '#Trim(URL.NavMethod)#';
      </CFIF>
</CFQUERY>
```

To Do: Creating a Navigation Report

▼ To Do

Follow these steps to create a Navigation Report that uses the URL parameter to generate the dynamic SQL.

1. Return to HomeSite and make sure that the Local Files tab is pointing to the /learncfe/hour14 directory.

2. Create a new page using the default template.

3. Change the `<TITLE>` text to `"Navigation Report"`.

4. Save the file as **navigation_report.cfm**.

5. Create a level 2 header for the page called Navigation Report.

6. Between the `<BODY>` and `</BODY>` tags, create a `<CFQUERY>` tag that returns the GuestName and Email columns from the Guestbook table. Refer to the following code if you need help:

   ```
   <CFQUERY NAME="qGetNavigationReport" DATASOURCE="learncfe">
       SELECT GuestName, Email
       FROM Guestbook
   </CFQUERY>
   ```

7. Use the `<CFOUTPUT>` tag to print out the columns you've selected. Refer to the following code for help:

   ```
   <!---Print out the results from the qGetGuests query --->
   <CFOUTPUT QUERY="qGetNavigationReport">
       #qGetNavigationReport.GuestName# #qGetNavigationReport.Email#<BR>
   </CFOUTPUT>
   ```

8. Save the page and test it by browsing the navigation_options.cfm page. Choose any hyperlink and you should see all rows displayed. You will now make it return only the data for the navigation method chosen.

9. Return to the navigation_report.cfm page.

10. Add a `<CFPARAM>` tag to the top of the page that creates and initializes the variable URL.NavMethod if it doesn't exist. Set the default to the empty string (`""`).

    ```
    <CFPARAM NAME="URL.NavMethod" DEFAULT="">
    ```

▼

14

▼ 11. Change the `<CFQUERY>` tag to add a `WHERE` clause that uses the `URL.NavMethod` variable in a search for the `GotHere` column. Refer to the following code for help:

```
<CFQUERY NAME="qGetNavigationReport" DATASOURCE="learncfe" DEBUG>
    SELECT GuestName, Email
    FROM Guestbook
    WHERE GotHere = '#Trim(URL.NavMethod)#'
</CFQUERY>
```

12. Surround the `WHERE` clause with a conditional block. Only include the `WHERE` clause if the URL parameter isn't empty.

13. Save the file and browse through navigation_option.cfm. Try each of the hyperlinks to be sure that they all work and the resulting SQL is as expected. The complete code is shown in Listing 14.5.

LISTING 14.5   Final Navigation Report Code

```
 1: <!DOCTYPE HTML PUBLIC "-//W3C//DTD HTML 4.0 Transitional//EN">
 2:
 3: <html>
 4: <head>
 5:     <title>Navigation Report</title>
 6: </head>
 7:
 8: <body>
 9:
10: <CFPARAM NAME="URL.NavMethod" DEFAULT="">
11:
12: <CFQUERY NAME="qGetNavigationReport" DATASOURCE="learncfe">
13:     SELECT GuestName, Email
14:     FROM Guestbook
15:     <CFIF Trim(URL.NavMethod) IS NOT "">
16:         WHERE GotHere = '#Trim(URL.NavMethod)#'
17:     </CFIF>
18: </CFQUERY>
19:
20: <!---Print out the results from the qGetGuests query --->
21: <CFOUTPUT QUERY="qGetNavigationReport">
22:     #qGetNavigationReport.GuestName# #qGetNavigationReport.Email#<BR>
23: </CFOUTPUT>
24: </body>
25: </html>
```

▲

Summary

During this hour, you learned that you can use variables and conditional logic inside the `<CFQUERY>` tag to create dynamic queries. You used both page variables and URL variables to generate dynamic SELECT statements. You will take this further in the next few hours to incorporate user input from forms that enable you to create rich search interfaces.

Q&A

Q In the Navigation Methods report, the hyperlinks were hardcoded. How could I see other methods in the returned data if I added the options to the Guest Book form?

A Because the Navigation Options page is hardcoded with hyperlinks, you would need to manually add any options and hyperlinks to this page to see additional data. Whenever you have a hardcoded page that goes against a database, we suggest making all of it dynamic when possible. You will begin to learn in the next hour how to make even the hyperlink page dynamic.

Q You showed using `<CFIF>` statement inside of a `<CFQUERY>` tag. Can other tags be used there too?

A Actually, yes. Other flow control tags (like `<CFLOOP>`) can be used within your SQL statement.

Workshop

The Workshop contains quiz questions and an exercise to help reinforce what you've learned in this hour. If you get stuck, the answers to the quiz questions can be found in Appendix A, "Answers to Quiz."

Quiz

1. What kind of ColdFusion variable types can you use in constructing SQL statements?

2. *True or false*: Whitespace is insignificant in SQL statements.

3. How can you determine how long it took to execute a query?

14

Exercise

1. Create a <CFQUERY> tag that prints out a few columns from the Guestbook table. Make each column heading a hyperlink that points to the same page. For each clickable column, create a URL parameter to pass in the name of the column to order the data by. Inside the <CFQUERY> tag, use the URL parameter to sort the data using an ORDER BY clause. Hint: You need to be able to handle a default sort order (for when one is not specified).

HOUR 15

Displaying Dynamic Pages

During Hour 14, you created an interface that allowed a narrow selection of choices for grouping guests by how they arrived at your site. In that example, you allowed users to drill down from a narrow set of data to see more details. In this hour, you'll create more interfaces like these, known as a drill-down interface.

In this lesson, you'll learn the following:

- When to create drill-down interfaces
- How to use URL parameters in SELECT statements
- Creating drill downs using frames
- Using Next-N interfaces

Understanding Drill-Down Interfaces

Good user interface design dictates that you should be careful not to overwhelm the user with too much information at once. Common sense dictates that a screen packed with information is hard to read and might contain more data than is necessary at the time. Retrieving too much data can also slow down the performance of the application and sour the user experience.

Consider the page of guest information shown in Figure 15.1. This page shows all guests who have signed the guest book. There is a lot of data on the page, which will only get worse as more guests sign the guest book.

FIGURE 15.1

This page shows too much information, and the user is likely to be overwhelmed with data she doesn't need to see all at once.

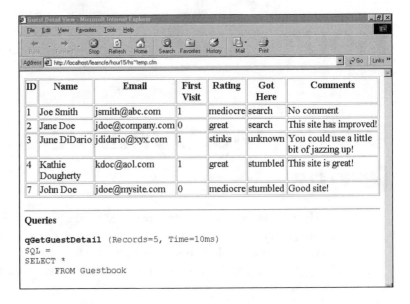

The key to interface design is to know your users and understand their needs. You need to determine what data they need, and when. For instance, perhaps the key data for looking at the guests is to see their name and email. These two columns of data won't overwhelm the user, but will contain the key information she needs. This page is depicted in Figure 15.2.

If you wanted to show this abbreviated list of guest information and then allow the user to get more details, you could create an interface called a drill-down interface. A *drill-down interface* displays an abbreviated list of information and allows the user to click on the row he wants to see more information about. Clicking on the row will then display the full detail about that row. Figure 15.3 shows a simple drill-down interface.

FIGURE 15.2

Showing only the data that the user needs makes for a cleaner, more readable interface.

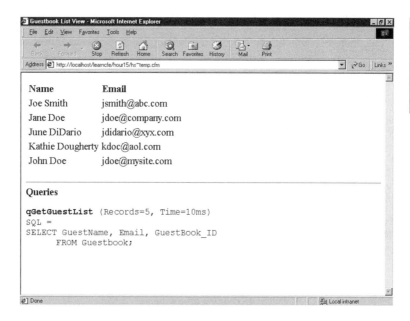

FIGURE 15.3

By clicking on a row of data, the details about that row are displayed.

As you learned in the last hour, you can use the anchor (<A>) tag and pass URL parameters to tell the target page what information you want to be displayed. Here we will use anchor tags to allow navigation through a drill-down interface.

Drill-Down Pages

A drill-down interface involves creating two pages:

- List view of data
- Detail view about one item on the List view

The List view page contains an abbreviated set of information about some data in your database. This list will be used as a set of hyperlinks that allow the display of the full details about the selected row.

The List Page

With guest book information, the most necessary pieces of data are made into a list. A List view might be as shown in Figure 15.4.

FIGURE **15.4**

The List view of guest book information includes the guest's name and email address.

Start by selecting the two columns in a <CFQUERY> tag. Print out each row of data. (We've made it easier to read by using simple formatting, but you would probably want to create a table.)

```
<CFQUERY NAME="qGetGuestList" DATASOURCE="learncfe">
    SELECT GuestName, Email
    FROM Guestbook;
</CFQUERY>

<CFOUTPUT QUERY="qGetGuestList">
    #qGetGuestList.GuestName# #qGetGuestList.Email#<BR>
</CFOUTPUT>
```

Each row of data (or at least one column in one row) is created as a hyperlink. This hyperlink points to the Detail view page. Here we will surround all three columns with an <A> tag to create a hyperlink that points to a detail page.

```
<CFQUERY NAME="qGetGuestList" DATASOURCE="learncfe">
    SELECT GuestName, Email, GotHere
    FROM Guestbook;
</CFQUERY>

<CFOUTPUT QUERY="qGetGuestList">
    <A HREF="guest_detail.cfm">
        #qGetGuestList.GuestName# #qGetGuestList.Email#
    </A><BR>
</CFOUTPUT>
```

The output is a list of data created as hyperlinks to the detail page, as shown in Figure 15.5.

FIGURE 15.5

Each row of data is created as a hyperlink to link to the detail information.

We are now ready to create the Detail view page and get information passed between the two pages.

To Do: Creating a Dynamic Query

Follow these steps to create a List view page in a drill-down interface.

1. Go into HomeSite and make sure that your Local Files tab is pointing to the /learncfe/hour15 directory under your Web root directory.

2. Create a new page using the default template.

3. Change the <TITLE> text to "Guest Book List View".

4. Save the page as **guest_list.cfm**.

5. Create a query to return the following two columns from the Guestbook table: GuestName and Email. Refer to Listing 15.1 for any help.

6. After the <CFQUERY> tag, create a <CFOUTPUT> tag to print out these two columns, using a simple <BR> tag to separate each line of data.

7. Save the file and browse to it to be sure that it works.

8. Return to HomeSite and put an <A> tag around both the name and email displayed columns. This will be the text in between the opening <A> and the closing </A> tags. Set the HREF attribute to the following page: guest_detail.cfm.

You will be modifying this page in the next section.

LISTING 15.1   Drill-Down Interface

```
 1: <!DOCTYPE HTML PUBLIC "-//W3C//DTD HTML 4.0 Transitional//EN">
 2:
 3: <html>
 4: <head>
 5:     <title>Guestbook List View</title>
 6: </head>
 7:
 8: <body>
 9: <CFQUERY NAME="qGetGuestList" DATASOURCE="learncfe">
10:     SELECT GuestName, Email
11:     FROM Guestbook;
12: </CFQUERY>
13:
14: <CFOUTPUT QUERY="qGetGuestList">
15:     <A HREF="guest_detail.cfm">
16:         #qGetGuestList.GuestName# #qGetGuestList.Email#
17:     </A><BR>
18: </CFOUTPUT>
19: </body>
20: </html>
```

▲

Detail View Page

The Detail view page will display the full details about the one row of data that was selected. Consider the SELECT statement to return all columns from the Guestbook table for one particular row:

```
<CFQUERY NAME="qGetGuestList" DATASOURCE="learncfe">
    SELECT *
    FROM Guestbook
    WHERE ...;
</CFQUERY>
```

In the WHERE clause, you need to specify which row to return. In order to find a particular row, this requires that you know a unique identifier for the row (hyperlink) you have clicked for use in the WHERE clause. Can you remember what we described as a unique identifier for each row in a table? Back in Hour 11, "Connecting to a Database," you learned about a primary key. A *primary key* is a column or set of columns that uniquely identifies each row in a table. Therefore, the primary key is well suited to identify the row to view details about. The primary key for the Guestbook table is a auto-generated number called GuestBook_ID. The List view page SELECT statement should be amended to include this identifier:

```
<CFQUERY NAME="qGetGuestList" DATASOURCE="learncfe">
    SELECT GuestName, Email, GuestBook_ID
    FROM Guestbook;
</CFQUERY>
```

Because we are using hyperlinks to navigate between the two pages, passing this key as a URL parameter works nicely. The List view page can be changed to include this GuestBook_ID identifier as a URL parameter. In this case, we are creating a URL parameter called GID and setting it equal to the value of the GuestBook_ID column for each hyperlink created.

```
<CFOUTPUT QUERY="qGetGuestList">
    <A HREF="guest_detail.cfm?GID=#qGetGuestList.GuestBook_ID#">
        #qGetGuestList.GuestName# #qGetGuestList.Email#
    </A><BR>
</CFOUTPUT>
```

Now the Detail view page can use the URL parameter in the SELECT statement in the dynamic query, as in the following:

```
 <CFQUERY NAME="qGetGuestDetail " DATASOURCE="learncfe" DEBUG>
    SELECT *
    FROM Guestbook
    WHERE GuestBook_ID = #URL.GID#;
</CFQUERY>
```

You will always want to fool-proof your applications, just in case a user navigates to the Detail page without going through the List page. In this case, the URL parameter won't exist, and an error will occur. Add a test to see if the URL parameter exists, and if it doesn't, display "No guest selected". (You learned about URL parameters and testing for existence in Hour 8, "Working with Links.") This test should be placed above the <CFQUERY> tag, and the query should not be performed if it doesn't exist. The following <CFIF> logic will do this for you:

```
<CFIF NOT IsDefined("URL.GID")>
    No guest selected!
<CFELSE>
    <CFQUERY NAME="qGetGuestDetail" DATASOURCE="learncfe" DEBUG>
        SELECT *
        FROM Guestbook
        WHERE GuestBook_ID = #URL.GID#;
    </CFQUERY>
    <!---print out the guest detail --->
</CFIF>
```

To Do: Creating the Detail View Page

Follow these steps to create a Detail view page in a drill-down interface.

1. Go into HomeSite and make sure that your Local Files tab is pointing to the /learncfe/hour15 directory under your Web root directory.

2. Create a new page using the default template.

3. Change the <TITLE> text to "Guest Book Detail View".

4. Save the page as **guest_detail.cfm**.

5. Create a query to return all columns from Guestbook. Refer to the following code for any help.

```
<CFQUERY NAME="qGetGuestDetail" DATASOURCE="learncfe">
    SELECT *
    FROM Guestbook;
</CFQUERY>
```

6. Surround the <CFQUERY> tag with a <CFIF> block. Put the <CFQUERY> inside the <CFELSE> condition.

7. Make the <CFIF> condition test for existence of the URL.GID parameter using the IsDefined() function. If it doesn't exist, display the message "No guest selected!".

▼ 8. Following the <CFQUERY> tag, create a <CFOUTPUT> tag to print out all columns, using a simple <BR> tag to separate each line of data.

```
<CFOUTPUT QUERY="qGetGuestDetail">
    #qGetGuestDetail.GuestBook_ID# #qGetGuestDetail.GuestName#
    #qGetGuestDetail.Email# #qGetGuestDetail.FirstVisit#
    #qGetGuestDetail.Rating# #qGetGuestDetail.GotHere#
    #qGetGuestDetail.Comments#<BR>
</CFOUTPUT>
```

9. Save the file and browse to it to be sure that it works. Browse from the guest_list.cfm page and click any hyperlink. The Detail view should be displayed, but should display all rows at this time.

10. Return to the guest_list.cfm page.

11. Amend the SQL statement to add the GuestBook_ID column to the SELECT list. Refer to Listing 15.2 for help.

12. Amend the <A> tags to pass a URL parameter called GID. Set this parameter equal to the query's GuestBook_ID column. See Listing 15.3 for help.

13. Save the file and browse it. Each hyperlink should now pass the GuestBook_ID value for the row when clicked.

14. Return to the guest_detail.cfm page.

15. Add a WHERE clause to the SELECT statement that uses the URL.GID parameter to return only one row of data.

16. Save the file and browse from guest_list.cfm. You should now be able to click each row and return only that row's full details in the Detail view page.

You'll probably want to clean up the look of the output, but the drill-down interface should be fully functional.

LISTING 15.2   Guest Book List View

```
1:<!DOCTYPE HTML PUBLIC "-//W3C//DTD HTML 4.0 Transitional//EN">
2:
3:<html>
4:<head>
5:<title>Guestbook List View</title>
6:</head>
7:
8:<body>
9:<CFQUERY NAME="qGetGuestList" DATASOURCE="learncfe">
▼ 10:SELECT GuestName, Email, GuestBook_ID
```

▼

LISTING 15.2   continued

```
11:FROM Guestbook;
12:</CFQUERY>
13:
14:<CFOUTPUT QUERY="qGetGuestList">
15:<A HREF="guest_detail.cfm?GID=#qGetGuestList.GuestBook_ID#">
16:#qGetGuestList.GuestName# #qGetGuestList.Email#
17:</A><BR>
18:</CFOUTPUT>
19:</body>
20:</html>
```

LISTING 15.3   Guest Detail View

```
 1:<!DOCTYPE HTML PUBLIC "-//W3C//DTD HTML 4.0 Transitional//EN">
 2:
 3:<html>
 4:<head>
 5:<title>Guest Detail View</title>
 6:</head>
 7:
 8:<body>
 9:<CFIF NOT IsDefined("URL.GID")>
10:No guest selected!
11:<CFELSE>
12:<CFQUERY NAME="qGetGuestDetail" DATASOURCE="learncfe">
13:SELECT *
14:FROM Guestbook
15:WHERE GuestBook_ID = #URL.GID#;
16:</CFQUERY>
17:
18:<CFOUTPUT QUERY="qGetGuestDetail">
19:Guest Book ID: #qGetGuestDetail.GuestBook_ID# <BR>
20:Guest Name: #qGetGuestDetail.GuestName#<BR>
21:Email: #qGetGuestDetail.Email#<BR>
22:First Visit: #qGetGuestDetail.FirstVisit#<BR>
23:Rating: #qGetGuestDetail.Rating#<BR>
24:Got Here: #qGetGuestDetail.GotHere#<BR>
25:Comments: #qGetGuestDetail.Comments#<BR>
26:</CFOUTPUT>
27:</CFIF>
28:
29:</body>
30:</html>
```

▲

Creating Drill Downs Using Frames

One problem with the drill down we've just created is that every time you view a guest's details, you have to click the browser's Back button to return to the List page. A more usable approach would be to display the guest list and details at the same time. Fortunately, you can do so easily by using a browser feature called frames. Using frames, you can split your browser window in two or more windows and control what gets displayed within each. ColdFusion Express templates are well suited for use within frames. Figure 15.6 depicts a frame set with two windows.

FIGURE 15.6

This frame set has two windows that allow you to view two templates at once.

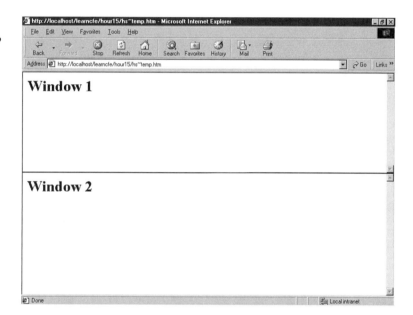

Frame Options

In Figure 15.6, the frames were created with scroll bars and borders. Frames allow you to use many different attributes to control the look and feel of your frames. Refer to the *Sams Teach Yourself HomeSite 4 in 24 Hours* (ISBN: 0672315602) book for more details.

Creating frames involves creating multiple templates. Each window in a frame typically displays a different template. If you have two windows, you need two templates. In addition, you always need one more page that is used to lay out and create the frames. In our example, there would be a total of three pages needed, one for each frame and one for the frame set definition.

When you create the frames, each window is named with a unique name. In a non-framed window, every time you select a hyperlink, the new page is opened in the same window, replacing whatever contents were there previously. In a framed window, you can use the window name to control the destination for any output. The key here is that by using frames, a single browser can display multiple Web pages at once, one in each frame; and each frame can be updated independently of the others.

The Frame Tags

Frames, either using straight HTML or using CFML, are created by using the following tags:

- The <FRAMESET> tag creates a new set of frames and defines the number of frames in a frame set. This is a block tag and should be terminated by using the </FRAMESET> tag.

- Within a frame set, individual frames are defined with the <FRAME> tag. One is specified for each frame in the set.

- The optional <NOFRAMES> and </NOFRAMES> tags can be used to specify text and HTML to be displayed by browsers that don't support frames.

There are other frame tags, but these are more specific to particular browsers and versions, so we'll skip those tags for now.

To demonstrate, let's look at the code for the two window frame set. This first block of code creates a simple frame set with two windows:

```
<FRAMESET ROWS="45%,*" FRAMEBORDER="1" BORDERCOLOR="Black">
    <FRAME SRC="frame1.cfm" NAME="Frame1" FRAMEBORDER="0" SCROLLING="Yes"
    ➥MARGINWIDTH="10" MARGINHEIGHT="10">
    <FRAME SRC="frame2.cfm" NAME="Frame2" FRAMEBORDER="0" SCROLLING="Yes"
    ➥MARGINWIDTH="10" MARGINHEIGHT="10">
</FRAMESET>
```

This frame set creates two rows, or windows, for displaying separate pages. Each of the two pages are defined by the <FRAME> tags, which call the CFML pages named frame1.cfm and frame2.cfm, respectively. The first frame window takes up 45% of the vertical browser window space, and the second takes up the rest (specified using the asterisk) at 55%.

Guest Drill Down

Our goal will be to put the Guest List view in the top frame, and the detail about the selected guest in the bottom frame. In this interface, the user would need only to click different guests to see their detail on the same window. Figure 15.7 shows how this might look.

FIGURE 15.7

The Guest List is shown in the top frame, and the detail of the selected guest is shown in the bottom frame.

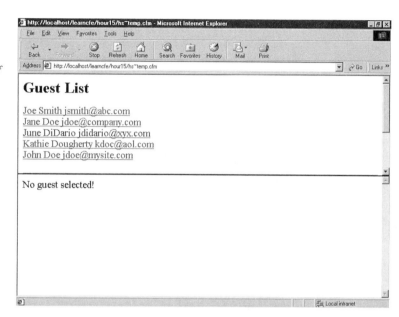

When the frame set first loads, both pages are loaded into the frame set. Because the user hasn't chosen a specific guest to look at, the text in the bottom frame is "No guest selected!". Each time a user chooses a guest by clicking the hyperlink, the bottom frame will get reloaded with the newest guest detail information.

Create the Frame Set

The first thing you'll need to do is create the frame set for use in the drill down. In this case, you will need to create three pages, one for the frame set itself and the other two for each frame's content. Because you have already created guest_list.cfm and guest_detail.cfm, you need only create the frameset page.

To create the frameset, create a new page, but do not use the default template. Other HTML tags are not allowed inside a frame definition file. Use the blank document and create the frame set. Design the look of the frame by deciding how big each frame will be. In our case, the List view will be slightly smaller than the Detail view frame. In this example, two frames are created:

```
<FRAMESET ROWS="45%,*" FRAMEBORDER="1" BORDERCOLOR="Black">
    <FRAME SRC="guest_list.cfm" NAME="List" FRAMEBORDER="0" SCROLLING="Yes"
    ➥MARGINWIDTH="10" MARGINHEIGHT="10">
```

```
<FRAME SRC="guest_detail.cfm" NAME="Details" FRAMEBORDER="0" SCROLLING="Yes"
➥ MARGINWIDTH="10" MARGINHEIGHT="10">
</FRAMESET>
```

The first frame uses the guest_list.cfm page as the source (SRC attribute). The name of the frame is designated as List, which will be used to target the pages. The second frame specifies the guest_detail.cfm page, and names the frame Details. Creating this frame set and browsing to it will yield the output as seen in Figure 15.8.

FIGURE 15.8

The Guest List is shown in the top frame, and the detail of the selected guest is shown in the bottom frame. For now, only the text "No guest selected!" *will appear in the bottom frame.*

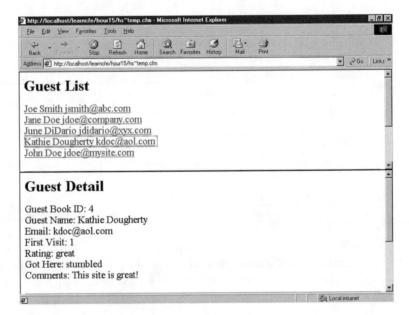

Change the Target Frame

The only change you have to make to the pages is to use the TARGET attribute of the <A> tag. This attributes specifies the frame to load the target page. The <A> tag is used in the List view page and specifies which page to load when you click a particular guest. Adding the TARGET attribute specifies where to put that target page. Assuming that the target frame is named Details, the following <A> tag will target that frame:

```
<CFOUTPUT QUERY="qGetGuestList">
    <A HREF="guest_detail.cfm?GID=#qGetGuestList.GuestBook_ID#"
TARGET="Details">
        #qGetGuestList.GuestName# #qGetGuestList.Email#
    </A><BR>
</CFOUTPUT>
```

Browsing to the frame set page will display both the List view and Detail view pages. For each list row that is clicked, the detail portion of the page will update with the latest information about that row.

To Do: Creating the Drill Down Using Frames

▲ To Do

Follow these steps to create a frame set for the drill down. Alter the guest_list.cfm page to add the TARGET attribute to the hyperlink for the detail page.

1. Go into HomeSite and make sure that your Local Files tab is pointing to the /learncfe/hour15 directory under your Web root directory.

2. Create a new page using the blank template.

3. Create a frame set with two frame windows, as specified in the following code. This can be made easier by using HomeSite's Frame Wizard, which can be found on the Frames Quick Bar. This wizard allows you to create the frame set by selecting options in a series of dialogs, the first of which is shown in Figure 15.9.

```
<FRAMESET ROWS="45%,*" FRAMEBORDER="1" BORDERCOLOR="Black">
    <FRAME SRC="guest_list_frame.cfm" NAME="List" FRAMEBORDER="0"
        SCROLLING="Yes" MARGINWIDTH="10" MARGINHEIGHT="10">
    <FRAME SRC="guest_detail.cfm" NAME="Details" FRAMEBORDER="0"
        SCROLLING="Yes" MARGINWIDTH="10" MARGINHEIGHT="10">
</FRAMESET>
```

FIGURE 15.9

HomeSite's Frame Wizard can simplify the creation of your frame sets.

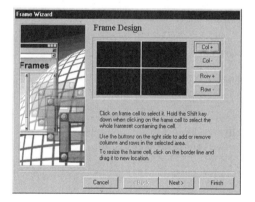

4. Save the page as **guest_drilldown.cfm**.

5. Browse the page to see that both pages are displayed in the frame windows. If you click a hyperlink, the incorrect frame window is changed.

6. Return to HomeSite. Open the file guest_list.cfm.

7. Select File, Save As and save the file as **guest_list_frame.cfm**.

▼ 8. Alter the `<A>` tag to add the TARGET attribute. Set the attribute equal to Details. (Be sure that this is what you named your frame window.)

9. Save the page and browse to it. When you click a hyperlink, the bottom frame should reload with the currently selected guest's details.

The full code listings for all three pages appear in Listings 15.4–15.6.

LISTING 15.4   guest_drilldown.cfm

```
1: <FRAMESET ROWS="45%,*" FRAMEBORDER="1" BORDERCOLOR="Black">
2:     <FRAME SRC="guest_list_frame.cfm" NAME="List" FRAMEBORDER="0"
   ➥SCROLLING="Yes" MARGINWIDTH="10" MARGINHEIGHT="10">
3:     <FRAME SRC="guest_detail.cfm" NAME="Details" FRAMEBORDER="0"
   ➥SCROLLING="Yes" MARGINWIDTH="10" MARGINHEIGHT="10">
4: </FRAMESET>
```

LISTING 15.5   guest_list_frame.cfm

```
1: <!DOCTYPE HTML PUBLIC "-//W3C//DTD HTML 4.0 Transitional//EN">
2:
3: <html>
4: <head>
5:     <title>Guestbook List View</title>
6: </head>
7:
8: <body>
9: <CFQUERY NAME="qGetGuestList" DATASOURCE="learncfe">
10:    SELECT GuestName, Email, GuestBook_ID
11:    FROM Guestbook;
12: </CFQUERY>
13:
14: <H2>Guest List</H2>
15: <CFOUTPUT QUERY="qGetGuestList">
16: <A HREF="guest_detail.cfm?GID=#qGetGuestList.GuestBook_ID#"
   ➥TARGET="Details">
17:        #qGetGuestList.GuestName# #qGetGuestList.Email#
18: </A>
19:   <BR>
20: </CFOUTPUT>
21: </body>
22: </html>
```

▼

LISTING 15.6   guest_detail.cfm

```
 1: <!DOCTYPE HTML PUBLIC "-//W3C//DTD HTML 4.0 Transitional//EN">
 2:
 3: <html>
 4: <head>
 5:     <title>Guest Detail View</title>
 6: </head>
 7:
 8: <body>
 9: <CFIF NOT IsDefined("URL.GID")>
10:     No guest selected!
11: <CFELSE>
12:     <CFQUERY NAME="qGetGuestDetail" DATASOURCE="learncfe">
13:         SELECT *
14:         FROM Guestbook
15:         WHERE GuestBook_ID = #URL.GID#;
16:     </CFQUERY>
17:     <H2>Guest Detail</H2>
18:     <CFOUTPUT QUERY="qGetGuestDetail">
19:         Guest Book ID: #qGetGuestDetail.GuestBook_ID# <BR>
20:         Guest Name: #qGetGuestDetail.GuestName#<BR>
21:         Email: #qGetGuestDetail.Email#<BR>
22:         First Visit: #qGetGuestDetail.FirstVisit#<BR>
23:         Rating: #qGetGuestDetail.Rating#<BR>
24:         Got Here: #qGetGuestDetail.GotHere#<BR>
25:         Comments: #qGetGuestDetail.Comments#<BR>
26:     </CFOUTPUT>
27: </CFIF>
28: </body>
29: </html>
```

Using Next-N Interfaces

Search sites such as Yahoo and AltaVista are used to search the entire Web to find text that you specify. There is an endless list of possible sites and references that can be returned. They don't show you a long, scrolling page of hyperlinks, but instead show you one page of links at a time. It is common to see text at the top of the page such as "Web Pages (1-20 of 841)". You click through the pages as you need them.

This is another form of data drill down, and is known as a next-n interface. A *next-n* interface displays only a small set of rows, but allows the users to go through the rows a set at a time. This functionality allows you to choose Next or Previous to move through the rows. This interface is useful when there are many rows in a database table. If the data rows were constantly being added, all rows might make for a very long scrolling page.

If you've been shopping on the Web, you've probably seen next-n interfaces. Most product catalogs are too long to display all at once. So the Web site categorizes the products as best they can, and then enables a next-n type interface to look through several products at a time.

Taking the Guest List view page, the interface could be modified to view only the first three guests at a time. The first page of data would resemble Figure 15.10.

FIGURE 15.10

A next-n interfaces displays a few rows at a time and allows the users to move through the rest using Next and Previous.

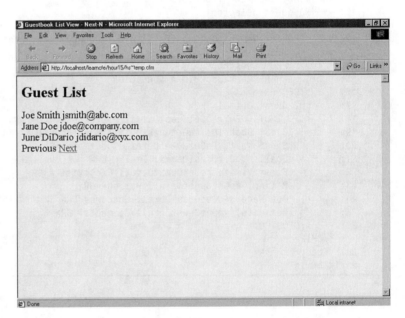

To create such an interface, you need to have the following two pieces of information:

- Start row—This number is the starting row number of the group that needs to be displayed.
- Max rows—This number is the number of rows to be displayed at one time.

As the user clicks through the application, you would have to make the program aware of the starting row number, and how many rows to display. For instance, to navigate through a list of 10 rows, the information supplied would be

- Page 1: Start Row = 1, Max Rows = 3
- Page 2: Start Row = 4, Max Rows = 3

- Page 3: Start Row = 7, Max Rows = 3
- Page 4: Start Row = 10, Max Rows = 3

In order to specify the starting row and how many rows to display at once, use the STARTROW and MAXROWS attributes of the <CFOUTPUT> tag, as shown in this code fragment:

```
<CFOUTPUT QUERY="qGetGuestList"
          STARTROW = 1
          MAXROWS = 3>
```

The number of rows to display at one time is fixed at 3 for this example. But the starting row will change for every time the user chooses to navigate backward or forward through the resultset. For this reason, the STARTROW attribute must be a variable, here named startrow:

```
<CFOUTPUT QUERY="qGetGuestList"
          STARTROW = #startrow#
          MAXROWS = 3>
```

Because the Next and Previous options are hyperlinks, the start row information can be sent as a URL parameter. For the first page load, initialize the URL.StartRow variable to 1:

```
<CFPARAM NAME="URL.StartRow" DEFAULT="1">
```

You want to return to the same page and just show a different set of rows. Create a set of hyperlinks that point back to the same page, as in the following:

```
<A HREF="guest_nextn.cfm">Previous</A>
<A HREF="guest_nextn.cfm">Next</A>
```

Now let's figure out how to calculate the starting row to pass on the URL. To move back to the previous page, you want to take the current starting row and subtract three. To move forward, add three. The <CFOUTPUT> tag is necessary to allow ColdFusion Express to resolve the value to put in the URL parameter:

```
<CFOUTPUT>
<!---Move backward through the Rows --->
<CFSET Previous = URL.StartRow - 3>
<A HREF="guest_nextn.cfm?StartRow=#Variables.Previous#">Previous</A>

<!---Move forward through the rows --->
<CFSET Next = URL.StartRow + 3>
<A HREF="guest_nextn.cfm?StartRow=#Variables.Next#">Next</A>
</CFOUTPUT>
```

The next point to take into consideration is to be sure that you don't move past the end of the resultset, or before it. Therefore, you need to make sure that Variables.Previous doesn't get below 1, and that Variables.Next doesn't get above the number of rows returned. We can get the rows returned by using the query's RECORDCOUNT variable. Using the <CFIF> tag, make the test prior to creating the hyperlink. You'll want to put in the Previous or Next text, but don't make them active to show the user he is at the beginning or end of the resultset.

```
<CFOUTPUT>
<!---Move backward through the Rows --->
<CFSET Previous = URL.StartRow - 3>
<CFIF Variables.Previous GTE 1>
    <A HREF="guest_nextn.cfm?StartRow=#Variables.Previous#">Previous</A>
 <CFELSE>
    Previous
 </CFIF>
<!---Move forward through the rows --->
<CFSET Next = URL.StartRow + 3>
<CFIF Variables.Next LT qGetGuestList.RecordCount>
    <A HREF="guest_nextn.cfm?StartRow=#Variables.Next#">Next</A>
 <CFELSE>
Next
 </CFIF>
</CFOUTPUT>
```

The final code, contained within one page, would resemble Listing 15.7.

LISTING 15.7   Final Guestbook List Page

```
 1: <!DOCTYPE HTML PUBLIC "-//W3C//DTD HTML 4.0 Transitional//EN">
 2: <html>
 3: <head>
 4:     <title>Guestbook List View - Next-N</title>
 5: </head>
 6:
 7: <body>
 8:
 9: <!---Initialize the starting row for the first time in --->
10: <CFPARAM NAME="URL.StartRow" DEFAULT="1">
11:
12: <CFQUERY NAME="qGetGuestList" DATASOURCE="learncfe">
13:     SELECT GuestName, Email, GuestBook_ID
14:     FROM Guestbook;
15: </CFQUERY>
16:
17: <H2>Guest List</H2>
18: <CFOUTPUT QUERY="qGetGuestList"
19:          STARTROW=#URL.StartRow#
20:          MAXROWS=3>
21:      #qGetGuestList.GuestName# #qGetGuestList.Email#<BR>
22: </CFOUTPUT>
23: <CFOUTPUT>
```

LISTING 15.7   continued

```
24: <!---Move backward through the Rows --->
25: <CFSET Previous = URL.StartRow - 3>
26: <CFIF Variables.Previous GTE 1>
27:     <A HREF="guest_nextn.cfm?StartRow=#Variables.Previous#">Previous</A>
28: <CFELSE>
29:     Previous
30: </CFIF>
31:
32: <!---Move forward through the rows --->
33: <CFSET Next = URL.StartRow + 3>
34: <CFIF Variables.Next LT qGetGuestList.RecordCount>
35:     <A HREF="guest_nextn.cfm?StartRow=#Variables.Next#">Next</A>
36: <CFELSE>
37:     Next
38: </CFIF>
39: </CFOUTPUT>
40: </body>
41: </html>
```

All Rows Are Returned

Each time the page is called, all rows are returned in the query. We are only restricting the number of rows displayed. You cannot specify a start row for a query, but you can limit the rows returned. You can calculate the number of rows you need by taking the start row and adding the maximum number of rows needed to it. This you can specify in the <CFQUERY> tag's MAXROWS attribute to return only **up to** the row you want to see on that page.

Make MAXROWS a Variable

I wanted to keep the example as simple as possible. But you might want to make the MAXROWS attribute a variable just like the STARTROW. In this way, it would be easy to change this value to display more rows, or even prompt the user for how many rows to display at one time.

Summary

During this hour, you learned how to create usable interfaces for data using various drill-down methods. In the next hour, you will build upon the knowledge of dynamic queries to create rich search interfaces using forms.

Q&A

Q You explained how to pass a primary key to a detail page for data drill down. Is there a way to pass multiple keys?

A You can pass them in a list format (1,2,3). The SELECT statement could then use the IN clause to find all matches in this list.

Q Reading the query every time for a next-n interface seems like a lot of unnecessary database access. Is there a way to cache the results to prevent this?

A Yes, actually there is. We'll cover this in Hour 22, "Improving Application Performance."

Q In a framed environment, is there a way to update more than one window with a single click?

A Yep, using JavaScript. Basically, you update one window, and send it a one line JavaScript call that forces a refresh or update in another window.

Workshop

The Workshop contains quiz questions and exercises to help reinforce what you've learned in this hour. If you get stuck, the answers to the quiz questions can be found in Appendix A, "Answers to Quiz."

Quiz

1. Why is the drill-down interface popular in Web-based applications?
2. When would you use a next-n style interface?
3. In what part of the URL are parameters passed?
4. *True or false*: Frames are not safe to use when performing data drill-down interfaces.

Exercises

1. As a rule, you are almost always better off helping users rather than telling them they made a mistake. Users should never get to the guest_detail.cfm page directly, but if they somehow did, they'd see an error message. A more friendly interface would be to send the user to where they really should have been, the guest_list.cfm page. Modify the guest_detail.cfm page so that if no GID was specified, the page would redirect to the guest_list.cfm page automatically.

2. Data drill down is used by almost every major search engine. Visit your favorite search engine, and do a search (one that you know will retrieve lots of records). Look at the URL as you browse the results pages and see if you can find how the position is being passed from one page to the next. Hint: Some sites use page numbers instead of record or row numbers.

HOUR 16

Creating Rich Search Interfaces

In the last three hours, you've learned to use dynamic queries and URL parameters to create flexible displays of your database output. In all these cases, all rows were retrieved from the database and displayed in pages, in frames, and a set at a time in a next-n interface. During this hour, you'll use dynamic queries, but this time you'll allow the user to decide which rows she wants to view. Forms will be used to create search interfaces, much like the ones you might use often on the Web.

In this hour, you'll learn the following:

- What types of search interfaces are on the Web
- What are the components of a search interface
- How to create a search form
- How to use form data in dynamic queries

Search Types

If you've ever been on a search site, such as Yahoo! or Excite, you have used a search form. They prompt you for a single line of text and allow you to find results from any Web site in the world. However, when you use a Web site to purchase products, such as housewares from Williams-Sonoma, you are searching through their private catalog. These are two different types of searches:

- Page searches—Most sites allow you to look through all their stored pages for text strings. The result is a list of pages that had a match. These sites search through the entire WWW for content that is stored in pages. This type of search is known as free text indexing and searching.
- Database searches—Sites that have product catalogs or other information they want you to browse will have search forms to let you choose what you want to see.

In this hour, we will be working with database searches. You will create search forms based on database tables and allow the user to choose which rows of data he wants to see.

Search Components

As with any type of form, there are two pages involved:

- Search form—Lets users choose what they want to see.
- Action page—Processes and displays that data.

The search form in this case will be based on columns that are in a database table (or more than one table). The user input into the forms will be used to dynamically create the query and customize the resulting output.

Creating the Search Form Page

To create a search form, you need to consider the data you will allow users to search on. Each column that you will allow the user to choose from will be created as a form control.

We will start with a simple example of searching on the Guest's name. To do this create an HTML form with a text control to capture the user's input for a guest name. Each form must have a submit button, so one should be created to start the search. A simple search is shown in Figure 16.1.

FIGURE 16.1

A simple search form is created by prompting for information in a database column.

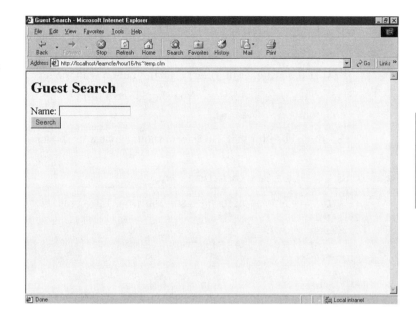

Naming Form Controls

Just as when you create a form for inserting information, you should try to name all form controls the same as the target database columns. This will make it easier to use in the action page because you'll know how to match up the form data with the database columns.

To Do: Create a Simple Search Form

▼ To Do

Follow these steps to create a simple search form to allow you to search through the Guestbook table by the guest's name.

1. Return to HomeSite and be sure that the Local Files tab is pointing to the /learncfe/hour16 directory.

2. Create a new page using the default template.

3. Change the <TITLE> text to "Guest Search Form".

4. Save the page as **guest_search_form.cfm**.

5. Inside the <BODY> and </BODY> tags, create a <FORM> tag with an ACTION of guest_search_action.cfm and a METHOD of post.

▼

▼   6. Inside the <FORM> and </FORM> tags, create a text control with a NAME of
        Guestname, a SIZE of 20, and a MAXLENGTH of 30. Use the Quick Bar from toolbar's
        text dialog to help you. Put a label of "Name:" in front of the text control.

     7. After the text control, create a submit button with the text as "Search".

     8. Save the page and browse. You should see a form with a text control and a submit
        button.

The resulting code for the search form should appear as shown in Listing 16.1.

LISTING 16.1   Guest Search Action Page

```
 1: <!DOCTYPE HTML PUBLIC "-//W3C//DTD HTML 4.0 Transitional//EN">
 2: <html>
 3: <head>
 4:     <title>Guest Search</title>
 5: </head>
 6:
 7: <body>
 8: <FORM ACTION="guest_search_action.cfm" METHOD="post">
 9:     <H2>Guest Search</H2>
10:
11:     Name:
12:     <INPUT TYPE="Text" NAME="GuestName" SIZE="20" MAXLENGTH="30">
13:     <INPUT TYPE="submit" NAME="Search" VALUE="Search">
14: </FORM>
15:
16: </body>
17: </html>
```

▲

Creating the Search Action Page

Now that we have a form to prompt for the guest name the user wants to look up, we can
use that data to create a dynamic query to return only those row(s) that match the search
criteria. The resulting page would display the resulting rows, possibly displayed as in the
output in Figure 16.2.

Assuming you have a form that prompts for a text value in a form control called
GuestName, you could use this control value in the action page to retrieve information
about the specified guest. To get all information about a row in which the GuestName column is equal to the data input into the form control, the following <CFQUERY> tag can be
used:

```
<CFQUERY NAME="qGetGuest" DATASOURCE="learncfe">
    SELECT *
    FROM Guestbook
    WHERE GuestName = '#FORM.GuestName#';
</CFQUERY>
```

FIGURE 16.2

A search performed to find John Doe would yield one row of output in our database.

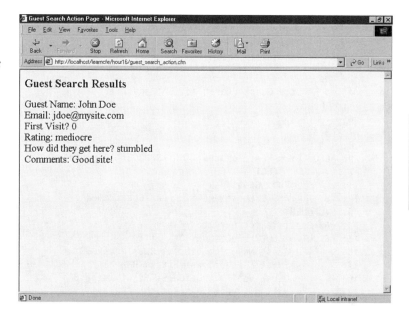

The #Form.GuestName# variable will be replaced with the name the user input into the form. Print out the data and voilà! You have a search interface. This will return all rows that match the user's input.

To Do: Create the Search Action Page

Follow these steps to create the action page for the search form. This action page will use the form variable sent by the form to create a dynamic query to return selected guests.

1. Return to HomeSite and create a new page using the default template.
2. Change the <TITLE> text to "Guest Search Action Page".
3. Inside the <BODY> and </BODY> tags, create a level 3 header with the text "Guest Search Results".
4. Create a <CFQUERY> tag under the heading. Return all columns from the Guestbook table in the learncfe datasource. Append a WHERE clause for the GuestName column and match it up with the value of the FORM.GuestName variable. If you struggle with this, refer to the code at the end of these instructions.
5. Use a <CFOUTPUT> tag to print out all resulting rows, using the appropriate label to specify what the column represents.
6. Browse to the guest_search_form.cfm page and submit a known guest name in the table. When you submit the form, you should see that row displayed.

▼ The resulting code for the action page should resemble Listing 16.2.

▼

LISTING 16.2 Guest Search Action Page

```
1: <!DOCTYPE HTML PUBLIC "-//W3C//DTD HTML 4.0 Transitional//EN">
2: <html>
3: <head>
4:     <title>Guest Search Action Page</title>
5: </head>
6:
7: <body>
8:
9: <CFQUERY NAME="qGetGuest" DATASOURCE="learncfe">
10:         SELECT *
11:         FROM Guestbook
12:         WHERE GuestName = '#FORM.GuestName#';
13: </CFQUERY>
14: <H3>Guest Search Results</H3>
15: <CFOUTPUT QUERY="qGetGuest">
16:         Guest Name: #qGetGuest.GuestName#<BR>
17:         Email: #qGetGuest.Email#<BR>
18:         First Visit? #qGetGuest.FirstVisit#<BR>
19:         Rating: #qGetGuest.Rating#<BR>
20:         How did they get here? #qGetGuest.GotHere#<BR>
21:         Comments: #qGetGuest.Comments#<BR>
22: </CFOUTPUT>
23: </body>
24: </html>
```

▲

Search Form Considerations

The pages that you have created work, but there are several other considerations that you will want to code for. For instance, how do your pages answer the following questions:

- What if the user mistakenly browses directly to the action page without going through the form? How can you make sure that this doesn't happen?
- What if no rows were found for the search criteria?
- What if the user submits the form without specifying any search criteria?
- What if the user submits the wrong type of search criteria, such as supplying a text string, when we're looking for a number?

There are no hard and fast answers to these questions because they are all part of how you want to design your application. Here we'll assume the following:

- If the user browses to the action page first, redirect her to the form.
- If the search doesn't yield any output, display a message to the user.

- If the user doesn't specify any search criteria, display all rows.
- Use validation to be sure that the correct type of search criteria is specified.

Redirect to the Form

If a user accidentally browses directly to an action page, you might want to help him out by redirecting him to the form within your code. This could easily happen if a user creates a favorite or bookmark of the action page. In this case, the form variables will not exist at all. To test if any form data is present, use the IsDefined() function on the FORM.GuestName variable as follows:

```
<CFIF NOT IsDefined("Form.GuestName")>
    <!---send them to the form--->
</CFIF>
```

You can redirect to another page by using the <CFLOCATION> tag. This tag, whenever encountered within a CFML page, will cause ColdFusion Express to halt processing of the current page, discard any HTML or text output that might have been generated thus far, and start processing a new page. It is the new page that will be sent back to the user.

> It will execute up to the <CFLOCATION> tag. That means if there were any server-side code above the <CFLOCATION>, they would be executed. Therefore, any inserts or updates into the database would be performed successfully. It is only the resulting HTML that will not be sent to the user.

This tag has two attributes, only one of which we will discuss here:

```
<CFLOCATION URL="page.cfm">
```

This process is generally depicted in Figure 16.3.

FIGURE 16.3

The <CFLOCATION> tag redirects processing from one page to another on the server.

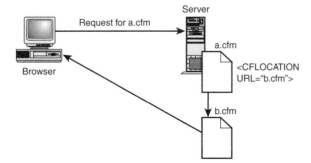

Refer to Hour 22, "Improving Application Performance," for more information on the <CFLOCATION> tag and performance.

Using the <CFLOCATION> tag within conditional logic, you can now detect users who bypassed the search form and send them there programmatically. This code would be as follows:

```
<!---Test to see if the user skipped the form --->
<CFIF NOT IsDefined("Form.GuestName")>
    <CFLOCATION URL="guest_search_form.cfm">
</CFIF>
```

You would need to put this code at the top of the action page, to be sure that no other processing occurs before this test.

To Do: Redirecting to the Form

▼ To Do

Follow these steps to detect if the user bypassed the search form and redirect her there.

1. Return to HomeSite and the guest_search_action.cfm page.

2. Before the <CFQUERY> tag, code conditional logic to test to see if the FORM.GuestName variable exists. Refer to Listing 16.3 if you experience problems.

3. Inside the <CFIF> and </CFIF> tags, use a <CFLOCATION> tag to redirect the user to the guest_search_form.cfm page if the FORM.GuestName variable does not exist.

4. Browse to the guest_search_action.cfm page, and you should be redirected to the guest_search_form.cfm page automatically.

The full action page is shown in Listing 16.3, with the addition to this exercise in bold.

LISTING 16.3 Guest Search Action Page

```
 1: <!DOCTYPE HTML PUBLIC "-//W3C//DTD HTML 4.0 Transitional//EN">
 2: <html>
 3: <head>
 4:     <title>Guest Search Action Page</title>
 5: </head>
 6:
 7: <body>
 8: <!---Test to see if the user skipped the form --->
 9: <CFIF NOT IsDefined("Form.GuestName")>
10:     <CFLOCATION URL="guest_search_form.cfm">
11: </CFIF>
12:
13: <CFQUERY NAME="qGetGuest" DATASOURCE="learncfe">
```

LISTING 16.3   continued

```
14:     SELECT *
15:     FROM Guestbook
16:     WHERE GuestName = '#FORM.GuestName#';
17: </CFQUERY>
18:
19: <CFOUTPUT QUERY="qGetGuest">
20:     Guest Name: #qGetGuest.GuestName#<BR>
21:     Email:  #qGetGuest.Email#<BR>
22:     First Visit? #qGetGuest.FirstVisit#<BR>
23:     Rating: #qGetGuest.Rating#<BR>
24:     How did they get here? #qGetGuest.GotHere#<BR>
25:     Comments: #qGetGuest.Comments#<BR>
26: </CFOUTPUT>
27: </body>
28: </html>
```

Handling No Rows Returned

You've already learned how to detect if a query has returned any rows in Hour 13, "Creating Data Driven Pages." Earlier in this hour, you learned that each query returns the number of rows in a variable named RecordCount. Use conditional logic to determine if any rows have been retrieved, and then give a friendly message if there were none. Using the qGetGuest query, the logic would be

```
<CFIF qGetGuest.RecordCount IS 0>
    <h3>No matches found.</h3>
<CFELSE>
    <!---Print out the resulting rows --->
</CFIF>
```

Be sure to put the printing of the rows into the <CFELSE> section so that an empty table will not be displayed.

No Search Criteria

If the user fails to input any search criteria on the form and submits, you can code your action page to handle it in many different ways:

- Display an error message telling the user to put in some search criteria and let him click the browser's Back button to return to the form.
- Display all rows from the database on the action page.
- Display all rows from the database in a next-n interface as most search engine sites do.

- Display a warning message about how much data will be returned and that it might take some time.

- Only show up to a maximum number of rows and then tell the user to limit his search to be sure that he is getting the rows he wants.

It all depends on the volume of data you expect in your tables and what you have found that your users want to view. Each of these solutions is possible using CFML, and you've already learned all the components of this programming logic within this book.

In this example, we will simply display all rows if a guest name was not entered. Using the <CFIF> tag, the WHERE clause is dynamically appended only if it has been given a value by the user. This code is shown in the following, with the added code in bold:

```
<CFQUERY NAME="qGetGuest" DATASOURCE="learncfe">
    SELECT *
    FROM Guestbook
    <CFIF Trim(FORM.GuestName) IS NOT "">
        WHERE GuestName = '#FORM.GuestName#'
    </CFIF>
</CFQUERY>
```

Remember that the Trim() function will take off any leading or trailing spaces from the variable value.

Again, if there is more than one dynamic clause, use the dummy WHERE clause with the conditional logic. For instance, if we allowed the user to search on both GuestName and Email, the query would look as follows:

```
<CFQUERY NAME="qGetGuest" DATASOURCE="learncfe">
    SELECT *
    FROM Guestbook
    WHERE 0=0
    <CFIF Trim(FORM.GuestName) IS NOT "">
        AND GuestName = '#FORM.GuestName#'
    </CFIF>
    <CFIF Trim(FORM.Email) IS NOT "">
        AND Email = '#FORM.Email#'
    </CFIF>
</CFQUERY>
```

In this case, if the user inputs criteria into either or both of the GuestName or Email form controls, the query will be dynamically generated to use the appropriate criteria in the SELECT statement.

Validating Form Input

As you learned in Hour 10, "Validating Form Fields," you should always use form validation to be sure that users don't input the wrong information. CFML is a typeless language, but databases are not. Therefore, you need to make sure of your data types before you query a database. Each form control you create for a database column search should be validated using the proper validation logic.

One way to ensure that users input the correct format of data is to give them a list of valid choices for a particular column. The Guestbook table has the columns listed in Table 16.1.

16

TABLE 16.1   Guestbook Columns

Column	Description	Value
Guestbook_ID	Primary key	System generated number
GuestName	Name of the guest	Text string
Email	Email address of the guest	Text string
FirstVisit	Is this their first visit to your site?	Yes or No
Rating	How do they rate your site?	great, mediocre, or stinks
GotHere	How they got to your site	searched, stumbled, or unknown
Comments	Comments on your site	Text string

You might want to search on all columns except for the Guestbook_ID, which doesn't make much sense to a user. The GuestName, Email, and Comments columns are simple text strings, so text controls should be created to search them. The FirstVisit column is a Yes/No column, and can be searched using a check box control.

The Rating and GotHere columns are different, in that they both allow the selection of one option out of a set of three options. The user simply chooses the correct radio button or select list item, and a predetermined value is input into the database column. This type of data is a candidate for creating a code table to supply its value.

Code Tables

Whenever possible, it is recommended that you think about each column in your database table and the possible values they can contain. At design time, determine which columns might have a predetermined set of values. Perhaps you can create a code table for all possible values in that column.

For the `GotHere` column, the current values are searched, stumbled, or unknown. It is possible in the future that you would want to add another option, such as `"referred by a friend"`. If you had created all your forms with hard-coded values, updating them all with the new value will be no small task.

In this case, a table could be created to hold all possible values for a column. This table, known as a lookup or code table, can be used to dynamically generate the form controls to populate them with valid values. For information in the `GotHere` column, perhaps the table would be as seen in Figure 16.4.

FIGURE 16.4

The `GotHere` column has a predetermined set of values and therefore can be codified into a table.

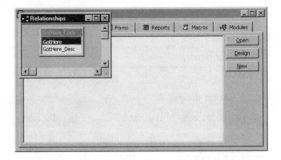

Because they are dynamically generated, it is easy to add another row to the database table, and all your forms will automatically receive those new values. For our three values, the data in the table will be created as shown in Figure 16.5.

FIGURE 16.5

The `GotHere_Code` table contains three rows of data for lookup. These values will be used in the form, both for insert and for query purposes.

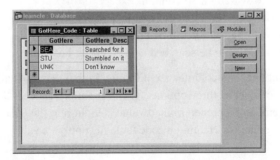

I have created the three rows with a three-character code column and a description column. The `GotHere` column will also serve as the primary key, and all values in this column must be unique. The description is just the longer description of how they got to the site.

Now that you have a table of options for the `GotHere` column, you'll need to change both your insert and your search forms to use these values. Both of these search forms will use a select control, but instead of hard-coding the options, you will use a <CFQUERY> tag to get all options and the <CFOUTPUT> tag to generate the necessary number of options in the list.

Start by retrieving the data from the database. Select both columns from the GotHere_Code table:

```
<CFQUERY NAME="qGetGotHere_Code" DATASOURCE="learncfe">
SELECT GotHere, GotHere_Desc
FROM GotHere_Code
</CFQUERY>
```

Inside the form, change the hardcoded values in the select control for how a person got to your site. Because you now want to dynamically generate an option in the select control for each row in the GotHere_Code table, surround the <OPTION> tag with a <CFOUTPUT QUERY="qGetGotHere_Code"> tag. This will generate an option for each row in the query. Use the GotHere column as the VALUE of the option, and the GotHere_Desc column as what the user will see in the select list:

```
How did you get here?
        <SELECT NAME="GotHere"
          SIZE="1">
        <CFOUTPUT QUERY="qGetGotHere_Code">
          <OPTION VALUE="#qGetGotHere_Code.GotHere#">
             #qGetGotHere_Code.GotHere_Desc#
          </OPTION>
        </CFOUTPUT>
        </SELECT>
```

To Do: Dynamically Generating a Select List

Follow these steps to alter the guest book form to create a dynamically generated select list.

1. Return to HomeSite and be sure that you are still pointing at the /learncfe/hour16 directory in the Local Files tab.

2. Open the page /learncfe/hour12/guestbook.cfm. Select File, Save As and save the file in the current directory (/learncfe/hour16).

3. Perform the same step to copy the file /learncfe/hour12/insert_guest.cfm page to the /learncfe/hour16 directory.

4. Before the select control for how the user got to the site, create the following <CFQUERY> tag:

```
<CFQUERY NAME="qGetGotHere_Code" DATASOURCE="learncfe">
SELECT GotHere, GotHere_Desc
FROM GotHere_Code
</CFQUERY>
```

▼   5. Modify the SELECT tag by removing any two of the three <OPTION> tags within it.

6. Surround the one remaining <OPTION> tag with a <CFOUTPUT> tag specifying the QUERY attribute to match the query above.

7. Change the VALUE attribute of the <OPTION> tag to #qGetGotHere_Code.GotHere#.

8. Change the text between the <OPTION> and </OPTION> tags to #qGetGotHere_Code.Got_Here_Desc#. The final code for the select control should be as follows:

```
How did you get here?
        <SELECT NAME="GotHere"
            SIZE="1">
        <CFOUTPUT QUERY="qGetGotHere_Code">
            <OPTION VALUE="#qGetGotHere_Code.GotHere#">
                #qGetGotHere_Code.GotHere_Desc#
            </OPTION>
        </CFOUTPUT>
        </SELECT>
```

9. Save the file and browse it. You should see the select list populated with the values from the table.

▲   10. Input more rows of data using this new input form.

Now that you've altered the input form to use the code table, you can create a control on the search form in the same manner to allow users to search for these values.

To Do: Generate a Select List for the Search Form

Follow these steps to alter the guest book search form to create a dynamically generated select list.

1. Return to HomeSite and the guest_search_form.cfm page.

▼   2. Before the submit button, create a <SELECT> tag. Set the NAME attribute to "GotHere" and the SIZE to "1".

3. Create the following <CFQUERY> tag:

```
<CFQUERY NAME="qGetGotHere_Code" DATASOURCE="learncfe">
SELECT GotHere, GotHere_Desc
FROM GotHere_Code
</CFQUERY>
```

4. Create a <SELECT> tag with the NAME set to "GotHere" and the SIZE set to "1".

5. Create one <OPTION> tag inside the <SELECT> tag. Surround it with a <CFOUTPUT> tag specifying the QUERY attribute to match the query you just created.

▼   6. Set the VALUE attribute of the <OPTION> tag to "#qGetGotHere_Code.GotHere#".

▼ 7. Put "#qGetGotHere_Code.Got_Here_Desc#" as the text between the <OPTION> and
</OPTION> tags. The final code for the select control should be as follows:

```
How did you get here?
        <SELECT NAME="GotHere"
            SIZE="1">
        <CFOUTPUT QUERY="qGetGotHere_Code">
            <OPTION VALUE="#qGetGotHere_Code.GotHere#">
                #qGetGotHere_Code.GotHere_Desc#
            </OPTION>
        </CFOUTPUT>
        </SELECT>
```

8. Save the file and browse it. You should see the select list populated with the values
from the table.

The form should still work, but the action page hasn't been altered to use this information in the query. The full guest_search_form.cfm page is shown in Listing 16.3, with the
changed code in bold.

LISTING 16.3   Guest Search Form Page

```
 1: <!DOCTYPE HTML PUBLIC "-//W3C//DTD HTML 4.0 Transitional//EN">
 2: <html>
 3: <head>
 4: <title>Guest Search</title>
 5: </head>
 6:
 7: <body>
 8: <FORM ACTION="guest_search_action.cfm" METHOD="post">
 9: <H2>Guest Search</H2>
10:
11: Name:
12: <INPUT TYPE="Text" NAME="GuestName" SIZE="20" MAXLENGTH="30">
13: <BR>
14: <CFQUERY NAME="qGetGotHere_Code" DATASOURCE="learncfe">
15: SELECT GotHere, GotHere_Desc
16: FROM GotHere_Code
17: </CFQUERY>
18: How did you get here?
19: <SELECT NAME="GotHere"
20: SIZE="1">
21: <CFOUTPUT QUERY="qGetGotHere_Code">
22: <OPTION VALUE="#qGetGotHere_Code.GotHere#"><
23: #qGetGotHere_Code.GotHere_Desc#
24: </OPTION>
25: </CFOUTPUT>
▼ 26: </SELECT>
```

16

LISTING **16.3**   continued

```
27: <BR>
28:
29: <INPUT TYPE="submit" NAME="Search" VALUE="Search">
30: </FORM>
31:
32: </body>
33: </html>
```

Now that you've allowed the users to search for how the guests got to your site, you'll have to change the action page to use that criteria in the query. However, you need to consider two things when creating a search form using code tables:

- When the user does not care which value was specified
- When the user wants to select more than one value for the column

In the current search form, the user is forced to choose one of the three options. That is okay for an input form, but you might not want to limit it to one value for searches. You might want to select without specifying a value or want to specify many values.

Adding an Any Option

You might want to manually create an option in your select control to allow the users to leave the select control unspecified. In this case, you simply manually code an <OPTION> tag, outside of the <CFOUTPUT> tag. This option will display in the select control along with the dynamically generated ones. This code would look as the bolded part of this excerpt from the guest_search_form.cfm page:

```
How did you get here?
    <SELECT NAME="GotHere"
        SIZE="1">
        <OPTION VALUE=""></OPTION>
    <CFOUTPUT QUERY="qGetGotHere_Code">
        <OPTION VALUE="#qGetGotHere_Code.GotHere#">
            #qGetGotHere_Code.GotHere_Desc#
        </OPTION>
    </SELECT>
```

When the select control is expanded, it will appear as shown in Figure 16.6.

This addition will leave the first option as a blank and pass the empty string as the value. This empty string could be detected in the action page and left off the search, as in the bolded part of the <CFQUERY> tag in guest_search_action.cfm:

```
<CFQUERY NAME="qGetGuest" DATASOURCE="learncfe">
    SELECT *
    FROM Guestbook
    WHERE 0=0
    <CFIF Trim(FORM.GuestName) IS NOT "">
        AND GuestName = '#FORM.GuestName#'
    </CFIF>
    <CFIF FORM.GotHere IS NOT "">
        AND GotHere = '#FORM.GotHere#'
    </CFIF>
</CFQUERY>
```

FIGURE 16.6

Adding a blank option will allow the user to leave off this criteria in her selection.

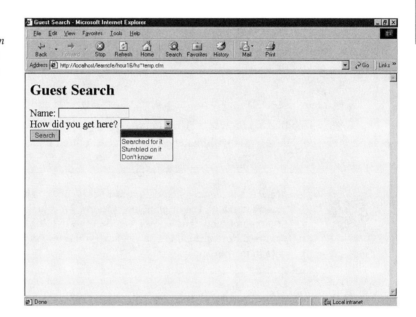

To Do: Add an Any Option

Follow these steps to alter the guest book search form to create an extra option to select any method of navigation.

1. Return to HomeSite and the guest_search_form.cfm page.

2. Right after the opening <SELECT> tag (before the <CFOUTPUT> tag), code an extra <OPTION> tag. Set the VALUE to the empty string and do not put any text between the <OPTION> and </OPTION> tags.

3. Save the file and browse. Be sure that the form loads with the blank option. If you submit the search, this will not affect the query.

4. Return to HomeSite and the guest_search_action.cfm page.

5. Alter the `<CFQUERY>` tag to add a dummy `WHERE 0=0` clause. Change the `WHERE` clause in the `<CFIF>` tag to the `AND` operator.

6. After the closing `</CFIF>` tag, create another `<CFIF>` tag to test if `FORM.GotHere` is empty. If it is not, create an `AND` clause using the `GotHere` form data. The resulting query is shown in the following:

```
<CFQUERY NAME="qGetGuest" DATASOURCE="learncfe">
    SELECT *
    FROM Guestbook
    WHERE 0=0
    <CFIF Trim(FORM.GuestName) IS NOT "">
        AND GuestName = '#FORM.GuestName#'
    </CFIF>
    <CFIF FORM.GotHere IS NOT "">
        AND GotHere = '#FORM.GotHere#'
    </CFIF>
</CFQUERY>
```

7. Create a `<SELECT>` tag with the `NAME` set to `"GotHere"` and the `SIZE` set to `"1"`.

8. Save the file and browse it. You should now be able to select a navigation option to see only those rows with matches, or leave the option blank and see all rows.

Are you not seeing much data returned? It could be because all rows that you created with the original insert form used values of search, stumbled, or unknown. Now that we've created this form using a code table, the values are different (SEA, STU, and UNK). I will show you how to update the old data in the next hour.

Selection of Multiple Values

The search form can be further amended to allow you to choose more than one option in the list to search on. Allowing users to select more than one option in a select control requires the use of a `MULTIPLE` keyword in the `<SELECT>` tag. In addition, you might want to show more than one option at a time by specifying a bigger value for `SIZE`. In this case, the select control is created to show two options at a time, with scroll bars for any other values, as shown in Figure 16.7.

Users might not be aware that they need to use Shift+click or Ctrl+click to select multiple options. You might want to put instructions on the form next to the select control.

FIGURE **16.7**

Adding the MULTIPLE *keyword and specifying a larger* SIZE *attribute allows the user to choose more than one option at a time.*

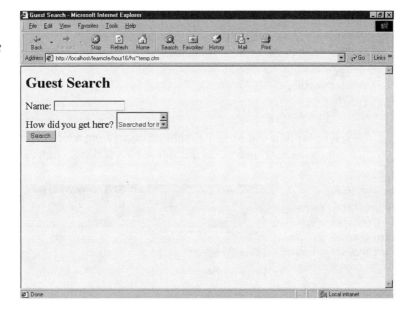

16

If you remember from Hour 9, "Using Forms," we talked about some types of form controls that don't create a variable if no value was input. This is true for a select control that allows multiple selections. If the user doesn't select any of them, the form variable isn't created and sent to the action page. Therefore, you must code around this by performing a workaround. One such workaround discussed was to use a <CFPARAM> tag in the action page to create the variable if it doesn't exist:

```
<CFPARAM NAME="FORM.GotHere" DEFAULT="">
```

In this way, the action page will treat a select control with no values selected as if the user chose not to restrict the output on that column.

However, you will soon discover that our current action page query cannot handle many choices at once for one column. If you wanted to select all rows in which the guest arrived by searching for it or stumbling on it, you would need the following SELECT statement:

```
SELECT *
FROM Guestbook
WHERE 0=0
AND GotHere = 'SEA'
OR GotHere = 'STU'
```

It would take some fairly complex logic to create this SELECT statement dynamically, if it weren't for the IN operator. The IN operator allows you to test for a column within a list of values. The list of values must be specified within parenthesis, and if the type is text, each element must be surrounded by single quotes. Thus, an equivalent statement to the previous could be rewritten using the following:

```
SELECT *
FROM Guestbook
WHERE 0=0
AND GotHere IN ('SEA', 'STU')
```

It just so happens that selecting multiple values from a select control creates a list in comma delimited format. This is displayed in the debug output as shown in Figure 16.8.

FIGURE 16.8

Debug output shows that multiple select lists generate a comma delimited list of values in the form variables.

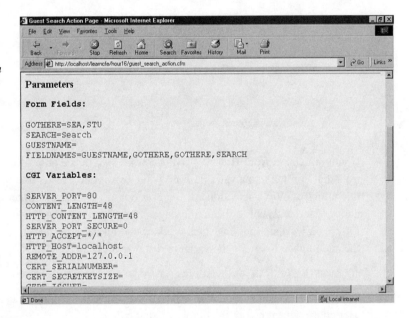

The only thing you need to do is use the ListQualify() function to put single quotes around each list item. The <CFQUERY> tag now looks as follows, with the change being bolded:

```
<CFQUERY NAME="qGetGuest" DATASOURCE="learncfe">
    SELECT *
    FROM Guestbook
    WHERE 0=0
    <CFIF Trim(FORM.GuestName) IS NOT "">
        AND GuestName = '#FORM.GuestName#'
    </CFIF>
    <CFIF FORM.GotHere IS NOT "">
        AND GotHere IN (#ListQualify(FORM.GotHere, "'")#)
    </CFIF>
</CFQUERY>
```

To Do: Allowing Multiple Selections

To Do ▼

Follow these steps to alter the guest book search form to allow multiple selections for the navigation method.

1. Return to HomeSite and the `guest_search_form.cfm` page.

2. Alter the `<SELECT>` tag by adding the `MULTIPLE` keyword and changing the `SIZE` attribute to `"2"`.

3. Save the file and browse. Be sure that the form loads and you see the multiple options. You can select more than one option by holding down the Control key and clicking on multiple rows.

4. Return to HomeSite and the guest_search_action.cfm page.

5. Above the `<CFQUERY>` tag, create the following `<CFPARAM>` tag to create the `FORM.GotHere` variable if it doesn't exist.

```
<CFPARAM NAME="FORM.GotHere" DEFAULT="">
```

6. Alter the `<CFQUERY>` tag to change the clause that deals with the `GotHere` column as the following query:

```
<CFQUERY NAME="qGetGuest" DATASOURCE="learncfe">
    SELECT *
    FROM Guestbook
    WHERE 0=0
    <CFIF Trim(FORM.GuestName) IS NOT "">
        AND GuestName = '#FORM.GuestName#'
    </CFIF>
    <CFIF FORM.GotHere IS NOT "">
        AND GotHere IN (#ListQualify(FORM.GotHere, "'")#)
    </CFIF>
</CFQUERY>
```

7. Save the page and browse to the form. You should be able to select multiple options and return multiple rows.

> Refer to the full code listing at the end of this hour for the solution, or refer to the code on the CD.

Free Text Searches

The last consideration for search forms that we will explore is called a free text search. A *free text search* allows the user to specify a pattern for finding rows of data instead of having to match the exact contents of a column to return the row. This is accomplished using

- The LIKE operator
- SQL wildcards

The normal operator for finding matches in columns is the equal sign (=). However, if we want to find patterns of data, we'll need to change our operator to the LIKE operator. This allows free text searches.

Now you can use SQL wildcards in your SQL. A wildcard is just a placeholder for text that might or might not be there. SQL has the following two wildcards:

- % (percent sign) that represents 0 or more characters
- _ (underscore) that represents exactly one character

For instance, if you wanted to find anyone with the first name of John, without caring about his last name, you could use the percent sign as a placeholder for any number of characters after the string "John":

```
SELECT *
FROM Guestbook
WHERE GuestName LIKE 'John%'
```

In this case, it doesn't matter if the person only put in John, or used John with any last name, all those rows would be returned. This wildcard can be used anywhere within the string to hold places for characters. If you wanted to find anyone with John in his name, you would use

```
SELECT *
FROM Guestbook
WHERE GuestName LIKE '%John%'
```

This would find matches for names like "Jacob John Smith" or "John Smith" or "Thomas John"...you get the picture.

The underscore (_) wildcard represents exactly one character. For instance, you might want to find matches on a phone number with a area code of 617 and exactly seven digits after it using the following SQL:

```
SELECT *
FROM Employee
WHERE Phone LIKE '617_____'
```

It's tough to count underscores in print, but there are seven of them to hold each digit's place.

To Do: Allowing a Free Text Search

▼ To Do

Follow these steps to alter the guest book search form to allow a free text search on the GuestName column.

1. Return to HomeSite and the guest_search_action.cfm page.

2. Alter the clause that searches on the GuestName column to use the LIKE keyword instead of the equal sign. Around the #FORM.GuestName# variable, but within the single quotes, use the percent sign as a wildcard. The result <CFQUERY> tag will look as follows, with the change bolded:

```
<CFQUERY NAME="qGetGuest" DATASOURCE="learncfe">
    SELECT *
    FROM Guestbook
    WHERE 0=0
    <CFIF Trim(FORM.GuestName) IS NOT "">
        AND GuestName LIKE '%#FORM.GuestName#%'
    </CFIF>
    <CFIF FORM.GotHere IS NOT "">
        AND GotHere IN (#ListQualify(FORM.GotHere, "'")#)
    </CFIF>
</CFQUERY>
```

3. Save the file and browse.

It will depend on the data in your table, but try to use a free text search. Perhaps you can just specify a single character and find more than one match. If you don't have any patterns to your data, try inserting a couple of rows to test it out.

> Refer to the full code listing at the end of this hour for the solution, or refer to the code on the CD.

▲

The Completed Code

The completed code for this hour for the guest_search_form.cfm page is shown in Listing 16.4.

LISTING 16.4 Complete Guest Search Form Page

```
1: <!DOCTYPE HTML PUBLIC "-//W3C//DTD HTML 4.0 Transitional//EN">
2: <html>
3: <head>
4: <title>Guest Search</title>
5: </head>
6:
```

LISTING 16.4   continued

```
 7: <body>
 8: <FORM ACTION="guest_search_action.cfm" METHOD="post">
 9: <H2>Guest Search</H2>
10:
11: Name:
12: <INPUT TYPE="Text" NAME="GuestName" SIZE="20" MAXLENGTH="30">
13: <BR>
14: <CFQUERY NAME="qGetGotHere_Code" DATASOURCE="learncfe">
15: SELECT GotHere, GotHere_Desc
16: FROM GotHere_Code
17: </CFQUERY>
18:
19: How did you get here?
20: <SELECT NAME="GotHere"
21: SIZE="2"
22: MULTIPLE>
23: <OPTION VALUE=""></OPTION>
24: <CFOUTPUT QUERY="qGetGotHere_Code">
25: <OPTION VALUE="#qGetGotHere_Code.GotHere#">
26: #qGetGotHere_Code.GotHere_Desc#
27: </OPTION>
28: </CFOUTPUT>
29: </SELECT>
30: <BR>
31: <INPUT TYPE="submit" NAME="Search" VALUE="Search">
32: </FORM>
33:
34: </body>
35: </html>
```

The completed code for this hour for the guest_search_action.cfm page is shown in
Listing 16.5.

LISTING 16.5   Complete Guest Search Action Page

```
1: <!DOCTYPE HTML PUBLIC "-//W3C//DTD HTML 4.0 Transitional//EN">
2:
3: <html>
4: <head>
5: <title>Guest Search Action Page</title>
6: </head>
7:
8: <body>
9:
```

LISTING 16.5   continued

```
10: <!---Test to see if the user skipped the form --->
11: <CFIF NOT IsDefined("FORM.GuestName")>
12: <CFLOCATION URL="guest_search_form.cfm">
13: </CFIF>
14:
15: <!---Create the FORM.GotHere variable if it doesn't exist --->
16: <CFPARAM NAME="FORM.GotHere" DEFAULT="">
17:
18: <!---Query the database using the IN operator, the LIKE operator and SQL
19: ➥wildcards --->
20: <CFQUERY NAME="qGetGuest" DATASOURCE="learncfe">
21: SELECT *
22: FROM Guestbook
23: WHERE 0=0
24: <CFIF Trim(FORM.GuestName) IS NOT "">
25: AND GuestName LIKE '#FORM.GuestName#%'
26: </CFIF>
27: <CFIF FORM.GotHere IS NOT "">
28: AND GotHere IN (#ListQualify(FORM.GotHere, "'")#)
29: </CFIF>
30: </CFQUERY>
31:
32: <!---Display a message if no rows were found. Otherwise, print out the rows
     ➥--->
33: <CFIF qGetGuest.RecordCount IS 0>
34: <H3>No matches found.</H3>
35: <CFELSE>
36: <H3>Guest Search Results</H3>
37: <CFOUTPUT QUERY="qGetGuest">
38: Guest Name: #qGetGuest.GuestName#<BR>
39: Email:   #qGetGuest.Email#<BR>
40: First Visit? #qGetGuest.FirstVisit#<BR>
41: Rating: #qGetGuest.Rating#<BR>
42: How did they get here? #qGetGuest.GotHere#<BR>
43: Comments: #qGetGuest.Comments#<BR><BR>
44: </CFOUTPUT>
45: </CFIF>
46: </body>
47: </html>
```

Summary

It's been an exciting hour of creating search interfaces as a window into the data in your databases. What you learned here can help you create rich search interfaces and powerful applications.

Q&A

Q **How could I enable my Web site to use free text indexing and searching for my pages and not just search against my database?**

A ColdFusion Express doesn't allow you to use the integration with a indexing and searching engine such as Verity Search 97. You would need to purchase the full ColdFusion Professional or ColdFusion Enterprise versions for this integration.

Q **You showed me how to make a select control driven by a database, but can I do the same for radio buttons?**

A Yes, you can dynamically generate a set of radio buttons based on code table values. However, because your code table has the capability to grow over time, this might mess up formatting of your form. If the list of radio buttons was dynamic, you could not control the layout of the form. It is best when using dynamic lists of data from a code table to use the select control instead.

Q **Can I control the order of the options in a dynamically generated select control?**

A You can sort the data when you query it from the database table. This will help you sort the data in the select box to a more desirable order, such as alphabetically. Otherwise, you could not control the order.

Workshop

The Workshop contains quiz questions and exercises to help reinforce what you've learned in this hour. If you get stuck, the answers to the quiz questions can be found in Appendix A, "Answers to Quiz."

Quiz

1. Which operator would you use to find matches between a list of values and a database column?

2. *True or false:* A select control can create many form variables.

3. What are the advantages of using code tables for columns?

4. What tag can redirect processing to another page on the server?

Exercises

1. Explore the Web, especially e-commerce sites, to see how they enable you to search through their catalog. What form controls do they allow you to search with?

2. Alter the guest_search_form.cfm page to allow the users to select if it's their first visit. Consider this addition because a check box only allows you to request seeing all guests on their first visit or not. Therefore, you'll want to allow them to specify if they don't care whether it was their first visit or not. What control would you use to allow them to choose yes, no, or n/a?

16

HOUR 17

Updating Database Data

You've learned how to insert data, search for it, and display it to users. In this hour, you'll learn how to create interfaces to update and delete data in tables.

In this lesson, you'll learn the following:

- How to create a table maintenance interface
- How to create an update form
- How to update rows in a database from form data
- How to create a delete confirmation page
- How to delete rows from a table

Understanding Maintenance Interfaces

Before you can update or delete a row of data from a database, you must allow the user to select the row(s) to change or delete. This requires some planning for the interface. There are two general ways to create a maintenance interface:

- Display all the rows in a list and allow the user to choose which ones she wants to update or delete

- Allow the users to search for rows; then determine which rows to update or delete based on the result

In this hour, we will create a simple list display of all rows in the Guestbook table. The user will choose a row to update or delete; then the processing will split based on which operation she chooses. The user will then be redirected back to the list page to continue with maintenance. This process is depicted in Figure 17.1.

FIGURE 17.1

Maintenance of database tables should be designed before coding. In this case, a list of rows will be displayed and the user will choose one to update or delete.

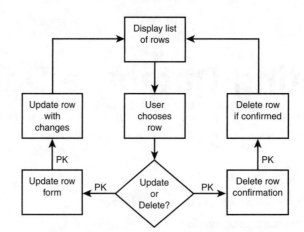

In order to update or delete a row, you must uniquely identify it. In this case, the primary key of the Guestbook table will be passed from page to page to be sure to display and update or delete the correct row.

As depicted, this requires the creation of five separate pages:

- Guestbook List view page
- Update form
- Update action page
- Delete confirmation page
- Delete action page

But let's see if we can consolidate this processing into fewer pages by detecting an operation type within one page. Fewer pages need to be created if you build in conditional logic for the type of operation you want to perform. For instance, you could create the following three pages:

- Guestbook List view page
- Maintenance page that will either display the row in a form for an update or display a confirmation message if deleted
- Maintenance action page that will either update the row given the user's input into the form or delete the row if the user confirms the deletion

Creating the List View

You've already created a Guest List View page in Hour 15, "Displaying Dynamic Pages." In that hour you listed only a few pertinent details about each guest and then allowed the user to drill down for more detailed information. The List view page and Drill Down page are displayed in Figure 17.2.

17

FIGURE 17.2

The Guest List View and Drill Down pages have been created in Hour 15.

Because we need to be able to pass the primary key of each row to either update or delete, we need to pass it either via the URL as a URL parameter or as a FORM variable using a form. These two scenarios are shown in Figure 17.3.

FIGURE 17.3

You can either pass information about a row to delete or update using a URL parameter or a FORM variable.

We will use the URL parameter scenario, but the processing is similar to using FORM variables.

Start by querying a subset of information from the Guestbook table:

```
<!---Get all rows from the table --->
<CFQUERY NAME="qGetGuestList" DATASOURCE="learncfe">
    SELECT GuestName, Email, GuestBook_ID
    FROM Guestbook;
</CFQUERY>
```

Then display the GuestName and Email information in an HTML table. If you want, you could create the hyperlink on the data to drill down as you did in Hour 15. I'm going to keep it simple here without the drill down:

```
<!---Print out the rows --->
<H2>Guest List View</H2>
<TABLE>
    <CFOUTPUT QUERY="qGetGuestList">
    <TR>
       <TD>
          #qGetGuestList.GuestName# #qGetGuestList.Email#
       </TD>
    </TR>
    </CFOUTPUT>
</TABLE>
```

Next, add two hyperlinks to the maintenance page. The hyperlink text should read either Update or Delete. The bolded code exhibits this change:

```
<H2>Guest List View</H2>
<TABLE>
    <CFOUTPUT QUERY="qGetGuestList">
    <TR>
       <TD>
       #qGetGuestList.GuestName# #qGetGuestList.Email#
       </TD>
       <TD><A HREF="guest_maint.cfm">Update</A></TD>
       <TD><A HREF="guest_maint.cfm">Delete</A></TD>
    </TR>
    </CFOUTPUT>
</TABLE>
```

Because both operations are going to the same page, we need to pass two pieces of information. The first is the operation type so that the page can distinguish what needs to be done. The second is the value of the GuestBook_ID column, which is the primary key. This will be used in the maintenance page to find the correct row to update or delete. I've created two URL parameters called op and gid that contain the operation code (u for update, d for delete) and the primary key column (guest ID), respectively. This change is shown as follows in bold:

```
<H2>Guest List View</H2>
<TABLE>
    <CFOUTPUT QUERY="qGetGuestList">
    <TR>
        <TD>
        #qGetGuestList.GuestName# #qGetGuestList.Email#
        </TD>
        <TD><A HREF="guest_maint.cfm?op=u&gid=#qGetGuestList.GuestBook_ID#">
        Update</A></TD>
        <TD><A HREF="guest_maint.cfm?op=d&gid=#qGetGuestList.GuestBook_ID#">
        Delete</A></TD>
    </TR>
    </CFOUTPUT>
</TABLE>
```

To Do: Create a Guest List View

To Do ▼

Follow these steps to create Guest List view page that displays the guest's name and email address. Add hyperlinks that allow you to go to the maintenance page.

1. Return to HomeSite and be sure that the Local Files tab is pointing to the /learncfe/hour17 directory.

2. Create a new page using the default template.

3. Change the <TITLE> text to "Guest List View Page".

4. Save the page as guest_list_url.cfm.

5. Write a query to return the following three columns from the Guestbook table: GuestBook_ID, GuestName, and Email.

6. Use the <CFOUTPUT> tag and table tags to display this information. Refer to the full code listing at the end of these instructions for help.

7. Inside the <CFOUTPUT> tag, create two more table cells. Inside one cell create a hyperlink to the guest_maint.cfm page and the hyperlink text of "Update". Create another hyperlink within the second table cell for "Delete" that points to the same page.

8. Save the file and browse. Make sure that both hyperlinks are displayed and they both take you to the guest_maint.cfm page. (You will receive an error until you create this page.)

9. Return to HomeSite and the guest_list_url.cfm page.

10. Create a URL parameter on the end of the Update hyperlink and pass a variable called op with a value of u. Create a second URL parameter called gid and give it a value of the query's GuestBook_ID column.

▼

17

▼   11. Create a URL parameter at the end of the Delete hyperlink and pass op as d and gid as the query's GuestBook_ID column.

12. Save the page and browse, taking note that the correct URL parameters are being passed in the debug information.

The full code listing for the guest_list_url.cfm page is shown in Listing 17.1.

LISTING 17.1   Guest List View Page

```
 1: <!DOCTYPE HTML PUBLIC "-//W3C//DTD HTML 4.0 Transitional//EN">
 2:
 3: <html>
 4: <head>
 5:     <title>Guestbook List View - URL</title>
 6: </head>
 7:
 8: <body>
 9: <!---Get all rows from the table --->
10: <CFQUERY NAME="qGetGuestList" DATASOURCE="learncfe">
11:     SELECT GuestName, Email, GuestBook_ID
12:     FROM Guestbook;
13: </CFQUERY>
14:
15: <!---Print out the columns and make each row a hyperlink --->
16: <H2>Guest List View</H2>
17: <TABLE>
18:     <CFOUTPUT QUERY="qGetGuestList">
19:     <TR>
20:         <TD>
21:         #qGetGuestList.GuestName# #qGetGuestList.Email#
22:         </TD>
23:         <TD><A HREF="guest_maint.cfm?op=u&gid=#qGetGuestList.GuestBook_ID#">
24:         Update</A></TD>
25:         <TD><A HREF="guest_maint.cfm?op=d&gid=#qGetGuestList.GuestBook_ID#">
26:         Delete</A></TD>
27:     </TR>
28:     </CFOUTPUT>
29: </TABLE>
30: </body>
31: </html>.
```

▲

Now that you've create the List view, you are ready to code the maintenance page.

Maintenance Page Processing

The maintenance page can detect the type of operation that is requested and provide the correct functionality. The first step is to detect the URL parameters. If none are supplied, redirect the user to the Guest List View page. This code is shown as follows:

```
<!---If a URL parameter for the operation was not sent, redirect the user back
 to the Guest List View page --->
<CFIF NOT IsDefined("URL.op") OR NOT IsDefined("URL.gid")>
    <CFLOCATION URL="guest_list_url.cfm">
</CFIF>
```

If the URL parameters do exist, the next step will be to retrieve the row. With either operation, you first need to retrieve the row requested. The following <CFQUERY> tag will retrieve the row to either update or delete:

```
<!---Get all columns for the chosen row from the table --->
<CFQUERY NAME="qGetGuest" DATASOURCE="learncfe">
    SELECT *
    FROM Guestbook
    WHERE GuestBook_ID = #URL.GID#;
</CFQUERY>
```

This is where the processing starts to differ between the update and delete operations. Begin by creating a conditional logic block to differentiate between the processing type, as shown in the following code. The <CFELSE> isn't really necessary, but it helps for those maintaining the code later on to know all possible scenarios:

```
<CFIF URL.op IS "u">
    <!---update processing --->
    Update!
<CFELSEIF URL.op IS "d">
    <!---Delete processing --->
    Delete!
<CFELSE>
    <!---Unknown processing operation --->
    Error, invalid processing type!
</CFIF>
```

You could use the <CFSWITCH> tag instead of the <CFIF> tag because both conditions evaluate the same variable. <CFSWITCH> processing is known to be slightly faster than using <CFIF>. This tag was introduced in Hour 6, "Implementing Conditional Processing."

17

To Do: Create the Maintenance Processing Page

Follow these steps to create the start of the Guest Maintenance page to process both updates and deletes.

1. Return to HomeSite and be sure that the Local Files tab is pointing to the /learncfe/hour17 directory.

2. Create a new page using the default template.

3. Change the <TITLE> text to "Guest Maintenance".

4. Save the page as **guest_maint.cfm**.

5. Test to see if either the op or the gid URL parameters are missing. If so, redirect the user to the Guest List view page using the <CFLOCATION> tag.

6. After the </CFIF> tag, create a <CFQUERY> tag that returns all columns from the Guestbook table using the URL.gid parameter to limit it to one row.

7. After the </CFQUERY> tag, create conditional logic to test for the value of URL.op. It could either be u, d, or unknown.

The full listing of the guest_maint.cfm page so far is shown in Listing 17.2.

LISTING 17.2 Guest Maintenance Page

```
 1: <!DOCTYPE HTML PUBLIC "-//W3C//DTD HTML 4.0 Transitional//EN">
 2:
 3: <html>
 4: <head>
 5:     <title>Guest Maintenance Page</title>
 6: </head>
 7:
 8: <body>
 9:
10: <!---If a URL parameter for the operation was not sent, redirect the user
11: back to the Guest List View page --->
12: <CFIF NOT IsDefined("URL.op") OR NOT IsDefined("URL.gid")>
13:     <CFLOCATION URL="guest_list_url.cfm">
14: </CFIF>
15:
16: <!---Get all columns for the chosen row from the table --->
17: <CFQUERY NAME="qGetGuest" DATASOURCE="learncfe">
18:     SELECT *
19:     FROM Guestbook
20:     WHERE GuestBook_ID = #URL.GID#;
21: </CFQUERY>
22:
23: <CFIF URL.op IS "u">
24:     <!---update processing --->
```

```
25:     Update!
26: <CFELSEIF URL.op IS "d">
27:     <!---Delete processing --->
28:     Delete!
29: <CFELSE>
30:     <!---Unknown processing operation --->
31:     Error, invalid processing type!
32: </CFIF>
33: </body>
34: </html>
```

We will now focus on the section for update processing and return to the delete processing later on this hour.

Update Processing

The bottom line for update processing is that you want to make changes to the column values for a row of data. The user chooses the row to update and then should be shown a form with all the current row values displayed. The user will update any values he chooses and leave other column values alone. Once submitted, the form data will be used to update the values in the database row.

Creating the Update Form

We need to create a form and default all the values to those stored in the database row. We can do this by starting with the insert form we modified in the last hour, as shown in Figure 17.4.

In order to set the row's values into the form, you need to learn how to default form controls.

Text Controls

To default a text control, simply set the VALUE attribute. In our case, we are setting it equal to a query result column, so it will need to be surrounded by a <CFOUTPUT> and specify the query name. You might need to use the Trim() function with some databases that return fixed-length fields. Those fields will pad the column with spaces that you will need to trim off.

```
<CFOUTPUT>
<INPUT TYPE="text" NAME="GuestName"
 VALUE= "#Trim(qGetGuest.GuestName)#">
</CFOUTPUT>
```

17

FIGURE 17.4

The Guest Book insert form can be used as a starting point to fill in the row's values into the form for an update process.

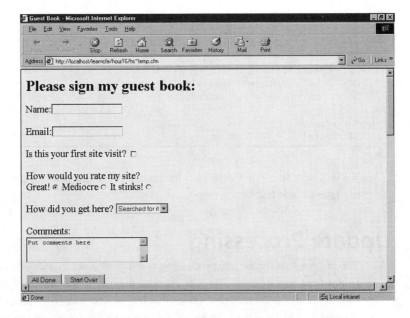

Check Box Controls

To prefill check box controls, embed the <CFIF> tag directly inside the control for the check box. If the row we want to display has the check box checked, the value will be "Yes". Here we can test and if the FirstVisit column is "Yes", we can default the check box to one using the CHECKED attribute. Notice that the <CFIF> tag is embedded inside the ending >, which closes the entire <INPUT> tag. Again, this would need to be inside a <CFOUTPUT> tag to resolve the query variable.

```
Is this your first site visit?
    <INPUT TYPE="checkbox"
        NAME="FirstVisit"
        VALUE="Yes"
        <CFIF qGetGuest.FirstVisit IS "Yes">
            CHECKED
        </CFIF>
        >
```

Radio Buttons

You can also embed a <CFIF> inside a radio button control to default it to a specific option based on information in the current row of the database. Each radio button will contain a test against the query column value to see which one is set in the database, and the entire set of radio buttons must be within a `<CFOUTPUT>` tag.

```
How would you rate my site?<BR>
   Great!<INPUT TYPE="radio"
      NAME="Rating"
      VALUE="Great"
         <CFIF qGetGuest.Rating IS "great">
            CHECKED
         </CFIF>
      >
   Mediocre<INPUT TYPE="radio"
      NAME="Rating"
      VALUE="Mediocre"
         <CFIF qGetGuest.Rating IS "mediocre">
            CHECKED
         </CFIF>
      >
   It stinks!<INPUT TYPE="radio"
      NAME="Rating"
      VALUE="Stinks"
         <CFIF qGetGuest.Rating IS "stinks">
            CHECKED
         </CFIF>
      >
```

Select Controls

Two tables are involved with the select control on the guestbook page. There is the Guestbook table that contains the rows of data users entered, and there's the GotHere_Code table that enabled the dynamic generation of the select control. Therefore, you will need to compare the row to update with the option that is being created by the GotHere_Code table to see if there is a match. When there is, the SELECTED attribute will be used to make that option the currently selected option on the update form. Assuming the row to update is retrieved into qGetGuest, a second query can be executed to find all possible values:

```
<CFQUERY NAME="qGetGotHere_Code" DATASOURCE="learncfe">
SELECT GotHere, GotHere_Desc
FROM GotHere_Code
</CFQUERY>
```

Now the select control can have an embedded `<CFIF>` tag to set the SELECTED attribute on the matching row as each option is created:

```
How did you get here?
   <SELECT NAME="GotHere"
         SIZE="1">
```

```
<CFOUTPUT QUERY="qGetGotHere_Code">
    <OPTION VALUE="#qGetGotHere_Code.GotHere#"
        <CFIF qGetGotHere_Code.GotHere IS qGetGuest.GotHere>
            SELECTED
        </CFIF>
        >
        #qGetGotHere_Code.GotHere_Desc#
    </OPTION>
</CFOUTPUT>
</SELECT>
```

TextArea Controls

Putting data into a TextArea control is just like printing it out to the page. Simply put the variable between the <TEXTAREA> and </TEXTAREA> tags using pound signs and a <CFOUTPUT> tag. Remember not to put any lines or spaces in between the opening and closing <TEXTAREA> tags and use the Trim() function to trim off spaces:

```
Comments:<BR>
        <TEXTAREA COLS=30
            ROWS=3
            NAME="Comments"><CFOUTPUT>#Trim(qGetGuest.Comments)
            #</CFOUTPUT></TEXTAREA>
```

Hidden Controls

As stated earlier, you allow the user to choose a row to update and display the row in a prefilled HTML form. However, users should not be allowed to update the primary key. This is the case with most well designed databases. In the case in which the primary key is system-generated, this column has no meaning to the user anyway; therefore, it is not displayed on the form.

In order to know which row to update, we must pass the primary key to the action page. Therefore, we must supply the primary key in a hidden form control. To put the value into a form control, simply create the hidden control with the appropriate NAME and VALUE attributes and use a <CFOUTPUT> tag:

```
<INPUT TYPE="Hidden" NAME="GuestBook_ID" VALUE="#qGetGuest.GuestBook_ID#">
```

Because we are using the same action page for both the update and the delete processing, we'll also need to add another hidden form control to pass the operation type to perform:

```
<INPUT TYPE="Hidden" NAME="op" VALUE="u">
```

After you prefill all form controls, you should be able to see the row in the database reflected on the form as displayed in Figure 17.5.

FIGURE 17.5

When a user selects a row to update, she should receive a pre-filled form with the data.

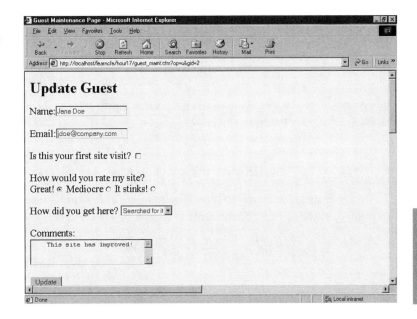

To Do: Create the Update Form

Follow these steps to create the form that will enable users to update a row in the Guestbook table.

1. Return to HomeSite and be sure that the Local Files tab is pointing to the /learncfe/hour17 directory.

2. Return to the file guest_maint.cfm.

3. Open the file /learncfe/hour16/guestbook.cfm.

3. Highlight and copy all the code within and including the <FORM> and </FORM> tags.

4. Paste in the copied form to the new page within the block for <CFIF URL.op IS "u">. Change the ACTION attribute to guest_maint_action.cfm.

5. Use the qGetGuest query information to prefill each control with the appropriate value. Don't forget to use the <CFOUTPUT> tag. Refer to the code at the end of this hour for help.

6. Set two hidden form controls: one for GuestBook_ID from the query, and another for op="u" for the operation.

7. Change the text on the button to "Update".

▼ 8. Save the file and browse from guest_list_url.cfm.

▼ You should now be able to select an Update link from the list page and get a prefilled
form with that row's information. Test it and compare it to what is in the database to
▲ make sure that the form is fully functional and prefilled.

> Refer to the end of this hour or the CD-ROM to see the full code listing for
> this form.

Creating the Maintenance Action Page

As with the maintenance form, the action page must also be sure that the user is navigat-
ing through the form. If not, redirect him to the list page:

```
<CFIF NOT IsDefined("FORM.op")>
    <CFLOCATION URL="guest_list_url.cfm">
</CFIF>
```

Using the Form.op hidden control value, we can then detect if this is an update or a
delete process:

```
<CFIF FORM.op IS "u">
    <!---Perform update processing --->
<CFELSEIF FORM.op IS "d">
    <!---Perform delete processing --->
<CFELSE>
    Error, unknown processing type!
</CFIF>
```

For the update processing, there are two options you can use to update the data in a database table:

- Using the <CFUPDATE> tag
- Using the <CFQUERY> tag with UPDATE

Using <CFUPDATE>

Just as the <CFINSERT> tag is a shortcut to inserting data, the <CFUPDATE> >tag is a shortcut for updating data. <CFUPDATE> is syntactically similar to <CFINSERT> and can be used
to handle simple updates:

```
<CFUPDATE DATASOURCE="learncfe" TABLENAME="Guestbook">
```

This tag does the following steps for you:

- Matches up form variables, which are submitted from a form to related database
  columns, by how they are named.
- Detects the data types of each column, puts single quotes around text form values,
  and formats dates into ODBC format.

- Detects the primary key column(s) and uses them in the WHERE clause to be sure to update only one row.
- Creates an UPDATE statement and sends it to the database for processing.

This is an easy way to update data quickly. But it does have limitations that you need to be aware of:

- Only data coming from a form can be used.
- Each form control must be named the same as the corresponding table column.
- All columns that make up the primary key must be in a form control.
- If your form has any other controls that don't have corresponding table columns, you must use the FORMFIELDS attribute to exclude them or you'll receive an error message.

In order to explicitly state the form controls that should be used to update, you can specify a comma-separated list of form variable names in the FORMFIELDS attribute:

```
<CFUPDATE DATASOURCE="learncfe" TABLENAME="Guestbook" FORMFIELDS="GuestName,
Email">
```

To Do: Update the Row Using <CFUPDATE>

Follow these steps to update a row in the Guestbook table.

1. Return to HomeSite and be sure that the Local Files tab is pointing to the /learncfe/hour17 directory.
2. Create a new page using the default template.
3. Change the <TITLE> text to "Guest Maintenance Action".
4. Save the page as **guest_maint_action.cfm**.
5. Inside the <BODY> and </BODY> tags, code the following conditional block to determine the operation:
   ```
   <CFIF NOT IsDefined("FORM.op")>
      <CFLOCATION URL="guest_list_url.cfm">
   </CFIF>

   <CFIF FORM.op IS "u">
      <!---Perform update processing --->
   <CFELSEIF FORM.op IS "d">
      <!---Perform delete processing --->
   <CFELSE>
      <CFLOCATION URL="guest_list_url.cfm">
   </CFIF>
   ```

17

▼ To Do

▼   6. Inside the <CFIF "FORM.op IS "u"> section, code a <CFUPDATE> tag to update the
       GuestBook table with the information from the submitted form. (Hint: If you
       receive errors, you might have to use the FORMFIELDS attribute to tell it which
       columns to update.)

    7. Save the page. Browse from the guest_list_url.cfm page. Be sure that you can
       choose a row, receive a prefilled page, and successfully update a row.

    8. After you have determined that updating each column is successful, add a
       <CFLOCATION> to redirect the user back to the guest_list_url.cfm page.

   Look at the data in the database to be sure that the update was successful. Refer to the
▲ code at the end of this hour or on the CD-ROM for help.

Using <CFQUERY> with UPDATE

With any application programming language, you update data in database tables using
the UPDATE SQL statement. This statement allows you to update one or more rows of data
at a time in a database table.

The UPDATE statement has the following general syntax:

```
UPDATE tablename
SET col1 = val1,
    Col2 = val2
    ...
WHERE PKColumn = PKValue
```

The tablename value should say which table you want to update information in. Specify
each "column=value" pair in the SET clause separated by commas. If you omit the WHERE
clause, **every row** in the table will be updated with this information. Sometimes that is
the intent, but more often than not problems are caused by forgetting to use a WHERE
clause.

As an example, to update a guest's email address, you would need to know the
GuestBook_ID primary key value for that row in the following UPDATE statement:

```
UPDATE Guestbook
SET Email = 'jdoe@company.com'
WHERE GuestBook_ID = 3;
```

Don't forget that you must follow the rules with data types within an
UPDATE statement just as you did with the INSERT statement. Text values
should always be surrounded with single quotes.

Using <CFUPDATE> is a quick and dirty way to update the table row. Using the <CFQUERY> tag with the SQL UPDATE statement might seem more complex, but it also makes it more flexible and powerful.

> Take care that you always use a WHERE clause on an UPDATE or DELETE statement or you'll effect all rows in the table.

To Do: Update Table Rows Using <CFQUERY> with UPDATE

Follow these steps to update rows in the Guestbook table. In the last hour, you used a code table for the values in the GotHere column. These values are different from the original form, which stored search, stumbled, and unknown. The new values are SEA, STU, and UNK. In this exercise, you will update the rows in the table to use these new values.

1. Return to HomeSite and be sure that the Local Files tab is pointing to the /learncfe/hour17 directory.

2. Create a new page using the default template.

3. Change the <TITLE> text to "Update Guestbook".

4. Save the file as **update_gothere.cfm**.

5. Inside the <BODY> and </BODY> tags, code a <CFQUERY> tag to find out how many rows we are going to update for the "searched" string:
```
<CFQUERY NAME="qGetGuest" DATASOURCE="learncfe">
    SELECT Count(*) AS SearchCount
    FROM Guestbook
    WHERE GotHere = 'search'
</CFQUERY>
<CFOUTPUT>Number of rows: #qGetGuest.SearchCount#</CFOUTPUT>
```

6. Save the template and run it. Note how many rows you will update.

7. Return to the HomeSite. After the ending </CFQUERY> tag, write another query that will update the rows as shown in the following:
```
<CFQUERY NAME="qUpdGuest" DATASOURCE="learncfe">
    UPDATE Guestbook
    SET GotHere = 'SEA'
    WHERE GotHere = 'search'
</CFQUERY>
```

8. Save the file and run it. It should update the rows successfully. Check the database to see that the rows were updated.

▲ Repeat these steps to update the GotHere value of stumbled to STU and unknown to UNK.

Delete Processing

Because deleting data can be harmful, you need to make sure that it was your user's true intent. Most deletions require that you respond to a confirmation message before deleting. After the data is gone, it's gone for good. So the process will be

1. The user selects a row to delete from the list page
2. The user receives a confirmation page.
3. If the user chooses to delete, the row is removed.
4. If the user cancels the action, no delete is made.

Creating the Confirmation Page

When the user clicks on the Delete hyperlink in the Guest List View page, she should receive a deletion confirmation, such as listed in Figure 17.6:

FIGURE 17.6

When the user chooses to delete a row, she should receive a delete confirmation page.

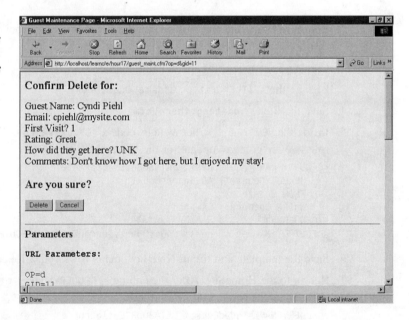

This page contains an HTML form with two submit buttons. A Delete button tells the action page to delete, and a Cancel button tells the action page to redirect back to the list view without deleting.

We can do this by creating submit buttons in a form:

```
<INPUT TYPE="Submit" NAME="Delete" VALUE="Delete">
<INPUT TYPE="Submit" NAME="Cancel" VALUE="Cancel">
```

Then, in the action page, you can detect which button was pressed. If you remember, submit buttons don't exist on the action page if they weren't clicked. Because it isn't possible for more than one button to be clicked, you can use the IsDefined() function to detect which condition is true, as in the following code:

```
<!--- If the user chose to cancel, go to the list view --->
   <CFIF IsDefined("Form.Cancel")>
       <CFLOCATION URL="guest_list_url.cfm">
   <CFELSEIF IsDefined("Form.Delete")>
       <!---Delete the row --->
   </CFIF>
```

You will also need to take the primary key of the column to delete from the query in this page and put it into a hidden form control. This will be used in the delete statement in the action page.

To Do: Create the Delete Processing

Follow these steps to create the delete confirmation window and detect the users choice to go ahead and delete or cancel.

1. Return to HomeSite and be sure that the Local Files tab is pointing to the /learncfe/hour17 directory.

2. Return to the guest_maint.cfm page.

3. Inside the <CFELSEIF URL.op IS "d"> block, print out the contents of the row. (The row was queried at the top of the page.)

4. Create a form with an action page of guest_maint_action.cfm.

5. Inside the form, create a submit button with a NAME of Delete and a text (VALUE) of Delete.

6. Create a submit button with a NAME of Cancel and a text (VALUE) of Cancel.

7. Create a hidden form control called GuestBook_ID and set it equal to the value of the query's matching column. Don't forget to use pound signs and the <CFOUTPUT> tag.

8. Save the page. To test, browse the guest_list_url.cfm page. Choose any Delete hyperlink and be sure that you see the confirmation page with the correct row.

Try submitting the form. You haven't coded the deletion logic yet, but you should see which primary key row you will be deleting within the form debug output.

Deleting Rows Using DELETE

Unlike with INSERT and UPDATE, there is no such tag as <CFDELETE>. If you want to remove a row or rows of data from a database table, you need to use the <CFQUERY> tag with the DELETE statement.

The DELETE statement has the following syntax:

```
DELETE FROM tablename
WHERE condition
```

The DELETE statement can also be dangerous because it can delete all rows in the table if you omit the WHERE clause.

> I always first write a SELECT statement using the same WHERE clause that I intend to use for the UPDATE or DELETE. I see how many rows will be affected before I change it to UPDATE or DELETE. This saves me headaches from updating or deleting more rows than I want to.

Using the DELETE within a <CFQUERY> tag, you don't need to name the query because it doesn't return any rows. For instance, if you wanted to delete the guest John Doe from the database, you could use the following tag:

```
<CFQUERY DATASOURCE="learncfe">
    DELETE FROM Guestbook
    WHERE GuestName = 'John Doe'
</CFQUERY>
```

If you have more than one John Doe in your database, you have just deleted them all. So using the primary key to delete them is recommended because it will only delete one row.

To Do: Delete the Row

Follow these steps to delete the row if confirmed or cancel the operation and move to the List view page.

1. Return to HomeSite and be sure that the Local Files tab is pointing to the /learncfe/hour17 directory.

2. Return to the guest_maint_action.cfm page.

3. Inside the <CFELSEIF FORM.op IS "d"> block, code the following logic:

```
<!--- If the user chose to cancel, go to the list view --->
    <CFIF IsDefined("Form.Cancel")>
        <CFLOCATION URL="guest_list_url.cfm">
```

```
    <CFELSEIF IsDefined("Form.Delete")>
        <!---Delete the row --->
    </CFIF>
<CFELSE>
    <CFLOCATION URL="guest_list_url.cfm">
</CFIF>
```

4. Save the page and browse from the guest_list_url.cfm page. Select Delete for a row and receive the confirmation page. Choose Cancel and you should be redirected back to the list view page.

5. Return to the guest_maint_action.cfm page.

6. Inside the `<CFELSEIF IsDefined("Form.Delete")>` block, code the following DELETE statement:

```
<CFQUERY DATASOURCE="learncfe">
    DELETE FROM Guestbook
    WHERE GuestBook_ID = #FORM.GuestBook_ID#
</CFQUERY>
```

7. Save the file and test it. If it works, the row will be deleted.

When you are satisfied that the delete works, add a `<CFLOCATION>` tag to redirect the user to the guest_list_url.cfm page after the deletion.

Summary

In this hour, you learned how to make a maintenance page that allows you to list, update, and delete information from a database table. This type of interface could be combined with the drill-down interface to get more information about each row, as well as the insert interface to add data. In this way, a fully-functional maintenance application can be built. When you get a standard set of templates for maintenance, it will be easier to build them for any table you need to maintain via the Web.

Q&A

Q How would I combine the update and delete functionality with the insert functionality?

A You could have a list page that shows all rows and allows updates and deletes as you've done in this hour. Then add a single submit button on this window to add. This will take you to a blank form to fill in and then submit to add. After addition, the user should be returned to the list page again. You can even combine the processing for inserts into the current three pages. The maintenance page could have additional conditional logic for the operation of insert (op="i"). In this section of code, a blank form could be displayed. When submitted, it would go to the same maintenance action page where another conditional block could be added for handling inserts using either <CFINSERT> or <CFQUERY> with INSERT.

Q Isn't using URL parameters on the URL rather insecure?

A Yes. It is my assumption in this example that if a user has the rights to see the guest list, he has the right to update any row. If you have rights based on different rows in the table, you would not want to use URL parameters to pass the guest primary key. The user could easily highlight and overwrite this value and might get to data he doesn't have the right to update or delete. You must always consider security in your application design.

Workshop

The Workshop contains quiz questions and exercises to help reinforce what you've learned in this hour. If you get stuck, the answers to the quiz questions can be found in Appendix A, "Answers to Quiz."

Quiz

1. What is the difference between using <CFUPDATE> and <CFQUERY> with UPDATE?
2. What is the difference between an insert form and an update form?
3. Why would you have to use the FORMFIELDS attribute of the <CFUPDATE> tag?
4. *True or false*: The DELETE statement always deletes one row in a table.

Exercises

1. Write a maintenance interface against the GotHere_Code table that allows you to insert, update, and delete the rows.
2. Explore e-commerce Web sites for how they allow you to maintain information in your shopping cart. (The shopping cart information will eventually be put into the database anyway, and can be thought of maintaining in the same way.) How do they allow you to remove items from their shopping cart? How can you update information, like quantity? What about adding? You can learn things from finding out how other sites do maintenance of data.

HOUR 18

Using Advanced Variable Types

You have created simple page variables, URL parameters, and FORM variables. Each of these variable types are atomic; they contain only one piece of information. There are cases where you have the need to group information together into a more complex type. This hour will explore some formats for complex data for grouping.

In this lesson, you'll learn the following:

- How to create, manipulate, and use lists
- What arrays are and how to use them within your CFML pages
- What structures are and how they differ from arrays

Understanding Complex Data Types

ColdFusion Express allows you to store your variables in more than just single values.
There are data needs that exceed the limits of simple variable types, so ColdFusion
Express enables you to work with data in the following formats:

- Lists
- Arrays
- Structures

Understanding Lists

Lists consist of a set of values, separated by a delimiter, usually a comma by default. A
simple list might be

```
<CFSET lMyFriends = "Kathie,June,Marjorie,Kristen">
```

 I have named my list with a prefix of the letter l. This represents a list. Using
this prefix makes it very easy to see what should be contained in that variable.

This might be more efficient than using separate variables for these names, such as

```
<CFSET MyFriends1 = "Kathie">
<CFSET MyFriends2 = "June">
<CFSET MyFriends3 = "Marjorie">
<CFSET MyFriends4 = "Kristen">
```

As you can see from this simple example, a list is easier to understand and easier to create and manipulate. If I wanted to add more friends to my list, I'd have to create a new
variable called MyFriends5, and so on. Creating variables with dynamic names is complicated. Lists enable you to easily group information together.

There are times when HTML naturally forms lists, and manipulating them becomes very
easy with ColdFusion Express' list functions, as follows:

- When you choose multiple selections from an HTML select form control, the
  result is a variable that contains a list of the options you selected.
- If you ever have more than one form control that has the same name, a single variable gets created with a list of the values for each of them.

At current count, there are at least 21 functions that help you manipulate, sort, delete, and manage lists. We will discuss several of the list functions here. Refer to the function reference for full coverage of list functions.

Creating Lists

Lists can be created using a simple <CFSET> tag and a value with a delimiter. A *delimiter* is just a constant character used to separate values. Most of the time, it is a comma, but you can use other delimiters as well. Another common delimiter is the pipe symbol (|). Each list function allows you to specify the delimiter.

The following <CFSET> tag creates a simple list with four elements using a comma as the delimiter:

```
<CFSET lMyFriends = "Kathie,June,Marjorie,Kristen">
```

When you have a list, you can add items to it using specific functions. These functions keep you from having to manually maintain the list yourself.

The ListAppend() function allows you to add a value to the end of the list:

```
<CFSET lMyFriends = ListAppend(lMyFriends, "Mike")>
```

This function does not alter the original list, but returns the list with the added element. I have chosen to overwrite the original list with the new list including the added element. There is a third optional attribute to specify an alternate delimiter, if the list is not delimited with commas.

You can also add elements to the front of the list using the ListPrepend() function. This function's syntax is identical to the ListAppend() function.

If you want to insert a list item within the list (not on the beginning or the end), you can use the ListInsertAt() function. This function refers to the first element in the list as 1. In this example, I'm inserting "Robert" into the second position in the list. The result would be "Kathie,Robert,June,Marjorie, Kristen,Mike":

```
<CFSET lMyFriends = ListInsertAt(lMyFriends, 2, "Robert")>
```

There is also a function ListSetAt() that enables you to overwrite the contents of a list element.

To easily find the syntax for functions, type them on a page in HomeSite, put your cursor on top of the function, and press F1. This will bring up help on that specific function or tag.

Lists from Other Sources

Lists are naturally created by using HTML form controls, as previously discussed. You can also create lists from other data types, such as queries and arrays:

- The ValueList() and QuotedValueList() functions can be used to take a query result column and create a list, either with quoted values or not. This is useful for sending into a SELECT statement using the IN clause. This allows you to take a resulting column from one query and use it in the formation of another query.

- The ArrayToList() function will take an array and dump it into a list. You will learn about arrays later this hour.

There are many other list functions that we have not discussed. Use the ColdFusion Express CFML Language Reference to learn more about list functions.

Looping over Lists

You can always refer to and use lists as a whole, but you can also separate them out into their individual elements by looping over the list. The <CFLOOP> tag enables you to loop over a list. This example loops through the lMyFriends list and puts each element into the ListItem variable for each iteration of the loop. The ListItem variable is simply printed out with a line break after each element in the list:

```
<h3>My friends:</h3>
<CFLOOP LIST="#lMyFriends#" INDEX="ListItem">
   <CFOUTPUT>#ListItem#<BR></CFOUTPUT>
</CFLOOP>
```

The display would show each name on a separate line, as in Figure 18.1.

FIGURE 18.1

Looping over the list separates the elements so you can work with them individually. Here they are just printed on separate lines.

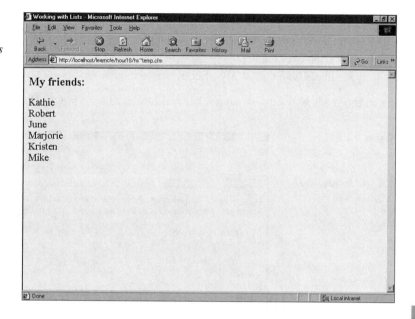

To Do: Create and Work with a List

Follow these steps to create a list and manipulate it using list functions:

1. Return to HomeSite and be sure the Local Files tab is pointing to the /learncfe/hour18 directory.

2. Create a new page using the default template.

3. Change the <TITLE> text to **"Working with Lists"**.

4. Save the page as lists.cfm.

5. Between the <BODY> and </BODY> tags, create a list of a few of your friends. Name the list lMyFriends.

6. Use the ListAppend() function to add another friend to the original list.

7. Use the ListPrepend() function to add a friend to the front of the list.

8. Use the ListInsertAt() function to insert another friend in the second position.

9. Use the <CFOUTPUT> tag to print out the value of the lMyFriend variable. Put the text of Original list in front of the output. Put a <BR> tag at the end of the output.

10. Use the ListSort() function to sort the list.

18

To Do

▼   11. Use another `<CFOUTPUT>` tag to print out the altered `lMyFriends` list. Use the text Sorted list in front of the output. Put a `<BR>` tag at the end of the output.

12. Loop over the list using the `<CFLOOP>` tag and print out each element on a separate line. Use a text of My Friends before the list.

Your code will vary by names, but will look similar to Figure 18.2.

FIGURE 18.2

Output from printing out a list, sorting a list, and looping over a list.

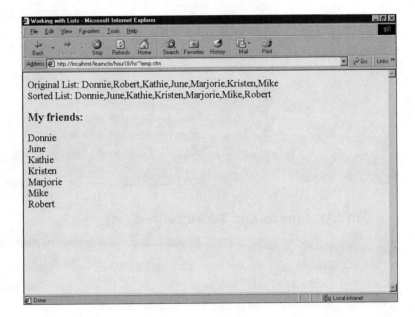

LISTING 18.1 Working with Lists

```
 1: <!DOCTYPE HTML PUBLIC "-//W3C//DTD HTML 4.0 Transitional//EN">
 2:
 3: <html>
 4: <head>
 5:     <title>Working with Lists</title>
 6: </head>
 7:
 8: <body>
 9: <!---Create a list with a simple CFSET tag --->
10: <CFSET lMyFriends = "Kathie,June,Marjorie,Kristen">
11:
12: <!---Add an element to the end of the list --->
13: <CFSET lMyFriends = ListAppend(lMyFriends, "Mike")>
14:
15: <!---Prepend an element to the front of the list --->
```

LISTING **18.1** contined

```
16: <CFSET lMyFriends = ListPrepend(lMyFriends, "Donnie")>
17:
18: <!---Insert an element into the 2nd position of the list --->
19: <CFSET lMyFriends = ListInsertAt(lMyFriends, 2, "Robert")>
20:
21: <!---Print out the list --->
22: <CFOUTPUT>#lMyFriends#</CFOUTPUT>
23:
24: <!---Sort the list --->
25: <CFSET lMyFriends = ListSort(lMyFriends, "text")>
26:
27: <!---Print out the list --->
28: <CFOUTPUT>#lMyFriends#</CFOUTPUT>
29:
30: <!---Loop over the list --->
31: <H3>My friends:</H3>
32: <CFLOOP LIST="#lMyFriends#" INDEX="ListItem">
33:     <CFOUTPUT>#ListItem#<BR></CFOUTPUT>
34: </CFLOOP>
35:
36: </body>
37: </html>
```

18

Understanding Arrays

Arrays are another way to group data in CFML. Most programming languages allow you to group information into arrays. Unlike lists, arrays are actually a separate data storage mechanism. (Lists are just string variables after all.) Instead of saving information into one variable, an array allows you to group a set of information under one name. For instance, an array called aMyFriends that contains my friends' names might visually be represented by Figure 18.3.

FIGURE **18.3**

An array is a grouping of information accessed through a common name.

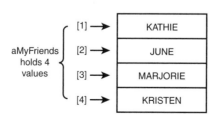

aMyFriends holds 4 values

[1] → KATHIE

[2] → JUNE

[3] → MARJORIE

[4] → KRISTEN

An *array* is a series of values that can be accessed by an index. An *index* is a numeric offset into the array where the value is stored. My array has four elements, therefore you would access them using numeric offsets of 1 through 4, which is the index. Specify the index by using square brackets surrounding the number, as in the following:

```
<CFOUTPUT>
My first friend in the list is #aMyFriends[1]#
</CFOUTPUT>
```

Notice that I named my array with a small letter 'a' followed by MyFriends. The small 'a' enables me to see right away that this is an array I'm working with. These naming conventions can help with maintenance of code.

The benefits of using arrays are similar to those of lists, in that arrays can be manipulated, sorted, and managed using functions.

Creating Arrays

Create an array using the ArrayNew() function. This function expects one attribute, which is the dimension of the array. An array that has a single column of information, such as aMyFriends, is considered a one-dimensional array. We'll talk about other dimensions in a little while.

To create the aMyFriends array, use the ArrayNew() function with a dimension of 1 within a <CFSET> tag:

```
<CFSET aMyFriends = ArrayNew(1)>
```

This sets up the array, an action called *array initialization*. Now you are ready to put data into the array. You can create the first item in the array using the array syntax, which consists of using index notation and square brackets:

```
<CFSET aMyFriends[1] = "Kathie">
```

Now you have an array with one element at the first position. You can continue to add elements, using this array syntax:

```
<CFSET aMyFriends[2] = "June">
<CFSET aMyFriends[3] = "Marjorie">
<CFSET aMyFriends[4] = "Kristen">
```

Adding to an Array

You can also use functions to add elements to an array. As with lists, there are corresponding `ArrayAppend()`, `ArrayPrepend()`, and `ArrayInsertAt()` functions. Here are some examples of their use:

```
<!---Add an element to the end of the array --->
<CFSET tmp = ArrayAppend(aMyFriends, "Mike")>

<!---Prepend an element to the front of the array --->
<CFSET tmp = ArrayPrepend(aMyFriends, "Donnie")>

<!---Insert an element into the 2nd position of the array --->
<CFSET tmp = ArrayInsertAt(aMyFriends, 2, "Robert")>
```

You might notice a difference right away between the list functions and array functions. I have set a variable called `tmp` to the result of these functions. The difference is that list functions **do not** change the list that is used as an argument, whereas the array functions **do**. Therefore, there is no need to put the result into another variable. In this case, the resulting value of the `tmp` variable is always "YES". This is considered a dummy variable that just is a placeholder to enable you to use a function.

It is recommended to use a variable that is obviously a dummy variable, such as tmp or dummy. This will help you and those after you to understand what the code is doing.

These functions will automatically handle the numeric index of the values and the order for you.

Arrays also allow you to create each element in the array and set default values for them using the `ArraySet()` function. When an array is created using `ArrayNew()`, you can put in default values for each element you want. This example creates an array and creates four elements initialized to 0:

```
<CFSET aTotalsByQuarter = ArrayNew(1)>
<CFSET tmp = ArraySet(aTotalsByQuarter, 1, 4, 0)>
```

Now you can set the individual elements of this array using `<CFSET>`.

18

Array Calculations

Arrays enable you to perform numeric functions on them, whereas lists do not. You can get the following information about an array:

- The sum of all elements in an array using `ArraySum()`
- The average of all elements in an array using `ArrayAvg()`
- The minimum value of all elements in an array using `ArrayMin()`
- The maximum value of all elements in an array using `ArrayMax()`

These operations can only be used on array elements that contain numeric data.

Printing Out Arrays

You can print out array elements by explicitly specifying the index. This code prints out the first element of the array:

```
<CFOUTPUT>#aMyFriends[1]#</CFOUTPUT>
```

However, if you do not know the exact number of elements in the array, you can loop through and print out all values using the `<CFLOOP>` tag. You use the index loop from 1 to the total number of array elements using the `ArrayLen()` function:

```
<h3>My friends:</H3>
<CFLOOP FROM="1" TO="#ArrayLen(aMyFriends)#" INDEX="i">
    <CFOUTPUT>#aMyFriends[i]#<BR></CFOUTPUT>
</CFLOOP>
```

The `INDEX` attribute (`i`) will get set to each number from 1 to the length of the array for each iteration of the loop. Because this value contains the current array index, it will be used to print out the array item for each time through the loop.

Sorting Arrays

Another benefit of working with data as grouped in arrays is the ability to sort the data. There three ways to sort the data:

- Alphabetically as case sensitive
- Alphabetically as not case sensitive
- Numerically

You can also sort the list as ascending or descending values. All of this can be accomplished through the use of the `ArraySort()` function. This function takes three arguments, the array to sort, the sorting type, and the sorting order. This code takes the aMyFriends array and sorts it alphabetically (case sensitive) starting with A and going through Z:

```
<CFSET tmp = ArraySort(aMyFriends, "text", "asc")>
```

Other values for the sorting type are textnocase and numeric. The sorting order might be designated as "desc" for descending.

To Do: Create and Work with Arrays

▼ To Do

Follow these steps to create and manipulate arrays using functions:

1. Return to HomeSite and be sure the Local Files tab is pointing to the /learncfe/hour18 directory.

2. Create a new page using the default template.

3. Change the <TITLE> text to "Working with Arrays".

4. Save the page as arrays.cfm.

5. Between the <BODY> and </BODY> tags, create an array to hold a few of your friends' names. Name the list aMyFriends.

6. Use array syntax to create four or so elements with your friends' names.

7. Use the ArrayAppend() function to add another friend to the original array.

8. Use the ArrayPrepend() function to add a friend to the front of the array.

9. Use the ArrayInsertAt() function to insert another friend in the second position.

10. Use the <CFLOOP> tag to loop through each array element in aMyFriends and print it out. Label the output with an <H3> tag containing "My Friends".

11. Use the ArraySort() function to sort the array.

12. Use another <CFLOOP> tag to loop through each array element in aMyFriends and print it out. Label the output with an <H3> tag containing "Sorted Friends".

▲

Your code will vary by names, but will look similar to Listing 18.2.

LISTING 18.2 Working with Arrays

```
1: <!DOCTYPE HTML PUBLIC "-//W3C//DTD HTML 4.0 Transitional//EN">
2:
3: <html>
4: <head>
5:     <title>Working with Arrays</title>
6: </head>
7:
8: <body>
9: <!---Create the array --->
```

18

LISTING 18.2   continued

```
10: <CFSET aMyFriends = ArrayNew(1)>
11:
12: <!---Add elements to the array using array syntax --->
13: <CFSET aMyFriends[1] = "Kathie">
14: <CFSET aMyFriends[2] = "June">
15: <CFSET aMyFriends[3] = "Marjorie">
16: <CFSET aMyFriends[4] = "Kristen">
17:
18: <!---Add an element to the end of the array --->
19: <CFSET tmp = ArrayAppend(aMyFriends, "Mike")>
20:
21: <!---Prepend an element to the front of the array --->
22: <CFSET tmp = ArrayPrepend(aMyFriends, "Donnie")>
23:
24: <!---Insert an element into the 2nd position of the array --->
25: <CFSET tmp = ArrayInsertAt(aMyFriends, 2, "Robert")>
26:
27: <h3>My friends:</H3>
28: <CFLOOP FROM="1" TO="#ArrayLen(aMyFriends)#" INDEX="i">
29:     <CFOUTPUT>#aMyFriends[i]#<BR></CFOUTPUT>
30: </CFLOOP>
31:
32: </body>
33: </html>
```

The printout will be similar to Figure 18.4.

FIGURE 18.4

Printing out the array values as per the previous code will yield these results.

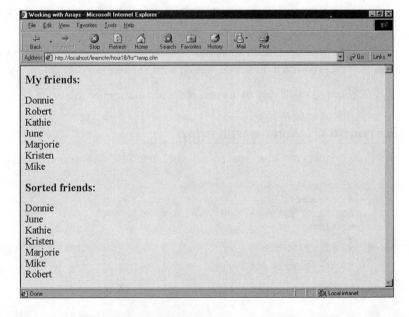

Two-Dimensional Arrays

The aMyFriends array is only one dimensional, because it just stores one group of information. If you wanted to store related information in an array, you would need to create another dimension. For instance, perhaps you wanted to also store your friends' last names in the array (but didn't want to store the last name and first name together). You could create a two-dimensional array. This is depicted in Figure 18.5.

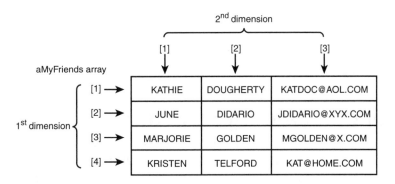

In order to create a two-dimensional array, use 2 as the argument to the ArrayNew() function:

```
<CFSET aMyFriends = ArrayNew(2)>
```

Now you can populate the array by specifying both indexes in the first and second dimension. If you think of the array as a table, the first dimension is the row number, and the second dimension is a column number. To create the first element in the first row, use the following:

```
<CFSET aMyFriends[1][1] = "Kathie">
```

To fill in the associated last name, use the second element in the first row:

```
<CFSET aMyFriends[1][2] = "Dougherty">
```

And the email address as the third element in the first row:

```
<CFSET aMyFriends[1][3] = "katdoc@aol.com">
```

You would print out the individual array elements also using the two array indexes. If you wanted to print out the entire array, you will have to use two loops, as in this pseudocode:

```
FOR EACH ROW
    FOR EACH COLUMN
        Print Row, Column position
    GET NEXT COLUMN
GET NEXT ROW
```

18

What this pseudocode represents is that you must loop through the row, and within the row loop through all columns. To do this, you could use two <CFLOOP> tags, one nested within the other:

```
<h3>My friends:</H3>
<CFLOOP FROM="1" TO="#ArrayLen(aMyFriends)#" INDEX="i">
    <CFLOOP FROM="1" TO="#ArrayLen(aMyFriends[i])#" INDEX="j">
        <CFOUTPUT>#aMyFriends[i][j]#</CFOUTPUT>
    </CFLOOP><BR>
</CFLOOP>
```

The first <CFLOOP> tag represents the row, and the inner <CFLOOP> tag represents each column in that row. The nested <CFLOOP> tag uses the ArrayLen(aMyFriends[i]) function. This represents the number of "columns" in the current dimension (i).

Understanding Structures

A structure is also a data type that allows you to group related information under one variable name. However, structures are designed to hold a group of related information about one thing. For instance, a structure would be useful to contain all the information about one of your friends, and not about all your friends together. This is analogous to a database row, where all columns are related to one particular thing. This is depicted in Figure 18.6.

FIGURE 18.6

A structure contains pieces of information about one thing.

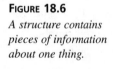
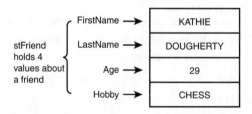

Another difference you might have noticed from arrays is that structures have a different type of index. Array indexes are always numeric, whereas structures can have strings as their index. Because this is different, indexes in structures are called *keys*. The keys for the structure shown in Figure 18.5 are FirstName, LastName, Age, and Hobby. This makes structures easy to work with, because these keys actually mean something and describe the data stored in those positions.

Creating Structures

You can create structures using the `StructNew()` function. This function does not take any arguments:

```
<CFSET stFriend = StructNew()>
```

Now you can create structure elements by creating both the key and the value within the `<CFSET>` tag:

```
<CFSET stFriend.FirstName = "Kathie">
<CFSET stFriend.LastName = "Dougherty">
<CFSET stFriend.Age = "29">
<CFSET stFriend.Hobby = "chess">
```

This type of syntax, in which the structure name is followed by a dot (.) and the key, is called *dot notation*.

Another option for inserting structure elements into a structure is by using structure functions. The `StructInsert()` function allows you to insert elements:

```
<CFSET tmp = StructInsert(stFriend, "FirstName", "Kathie")>
```

In this case, the `tmp` variable is a dummy variable that always equals `"yes"`.

A third option is to set structure elements by using array syntax, with the brackets. The difference from using arrays is that the index can be non-numeric:

```
<CFSET stFriend["FirstName"] = "Kathie">
```

> Array syntax on structures allows the key to be a variable, because it will be resolved by ColdFusion Express if it is not surrounded by quotes, as follows:
> ```
> <CFSET KeyName = "FirstName">
> <CFSET stFriend[Key] = "Kathie">
> ```
> It also allows spaces and special characters in the key names. However, using spaces and special characters is not recommended.

Looping over Structures

Just as with arrays and lists, you can loop over a structure and print out all values. Again, use the `<CFLOOP>` tag, but use yet another type of loop called a *collection loop*. The collection is the structure

```
<CFLOOP COLLECTION="#stFriend#" ITEM="keyname">
    <CFOUTPUT>#Keyname#: #stFriend[Keyname]#</CFOUTPUT><BR>
</CFLOOP>
```

18

This displays the key name, which is the label for the element, and the element value itself. The output would resemble Figure 18.7.

FIGURE **18.7**

Printing out the structure key and the value produces this display.

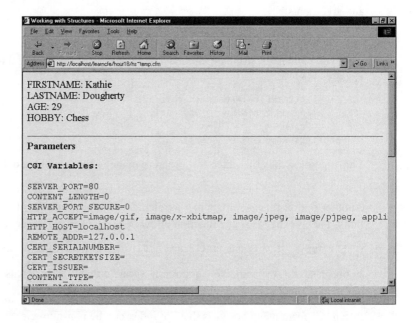

We have just began to learn about these different data types. Please consult the ColdFusion Express documentation for full listings of all list, array, and structure functions.

To Do: Create and Work with Structures

Follow these steps to create and manipulate structures using functions:

1. Return to HomeSite and be sure that the Local Files tab is pointing to the /learncfe/hour18 directory.

2. Create a new page using the default template.

3. Change the <TITLE> text to **"Working with Structures"**.

4. Save the page as structures.cfm.

5. Between the <BODY> and </BODY> tags, create a structure. Name the structure **stMyFriends**.

▼   6. Use dot notation to store a friend's first and last name in the structure. (Name the keys FirstName and LastName, respectively.)

7. Use the StructInsert() function to insert another key of Age with the value being the age of your friend.

8. Use array syntax to add a fourth element to the structure for your friend's hobby. Name the key Hobby.

9. Use a <CFLOOP> tag to loop through the structure (as the COLLECTION attribute) to print out the two values you have set. Label the output with an <H3> tag contain-

▲   ing "My Friend".

Your code will vary by names, but will look similar to Listing 18.3.

LISTING 18.3   Working with Structures

```
 1:  <!DOCTYPE HTML PUBLIC "-//W3C//DTD HTML 4.0 Transitional//EN">
 2:
 3:  <html>
 4:  <head>
 5:    <title>Working with Structures</title>
 6:  </head>
 7:
 8:  <body>
 9:
10:  <!---Create the structure --->
11:  <CFSET stFriend = StructNew()>
12:
13:  <!---Initialize the structure using dot notation --->
14:  <CFSET stFriend.FirstName = "Kathie">
15:  <CFSET stFriend.LastName = "Dougherty">
16:
17:  <!--Initialize another structure element using StructInsert()--->
18:  <CFSET tmp = StructInsert(stFriend, "Age", "29")>
19:
20:  <!---Yet another using array syntax --->
21:  <CFSET stFriend["Hobby"] = "Chess">
22:
23:  <h3>My Friend:</H3>
24:
25:  <CFLOOP COLLECTION="#stFriend#" ITEM="keyname">
26:      <CFOUTPUT>#Keyname#: #stFriend[Keyname]#</CFOUTPUT><BR>
27:  </CFLOOP>
28:
29:  </body>
30:  </html>
```

The printout will be similar to Figure 18.8.

18

FIGURE 18.8

Printing out the structure values as per the previous code will yield these results.

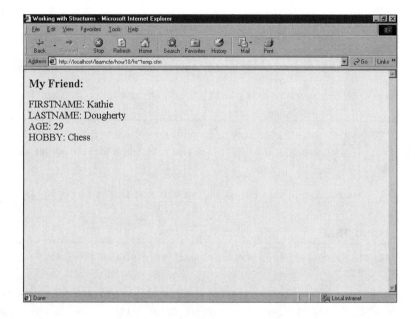

Comparing Advanced Variable Types

There are several differences between arrays, lists, and structures that might help you decide which format to use:

- Lists occur naturally in HTML forms, and therefore can be worked with directly using list functions.
- Lists enable you to perform string searches by using functions such as ListFind(), ListContains(), and ListQualify().
- Lists can be used in a SELECT statement's WHERE clause using the IN operator.
- Arrays can store related columns of information using more dimensions.
- Arrays enable computations such as sum, min, max, and average.
- Structures enable you to group different pieces of related information into a whole.

The difference between arrays and structures is that arrays store lists of like information, whereas structures store groups of related data about one particular thing. The best news is that there are functions to enable you to cast an array to a list, ArrayToList() and a list to an array, ListToArray().

Summary

These more complex data types can be used to keep data together in logical groupings. These groupings of data enable you to perform manipulations on them as a whole, instead of tracking individual variables.

Q&A

Q Does ColdFusion Express use any advanced variable types internally?

A Yes, ColdFusion Express often uses structures to store related data. For instance, all form data in the action page are put into a structure called FORM. This means you can act on the form data as a group, including the use of all structure functions. If you wanted to determine if a form was submitted to the action, you could simply test for IsDefined("Form"). The same is true for URL parameters.

Q A list looks like a row of data from a comma-separated file (.csv). Can I use it to loop through a data file and go through each item?

A This is a common use of lists within ColdFusion. Unfortunately, ColdFusion Express doesn't provide the capability to manipulate files. You will need to obtain the full ColdFusion Professional or ColdFusion Enterprise to get access to the <CFFILE> tag.

Q Query resultsets consist of rows and columns of data. Are they just two-dimensional arrays?

A Query resultsets are not arrays; however, in some ways they behave as one. For instance, you can access query rows by using array syntax such as qQuery.Column[1]. But you cannot use array functions on them. You could loop through a query and put it into an array as well.

18

Workshop

The Workshop contains quiz questions and activities to help reinforce what you've learned in this hour. If you get stuck, the answers to the quiz questions can be found in Appendix A, "Answers to Quiz."

Quiz

1. How can you create a list?
2. *True or false:* The following code creates a two-dimensional array:
   ```
   <CFSET aTestArray[1][2] = "Foo">.
   ```

3. Structure data resemble what part of a database?

4. What is the difference in how arrays and structures are referenced?

Exercises

1. Perform a query to return the Guest_Name column from the learncfe data source. Loop through the resultset and put each column value into a one-dimensional array.

2. Create a small form to capture a few pieces of information (any types of controls). Create an action page and use the IsDefined() function to see if the form structure exists. If it doesn't, redirect the user to the form. Test this by browsing the action page without going through the form.

HOUR 19

Personalizing Your Web Site

Have you ever visited a Web site and had it welcome you as a new visitor? Or have you ever returned to a site to be greeted by a welcome back message? Personalization is the mechanism used to track information about your visitors, and personalization is an important part of creating a pleasant user experience.

In this hour, you'll learn the following:

- What personalization is, and how it works
- What the terms *state* and *statelessness* mean, and why these affect you
- How to use persistent client cookies
- How to use ColdFusion client variables

Understanding Personalization

Whether you are aware of it or not, if you surf the Web regularly you have experienced personalization. E-commerce sites welcome you back and make book suggestions based on prior purchases. Secure sites remember your login but prompt for your password. Portals let you customize home pages so that they contain just the content you want. Online trading sites require that you log in once, and then remember you for the entire session.

What all these sites and interactions have in common is personalization—the capability for a site to adapt to a user thereby customizing and personalizing the user's experience. Using personalization is an important part of creating an appealing Web presence. By using ColdFusion Express, implementing personalization is a very painless process indeed.

Before we can play with personalization, it is important to understand how this technology works. Or rather, it is important to understand the inherent limitations of the Web, and how to work around them.

Understanding Statelessness

The Web is *stateless*. What this means is that when a user connects to a Web server, there is no connection that stays open between the client (the browser) and the server. When a browser makes a request, a connection is made for that specific request, and then the connection is immediately broken.

As a matter of fact, if a Web page contains five graphic images, a Web browser must make at least six connections to retrieve the page (one for the page, and one per image).

This is why hits are a useless measure of server activity. A *hit* is a request, and requesting a page could involve dozens of hits. The more buttons, images, graphics, and icons, the more hits.

In the early days of the Web (not that long ago actually), sneaky Web masters learned that if they broke their logo into five separate images, they could add five extra hits per page request. Armed with that little trick, sites could suddenly boast of millions of hits a day, even though their traffic had not increased at all.

Hits have nothing to do with how many pages were viewed. They also have nothing to do with how many visitors a site gets. The next time you hear someone boast that their site got millions of hits, don't be impressed.

This is very different from company networks, for example. When you log in to your network at work, you have an open connection to the network server. The server knows when you are connected and when you aren't, and a network administrator can see all connected users and interact with them as needed.

There's a very good reason for this behavior. If Web servers kept open connections to all connected clients (like office networks), you'd only be able to support tens or hundreds of simultaneous connections at any time (like office networks). Because Web browser connections only need to remain open for milliseconds (as much time as it takes to retrieve a single request), Web servers can handle thousands of clients simultaneously. Although in truth, they are not simultaneous at all; it only appears that way.

When a server is aware of what the client is doing, that server is aware of the client's *state*. The Web is *stateless*; Web servers are not aware of client state.

State in a Stateless World

The Web's statelessness helps ensure that your Web server can handle lots of users. But this behavior is highly problematic too. Because clients have no open connection, there is no simple way to track client requests. Every request stands on its own two feet with no knowledge of any prior requests.

Why is this problematic? Well, if requests are unaware of prior requests, how can actions be tracked across requests? How can items be placed in a shopping cart while ensuring that the cart's contents are still present on the next page? How can online retailers remember users to make recommendations?

Yet Web servers *do* track state. Obviously shopping carts *do* work. And online retailers *do* accurately remember users. So how are they doing this? The answer is they are using technologies that create state in an essentially stateless world.

19

Using Cookies

Cookies are one of the most misunderstood technologies on the Web (and the fact that they have a funny name does not help one bit). Unfortunately, lots of unfounded hype and conspiracy theories have tarnished the reputation of these invaluable tools. Cookies are simply variables that are stored on your computer by your browser.

Cookies are actually not a ColdFusion feature, they are supported by almost all Web servers and browsers as well as by most Web development languages. ColdFusion does, however, greatly simplify the use of cookies.

Understanding Cookies

The simplest way to understand cookies is to walk through a usage scenario:

1. A user visits your site for the first time.

2. Your Web server asks the user's browser to save a variable for future use somewhere on the user's hard disk.

3. The next time the user visits your site, the browser sends back that variable automatically to your Web server.

4. Your Web server knows that this is a user who has visited the site once before because the variable is present.

The variable that the browser saved is called a *cookie*. Because cookies are saved on the client (the browser), they provide a simple solution to the statelessness problem.

> It is important to remember that Web servers do not write information on users' hard disks, browsers do. And Web servers do not read users' hard disks either, Web browsers do. Web browsers are very careful to only send cookies to the server that set them. There is no way for a Web server to read cookies set by other Web servers.

> Because cookies are sent to the server on every request, and because they can be read and manipulated on the client machine, they are not suited for confidential information (like passwords or credit card numbers).

Working with Cookies

ColdFusion Express makes working with cookies very simple. Cookies are set using the <CFCOOKIE> tag. Cookies are accessed like other variables, but are prefixed with the type designator COOKIE.

Let's walk through an example based on the scenario we just looked at.

To Do: Read and Write Cookies

We'll create a simple file that will welcome a user. If the user has never visited the site before, he'll get a new user welcome message; if this is a return visit, he'll get a welcome back message. Here are the steps:

▼ 1. Open HomeSite (if it is not already open), and create a directory called hour19 under the learncfe directory.

2. Open a new blank document.

3. Type the code from Listing 19.1 in to the new page.

LISTING 19.1 Working with Cookies

```
 1: <HTML>
 2: <HEAD>
 3: <TITLE>Working With Cookies</TITLE>
 4: </HEAD>
 5:
 6: <BODY>
 7:
 8: <!--- Is this a new user? Check for the cookie --->
 9: <CFIF IsDefined("COOKIE.last_visit")>
10: <CFOUTPUT>
11: Welcome back, you were last here on #DateFormat(COOKIE.last_visit)#.
12: </CFOUTPUT>
13: <CFELSE>
14: Welcome new user, we hope you'll enjoy your visit.
15: </CFIF>
16:
17: </BODY>
18: </HTML>
19:
20: <!--- Set last_visited cookie --->
21: <CFCOOKIE NAME="last_visit" VALUE="#Now()#" EXPIRES="NEVER">
```

19

4. Save this file as **cookies.cfm** in the hour19 directory.

5. Open your Web browser and go to http://localhost/learncfe/hour19/ cookies.cfm. You should see a screen similar to the one shown on the left in Figure 19.1.

6. Now refresh the browser. You should see a screen similar to the one shown on the right in Figure 19.1.

FIGURE 19.1

On the left, the lack of a cookie is often used to assume that this is a first visit.
On the right, cookies can contain any information, including date and times.

Now that you've seen cookies in action, let's look at the code to see how it worked.

The first few lines of code are straight HTML. Then comes the following <CFIF> statement on line 9:

```
<CFIF IsDefined("COOKIE.last_visit")>
```

This statement checks to see whether a variable named COOKIE.last_visit exists. If it exists, the user is welcomed back, and the last visit is displayed (the cookie contains the date and time of the last visit) as follows:

```
Welcome back, you were last here on #DateFormat(COOKIE.last_visit)#.
```

If COOKIE.last_visit does not exist, a welcome new user message is displayed.

The last line of code actually sets the cookie. The cookie is reset every time the page is refreshed; that way it always contains the correct last visit date. As previously explained, setting cookies requires that you use the <CFCOOKIE> tag, as in line 21:

```
<CFCOOKIE NAME="last_visit" VALUE="#Now()#" EXPIRES="NEVER">
```

Here the cookie is named last_visit and the cookie value is the ColdFusion Now() function (which returns the current date and time, as explained in Hour 7, "Using Functions"). Cookies can be set to automatically expire after a specified amount of time (or at a specific time), or they can be set to **never** expire as is the case here. When the cookie is set, it'll be automatically sent back to the Web server on every subsequent request allowing the welcome message to be personalized.

There you have it: That's all there is to using cookies.

> Be careful where you set your cookies. In our example, if the <CFCOOKIE> tag would have been at the top of the page (before the <CFIF> statement), the test to see if the cookie existed would always return TRUE, even the first time around, because the <CFCOOKIE> tag would have already set the cookie.

Cookie Limitations

As wonderful as cookies are (and yes, contrary to popular belief, I firmly believe that cookies are indeed wonderful), there are some important limitations that you must be aware of:

- Not all Web browsers support cookies (although most newer ones do).
- Cookies can be disabled in most browsers. Even if your user's browser supports cookies, if the user has disabled cookies, your cookie will not be saved.

- Users can delete cookies. (There are even utilities available to simplify cookie deletion.)

- In many browsers there is a maximum of 20 cookies allowed per domain—try to set a 21st cookie, and it'll be ignored.

These are important limitations. If you use cookies, you must *never* assume that a cookie will be present just because you set it. Any code you write must first check for the presence of a cookie, and must be able to handle the cookie not being there.

> Many developers like to set default cookies before they use them to ensure that they exist. For example, they might include code like this at the top of the page:
>
> ```
> <CFIF NOT IsDefined("COOKIE.bgcolor")>
>   <CFCOOKIE NAME="bgcolor" VALUE="white">
> </CFIF>
> ```
>
> This way they could refer to #COOKIE.bgcolor# safely in their code.

Using Client Variables

Client variables are a special type of variable that is unique to ColdFusion. These variables were designed to compensate for some of the limitations inherent in cookies.

Understanding Client Variables

Unlike cookies that are stored on the client machine (via the Web browser), client variables are stored on the server. As such, they do not have the maximum number of variable restrictions, nor can users easily delete or disable them.

Now this raises an obvious question. I told you earlier that the Web is stateless. Cookies compensate for this because they are saved on the browser side. How can ColdFusion Express possibly store client variables on the server in a stateless environment?

The answer is actually pretty simple. Although client variables are stored on the server, an ID that is used to identify the client is stored on the browser. There are actually two ways that this ID is stored on the browser:

- As a cookie
- As a URL parameter

For the most part, this is all transparent. You as a developer can just read and write client variables, and ColdFusion worries about the details of passing IDs for you.

19

Actually, what gets saved to the browser is more than just an ID; that would be too easy for a user to change. Instead, ColdFusion sets two cookies or parameters, one named CFID (an ID number) and one named CFTOKEN (a random number). To access client variables, the CFID and matching CFTOKEN must be submitted together, making client variables safe to use.

Turning on Client Variables

Unlike cookies, before you can use client variables, support for them must be explicitly enabled. Client variable support is turned on with the <CFAPPLICATION> tag, a special tag used to set application level settings. The following line of code turns on client variables:

```
<CFAPPLICATION NAME="forta.com" CLIENTMANAGEMENT="Yes">
```

<CFAPPLICATION> requires that your application be named. Here I have named it forta.com. You can name your application with any name you like, although I'd recommend that you use something unique and descriptive. The reason applications must be named is that a single ColdFusion server often hosts many different applications. To prevent applications from reading and writing each other's client variables, a name is used to separate them. Because I named my application forta.com, only client variables set within the forta.com application will be visible to me. Similarly, any other applications will not have access to my variables.

To turn on client variables, the attribute CLIENTMANAGEMENT must be set to YES (as seen previously).

Be careful when naming your applications. If the name is too generic, another application might have the same name, and then your client variables will be shared.

The opposite is true too. Make sure that you don't use different names for the same application, or the client variables will not be shared properly.

So where do you put this <CFAPPLICATION> tag? It has to go inside every page in your application. If it is not present in one page, that page will not have access to the client variables.

And obviously, putting that tag in every page is both tedious and highly error prone. Fortunately there is a better way. Remember the hour on includes (Hour 4, "Creating

Your First ColdFusion Page")? You will recall that the <CFINCLUDE> tag allows you to include one ColdFusion Express page from within another. ColdFusion Express supports another type of include, one that is included automatically without having to use the <CFINCLUDE> tag. This is called the *application framework* file, a special file which, if present, is automatically included at the very top of your page.

This file must be named APPLICATION.CFM, and we'll look at it in greater detail in Hour 20, "Securing Your ColdFusion Pages." For now, it'll suffice to say that as this file is automatically included if present, it is an ideal place to turn on client variables.

Working with Client Variables

When client variables are turned on, using them is even easier than cookies. Like regular variables, client variables are set with the standard <CFSET> and <CFPARAM> tags. And like all other variable types, they can be accessed as regular variables: They just need the CLIENT prefix.

To Do: Use Client Variables

▼ To Do

In the next hour, we'll create a login system to secure administration of the guest book application. For now we'll create a simple login screen. (It won't actually secure anything yet: It won't even perform real authentication for now. We'll add that in the next hour.) What is special about this form is that it'll remember the username when you come back to the form again. (It does not remember passwords though; that would be highly insecure.) Here are the steps to follow:

1. Open HomeSite (if it is not already open), select the hour19 directory, and open a new blank document.

2. Type the following code into the new page (of course you can use your own name instead of mine):

   ```
   <CFAPPLICATION NAME="forta.com" CLIENTMANAGEMENT="Yes">
   ```

3. Save the file as **application.cfm**.

4. Open another blank document, and type the code from Listing 19.2.

LISTING 19.2   login.cfm

```
1: <HTML>
2: <HEAD>
3: <TITLE>Login</TITLE>
4: </HEAD>
5:
6: <BODY>
7:
```

▼

19

LISTING 19.2   continued

```
 8: <!--- Initialize client variable --->
 9: <CFPARAM NAME="CLIENT.username" DEFAULT="">
10:
11: <!--- Login form, populate username with client variable --->
12: <CFOUTPUT>
13: <FORM ACTION="authenticate.cfm" METHOD="post">
14: <TABLE BORDER="1">
15: <TR>
16: <TD>Login Name:</TD>
17: <TD><INPUT TYPE="text" NAME="username" VALUE="#CLIENT.username#">
    ➥</TD>
18: </TR>
19: <TR>
20: <TD>Password:</TD>
21: <TD><INPUT TYPE="password" NAME="password"></TD>
22: </TR>
23: <TR>
24: <TD COLSPAN="2" ALIGN="center">
25: <INPUT TYPE="submit" VALUE="Login">
26: </TD>
27: </TR>
28: </TABLE>
29: </FORM>
30: </CFOUTPUT>
31:
32: </BODY>
33<: /HTML>
```

5. Save the file as **login.cfm**.

6. To test the page go to http://localhost/learncfe/hour19/login.cfm. You should see a login screen like the one shown in Figure 19.2.

Don't submit the form yet; you'll get an error because we have yet to create the ACTION page. But before we do that, let's quickly look at the files we just created.

The APPLICATION.CFM file turns on client variable management as explained above. Because this file is always automatically included (and always processed first), it'll be processed when login.cfm is requested.

File login.cfm contains a simple login form in an HTML table. There are just two lines of code of special interest here. The <INPUT> field for username uses the VALUE attribute to populate the form field with a username—if one exists—as follows:

```
<INPUT TYPE="text" NAME="username" VALUE="#CLIENT.username#">
```

FIGURE 19.2

Client variables should always have default values so that your code does not break if the variable does not exist.

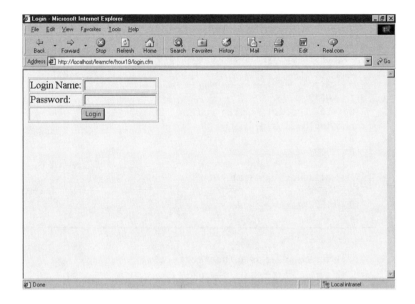

`CLIENT.username` will contain the previously specified username, if there was one. But what if there wasn't one because this is the first time the form is requested? To solve this problem, the following line of code appears above the form on line 9:

```
<CFPARAM NAME="CLIENT.username" DEFAULT="">
```

This `<CFPARAM>` call initializes the `CLIENT.username` variable if it does not exist. It sets the variable to `""` (an empty string) so that it can safely be used even if it has not previously been set. As soon as this line is processed, that client variable exists. (If you were to refresh the page, you'd actually be using the previously saved client variable, even though the form would look the same.)

To Do: Save Client Variables

The form in login.cfm submits form fields to authenticate.cfm, so we'll create that file next. Here are the steps to follow:

1. Open HomeSite (if it is not already open), select the hour19 directory, and open a new blank document.

2. Type the code from Listing 19.3 into the new page.

19

Listing 19.3 authenticate.cfm

```
 1: <!--- Save user name --->
 2: <CFSET CLIENT.username=FORM.username>
 3:
 4: <HTML>
 5: <HEAD>
 6: <TITLE>Login</TITLE>
 7: </HEAD>
 8:
 9: <BODY>
10:
11: <H1>Access granted!</H1>
12:
13: </BODY>
14: </HTML>
```

3. Save the file as **authenticate.cfm**.

4. Do not execute this file directly. Instead, go to
   http://localhost/learncfe/hour19/login.cfm and fill in the form. (Any username and password will do for now.)

5. Now go back to http://localhost/learncfe/hour19/login.cfm and refresh the
   page. The username you specified last time will be prefilled in the username field
   for you as seen in Figure 19.3.

Figure 19.3

Client variables can be used to prefill form fields.

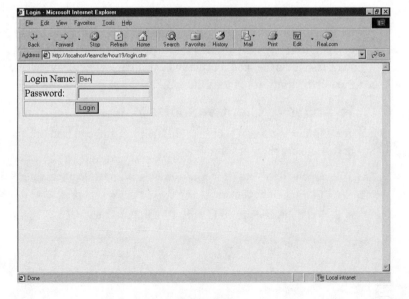

▼ Let's take a look at authenticate.cfm. The code here does not do any actual authentication yet. (We'll add that in the next hour.) For now it always says Access granted!.

The interesting line of code is the one at the top of the page:

```
<CFSET CLIENT.username=FORM.username>
```

This <CFSET> statement saves whatever the user typed in the username field to CLIENT.username so that when the login.cfm page is displayed next, that value can be used to prefill the username field.

That'sall there is to using client variables.

> Client variables cannot contain complex data types like arrays and structures. Client variables can, however, contain lists.

Summary

Personalization is an important part of creating polished Web applications. In this hour, you learned what personalization is and why implementing personalization on the Web requires special care. You learned how to use cookies and client variables, and how to work with and read and write both. In the next hour, we'll build a security system based on the techniques you learned here.

Q&A

19

Q Is there a way to delete cookies after they have been set?

A To delete a cookie, simply set it with EXPIRES="NOW". This will expire the cookie immediately, which in effect deletes it.

Q Is there a way to determine if a browser cannot accept cookies (either because the browser does not support cookies or because the user has disabled them)?

A The only way to detect this is by setting a cookie in one page and then checking to see if it was actually set in another. Obviously this is not ideal, which is why client variables are more compelling.

Q If client variables are stored on the server instead of the browser, does this mean that if the server is restarted, all the variables are lost?

A No, not at all. Client variables are written to disk so that even after a restart, they are available. On Windows NT, they are written to the registry.

Workshop

The Workshop contains quiz questions and exercises to help reinforce what you've learned in this hour. If you get stuck, the answers to the quiz questions can be found in Appendix A, "Answers to Quiz."

Quiz

1. What is the primary limitation of cookies?
2. *True or false:* Cookies are a good place to store passwords.
3. *True or false:* Client variables are a good place to store passwords.
4. Why are client variables safe to use if they rely on cookies?

Exercises

1. Go back to the guest book you created in Hour 12, "Collecting Data," and change the code so that users can only fill in the guest book once. Hint: You need to set a cookie after the guest book has been filled in. You can check for the presence of this cookie to determine whether the guest book has been filled in before.
2. Many browsers let you turn on an option that notifies you of every cookie as it is received. Turn this option on and browse some of your favorite Web sites. See if you can work out who is using cookies, and what for.
3. Make a copy of the cookies.cfm file and name it `client.cfm`. Change the code so that it achieves the same result as it does now, but using client variables instead of cookies.

Hour **20**

Securing Your ColdFusion Pages

Any discussion about the Internet and Internet-based applications sooner or later turns to the subject of security. The openness of the Internet, the fact that so many hosts are connected to each other, the sheer amount of data and users online at any time—all of these make security a legitimate concern, and one that you, as a developer, must address. But doing so requires an understanding of the risks and how they can be minimized.

In this hour you'll learn the following:

- What the security risks on the Internet really are
- What access control is
- How to secure your ColdFusion applications

Understanding Security

Security on the Internet is a complicated subject. Or rather, security on the Internet is actually a series of subjects—subjects that often get lumped together in one mass of usually unfounded hysteria.

Before you can address legitimate security concerns, it is important to understand the risks and what you can do about them. And the risks fall into three main categories.

Hacking

Hacking is a generic term that encompasses all sorts of malicious attacks against your servers. The most common forms of hacking include

- Denial of service attacks—Bombarding servers with bogus requests making it impossible for them to respond to legitimate ones
- Content alteration—Changing site content without authorization
- Content theft—Unauthorized access to servers with the purpose of stealing content (financial data, personal user information, and so on)

Hacking is a serious problem, and preventing hacking is a complicated process. There is no way I can cover all there is to know about hacking and hacking prevention in this chapter (there are entire books on the subject). For now, suffice it to say that hacking prevention is *not* an application development concern. The primary tools against hacking involve the use of firewalls, proxy servers, and sophisticated authentication systems. Server administrators must protect their servers against hacking, and then the ColdFusion Express applications running on those servers will be protected automatically, along with any other content on the server.

 For more information on how to secure your sites from hackers, you might want to take a look at *Maximum Security: A Hacker's Guide to Protecting Your Internet Site and Network* (ISBN: 0672313413).

Eavesdropping

Eavesdropping is the most glamorous form of security breach, the kind that makes for great movies and talk show topics. It is also less of a concern than the other security risks, and it's also the easiest one to address.

The word *eavesdropping* means listening in on a conversation to hear information that is probably not supposed to be heard. And eavesdropping on the Internet is very similar. Back in Hour 1, "Understanding ColdFusion Express," I explained that the Internet was one big network, and that data traveled across it in the form of IP packets. If someone were to eavesdrop on an Internet connection, he could steal the data being sent in those packets.

The scenario that most people fear is that they'll type a credit card number into an online form, and someone will steal it while it is in transit between the Web browser and Web server.

Fortunately there is a simple solution to this problem, and once again, it is not an application-level solution. There are technologies (most notably SSL) that can be used to encrypt the data being sent back and forth between browser and server. Encrypted data can still be eavesdropped on, but, as it is encrypted, it'll be useless to the cyberthief. Encryption is installed at the Web-server level, and, if present, any data sent to and from the server can be encrypted. And not just static data—even dynamic content (such as ColdFusion Express content) can be safely encrypted in this way.

Don't misunderstand me. I am not saying there is no real risk of eavesdropping. There is, and encryption should be used where appropriate. But it is important to understand that encryption does not solve all problems. In fact, far more data is stolen by hacking into servers, or by breaking access control (which we'll talk about next), than by eavesdropping. Encryption is important, and your users will expect to see the little key or padlock symbol in their browser telling them that the page is encrypted. But don't assume that after you enable encryption your work is done. It's not; in fact, it's just beginning.

Encryption should be used with care and not overused. Page encryption and decryption takes time, and encrypted data is larger than unencrypted data. Encryption has an impact on performance and should only be used when absolutely necessary.

Unauthorized Access

20

The real risk for Web application developers is unauthorized access. Because Web-based applications often have access to entire databases, it is up to the developers to ensure that users have access to the right data. Consider these examples:

- Secure sites must only allow access to authorized users.
- Online banks and trading sites must ensure that users only access their own accounts and no one else's.

- Intranets often display different sets of options based on the user logged in. Users in different departments might see options applicable to their own departments. Management and administrators might have access to options that most users don't.
- Customers on e-commerce sites can update their own profiles, but no one else's.

The common theme here is that the same application must behave differently based on the logged-in user. This is known as *access control*, and this is very much a Web application developer's concern.

Understanding Authentication

As I just explained, access control is based on user logins. Without the ability to authenticate, users' access control cannot be implemented. There are many forms of access control, and whether you know it or not, you probably use them every day. Typical uses are when

- Your email program prompts you for a password.
- Your ISP requires that you log in.
- Your ATM machine prompts you for an ID number.
- Your phone-based banking asks you for personal information.

All of these are forms of access control, and all are built on a system known as *challenge and response*. You are challenged to prove you are who you say you are, and you respond accordingly. If the response is the one that was expected, you have been authenticated; if not, then not.

Authentication requires that there be a list of users to validate against. One of the simplest types of lists is a database table, like the users tables in the learncfe database. We'll use this one to build our own security system.

Implementing Access Control

Earlier in this book, you created a guest book application that allows visitors to post comments about your site. To demonstrate the use of access control, we'll build a secure administrative interface to this guest book so that you, the system administrator, can remove entries you deem inappropriate.

Creating the Administration Pages

The first thing we need to do is build the administration pages. There are just two pages in this application; guestbook_admin.cfm is the form that prompts for the entries to be deleted, and guestbook_admin_process.cfm performs the deletion.

To Do: Create the Guest Book Administration Page

The guest book administration page displays a list of all the guest book entries, with a check box next to each one. You can check as many check boxes as needed, and then click the Process button to delete the checked entries. Here are the steps needed to create this page:

1. Open HomeSite (if it is not already open) and create a directory called hour20 under the learncfe directory.

2. Open a new blank document.

3. Type the code from Listing 20.1 into the new page.

LISTING 20.1 Guestbook Administration Login Page

```
1: <!--- Retrieve guestbook --->
2: <CFQUERY DATASOURCE="learncfe" NAME="guestbook">
3: SELECT GuestBook_ID, GuestName, Email, Comments
4: FROM GuestBook
5: ORDER BY GuestName
6: </CFQUERY>
7:
8: <HTML>
9: <HEAD>
10:  <TITLE>Guestbook Administration</TITLE>
11: </HEAD>
12:
13: <BODY>
14:
15: <!--- Create form --->
16: <FORM ACTION="guestbook_admin_process.cfm" METHOD="post">
17:
18: <TABLE>
19:
20: <TR>
21:  <TH COLSPAN="2">
22:   Check the entries to be deleted, and then click the Process
button
23:  </TH>
24: </TR>
25:
26: <!--- Display entries --->
```

20

▼

LISTING 20.1   continued

```
27: <CFOUTPUT QUERY="guestbook">
28: <TR>
29:  <TD><INPUT TYPE="checkbox" NAME="GuestBook_ID" VALUE="#GuestBook_ID#"></TD>
30:  <TD><A HREF="mailto:#Email#">#GuestName#</A><BR>#Comments#</TD>
31: </TR>
32: </CFOUTPUT>
33:
34: <!--- Submit button --->
35: <TR>
36:  <TH COLSPAN="2"><INPUT TYPE="submit" VALUE="Process"></TH>
37: </TR>
38:
39: </TABLE>
40:
41: </FORM>
42:
43: </BODY>
44: </HTML>
```

4. Save this file as **guestbook_admin.cfm** in the hour20 directory.

5. Open your Web browser and go to `http://localhost/learncfe/hour20/guestbook_admin.cfm`. You should see a screen similar to the one shown in Figure 20.1.

FIGURE 20.1

The guest book administration page is used to delete guest book entries.

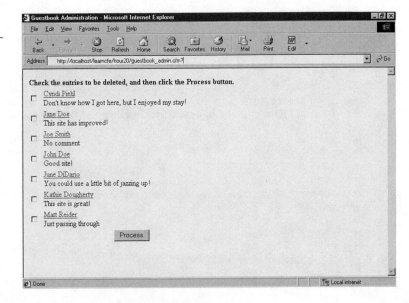

▲

Let's take a quick look at the code in guestbook_admin.cfm. The code starts with a simple SQL query, which retrieves all the rows from the GuestBook table. Then it creates the page head and body using standard HTML. The page body contains a form, which is used to allow guest book entry selection. The form contains a table with one table row for each guest book entry. Each row contains two cells, the left cell contains a check box and the right cell displays the guest book entry itself. Let's take a better look at the check box code:

```
<INPUT TYPE="checkbox" NAME="GuestBook_ID" VALUE="#GuestBook_ID#">
```

This <INPUT> tag creates a check box named GuestBook_ID (which is the name of the GuestBook table's primary key). And every check box, regardless of how many there are, all have that same name.

So how does ColdFusion Express know which entries you want to delete if the field names are all the same? Take a look at the VALUE attribute. The check box VALUE attribute is dynamically populated, so for the first entry the <INPUT> might be

```
<INPUT TYPE="checkbox" NAME="GuestBook_ID" VALUE="1">
```

When HTML forms contain multiple elements with the same name, results are returned to ColdFusion Express as a single comma delimited list. So if you checked entries 1, 17, and 43, the GuestBook_ID value would appear in ColdFusion Express as 1,17,43. That format is very useful as you'll see in a moment.

It is worth noting that when *no* check boxes are checked, you'll not end up with an empty variable. Rather, you'll end up with no variable at all. This is the way check boxes (and radio buttons) behave in HTML.

To Do: Create the Guest Book Administration Processing Page

The guestbook_admin.cfm page creates a form that allows you to select entries to delete. The actual deletion is handled by the <FORM> ACTION page, guestbook_admin_process.cfm. Here are the steps needed to create this page:

1. Open a new blank document.

2. Type the code from Listing 20.2 in to the new page.

▼ To Do

20

LISTING 20.2 Guestbook Deletion Code

```
 1: <!--- Make sure GuestBook_ID is present --->
 2: <CFIF NOT IsDefined("FORM.GuestBook_ID")>
 3:  <CFLOCATION URL="guestbook_admin.cfm">
 4: </CFIF>
 5:
 6: <!--- Make sure GuestBook_ID is not empty --->
 7: <CFIF FORM.GuestBook_ID IS "">
 8:  <CFLOCATION URL="guestbook_admin.cfm">
 9: </CFIF>
10:
11: <!--- Delete the entries --->
12: <CFQUERY DATASOURCE="learncfe">
13: DELETE FROM GuestBook
14: WHERE GuestBook_ID IN (#FORM.GuestBook_ID#)
15: </CFQUERY>
16:
17: <!--- ANd redisplay the guestbook admin page --->
18: <CFLOCATION URL="guestbook_admin.cfm">
```

3. Save this file as **guestbook_admin_process.cfm** in the hour20 directory.

4. Open your Web browser and go to http://localhost/learncfe/hour20/ guestbook_admin.cfm. Select one or more guest book entries and click the Process button. The entries will be deleted, and the guestbook_admin.cfm page will reflect the changes made.

The code in page guestbook_admin_process.cfm is pretty simple. First, it uses an IsDefined() statement to make sure a form field named GuestBook_ID was passed. If not there will be nothing to delete, so the user is redirected back to the guestbook_admin.cfm page automatically. The same thing happens if GuestBook_ID exists but is empty.

Next, the <CFQUERY> tag performs the deletion. The SQL DELETE statement allows you to specify the rows to delete in a special format in the WHERE clause. What is that format? It's a comma-delimited list. So if entries 1, 7, and 43 were checked, the generated DELETE statement would be

```
DELETE FROM GuestBook
WHERE GuestBook_ID IN (1,7,43)
```

> Now you see why a comma-delimited variable, created by having multiple HTML form fields with the same name, is so useful. Because SQL uses this same comma-delimited format for a list of values, creating sophisticated data-driven SQL statements is a pretty simple process.

After the rows have been deleted, the user is redirected back to guestbook_admin.cfm.

Securing the Administration Application

You now have a working administrative application. You now also have a security hole. After all, anyone who knows the URL to this page will be able to delete entries out of your guest book.

In order to secure an application, you need to determine if a user is authorized to access the pages in it. The best way to do this is to set a variable that can be checked on each request. And as you will recall from Hour 19, "Personalizing Your Web Site," ColdFusion does allow you to create variables that persist from one request to the next using CLIENT variables.

So here's how the process works:

1. A CLIENT variable is created to store the name of the logged-in user (after the user logs in).

2. Each time a page is requested, that variable is checked. If it contains the name of a logged-in user, the page request will be processed. If the variable is empty (as it will be initially), the user is redirected to a login screen.

3. The login screen prompts the user for a login name and password, which are submitted to an authentication page.

4. The authentication page compares the specified login information to the user database. If the login is valid, the user ID is stored in the CLIENT variable. If not, the login screen is redisplayed.

5. This process is repeated on every request. Of course, when the CLIENT variable contains a valid user ID, it'll allow processing.

The key to making this work is to be able to check the CLIENT variable on each and every request. How can that be done? In Hour 19, I explained that the application.cfm file, if present, is always included automatically and processed first. This is, therefore, the perfect place to perform the security check.

20

To Do: Implement Security Checking

The first thing we need to do is create an application.cfm file to perform the security check. Here are the steps to follow:

1. Open a new blank document.

2. Type the following code in to the new page:

```
<!--- Enable client variable --->
<CFAPPLICATION CLIENTMANAGEMENT="Yes" NAME="SiteAdmin">

<!--- Initialize logged_in variable --->
<CFPARAM NAME="CLIENT.logged_in" DEFAULT="">

<!--- If not logged in, force login --->
<CFIF CLIENT.logged_in IS "">
 <CFLOCATION URL="login/login.cfm">
</CFIF>
```

3. Save this file as application.cfm in the hour20 directory. Do not try to run any code yet; you'll generate an error if you do so.

The code here first enables client state management. As explained in Hour 19, this is required to use CLIENT variables. Next a variable named CLIENT.logged_in is initialized. This is the variable that will contain the name of the logged-in user, if there is one. And finally a <CFIF> statement is used to check the contents of CLIENT.logged_in. If it is empty, the user is redirected to a login page (which we have yet to create). Otherwise, processing will continue

To Do: Implement Login Prompting

Now for the fun part, the authentication system. The application.cfm that we just created redirects users to a page called login.cfm in a subdirectory of hour 20 called login. First we'll create the application.cfm and login.cfm pages. Here are the steps to follow:

1. Create a subdirectory in the hour20 directory and name it login. Make sure this is the selected directory in HomeSite.

2. Open a new blank document.

3. Type the following code in to the new page:

```
<!--- Enable client variable --->
<CFAPPLICATION CLIENTMANAGEMENT="Yes" NAME="SiteAdmin">

<!--- Initialize logged_in variable --->
<CFPARAM NAME="CLIENT.logged_in" DEFAULT="">
```

▼   4. Save this file as application.cfm in the login directory (I'll explain why we need this file in a moment).

   5. Open another blank document, and type the code from Listing 20.3 in to the new page.

LISTING 20.3   Administration Login Page

```
 1: <HTML>
 2: <HEAD>
 3:   <TITLE>Login</TITLE>
 4: </HEAD>
 5:
 6: <BODY>
 7:
 8: <CENTER>
 9:
10: <!--- Login form --->
11: <FORM ACTION="authenticate.cfm" METHOD="post">
12: <TABLE BORDER="1">
13:  <TR>
14:   <TH COLSPAN="2">
15:    This is a secure page, please login to continue.
16:   </TH>
17:  </TR>
18:  <TR>
19:   <TD>Login Name:</TD>
20:   <TD><INPUT TYPE="text" NAME="UserID"></TD>
21:  </TR>
22:  <TR>
23:   <TD>Password:</TD>
24:   <TD><INPUT TYPE="password" NAME="UserPassword"></TD>
25:  </TR>
26:  <TR>
27:   <TD COLSPAN="2" ALIGN="center"><INPUT TYPE="submit" VALUE="Login"></TD>
28:  </TR>
29: </TABLE>
30: </FORM>
31:
32: </CENTER>
33:
34: </BODY>
35: </HTML>
```

20

   6. Save this file as **login.cfm** in the login directory.

   7. Now open your browser and go to http://localhost/learncfe/hour20/ guestbook_admin.cfm. You should see a login page like the one shown in
▼   Figure 20.2.

FIGURE 20.2
Users are redirected to the login page automatically if needed.

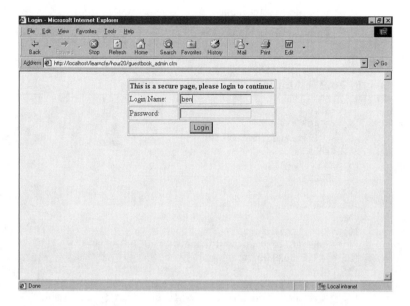

The login.cfm code is pretty simple (and very similar to the example in the last hour). It is straight HTML, and creates a form that prompts for two fields, `UserID` and `UserPassword`. This is the file that the application.cfm in the hour20 directory redirects users to if they are not logged in.

But why did we need an application.cfm file here? ColdFusion Express handles application.cfm files in a special way. Every time you request a ColdFusion page, ColdFusion Express looks for an application.cfm file in this order:

- If an application.cfm exists in the current directory, then it is used.
- If no application.cfm exists, ColdFusion Express will look in the directory above the current directory, and then the directory above that, and so on, until it finds one (or until there are no more directories).

Only one application.cfm is ever processed. If there are multiple application.cfm files in the directory tree, only the nearest one will be used.

So if we had not put an application.cfm in the login directory, the application.cfm file in the directory above it (the hour20 directory) would have been used automatically. And why would that have been a problem? Well, walk through the processing. The application.cfm checks to see if a user is logged in or not, and, if not, sends the user to the login directory. Requests to that directory would once again cause that same application.cfm to be processed, and so once again the user would be redirected. And then again. And again. And ..., you get the idea. You'd end up in an endless loop with every request being redirected over and over to the same place.

And so the solution is to put an application.cfm in the login directory. This application.cfm is the same as the one in the hour20 directory, except for the fact that it does not do any redirection (and does not even have the <CFIF> statement in it).

> If you have multiple application.cfm files for the same application, and need to share CLIENT variables among them, make sure the application name (specified in the <CFAPPLICATION> tag) is identical. If the names do not match, the CLIENT variables will not be shared.

To Do: Implement Authentication

▼ To Do

The final piece in the puzzle is the authentication itself. File login.cfm contains a form, the ACTION page authenticate.cfm. This page does the actual authentication and stores the CLIENT.logged_in variable, too. Here are the steps to follow:

1. Open a new blank document, and type the code from Listing 20.4 into the new page.

LISTING 20.4 Authentication Page

```
1: <!--- Initialize variables --->
2: <CFPARAM NAME="FORM.UserName" DEFAULT="">
3: <CFPARAM NAME="FORM.UserPassword" DEFAULT="">
4:
5: <!--- Authenticate user --->
6: <CFQUERY DATASOURCE="learncfe" NAME="authenticate">
7: SELECT *
8: FROM Users
9: WHERE UserID = '#FORM.UserID#'
10:  AND UserPassword = '#FORM.UserPassword#'
11: </CFQUERY>
12:
13: <!--- Check if authenticated --->
```

20

LISTING 20.4 continued

```
14: <CFIF authenticate.RecordCount IS 1>
15:   <!--- Authenticated, save user name --->
16:   <CFSET CLIENT.logged_in = authenticate.UserID>
17:   <CFLOCATION URL="..\guestbook_admin.cfm">
18: <CFELSE>
19:   <!--- Failed authentication, login again --->
20:   <CFLOCATION URL="login.cfm">
21: </CFIF>
```

2. Save this file as **authenticate.cfm** in the login directory.

3. Now try going to http://localhost/learncfe/hour20/guestbook_admin.cfm once again.

4. When prompted for the login and password, put your own name in the name and password fields, and submit the form. The authentication will fail (you are not a registered user), and the login screen will be redisplayed.

5. This time, log in with the login name of admin, and use cfexpress as the password (the only user actually in the database table). You'll now have access to the guest book administration program.

Let's take a look at the authenticate.cfm code. First the two FORM fields are initialized with default values. This is good programming practice—never assume that fields will be there, even if you know the form will submit them. This way if users somehow get to this page directly (bypassing the form), your code won't break.

Next a SQL query is performed against the users table to retrieve all users whose login name and password were specified. The <CFIF> statement then checks to see how many rows were returned. If 1 was returned, then the username and password must be valid. (Otherwise, no rows would have matched the search criteria.) The user ID is saved to CLIENT.logged_in, and the user is redirected to the guestbook_admin.cfm page (the original destination). If there were no matches (or too many matches, which should never happen), the user is sent back to the login.cfm page to try again.

When the user is logged in (meaning CLIENT.logged_in is not empty), the application.cfm in the hour20 directory will allow unrestricted access to the guest book administration application.

There you have it—a working access control system, all in under 50 lines of code.

Summary

Security on the Internet is important, but even more important is understanding the security risks (as well as the hype) and what to do about them. In this hour, you learned about the major categories of security risk, and how they are addressed. For application developers, the biggest concern is access control, and so you learned how to create an access control system of your own so that you can secure your applications as you see fit.

Q&A

Q The application.cfm file is processed before my page is processed. Is there a file that is processed after my file is processed?

A Yes, there is. The onrequestend.cfm file behaves just like application.cfm, but it is processed after your page is. All the same usage rules apply though (only one is ever processed, and the first one in the directory tree).

Q Is there any way to use my existing user directories with ColdFusion applications?

A That depends on what the user directory is. If you have a list of names in a database, ColdFusion Express will be able to use it. Full-blown directory services (like LDAP, or Windows 2000 Active Directory) are supported in the commercial versions of ColdFusion, but not in ColdFusion Express.

Q Your security system is pretty simple; it either grants access or doesn't. How could you create a more granular access control system?

A You are right—access control is seldom a simple *deny all* or *grant all* proposition. Usually you have different levels of access, and the application behaves differently based on those access levels. The simplest way to do this in ColdFusion Express is to create an additional CLIENT variable to store this information (which will most likely be retrieved from a database). Then you can use <CFIF> statements in your code and conditionally include or exclude parts of your application based on the values in those variables.

20

Workshop

The Workshop contains quiz questions and exercises to help reinforce what you've learned in this hour. If you get stuck, the answers to the quiz questions can be found in Appendix A, "Answers to Quiz."

Quiz

1. What is eavesdropping, and how is it prevented?

2. *True or false:* Access control is a ColdFusion developer's problem.

3. *True or false:* Every directory in a ColdFusion application must have its own application.cfm.

4. Why are CLIENT variables used in an access control system?

Exercises

1. Do you use any Web sites that require that you log in? How are they using access control?

2. Add additional users to the users table, starting with yourself.

3. Add a logout feature to the guest book administration program. Hint: You don't actually have to log out. You just need to make sure CLIENT.logged_in is empty, and then a new login will be required.

HOUR 21

Debugging and Troubleshooting

As much as we'd all like to write perfect code all the time, the sad truth is that problems do occur. And although there can be no substitute for bug-free code, knowing how to detect and troubleshoot problems when they do occur is an important part of the application development process.

In this hour, you'll learn the following:

- What can go wrong
- How to determine what has gone wrong
- How to use the built-in debugging options
- How to debug code
- How to use the ColdFusion Express log files

Understanding What Can Go Wrong

By now you should have discovered that lots of things have to be working properly for your application to run. A ColdFusion Express application typically involves many different applications and systems, and any of them could be the culprit when things start to fail.

So, what can go wrong? And when something does go wrong, how can you tell where the problem lies?

Web Server Problems

For the most part, Web servers just work. When your Web server is installed and working, about the only real problem that could arise is that somehow the Web server stops running. This generally only happens if the server was manually stopped (and not restarted) or somehow crashed (which does occasionally happen).

If your Web server is down, no requests will be responded to. When a page is requested from a Web server that is not running, an error will be displayed (like the one seen in Figure 21.1). Of course, the exact error screen varies from one Web browser to the next.

The solution to this problem is a simple one—restart the Web server, and you'll be back in business.

ColdFusion Express Problems

Like the Web server, ColdFusion Express must be running in order to process ColdFusion requests. If ColdFusion Express is not running, and a ColdFusion page is requested, you'll see an error like the one shown in Figure 21.2.

Again, the solution here is a simple one. Restart ColdFusion (see Hour 2, "Getting Started," for details on how to do this), and you'll be able to process requests once again.

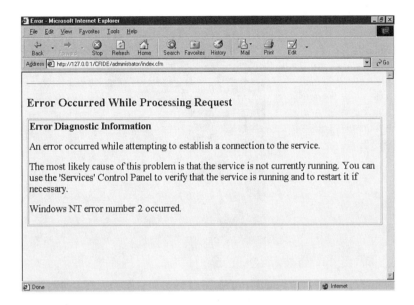

FIGURE 21.2

If ColdFusion Express is not running, the error screen will tell you so.

Database Problems

Most ColdFusion applications rely on databases, and so when database problems occur, most ColdFusion applications fail. And unlike Web server and ColdFusion Express server problems, database problems tend to be more difficult to diagnose and solve.

If you suspect that you are having database-related problems, the following To Do sections suggest some things you should do.

To Do: Verify That the Data Source Is Working

ColdFusion relies on data sources for all database access, and so the first thing to do is to verify that the data source being used is working. Here are the steps to follow:

1. Launch the ColdFusion Administrator (see Hour 2, if you need help with this).
2. Select the ODBC option to display the list of available data sources.
3. Click the Verify link to the right of the data source to be verified.
4. You'll see a screen like the one shown in Figure 21.3, if the data source is working, or like the one shown in Figure 21.4, if it is not.

▼ To Do

21

FIGURE 21.3

Successful ODBC data source verification means that the data source can be used within your applications.

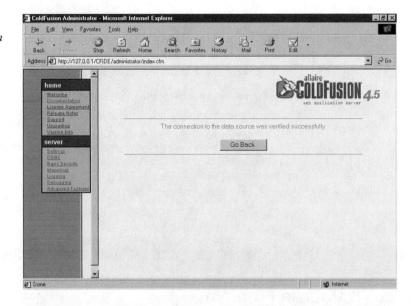

FIGURE 21.4

If data source verification fails, the ColdFusion Administrator will display a list of possible corrective actions.

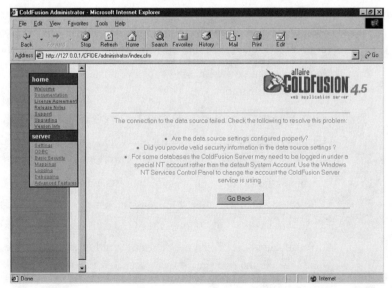

If verification fails you'll need to look at the data source settings to see what is wrong. Generally, if a data source was working and then it suddenly fails, the problem is one of the following:

- Security changes—Login or file permission changes can prevent access to databases.
- Database location changes—If a database file is moved to a new path, all data sources pointing to it will need updating.
- Database is in use—If another application has the same data file open, you might run into problems.
- Database corruption—This is one you hope never happens, but, when it does, you'd better have a good backup handy.

Backing up databases that are in use is not a trivial process. If you are using client/server databases, you should use database-specific backup options. If you are using client databases (such as Microsoft Access), you must make sure the file is not in use during the backup process (or it'll not be backed up properly). One way to do this is to uncheck the Maintain Database Connections check box in the ODBC driver settings screen. But, be warned—unchecking this box will negatively impact database access speed.

The ColdFusion Administrator ODBC page has a Verify All button, which, when pressed, will verify all listed data sources at once.

To Do: Make Sure ColdFusion Can Use the Data Source

After you have verified that the data source is in fact working, the next thing to do is to see if ColdFusion can actually use it. The best way to do this is as follows:

1. Create a new ColdFusion page and put a really simple <CFQUERY> in it, one that you know should work.
2. Execute the page and check for any errors.
3. If an error occurs, try executing the exact same SQL statement from some other application (such as Microsoft Query).

▼ To Do

▼

21

▼   4. If the error occurs in another application, too, you have some form of database or
         ODBC driver corruption. Restarting ColdFusion might help if the latter is the
         cause.

     5. If the error occurs only in ColdFusion, check the spelling, use of ColdFusion vari-
        ables, and use of single and double quotes. Syntactical errors will almost always be
▲   the culprit in this situation.

> There are known problems in some ODBC drivers that can cause gradual
> problems. Browse the knowledge base on the Allaire Web site
> (http://www.allaire.com) for more information on recommended drive
> versions.

Debugging Applications

Thus far we have looked at common system and server-related problems. These are relatively simple problems to solve, but they are also the less common type of problem.

More often than not when you find yourself troubleshooting, you'll be looking for bugs
in your code. Unfortunately, you'll probably find yourself doing this quite often.
Fortunately, ColdFusion Express takes much of the guesswork out of debugging.

Finding Coding Errors

ColdFusion Express is very kind to developers. When coding errors occur, ColdFusion
will display an error page like the one shown in Figure 21.5. The error messages are usually pretty self explanatory, and even list by number the line that an error occurred on,
and the position in the line.

Most ColdFusion coding errors fall into one of the following categories:

- Mismatched tags.
- Misspelled variable names.
- Mismatched quotes or pound signs.
- Misspelled function names. (Misspelled tags will never trigger ColdFusion errors,
  and they'll be ignored anyway.)
- Invalid attributes or parameters (or attribute and parameter values).
- Missing required attributes or parameters.
- Mismatched comments.

Look for any of these, and, more often than not, you'll find your problem.

FIGURE 21.5

ColdFusion displays detailed error messages complete with line numbers and text positions when coding errors occur.

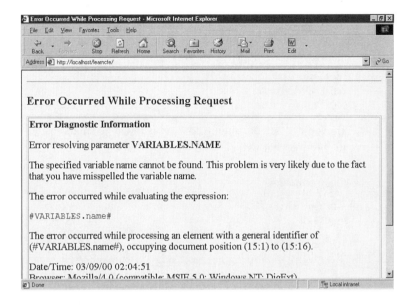

Finding Bugs

Bugs are a little different from coding syntax errors. Bugs usually don't cause errors because buggy code is usually syntactically correct code. What makes it buggy is that it does not work as intended.

ColdFusion Express can't flag buggy code as it can syntax errors—there is no way ColdFusion Express can know what you intended to write. If the code is syntactically correct, ColdFusion Express will execute it.

So, how do you find buggy code? The best way to isolate bugs is to break your code into smaller pieces. By testing your code in small, bite-sized chunks, you can determine exactly what works and what does not.

> You can *comment out* code by wrapping it within <!--- and --->. This way, ColdFusion Express can process just part of a page, allowing you to determine when the page works and when it doesn't.

21

Often bugs are caused by logic errors—invalid conditional statements or faulty expressions. One way to find these is to replace variables with hard-coded values one at a time. By seeing how a block of code behaves with known values and conditions, you can often determine exactly which values and conditions are valid and which are not.

A useful debugging trick is to look at the contents of variables at various points in the page. For example, if you had a counter variable named cnt and wanted to see what its value was, you could do the following:

```
<CFOUTPUT>
<!--Debug: cnt=#cnt# -->
</CFOUTPUT>
```

This code will add debugging comments to the generated page. These will not show up in the browser, but will be visible in the source (which can be seen by using the browser's View Source option). If cnt had a value of 5, the source would contain the following comment:

```
<!--Debug: cnt=5 -->
```

> Another useful technique is to stop processing at various locations in your code until you find exactly where it is failing. You can do this using the <CFABORT> tag, which instructs ColdFusion to abort processing immediately. So, to debug a page, you could perhaps place a <CFABORT> directly above the suspected trouble spot. If the error still occurs, you'll know that the problem is above the <CFABORT> tag and you'll move it up and try again. If it does not occur, you'll know the problem is lower down, and so on.

There are lots of ways to debug your code, but all involve the same basic concepts:

- Test smaller blocks of code first.
- Eliminate as many variables as possible. The less code can change, the easier it is to pinpoint problems.
- Try to learn what happens as your code is processed. The more you know about what is going on within your code at runtime, the more likely you are to find the bug.

Using the Debugging Options

To help you debug your code, ColdFusion can append debug output at the bottom of generated pages (as seen in Figure 21.6).

Debug output is enabled in the Debug Settings page in the ColdFusion Administrator (see Figure 21.7). To enable debug output, simply check the desired options and click the Apply button.

FIGURE 21.6
ColdFusion Express can append optional debug output to the bottom of every page.

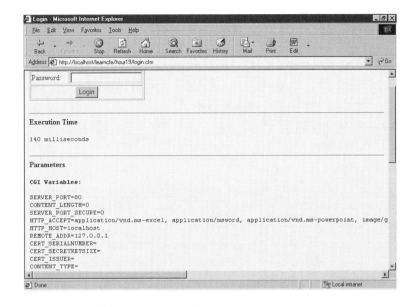

FIGURE 21.7
Debug output is enabled and disabled using the ColdFusion Administrator.

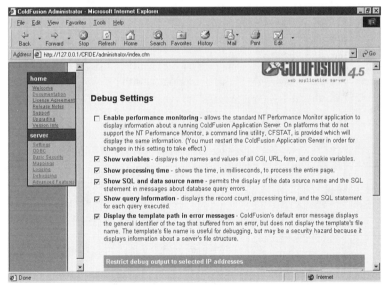

The various debugging options are described in the following sections.

Enable Performance Monitoring

Performance monitoring is not really a debugging option per se. If you have checked the Enable Performance Monitoring check box, ColdFusion will publish real-time statistics

21

to an external monitoring program (Performance Monitor on Windows NT, a utility named cfstat on Linux).

Show Variables

Turn on the Show Variable option to display a list of all CGI, FORM, URL, and COOKIE variables at the bottom of each page.

> Show Variables should always be checked when debugging your code.

Show Processing Time

Turn on the Show Processing Time option to display the amount of time (in milliseconds) that it took to process a page. This option is mostly used in troubleshooting performance related problems.

Show Processing Time—Detail View

The Show Processing Time option has a sub-option—Detail View. This option breaks down the processing time per component and displays the processing time for each one individually.

The only downside with this option (and the reason it is a separate option) is that, unlike the other debugging options, this one requires a ColdFusion restart to take effect.

Show SQL and Data Source Name

This is not really a debugging option; it's an error message option. If a database-related error occurs (for example, if an invalid SQL statement is executed), ColdFusion will display an error message. If you have checked Show SQL and Data Source Name, the error message will contain the data source name and the offending SQL statement. This is invaluable debugging information, but there are security risks associated with publishing this information.

Show Query Information

Turn on this option to display SQL query information in the debug output. You'll see the submitted SQL statement, the number of rows retrieved, and the execution time for each query.

> Show Query Information should always be checked when debugging your code.

Display the Template Path in Error Messages

This, too, is not really a debugging option; it's an error message option. When errors occur ColdFusion displays an error message. If you have checked this option, the error message will contain the path of the ColdFusion file that generated the error. This is invaluable debugging information, but there are security risks associated with publishing this information.

> If enabled, debug output will be displayed at the bottom of every ColdFusion page for every single user. ColdFusion Express lets you restrict debug output so that it is only sent to selected users. Users are selected by their IP addresses, which can be entered in the `Restrict Debug Output to Selected IP Addresses` box. Enter an IP address here and click the Add button to add it to the selected list. If any IP addresses are listed, debug output will only be sent to those addresses.
>
> To send debug output only to yourself (assuming you are running ColdFusion Express locally), you can specify the `localhost` IP address—`127.0.0.1`.

Using the Log Files

Sometimes problems aren't discovered until after the application is up and running. For this reason, it is a good idea to check ColdFusion's log files regularly. These are stored in a directory called Log under the ColdFusion installation directory (which is usually c:\cfusion).

There could be several log files in that directory, but the one you are most interested in is APPLICATION.LOG. This file contains the exact error messages that were sent to users, and reviewing it on a regular basis will let you know what errors users are running into.

The following is one entry from my own APPLICATION.LOG file:

```
"Error","TID=102","03/02/00","22:57:53","127.0.0.1","Mozilla/4.0 (compatible;
➡ MSIE 5.0; Windows NT; DigExt)","Error resolving parameter CLIENT.BEN
➡The client variable BEN does not exist. The cause of this error is very
➡ likely one of the following things:The name of the client variable has
➡been misspelled.The client variable has not yet been created or has
➡timed out.To set default values for client variables you should use the
➡ CFPARAM tag (e.g. &lt;CFPARAM NAME="Client.Color" DEFAULT="Red"&gt;)
➡The error occurred while evaluating the expression: #CLIENT.ben#  The
➡ error occurred while processing an element with a general identifier
➡of (#CLIENT.ben#), occupying document position (13:1) to
➡(13:12).Date/Time: 03/02/00 22:57:53Browser: Mozilla/4.0
➡(compatible; MSIE 5.0; Windows NT; DigExt)Remote Address:
➡ 127.0.0.1Template: C:\InetPub\wwwroot\learncfe\hour19\client.cfm"
```

21

As you can see, this is a comma-delimited record. The first field tells you whether the entry is an `Error` or a `Warning`. Next comes the thread ID (not that interesting), followed by the date and time that the error occurred. Next comes the IP address of the user who generated the error, and the browser identification (useful for detecting browser-specific problems). The final field is the complete error message. (In this example, I was referring to a variable that did not exist, usually indicative of a typo.)

> It's a good idea to schedule regular reviews of the log files. This way you'll know of errors, even when users don't report them. (Most users don't.)

Avoiding Bugs

I started this hour by saying that there is no substitute for writing bug-free code. Yes, it's a noble goal, but it is not an impossible one. Writing bug-free code requires that developers be very disciplined and methodical in their application development, and that involves creating rules and adhering to them.

Here are some of my own ColdFusion application development rules. Feel free to add your own to the list.

- Create small, reusable code blocks, rather than long, unmanageable pages.
- Organize your code, and use indentation to show that organization.
- Use descriptive file and directory names, and don't put your entire application in one big directory.
- Use descriptive variable names (x is not description).
- Don't nest code unnecessarily.
- Never hard-code anything; use shared variables where appropriate.
- Make no assumptions about the existence of variables. Always assign default values or test for their presence before using them.
- Comment your code in detail.
- Test, test, test. (Don't ever assume your code will work.)
- Make sure you have at least two setups, one for development and one for production. Even better, add a third for staging.
- Never make changes on live servers. No change is as minor as you expect, and no change is important enough to risk bringing down working applications.
- Use version control.

Summary

Debugging and troubleshooting are an unfortunate fact of life for us developers. Fortunately, ColdFusion Express provides all sorts of options and features to simplify this process. In this hour, you learned how to determine where problems have occurred and what to do about them. You also learned how to use the debugging and logging features, as well as how to go about finding bugs in your applications. And finally, because an ounce of prevention is worth more than a pound of cure, you also learned how to write code to avoid bugs in the first place.

Q&A

Q Does ColdFusion have an interactive debugger?

A The commercial versions of ColdFusion feature a full-blown interactive debugger (complete with expression viewing, watchpoints, breakpoints, stack traces, and more). This debugger is not available, however, in ColdFusion Express.

Q It's great to be able to read logs to find errors, but is there a way to programmatically respond to errors at runtime?

A This, too, is a feature only available in the commercial versions of ColdFusion. Custom error screens and the programmatic handling of errors are supported in ColdFusion Professional and ColdFusion Enterprise (but not in ColdFusion Express).

Q You mentioned performance monitoring in passing. Where can I find out more about monitoring and improving application performance?

A The next two hours cover application performance and server tuning in detail.

Workshop

The Workshop contains quiz questions and exercises to help reinforce what you've learned in this hour. If you get stuck, the answers to the quiz questions can be found in Appendix A, "Answers to Quiz."

Quiz

1. *True or false*: If ColdFusion Express is not running, a "Server not found" error will be displayed.

2. What is the first thing to do if errors are generated when trying to use a data source?

21

3. *True or false*: Debug output can be used to examine the execution time of each line of code.

4. What kind of information can you learn by examining the APPLICATION.LOG file?

Exercises

1. Experiment with shutting down and restarting your Web server and ColdFusion Express (first one, then the other). What kind of errors do you see when these conditions occur?

2. Look at your APPLICATION.LOG file and see if you can work out what caused any listed errors. (I'd be amazed if you have made it to Hour 21 without generating any errors at all.)

3. Look at my list of development rules. Are there any others you feel should be added to the list?

HOUR **22**

Improving Application Performance

Your applications can never run fast enough. As the size and complexity of your applications grow—the number of users increase, your site attracts greater numbers of visitors, and your application is used more—your application will undoubtedly start to slow down. This is normal and to be expected. There is something you can do about it.

In this hour, you'll learn the following:

- Where most bottlenecks occur
- How to improve database performance
- How to eliminate unnecessary database access
- How to improve the performance of your code

Improving Database Query Performance

I will start with a simple statement, one that I have learned by writing and helping developers with for thousands of different ColdFusion-based applications. More often than not, if your application is performing badly, the problem is at the database level.

Here are some of the most common database problems:

- **Poor database design**—If your underlying tables aren't designed properly, or if you are using large flat data files (instead of relational tables), your application will crawl.
- **Poorly written SQL**—A good working knowledge of SQL is required. Fortunately SQL isn't a complicated language; unfortunately most users learn just the basic statements and don't take the time to master some of the more complex language elements like aggregate functions, joins, and unions. Without these, your SQL operations won't perform as well as they could.
- **Failing to take advantage of database features**—Decent databases support stored procedures, triggers, scheduled events, and more. All of which must be used to fully leverage your database's potential.
- **Inadequate (or missing) indexes**—Indexes can improve the speed of SELECT operations. They can also negatively impact SQL operations. Indexes must be managed and maintained regularly.

When planning your application, you must take time to think through the database design properly. Failing to do so will only create problems for you later, and it is much easier to design a database properly upfront than it is to alter a database (and all the applications that use it) later on.

 Need to brush up on your SQL in a hurry? Then you might want to grab a copy of my book *Sams Teach Yourself SQL in 10 Minutes* (ISBN: 0672316641).

Don't Do the Database's Job

One sin that most beginning ColdFusion developers are guilty of is doing the database's job. Database software systems are complicated pieces of software, designed by massive development teams, and tested and used by hundreds of thousands of developers. It doesn't make sense to write code in ColdFusion (or any other language for that matter) to do something that the database can do already.

Here are some examples of what I mean:

- Don't ever write code to loop through query results to filter data (to find specific rows); the database system will always do a faster job of that than you can if you write your SELECT WHERE clauses properly.

- Don't ever retrieve rows to count them (or to obtain sums or averages). Using aggregate functions, the database system will do the task far quicker and more efficiently.

- Don't write data-entry validation rules yourself; set constraints at the database level. These will execute quicker, and can also be shared with other applications.

- Don't ever query for data that will only be used to pass to another query. If you find yourself doing that, you need a stored procedure.

What these examples have in common is that although you can perform all sorts of data manipulation tasks in your own code, if the task is one that the database can do, it will almost always do it quicker.

The bottom line is to take time to learn your database system and SQL: It will be an investment well worth making.

> If your database supports the use of *stored procedures*, use them. In addition to executing code quicker, they can secure your data, simplify application development, and can significantly shorten application development time.

Eliminate Unnecessary Queries

Database queries are an important part of every application. In fact, there aren't many applications that don't somehow use databases at some level. This is especially true of Web-based applications (like ColdFusion Express applications).

Your application should use databases extensively—data should never be hard-coded in your code—but at the same time, database access has performance costs. And as databases are usually where bottlenecks occur anyway, finding a way to eliminate these unnecessary queries can dramatically improve performance.

So, how can you do this in ColdFusion Express? You will recall (from Hours 19, "Personalizing Your Web Site," and 20, "Securing Your ColdFusion Pages") that ColdFusion features special variable types that persist across requests. We used CLIENT variables in those hours, but there is another variable type that we haven't used yet—APPLICATION variables. Like CLIENT variables, APPLICATION variables persist across requests. Unlike CLIENT variables, APPLICATION variables are visible to *all* users. And because they are shared, any data in them is shared too, even queries.

In other words, by using APPLICATION variables, it becomes possible to execute a query once, and then reuse the retrieved query results over and over. This is a much simpler process than you'd think. All it takes to turn a query into an APPLICATION scope query is inserting the prefix APPLICATION in front of the query name.

> Unlike APPLICATION variables, CLIENT variables cannot be used to store queries (or any data other than simple variables).

To Do: Create a Query That Can Be Reused Over and Over

▲ To Do

One of the tables you have used several times now is the SiteReference table—the table that contains a list of options used when prompting your visitors for how they found your site. Because the contents of that table change infrequently, it's a perfect candidate for saving to the APPLICATION scope. Here are the steps to follow:

> To see exactly what this example does, I recommend that you turn on debugging output. See Hour 21, "Debugging and Troubleshooting," if you need a reminder on how to do this.

1. Open HomeSite (if it isn't already open), and create a directory called hour22 under the learncfe directory.

2. Open a new blank document.

3. Type the following code in to the new page:

LISTING 22.1 application.cfm Code

```
 1: <!--- Name application --->
 2: <CFAPPLICATION NAME="GuestBook">
 3:
 4: <!--- Load site refs if not loaded --->
 5: <CFIF NOT IsDefined("APPLICATION.SiteRef")>
 6:  <CFQUERY DATASOURCE="learncfe" NAME="APPLICATION.SiteRef">
 7:  SELECT SiteRef_Code, SiteRef_Description
 8:  FROM SiteReference
 9:  ORDER BY SiteRef_Description
10:  </CFQUERY>
11: </CFIF>
```

▼

▼ 4. Save this file as **application.cfm** in the hour22 directory.

5. Open a new blank document, and type the following code into the page:

LISTING 22.2 Site Ref Codes

```
 1: <HTML>
 2: <HEAD>
 3:  <TITLE>Site Ref Codes</TITLE>
 4: </HEAD>
 5:
 6: <BODY>
 7:
 8: <UL>
 9: <CFOUTPUT QUERY="APPLICATION.SiteRef">
10:  <LI>#SiteRef_Description#</LI>
11: </CFOUTPUT>
12: </UL>
13:
14: </BODY>
15: </HTML>
```

6. Save this page as **siteref.cfm** in the hour22 directory.

7. Now test the page in your browser by going to
   http://localhost/learncfe/hour22/siteref.cfm. You should see a page like
   the one shown in Figure 22.1.

FIGURE 22.1

*When a query is read
into the APPLICATION
scope, the
APPLICATION prefix is
used.*

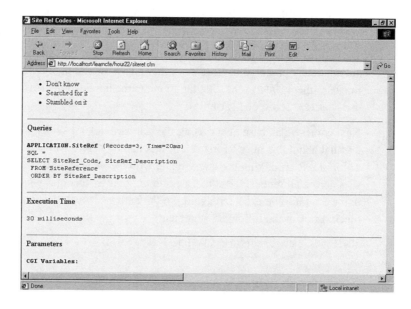

▼

▼   8. Click your browser's refresh button. This time you'll see a page like the one shown
        in Figure 22.2.

FIGURE 22.2

*When a previously cre-
ated query is used, it
won't be displayed in
the debug output.*

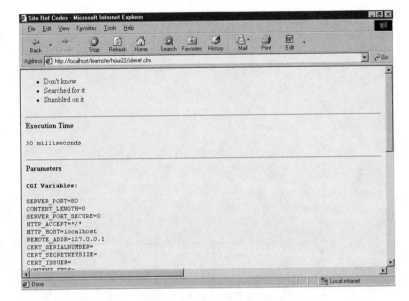

▲

The only difference between Figures 22.1 and 22.2 is the debug output. Figure 22.1
shows that a database query was executed, whereas Figure 22.2 lists no query at all. So
how was ColdFusion Express able to display the query results without executing a
query?

We will take a look at the code in the application.cfm file. You will recall that this file is
automatically processed before any other pages, including our siteref.cfm page. The first
line uses the <CFAPPLICATION> tag to name the application. This is required in order to
use APPLICATION scope variables.

Next comes a database query using the standard <CFQUERY> tag. But there are two things
unusual about this query. First of all, it is named APPLICATION.SiteRef (instead of just
SiteRef). By prefixing the query name with the APPLICATION scope, the query will persists across all requests. But that isn't enough; after this query has been executed, we
don't want it to be executed again. So the entire <CFQUERY> is enclosed within a <CFIF>
block. Look at the following statement:

```
<CFIF NOT IsDefined("APPLICATION.SiteRef")>
```

The IsDefined() function checks to see if a variable exists. IsDefined("APPLICATION.SiteRef") returns TRUE if APPLICATION.SiteRef exists, and FALSE if it doesn't. Using this function, the <CFIF> statement will only execute the <CFQUERY> if APPLICATION.SiteRef doesn't exist. This way, the query will only get executed once, the first time the application.cfm is processed. After that, the <CFIF> statement will prevent it from being executed again.

We now have a single query that, when executed, persists so that it can be used over and over. But how is the query used? Look at the code for siteref.cfm. The only thing unusual here is the query name in the <CFOUTPUT> tag. In order to use a query in the APPLICATION scope, that prefix must be specified. And that query can be used as often and as frequently as needed, without having to reread it from the database.

> When saving APPLICATION scope variables, make sure to always wrap the <CFQUERY> within a <CFIF> block that checks to see whether the query was already saved. If you forget to do this, the query will be re-run on every request (even though it is an APPLICATION scope variable), defeating the entire purpose of this exercise.

Saving queries in APPLICATION variables works well for queries that meet the following requirements:

- They contain static (not dynamically constructed) SQL
- The results change infrequently
- They are used throughout the application

Cache Query Results

Not all queries can be saved to APPLICATION variables. Indeed, queries that don't match the previously listed requirements *should not* be saved that way. For queries and data that are more dynamic (and narrower in scope), ColdFusion Express features another way to eliminate unnecessary database access—query caching.

Let's look at an example. In Hour 15, "Displaying Dynamic Pages," you learned how to create next-n style interfaces. These allow users to browse back and forth through query results one page at a time. As you will recall from the code there, each time a page is displayed, ColdFusion Express retrieves *all* the data. It is the output loop that restricts the data being displayed, but regardless of what is being displayed, *all* rows are being retrieved. If your visitor clicks the previous and next buttons ten times, you've just made ten additional database requests, all for the exact same data, and all using this same query:

```
<CFQUERY NAME="qGetGuestList" DATASOURCE="learncfe">
 SELECT GuestName, Email, GuestBook_ID
 FROM Guestbook;
</CFQUERY>
```

Obviously that is not efficient, and that's where query caching comes into play. Query caching allows you to request that a query be cached for a specific amount of time. When a query has been cached, ColdFusion Express will automatically use it when possible instead of executing the query again.

As if that were not exciting enough; it gets better. Caching queries involves only one minor change to your code.

To Do: Create a Query That Can Be Reused Over and Over

To demonstrate query caching, we'll update the next-n example from Hour 15. Here are the steps to follow:

> If you'd rather not edit the original files, you can copy the appropriate CFM files from the hour15 folder to a new hour22 folder (for this hour's To Dos).

> Again, to see exactly what this example does, I recommend that you turn on debugging output.

1. Select the hour15 folder and open file guest_nextn.cfm.

2. Locate the `<CFQUERY>` tag for the qGetGuestList query, and edit the `<CFQUERY>` line so that it looks like this:
   ```
   <CFQUERY NAME="qGetGuestList" DATASOURCE="learncfe"
   ➥ CACHEDWITHIN="#CreateTimeSpan(0,0,10,0)#">
   ```

3. Save the updated file.

4. Now test the page in your browser by going to http://localhost/learncfe/hour15/guest_nextn.cfm. You should see a page like the one shown in Figure 22.3.

FIGURE 22.3

Debug output doesn't indicate whether a query has been cached.

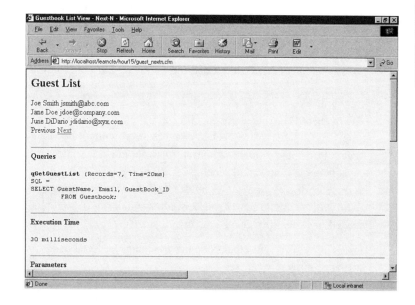

5. Click your browser's refresh button. This time you'll see a page like the one shown in Figure 22.4.

FIGURE 22.4

When a cached query is used, the debug output will so indicate.

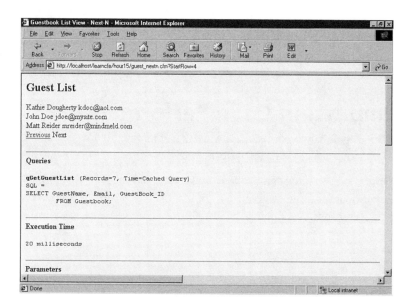

Once again, the only difference between Figures 22.3 and 22.4 is the debug output. Figure 22.3 shows that a database query was executed along with the execution time (in milliseconds). Figure 22.2 lists the query without an execution time. Instead, it says `Cached Query`, telling you that a cached copy was used.

So what changed here? We added the following attribute to the <CFQUERY> tag:

```
CACHEDWITHIN="#CreateTimeSpan(0,0,10,0)#"
```

The CACHEDWITHIN attribute specifies how long to cache the query for (or, how much time since the query was cached can it be used without needing to be reread). The CreateTimeSpan() function is used to create interval values. It takes four parameters; days, hours, minutes, and seconds. CreateTimeSpan(0,0,10,0) creates an interval of 10 minutes (0 days, 0 hours, 10 minutes, and 0 seconds). Using this interval, the cached query will be usable for 10 minutes, after which it will be reread from the database if needed (and possibly cached again).

That's all it takes. No other code has to change. All you need it the CACHEDWITHIN attribute, and you're all set.

It is important to note that requesting query caching doesn't guarantee the query will actually be cached. The ColdFusion Administrator can be used to restrict the maximum number of concurrent cached queries (or to disable this feature altogether), so queries might or might not get cached, and you can't control that. In fact, there is no way to even know whether a query has been cached. All you can determine is if a query was read from the cache (by looking at the debug output).

Improving Code Performance

Optimizing your database activity is important, but it isn't enough. How you write your code can also impact performance.

Code optimization is a lengthy subject, and I cannot cover all the material in a single hour (or in this whole book for that matter). There are some very important points that are worth mentioning.

Reuse, Reuse, Reuse

I introduced you to code reuse in Hour 4, "Creating Your First ColdFusion Page." As I explained, <CFINCLUDE> can be used to break code into smaller, reusable chunks. What does this have to do with performance?

- Smaller blocks of code can be cached more efficiently by the ColdFusion Express server. This in turn improves performance.
- Code designed for reuse can be shared across many applications so that as you fine tune and improve the performance of one application, all applications benefit.
- The very act of writing code with reuse in mind forces developers to write more structured and better organized code.

When all is said and done, there is nothing to lose by writing code for reuse. And at the same time, there's lots to gain.

If and when you upgrade to the full commercial version of ColdFusion, you'll find that it supports an additional form of code reuse—Custom Tags.

Variable Prefixes

As you have learned, there are two ways to refer to many variables—with the appropriate type prefix, and without. For example, to display a FORM variable named first_name, you could use the following code:

```
#FORM.first_name#
```

Or, you could do this:

```
#first_name#
```

This applies to FORM fields, URL parameters, and even local VARIABLES. So, which format do you use? The former will execute a bit quicker because ColdFusion Express will not have to try to determine which variables you are referring to.

There is one downside to using prefixes. If you refer to a variable without a prefix, you won't be limited to a single variable type. (The same code will work with FORM fields and URL parameters, for example.) After you use the prefix, you are limited to just the type specified.

Simplify Your Code

If you find your code difficult to read, chances are ColdFusion Express feels the same way. Here are some rules I'd suggest you try to follow:

- Don't nest code unnecessarily (this is true for <CFIF>, <CFLOOP>, and even <CFOUTPUT>). Nested statements (for example, a <CFIF> within a <CFIF>) take longer to process than statements not nested.
- Don't overuse lists. Arrays and structures are far more efficient—up to three or more times faster than lists. (These data types were covered in Hour 18, "Using Advanced Variable Types.")
- Don't overuse the dynamic expression evaluation functions DE() and Evaluate().
- Enable Strict Attribute Validation (more on this in the next hour) so that ColdFusion Express will force you to write better code.

Cleaner, simpler code will usually also be more efficient code.

Organize Your Code

A closely related subject is that of code organization. ColdFusion Express makes it easy to write applications. It also makes it easy to write applications poorly. The difference between the two usually centers around code organization.

When you write your code, you should have a standard format for all pages. Here's what I like to use (in order):

- Page header—A block of text (in a comment) that contains a description of the file, the date it was created, the developer's name and email address, a list of assumptions or dependencies, and a chronological list of changes made to the file.
- Variable initialization—If you expect URL parameters or FORM fields and want to assign default values, do them all in one place.
- Variable validation—As all your expected variables now exist, this is a good place to perform validation and error checking (aborting processing or redirecting if needed).
- Database queries—All database queries should be grouped together, even if they aren't needed until later in the page. Queries should never appear right in the middle of HTML output (in a FORM for example).
- Output—After all conditional processing is complete, you can start generating output using all the preceding variables and queries.

This format will not work for all files, and you may of course create your own (you don't have to use mine). But however you decide to do it, do it. Standardize on a format that works for you, and adhere to it. It'll make your development life that much simpler.

Monitoring Server Performance

ColdFusion Express provides a mechanism for monitoring server performance. You can use these to monitor queue size, response time, database response time, as well as to try and pinpoint bottlenecks.

> The tools described here are primarily oriented towards system administrators and advanced developers.

To facilitate performance monitoring, the ColdFusion Express server can publish real-time statistics and data. This option must be explicitly enabled in the ColdFusion Administrator (as shown in Figure 22.5). If Enable Performance Monitoring is not turned on, the monitoring tools will not display any information.

FIGURE 22.5

Enable Performance Monitoring must be checked in the ColdFusion Administrator to use the monitoring options.

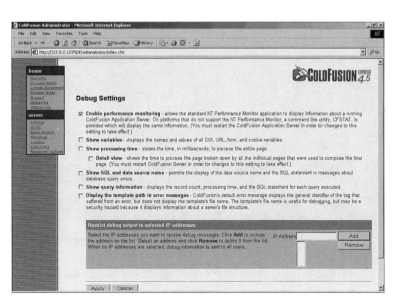

Why must Enable Performance Monitoring be explicitly enabled (as opposed to always being on)? Because there is a performance overhead in collecting and publishing this data. For this reason, do not turn this option on unless you actually need it.

The monitoring tools differ based on the platform being used (Windows or Linux), but the data displayed is the same. Table 22.1 lists the counters that are available for performance monitoring.

TABLE 22.1   Counters

Counter	Description
Avg DB Time (AvgDB Time)	Average database query response time (in milliseconds). The lower this number, the better. A high number indicates database-related problems.
Avg Queue Time (Avg Q Time)	Average request queued time (in milliseconds), or how long requests are queued before they are processed. The lower this number, the better. A high number means that users are experiencing slow page response time.
Avg Req Time (AvgReq Time)	Average request time (in milliseconds), or how long it takes a request to be processed. The lower this number, the better. A high number means that users are experiencing slow page response time.
Bytes In / Sec	Inbound data speed (in seconds). This is used to monitor load.
Bytes Out / Sec	Outbound data speed (in seconds). This is used to monitor load.
Cache Pops / Sec (CP/Sec)	Cache usage counter (in seconds). The higher this number, the better. A low number means that you need to increase the cache size.
DB Hits / Sec (DB/Sec)	Database hits per second. This is used to monitor load.
Page Hits / Sec (Pg/Sec)	Number of page requests per second. This is used to monitor load.
Queued Requests (Reqs Q'ed)	Number of queued requests. The lower this number, the better. A high number means that users are experiencing slow page-response time.
Running Requests (Reqs Run'g)	Number of running requests. This is used to monitor load.
Timed Out Requests (Reqs TO'ed)	Number of timed out requests. The lower this number, the better. (A value of 0 is best.)

Performance Monitoring on Windows

Windows features a Performance Monitoring tool called PerfMon (or Performance Monitor). This utility ships with Windows and is the standard mechanism for performance monitoring on Windows systems.

This option is for Windows NT and Windows 2000 only.

To launch the Performance Monitor for ColdFusion Express, select the ColdFusion Performance Monitor option from the ColdFusion program group. This will display the PerfMon window as shown in Figure 22.6.

FIGURE 22.6

ColdFusion Express for Windows uses the standard PerfMon tool for performance monitoring.

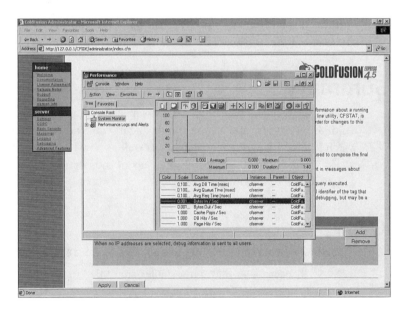

PerfMon displays a real-time graph or histogram showing performance data. You can select any of the counters to display real-time statistics as well as average, high, and low values. Refer to Table 22.1 for a list of the counters and what they contain.

Performance Monitoring on Linux

ColdFusion Express for Linux comes with a utility called cfstat which provides real time status information.

To launch cfstat, execute the command ./cfstat. This will display the status screen as shown in Figure 22.7.

PerfMon displays data in a grid format. Real-time statistics include average, high, and low values. Refer to Table 22.1 for a list of the counters and what they contain.

Summary

With a little care and planning, you can squeeze additional performance out of your ColdFusion Express applications. In this hour, you learned about some of the things to watch for in designing your database, as well as how to avoid unnecessary database access where possible. You also learned about code optimization and organization, and why these are so important.

Q&A

Q Do APPLICATION variables use cookies like CLIENT variables do?

A No, because APPLICATION variables aren't tied to specific clients, there is no need to do any client identification at all. As such, APPLICATION variables always work, regardless of client capabilities and features.

Q I'd like to use query caching, but I need my query to refresh at a fixed time every day instead of at an interval. Can ColdFusion Express do this?

A Instead of using CACHEDWITHIN in your <CFQUERY> tag, use the CACHEDAFTER attribute. This attribute lets you specify a period of time after which the cache will be refreshed. This is very useful when caching data that gets updated in a database at fixed times.

Q **How can I refresh the data in an APPLICATION scope query?**

A APPLICATION variables do time out, and when they do your query will be refreshed automatically the next time it is needed (because it won't exist). To refresh it manually, however, you could temporarily comment out the <CFIF> statement, or load it from another template.

Q **Can I cache queries that are made up of dynamic WHERE clauses (using <CFIF> statements as learned in Hour 14)?**

A Yes, the query caching engine is intelligent enough to distinguish queries that have the same name but differ because of dynamic SQL, and these queries are cached independently of each other. As such, cached queries are perfectly safe to use with dynamic SQL.

Q **I'd like to use standard templates for my code so that they are organized as you suggest above. Can HomeSite help me do this?**

A HomeSite lets you create your own code templates that are perfect for this. Here's what you need to do. Create a page in HomeSite that you'd like to use for your template, and then simply select the Save As Template option from the File menu. Whenever you want to start a new file, select File, New and double-click on your template.

Workshop

The Workshop contains quiz questions and exercises to help reinforce what you've learned in this hour. If you get stuck, the answers to the quiz questions can be found in Appendix A, "Answers to Quiz."

Quiz

1. What is the number one culprit in poorly performing ColdFusion Express applications?

2. How can unnecessary database retrieval be eliminated?

3. *True or false:* Cached queries are best suited for dynamic queries.

4. What is nesting?

Exercises

1. You have used the SiteRef table in several examples thus far. Change all those pages so that they use a single query (in the APPLICATION scope) instead of querying for the data over and over.

2. Open the two pages created in the beginning of this hour, and organize them as explained in Exercise 1.

HOUR 23

Managing the ColdFusion Server

You've seen and used much of ColdFusion Express by now. You've even used parts of the ColdFusion Administrator. It's now time to take a look at parts of the Administrator overlooked thus far.

In this hour, you'll learn the following:

- How to fine-tune server settings
- How to manage basic security
- How to manage logs and error handling

> You've learned how to use several of the ColdFusion Administrator pages in
> prior hours. In this hour, we'll primarily concentrate on the pages that we
> have not used thus far.

Launching the ColdFusion Administrator

The ColdFusion Administrator is a Web-based application. This is important because it
means that you can administer your ColdFusion server from anywhere—all you'll need
is a Web server, Internet access, and the appropriate password.

Launching the Administrator Locally

To launch the ColdFusion Administrator locally—on the computer running
ColdFusion—you can use one of the following URLs:

- `http://localhost/cfide/administrator/index.cfm`
- `http://127.0.0.1/cfide/administrator/index.cfm`

> If you are using ColdFusion Express on Windows, you might also select the
> ColdFusion Administrator menu option from the ColdFusion Express pro-
> gram group (under the Start button). This will launch a Web browser for
> you that will automatically go to the required URL.

Launching the Administrator Remotely

To launch the ColdFusion Administrator remotely, you'll need to know the DNS name or
IP address of the host running ColdFusion Express. This will typically be the same hostname or IP address that you'd use to access Web pages on the server. If you do not know
the hostname or IP address, contact your ISP or network administrator:

- `http://host/cfide/administrator/index.cfm` (replacing *host* with the appropriate hostname)
- `http://ip/cfide/administrator/index.cfm` (replacing *ip* with the appropriate
  IP address)

Logging In to the Administrator

For security reasons, access to the ColdFusion Administrator is password protected. The
default password will be whatever you specified at install time.

Passwords are encrypted and cannot be read. If you forget the password, you won't be able to access the administrator, so don't forget it (or change it to one you won't forget).

When you launch the ColdFusion Administrator, you'll be presented with a login screen, as seen in Figure 23.1. Enter the administrator's password and click the Password button. If the password is correct, you'll be presented with a welcome screen like the one shown in Figure 23.2.

23

FIGURE 23.1

The ColdFusion Express Administrator is password protected to protect against unauthorized access.

FIGURE 23.2

The Welcome page contains useful information as well as links to tutorials and sample applications.

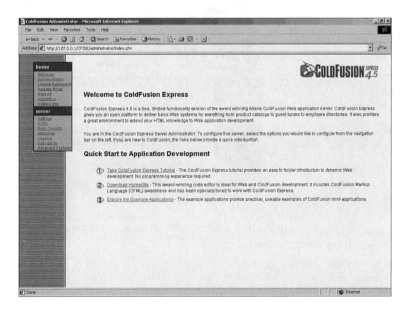

The left side of the Administrator screen contains two sets of menu options. The top set, titled Home, is a list of links to documentation, support, upgrade information, and version information. The latter is useful for you to determine the exact software version you are running in the event that you run into technical difficulties.

The bottom set, titled Server, is a list of links to the six Administrator screens. (The seventh option is a list of features available in ColdFusion Professional and related upgrade information and links.)

Using the Server Settings

The ColdFusion Administrator Server Settings page, seen in Figure 23.3, is used to manage and fine-tune server performance. These options should not be changed frequently, and a good understanding of what they do (and the impact they'll have) should precede changing and manipulating them.

FIGURE 23.3

The Server Settings page is used to manage and fine-tune the ColdFusion Express Administrator server.

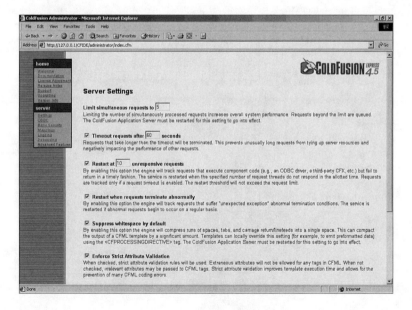

The page is made up of a set of options. After changes are made, you must click the Apply button to save them.

Some options require that the ColdFusion Express server be restarted before the new settings take effect. These are noted in the Administrator. Refer to Hour 2, "Getting Started," for instructions on how to stop and restart ColdFusion Express.

Limit Simultaneous Requests to *n*

ColdFusion Express processes multiple requests at once, and you can specify just how many. Depending on your system hardware, tweaking this value can improve system performance. The Allaire Web site contains knowledge base articles with recommendations on the use of this option. Most users will find that the default value works best.

If there are more requests waiting than allowed concurrently, those extra requests are not ignored. Rather, they sit in a queue until they can be processed (when another process finishes).

Timeout Requests After *n* Seconds

Every once in a while, you'll end up with a page that takes far too long to process. And although this is annoying to whoever requested the page, the bigger problem is that when this occurs the performance of the entire server can suffer.

You can specify a timeout value which instructs ColdFusion Express to terminate any pages that take longer than a specified amount of time to execute. You must also check the check box to enable this option.

Keep the Timeout Requests After option turned on. A good starting point for the timeout interval might be 30 or 60 seconds, depending on how your application performs normally. Obviously, you don't want to set this value too low, or valid requests will be terminated.

Restart After *n* Unresponsive Requests

If too many requests stop responding, you usually need to restart ColdFusion Express so that it'll free up any blocked resources. This option tells ColdFusion Express to restart itself in the event that too many requests stop responding. Of course, when the server restarts, all requests being processed will be lost, as will any data stored in variables.

You can specify the number of requests that must not be responding before a restart occurs. You must also check the check box to enable this option.

> Keep the Restart After option *always* turned on. That way, if a problem occurs, ColdFusion Express can try to fix itself.

Restart When Requests Terminate Abnormally

ColdFusion Express should always process requests methodically and in their entirety, and almost always does. But if for some reason a request is not completed because an internal error occurred, there is a risk that the server will become unstable. If that happens, the safest thing to do is to restart ColdFusion. This option tells ColdFusion Express to restart itself if a pattern of abnormally terminated requests is detected.

> I strongly recommend that you turn the Restart When Requests Terminate Abnormally option on. The only downside here is that restarting ColdFusion Express will cause any requests being processed to be terminated, and any data in memory to be lost. Although that is indeed a risk, the risks involved in running an unstable server are far worse. Plus, this will happen very rarely, if at all.

Suppress Whitespace by Default

As you have no doubt discovered by now, when ColdFusion Express processes the CFML tags in your code, it replaces much of them with empty lines (after all, CFML is processed by ColdFusion, not the browser). These lines, referred to by developers as *whitespace*, can increase the size of the data being sent to the browser. This option instructs ColdFusion Express to attempt to strip as much whitespace as possible from the outbound data to improve data transfer time.

Enable Strict Attribute Validation

ColdFusion validates your code before it executes it, and when errors occur ColdFusion tells you so. ColdFusion Express can be instructed to be far stricter when validating code. This is a good thing; it'll force you to write better code, and the code will execute quicker as well.

I strongly recommend that you turn the Enable Strict Attribute Validation option on, unless you have lots of legacy code that might break under stricter validation.

Using ODBC Data Sources

This screen is used to define and manage ODBC data sources. Refer to Hour 11, "Connecting to a Database," for complete details.

Using Basic Security

The full commercial versions of ColdFusion feature extensive security systems that provide an incredible amount of control over all aspects of ColdFusion (as well as the application you develop).

ColdFusion Express supports just a single security feature, password-protecting the ColdFusion Administrator. The Basic Server Security screen, seen in Figure 23.4, is used to enable or disable ColdFusion Administrator security, as well as to change the password.

FIGURE 23.4

The Basic Server Security screen is used to secure the ColdFusion Administrator.

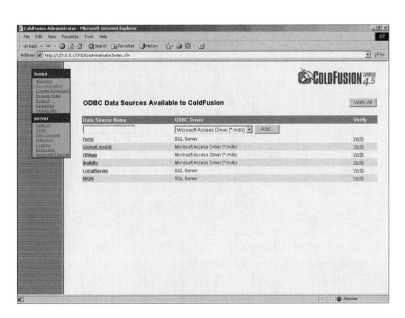

23

Leaving the ColdFusion Administrator unsecured is generally not a good idea. Without security enabled anyone could reconfigure the ColdFusion Express server and, in doing so, could break your applications.

After changes are made to this page, you must click the Apply button to save them.

Using Mappings

The Mappings page, seen in Figure 23.5, is used to define path mappings—sometimes known as *aliases*. A mapping is a mechanism by which you can refer to a path by an alternate name. For example, you might want /images/ to map to the path C:\inetpub\wwwroot\data\current\public\images. This way you can refer to /images/ within your ColdFusion code, and the right path will be used.

FIGURE 23.5

The General Mappings page is used to define aliases, or logical path mappings.

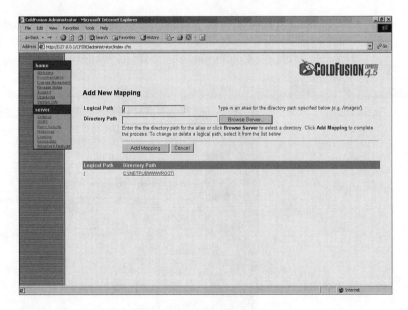

It is important to note that these mappings are ColdFusion mappings, not Web server mappings. They can be used *only* in conjunction with CFML tags, but not with HTML or any other client technology (such as JavaScript).

By default, a single mapping will be present. The alias / will be mapped to your Web server document root. This allows you to refer to that path in tags such as <CFINCLUDE>.

To add a mapping of your own, specify the Logical Path (the alias you want to use), the actual Directory Path, and then click the Add Mapping button.

Using General Error Logging

The General Error Logging page, seen in Figure 23.6, is a miscellaneous collection of options that can be used to help you find and track problems.

FIGURE 23.6

The General Error Logging page is used to configure error handling and logging options.

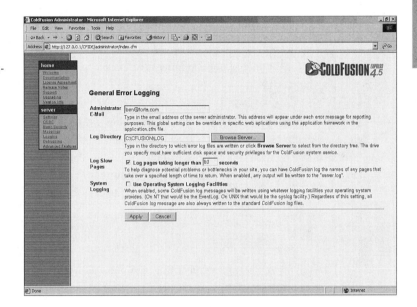

The page is made up of a set of options. After changes are made you must click the Apply button to save them.

Administrator E-Mail

When an error occurs, ColdFusion Express displays an error message. If an email address is specified in the Administrator E-Mail field, ColdFusion Express will display it along with the error message, and will ask the user to send a mail message describing what happened.

Unfortunately, most users don't do this when asked. For the few who do, this option is very useful. The faster you know of problems, the better. Users often find problems before you do.

> During testing you might want to use your address in the Administrator E-Mail field. After the application has been deployed, that address can be changed to a help desk or support department if needed.

Log Directory

We looked at ColdFusion's log files in Hour 21, "Debugging and Troubleshooting." This option lets you specify the location of the ColdFusion log files, should you want to write them elsewhere.

As a rule, I'd recommend not changing this option.

Log Slow Pages

To help diagnose problems after your application has been deployed, ColdFusion can log all pages that take longer than a specified amount of time to execute. If enabled, this information is written to a log file named server.log. You can then check this file regularly to see if any pages routinely take a long time to process. If some pages keep showing up in the log, you'll know where you need to concentrate your optimizing efforts.

If you specify an interval here, you must also check the check box.

> This is a very useful option, and one that should be used on all servers.

System Logging

ColdFusion maintains its own log files. But, if wanted, some log information can be written to the standard system log (for example, Windows NT's EventLog). To enable this option, check the check box.

Using Debug Settings

This screen is used to define and manage the debugging options. Refer to Hour 21 for complete details.

Summary

ColdFusion Express will run using all the default installation options. But for improved performance, you can manage all sorts of options so that the server behaves exactly the way you need. In this hour, you learned what all these options are and what they do.

Q&A

Q I see that ColdFusion can process multiple requests at once. Can it take advantage of multiprocessor systems?

A Yes, ColdFusion Express will automatically detect the presence of multiple processors, and will adapt to take advantage of them properly.

Q Can I specify multiple email addresses in the Administrator E-Mail field?

A No, only one address is allowed. If you'd like messages to be sent to multiple recipients, you should set up a mail group in your mail server, and use that address in this field.

Q Where can I get more information on fine-tuning these settings?

A Allaire has an online knowledge base with articles that explain these options in greater detail than I have done here. Go to `http://www.allaire.com` to access the knowledge base.

Workshop

The Workshop contains quiz questions and exercises to help reinforce what you've learned in this hour. If you get stuck, the answers to the quiz questions can be found in Appendix A.

Quiz

1. Can ColdFusion Express process multiple requests at once?
2. *True or false:* Strict validation slows system performance.
3. *True or false:* The ColdFusion Administrator password can be changed or removed altogether.
4. Which option can you use to help track poorly performing pages?

Exercises

1. If you haven't already done so, turn on the Log Slow Pages option. I'd also recommend that you turn on Strict Attribute Validation.

2. Specify your email address in the General Error Logging page. Then generate an error to see how the address is used.

HOUR **24**

Deploying Your Applications

By now you're a ColdFusion Express expert, and are creating applications of your own. The final step is to deploy your application to a publicly accessible server.

In this hour, you'll learn the following:

- What hosting options are available to you
- How to pick a hosting company
- How and why to use Projects
- How to handle updates to existing applications

Hosting ColdFusion Express Applications

When your application is complete, it needs to be put somewhere publicly accessible. Obviously, if the application is not accessible, it'll not be used, which defeats the point of having created it in the first place.

This is called *application hosting*, and you have two basic choices when it comes to hosting:

- Host the application yourself
- Have a service provider host the application for you

Both are valid options, and both are viable alternatives. To help you determine which will work best for you, here are some points to consider.

Adequate Horsepower

ColdFusion Express can run on almost any computer running Windows or Linux with the appropriate software installed. Indeed, ColdFusion Express is designed to be able to run on very basic hardware, so that application development is simpler and cheaper.

Hosting an application requires higher-end hardware. To efficiently process multiple concurrent requests, to respond to users in a timely fashion, to ensure guaranteed uptime so that the application you worked so hard to develop is always available, for all these reasons and more—selecting the right hardware is very important.

No two applications are the same, and what you'd consider acceptable performance varies just as much. As such, there is no simple formula to determine the ideal hardware configuration, but here are some pointers:

- Memory, lots of memory, is very important. The more memory you have, the better use you can make of caching. (I generally recommend that, if forced to choose between the latest, fastest processor with less memory, and a slower processor with more memory, go for the latter).
- ColdFusion Express is fully capable of leveraging the power of multiple processors (when the underlying operating system supports multiple processors properly).
- ColdFusion applications typically don't need lots of disk storage (your databases might, however). Massive hard drives are not usually necessary; fast hard drives are very beneficial however.
- If you are using a client/server database, the database should go on a dedicated server (optimized for the database software being used).

> The Allaire Web site at http://www.allaire.com contains documents and
> knowledge base articles with configuration recommendations.

Permanent Internet Connections

As explained back in Hour 1, "Understanding ColdFusion Express," the Internet is simply a big network. To be able to connect to a host, that host must obviously be connected
to the network.

This means that Web servers must be connected to the Internet at all times. If you connect to the Internet via a dial-up (modem) connection on an as-needed basis, your Web
server will be inaccessible whenever you are not connected. Hosting Web servers
requires that you have a permanent Internet connection.

This is the primary consideration when deciding whether or not to host your application
yourself. Permanent Internet connections are more expensive than simple dial-up connections, and, if you don't have a permanent connection, you really have no choice but to
host with an ISP.

> A related concern is that of connection speed. Even if you do have a perma-
> nent Internet connection, unless it is a very fast (high-bandwidth) connec-
> tion, you'll still not want to host the application yourself. Remember, every
> user who connects to your site connects via that same connection, so it had
> better be fast enough to handle the anticipated load.

Static IP Address

I explained static and dynamic IP addresses back in Hour 1. Dynamic IP addresses are
fine for hosts to which users do not have to connect. But publicly accessible hosts (such
as Web servers) must use static IP addresses.

Let me put it in different terms. A dynamic IP address is like having a phone number that
changes all the time. If all you do is call others, then that will not present a problem.
But, if others need to call you, they'll never be able to find you because your phone
number will have changed. Dynamic IP address are much the same. And Web servers
really require static IP addresses.

Whether you have a static or dynamic IP address is dependent on your service provider. Many service providers will allocate a range of IP addresses for your use, and you can then pick one to use for your Web server. If your ISP does not offer static IP addresses, then you cannot host public Web servers.

> You will recall that DNS is the mechanism used to allow users to specify host-names instead of IP addresses. If you host your application with an ISP, then DNS management is the ISP's responsibility. However, if you host your own applications, you might have to configure and manage your own DNS servers too.

Picking a Hosting Provider

If you do decide to host with a hosting provider (an ISP, Internet Service Provider, or an ASP, Application Service Provider), your next task is to pick one, and there are lots of them.

Although I cannot make explicit recommendations, here are some pointers to help you pick a hosting provider:

- Decide if you need shared hosting (your application runs on the same server as other applications) or dedicated hosting (you have your own dedicated box). Shared is cheaper, but other running applications could adversely impact your own application. Dedicated is more expensive, but you have total control over the computer on which it runs. Not all hosting companies offer both options.
- Determine what version of ColdFusion you need, and what database you will use. Pick a hosting provider that supports what you plan to use; do not change your application plans to match what a provider offers. The same is true for operating systems, Web servers, and any other software you use.
- Do you need physical access to the servers? If you do, make this very clear upfront. Some providers allow this; others don't.
- Find out what type of access is allowed. Is FTP enough? Do you need Telnet? If you are using the full version of ColdFusion, is RDS (remote development services) supported?
- Ask about support policies. If a server goes down at 3 o'clock in the morning, will there be a way to restart it?
- Do you need a domain setup? What about email accounts? Determine what you need, and find out if there are any additional charges for these services.

These are just some initial issues to consider. I'd encourage you to take your time when picking a provider, think through your application and what services you need, and try to project what future needs might be. And find out all you need upfront, before you sign up.

> Ask potential providers for references. Picking a provider is an important decision, and picking the wrong provider can negatively impact your online presence. The more you know about potential providers, the better.

Using Projects

Web applications, and Web sites for that matter, are typically made up of lots of different files. These might include

- HTML pages
- ColdFusion CFM files
- Images (GIF, JPEG, or others)
- Image maps
- Multimedia files
- Databases

When deploying an application to your server (regardless of whether you host yourself or are hosted by a provider), you must make sure that all the components and files are deployed. If files are missing, links won't work, errors will be displayed, and your entire application might not function properly.

To simplify working with sets of files, HomeSite features Projects. Projects were briefly introduced in Hour 3, "Using HomeSite," but it's worth taking a look at this feature in more detail.

Projects are simply ways to group files together as a single collection. Using Projects, it is possible to open, edit, manipulate, and upload entire sets of files at once. And Projects can contain files, folders (directories), and even folders within folders (subdirectories).

> HomeSite Projects are accessed via the Projects tab on the Resource Tab (if you can't find it, refer to Hour 3).

24

Creating A Project

Projects can be created at any time during the application development process. And HomeSite provides simple wizards to make Project creation very easy.

To Do: Create a Project

We'll create a project to contain all the code you've developed in this book. Here are the steps:

1. Open HomeSite (if it is not already open), and go to the Projects tab in the Resource tab (see Figure 24.1).

FIGURE 24.1

The Project tab is used to open and interact with Projects.

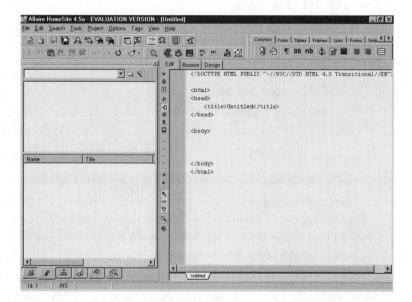

2. Click the New Project button (the one at the top with a picture of a magic wand) to display the New Project dialog (seen in Figure 24.2).

3. Name your project with a distinctive name. (I used learncfe.)

4. Next, specify the root location of the files in the Location field. You can also click the button to the right of the field to select the location by browsing the hard drive (as seen in Figure 24.3). (If you are using default Microsoft Web server settings and called your application root learncfe, the path will be `c:\inetpub\wwwroot\learncfe`).

FIGURE 24.2

Use the New Project wizard for simple Project creation.

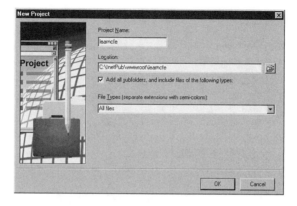

FIGURE 24.3

To prevent types or path errors, select the Project location manually by browsing the hard drive using the Select Directory dialog.

24

5. Make sure the Add All Subfolders check box is checked (refer to Figure 24.2). This way all the directories beneath the learncfe directory will be included as well.

6. You can filter the types of files to include in the Project. Use the default option All Files selected.

7. Click the OK button to create the Project. The new Project will automatically be opened as seen in Figure 24.4.

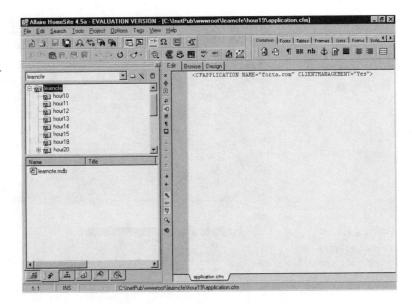

FIGURE 24.4

After they are created, Projects are automatically opened for immediate use.

You can now open and close folders and files as needed.

There is no limit to the number of Projects that you can create in HomeSite.

The bigger projects are, the slower they are to work with, and the longer deployment takes. For this reason many developers like to create multiple projects for the same application. They might create one project that contains the entire application, and other projects that contain parts of the application. This way they have the option of working with (and deploying) entire projects at once, or just parts of a project.

Using Projects

When a Project is open you can manipulate and edit its contents as you would any other files and folders. You can even perform search and replace on entire Projects using the Extended Find and Extended Replace options (both are in the HomeSite Search menu).

Opening Existing Projects

There are several ways to open existing projects:

- Select Open Project from the HomeSite Project menu to locate and open a specific Project.

- To reopen a recently used Project, select Reopen Project from the Project menu and select the desired Project from the displayed list.

- Click the Open Project button on top of the Projects tab. (It's the one with a picture of a folder on it.)

- Select a recently used Project from the drop-down list at the top of the Projects tab.

> Only one Project can be open at any time. If a Project is open, it will automatically be closed if a second Project is opened.

Closing Projects

To close a Project, do one of the following:

- Select Close Project from the Project menu.

- Right-click the Project name (the top-level item) in the Project tab, and select Close Project.

> If Project contents have been changed, you'll be prompted to save the Project when it is being closed. Make sure you answer Yes when prompted, or you'll lose your changes.

Adding Items to Projects

Projects contain all the files that were present when the Project was first created. If you add new files to a folder, or new folders within a folder, by default these will not be added to your Project. Here's how to add new items to a Project:

- In the Projects tab, right-click the folder containing the items to be added and select Add Folder or Add Files to Folder as needed.

- Enable Auto Include to have new items in existing folders automatically added to your Projects.

Auto Include is a very useful feature. If enabled, any files added to specified folders will automatically be added to your Project. To enable Auto Include, right-click a Project folder and select Properties to display the Edit Folder Properties dialog. Then check the Auto Include check box (and specify the types of files to include). You will need to do this for each and every folder in your Project individually.

Removing Items from Projects

Project items can be removed (as long as they are not included with Auto Include enabled). Here's how to remove items from a Project:

- To remove an entire folder, right-click that folder and select Remove Folder.
- To remove a file, right-click that file and select Remove From Project.

Uploading a Project

One of the most useful features of Projects is the capability to upload them to remote servers. Projects can be uploaded in two ways:

- Local Deployment is best suited for when you have local access to the server. If you can connect to (and browse) your server directly from your computer, then you should use this method.
- Remote Deployment must be used when you do not have direct access to the server. This method requires FTP access to the Web server. (You'll need the host-name and login information. Your hosting provider will give you this information).

 To use remote deployment via FTP, you must first define the FTP server in HomeSite. You can do this by selecting the File tab in the Resource tab, and then select Allaire FTP & RDS from the drop-down list at the top of the tab. This will display all available FTP servers. To add an FTP server, right-click the top item and select Add FTP Server. This will display the Configure FTP Server dialog (seen in Figure 24.5), which you must fill in using the information provided by your ISP. After your FTP server has been defined, you can use it in the Files tab as well with Projects.

FIGURE 24.5

HomeSite has integrated support for FTP so that you do not need to use an external FTP client.

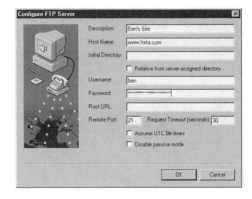

Here are the steps to upload your Project:

1. Click the Deployment Wizard button at the top of the Projects tab to display the Deployment Wizard (as seen in Figure 24.6). You can also select Deployment Wizard from the Project menu.

FIGURE 24.6

The Deployment Wizard can be used to deploy projects directly or to create deployment scripts.

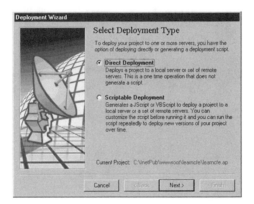

2. HomeSite allows you to deploy your Projects directly, or to use a script (which gives you greater control over the deployment process). You should usually select Direct Deployment. Then click the Next button.

3. Next you'll be prompted for the deployment destination (as seen in Figure 24.7). Select either Local/Network Deployment (to deploy directly) or Remote RDS/FTP Deployment (to deploy via FTP). You can also select any of the four options to further control the upload process. Of particular interest is the Upload Only Newer Files check box which, if checked, ensures that only updated files are uploaded (which can dramatically reduce upload time). When you have made your selections, click the Next button.

FIGURE 24.7

The Deployment Wizard supports a range of options that you can use to control the deployment process.

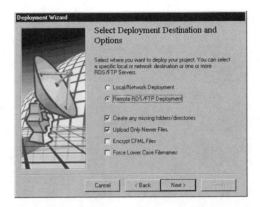

4. If you selected Remote RDS/FTP Deployment, you'll be prompted for the servers to deploy to (as seen in Figure 24.8). You can select as many servers as needed, and HomeSite will deploy the Project to all of them. After you have selected the servers (at least one must be selected), click the Next button.

FIGURE 24.8

You can select one or more FTP servers to deploy your projects to.

5. Click the Finish button to deploy your Project.

You might have noticed the deployment option Encrypt CFML Files (refer to Figure 24.7). This option lets you encode your CFM files so that they cannot easily be read. ColdFusion will still process them just as if they were plain text, but to casual browsers (who might come across your code if they had server access), the files would be unintelligible.

Handling Updates

Applications often need updating. And because Web sites are always live (there is no off-hours time on the Internet), special care must be taken when updating running applications.

- Always test changes thoroughly before deploying them. Development should never occur on production servers, and you should perform all testing on development (and testing) servers before you deploy updates. This will lessen the likelihood of breaking existing applications.

- Make backups of applications before you update them. This way if an error occurs you can roll back to a prior version if needed.

- Although not always possible, try to schedule updates for times when traffic is lowest. Although no two sites are the same, most Webmasters find that the sites are least busy at about 8:00 a.m. GMT (about 3:00 am East Coast U.S. time, midnight West Coast U.S. time, and 9:00 a.m. in most of Europe). Of course, depending on to whom your site appeals, its low-traffic time could be different. Your Web server's log files will help you determine when the low-traffic time is.

- Be very careful when updating databases because they cannot be rolled back as easily. In addition, if you are using a shared file–based database (such as Microsoft Access), you might have to shut down ColdFusion Express during the update so that the file is unlocked. (When ColdFusion has the file open, it'll be locked, and you'll not be able to overwrite it.)

- After you have deployed your updated application, test it for a while to ensure that it is working properly. The fact that it worked on one machine does not mean it'll work on another. Test it and, if there are problems, roll back to the previous version.

These are just some points to consider. And if I have scared you a bit, that's good. Too many developers pay lots of attention to development and not enough to deployment and updates. It's a real shame when good applications fail because extra care was not taken at deployment time. With extra care and planning, your applications can run and run well, which will help you accomplish the goals and objectives that started this project in the first place.

Summary

After you have finished developing your ColdFusion Express application, you'll need to host it somewhere. In this hour, you learned about different hosting options, and how to pick the one that works for you. You also explored Projects and how these can simplify application deployment. And finally, you learned about ongoing application maintenance and the care that this needs.

Q&A

Q **If I write my application using ColdFusion Express, can I host it with a provider that uses the complete commercial version of ColdFusion?**

A Yes, ColdFusion Express is a subset of the full ColdFusion, and any ColdFusion Express code can be executed by the full versions, too. This also presents a great upgrade path for your applications when you are ready for that.

Q **Where can I find a list of ISPs that offer ColdFusion hosting?**

A I host a provider-managed list on my personal ColdFusion site at `http://www.forta.com/cf`.

Q **Hosting seems like a complicated process. Why would I ever want to do it myself?**

A Hosting your own applications is expensive and time consuming, and is therefore not the right option for all developers. The reason that some organizations host their own applications is so that they have more control over them. Be it to have access to servers, to add more servers as needed, to have full control over DNS and email, or to secure application and data properly, the issue is one of control. The only way to completely control your application is to host it yourself. But then again, more Web sites and applications are being hosted by providers or online services than are self-hosted. The choice is yours.

Q **Can I use version control systems for my ColdFusion applications?**

A Version control systems are valuable tools for keeping track of code changes and development groups. HomeSite does not have its own version control system, but it does provide built-in support for popular version control applications (such as Microsoft Visual SourceSafe). Version control in HomeSite is accessed via Projects. See the HomeSite documentation for more details.

Q **Several of the screens used with Projects referred to RDS and FTP. I know what FTP is, but what is RDS?**

A *RDS* stands for *remote development services*, a mechanism used to facilitate remote application development. RDS is not supported in HomeSite or ColdFusion Express. (You need the commercial version of ColdFusion and ColdFusion Studio.) Using RDS you can upload files (just as with FTP) but you can also access SQL query building tools, debuggers, and other utilities and options.

Q Is there a way to prevent ColdFusion Express from locking my database files?

A Yes, there is, but use it with caution. The data source setup screen (in the ColdFusion Express Administrator) has a check box called Maintain Database Connections. If the option is checked (the default behavior), ColdFusion Express will maintain connections between requests so as to improve database access time (connecting to a database is a time-consuming process). This means that the database files will remain open and therefore locked. You can uncheck this option so that ColdFusion will close (and unlock) database files after each and every request, but doing so will impact the performance of all database operations.

Workshop

The Workshop contains quiz questions and exercises to help reinforce what you've learned in this hour. If you get stuck, the answers to the quiz questions can be found in Appendix A, "Answers to Quiz."

24

Quiz

1. Why is a permanent Internet connection needed to host ColdFusion applications?

2. *True or false*: HomeSite does not require the use of external FTP software.

3. What HomeSite feature must you use to be able to deploy entire applications at once?

Exercises

1. You've already created a Project for the entire learncfe directory structure. Now create additional projects for specific parts of the application (specific folders). Make sure each Project is uniquely named.

2. If you are not hosting your own applications, set up an FTP connection using the information provided by your hosting company. Try browsing the connection in the Files tab before you use it to deploy a Project.

APPENDIX **A**

Answers to Quiz

Answers for Hour 1

1. What's the difference between the Internet, intranets, and extranets?

   Who can access them, and where they can be accessed from. Internet sites are usually public, whereas Intranet sites are usually private for a single organization, Extranets are usually private for a distributed group.

2. *True or false*: Every page on the Internet has a unique address.

   True. This is its URL.

3. *True or false*: Every host connected to the Internet has a unique DNS name.

   False. DNS names aren't required, nor must they be unique. IP addresses must be unique, however.

4. Where does ColdFusion Express run: on the host running the Web server or on the host running the Web browser?

   On the Web server.

5. Why is HomeSite the editor of choice for ColdFusion Express development?

   It has built-in support for ColdFusion files and language features.

Answers for Hour 2

1. What platforms are supported by ColdFusion Express?

   Windows (including Windows 98, Windows NT, and Windows 2000) and Linux.

2. What is it that allows ColdFusion Express to be administered from anywhere?

   Web-based administration.

3. *True or false*: ColdFusion Express is a Web server.

   False. ColdFusion Express is an application server, and requires that a separate Web server be installed and running.

4. How can you check that IP is installed and that your Web server is running?

   Ping yourself (or use any other IP-based utility or application).

5. *True or false*: The ColdFusion Administrator must be accessed from the local machine only.

   False. The ColdFusion Administrator can be executed from any browser anywhere.

Answers for Hour 3

1. Why does HomeSite feature an integrated Web browser and support for multiple external browsers as well?

   To simplify the testing of HTML as well as testing on multiple browsers (always a recommended practice).

2. *True or false*: HomeSite's Design mode is a full-featured WYSIWYG design tool.

   False. HomeSite supports some interactive design features, but it is first and foremost a text editor.

3. Which HomeSite feature should be used to create and manage reusable blocks of code?

   Snippets.

4. Which HomeSite feature should be used to manage sets of files that make up a Web site or Web application?

Projects.

Answers for Hour 4

1. How does a Web server know that a page is to be processed by ColdFusion?

By the MIME type (specified by the file extension which will be CFM or CFML for ColdFusion Express).

2. *True or false*: CFML is made up only of tags.

False. CFML also includes a complete set of functions.

3. Why can't ColdFusion pages be viewed with HomeSite's integrated browser?

ColdFusion pages cannot be browsed as is; they must be processed by ColdFusion first.

4. How can aliases (path mappings) be used with `<CFINCLUDE>`?

By registering the aliases in the ColdFusion Administrator.

A

Answers for Hour 5

1. What prefix would you use to designate a variable as a page variable?

You would use the `Variables.` prefix.

2. *True or false*: CFML variables don't need to be initialized before they are used.

False. All variables must be initialized before they are used.

3. How would you describe a literal value?

A value that is taken as it is, without having to be processed or evaluated.

4. *True or false*: The `<CFPARAM>` tag will always create a variable and assign it a default value.

False. The `<CFPARAM>` tag will only create a variable if it doesn't already exist.

Answers for Hour 6

1. Study the following code:

```
<CFIF WeatherForecast IS "GoingToRain">
    Drive to work!
</CFIF>
Walk to work!
```

    A. What message will you see if `WeatherForecast` is `"GoingToRain"`?

        You would see both messages for `"Drive to work!"` and `"Walk to work!"`.

    B. What message will you see if `WeatherForecast` is **not** `"GoingToRain"`?

        You would see the message `"Walk to work!"`.

    C. How would you change this code to work properly?

        For either condition, this statement will display the `"Walk to work!"` message. In order to make this work properly, the `"Walk to work!"` message should be after the `<CFELSE>` tag within the `<CFIF>` and `</CFIF>` tags.

2. What is wrong with the following code?

```
<CFIF Name = "Sue">
```

You cannot use normal operators such as the equal (=) sign within the `<CFIF>` tag. You must use the `IS` operator instead.

Answers for Hour 7

1. What tells ColdFusion that an expression is a function and not a variable?

Functions have parentheses after them.

2. *True or false*: Every function returns a value.

True.

3. *True or false*: Functions must always be enclosed within pound signs.

False. Pound signs are only needed when functions are used within strings; the rules are just like any other variable or expression.

4. Why is HomeSite the editor of choice for ColdFusion Express development?

HomeSite has extensive integrated support for CFML; the language used to write ColdFusion Express applications.

Answers for Hour 8

1. What is the name of the text that appears after a ? in a URL?

The query string.

2. *True or false*: Every URL parameter must be separated by a ?.

False. URL parameters must be separated by ampersands (the & character).

3. Why is missing parameter handling so important when using URL parameters?

Without error checking and handling, any code that depends on the existence of a URL parameter will break if that parameter does not exist.

Answers for Hour 9

1. *True or false*: Form controls must be used in between <FORM> and </FORM> tags.

   True. In order for the form to work properly, all controls must be within the opening <FORM> and closing </FORM> tags.

2. What is the difference between check boxes and radio buttons?

   A check box alone is used to indicate a yes/no or on/off value. Radio buttons are designed to be used in a set of mutually exclusive options.

3. What field type would you use to ask an applicant their gender?

   Usually, radio button options of Male and Female are used to capture this type of information.

4. *True or false*: Check boxes don't generate form variables if they are not checked.

   True. If you do not check a check box on a form, the form variable does not get created and sent to the action page.

Answers for Hour 10

1. *True or false*: To validate a Social Security number, you can use a hidden form field.

   False. ColdFusion does not have server-side validation for Social Security numbers. You would have to code your own test within the action page as custom validation. You might also want to use JavaScript to validate on the client side.

2. What is the difference between the _date and _eurodate validation types?

   The European date format displays dates as day first, month, and then year.

3. *True or false*: Using _float will require the input number to have decimal places in the number.

   True. Using float server-side validation requires the use of a decimal point.

4. What is the difference between client-side and server-side validation?

   Client-side validation is performed by the browser using a scripting language, such as JavaScript. Server-side validation is performed by the ColdFusion Express application server on the server side.

Answers for Hour 11

1. *True or false*: A foreign key is a column or set of columns that uniquely identifies each row in the table.

   False. This defines a primary key.

A

2. Why did the relational database emerge?

   It emerged out of the need to store information in an ordered fashion in order to put data in and get data out effectively, without waste of storage.

3. What is the difference between a relational database and a Relational Database Management System?

   A relational database is a theory of how data should be ordered for efficient storage and retrieval. A Relational Database Management System is the software that was written to support the relational database.

Answers for Hour 12

1. *True or false*: You cannot insert a row into more than one table with one INSERT statement.

   True. An INSERT statement can only insert into one table at a time.

2. *True or false*: The <CFINSERT> tag can be used to insert data, and you don't have the need to use <CFQUERY> and INSERT.

   False. If you wanted to insert data from some source other than a form, like from a text file, you could not use the <CFINSERT> tag.

3. What are the rules about formatting text for insert into a database table column?

   It depends on your database software. But string or text columns should always be surrounded by single quotes. Date values will need to be formatted as the database expects them. The CreateODBCDate() function can be used to format the date correctly for you. Numbers should not be surrounded by quotation marks. Each data type has its own formatting rules, so be sure to look through your database documentation or help files if you experience problems.

Answers for Hour 13

1. *True or false*: The <CFQUERY> tag returns data from the database and displays it on the page.

   False. It only retrieves it, but doesn't display it.

2. How can I print out all rows resulting from a <CFQUERY> tag?

   Use the <CFOUTPUT> tag with the QUERY attribute to loop over all rows to print out.

3. What are some uses for aliasing?

   Aliases help to reduce typing in SQL statements and allows you to rename columns that ColdFusion Express would not be able to use, such as spaces in column names and aggregate functions.

Answers for Hour 14

1. What kind of ColdFusion variable types can you use in constructing SQL statements?

   You can use any type of variable inside a `<CFQUERY>` tag because it will be resolved prior to going to the database.

2. *True or false*: Whitespace is insignificant in SQL statements.

   False.

3. How can you determine how long it took to execute a query?

   Two ways: viewing the debug output and printing out `CFQUERY.ExecutionTime`.

Answers for Hour 15

1. Why is the drill-down interface popular in Web-based applications?

   Because of the nature of database data, it is dynamic and growing. Therefore, you can keep from getting too much data from the database and affecting performance, as well as overwhelming the user with too much information at once.

2. When would you use a next-n style interface?

   When the number of rows that can be returned are unknown, but the user might want to view each resulting row.

3. In what part of the URL are parameters passed?

   In the query string.

4. *True or false*: Frames are not safe to use when performing data drill-down interfaces.

   False.

Answers for Hour 16

1. Which operator would you use to find matches between a list of values and a database column?

   The `IN` operator allows you to search in a list, as in (STU, UNK).

2. *True or false*: A select control can create many form variables.

   False. It creates one variable with a comma-delimited list of values selected.

3. What are the advantages of using code tables for columns?

   If you can control what data goes into a database column, you can more easily search it because you know the possible values.

4. What tag can redirect processing to another page on the server?

The <CFLOCATION> tag can halt processing of one page and redirect the user to another.

Answers for Hour 17

1. What is the difference between using <CFUPDATE> and <CFQUERY> with UPDATE?

The <CFUPDATE> tag can only update using form data, whereas you can use the <CFQUERY> tag with UPDATE for any type of processing.

2. What is the difference between an insert form and an update form?

An insert form is built against a database table in which all fields are generally left blank, whereas the update form should be prefilled with a row of data. Also, the update form must supply the primary key of the row to update in a hidden form control for the action page.

3. Why would you have to use the FORMFIELDS attribute of the <CFUPDATE> tag?

You will have to use this attribute to make sure that ColdFusion Express doesn't try to match up any form controls with a database column that doesn't exist. One such example is the use of a submit button.

4. *True or false*: The DELETE statement always deletes one row in a table.

False. It will delete as many rows as there are matches in the WHERE clause. If there is no WHERE clause, it will delete all rows in the table.

Answers for Hour 18

1. How can you create a list?

Use <CFSET> and assign it a comma-separated (or otherwise delimited) list of values.

2. *True or false*: The following code creates a two-dimensional array:
`<CFSET aTestArray[1][2] = "Foo">`.

False. You must first create an array using the ArrayNew() function.

3. Structure data resemble what part of a database?

They resemble a single table row with related columns.

4. What is the difference in how arrays and structures are referenced?

Arrays are referenced, or indexed, using numbers. Structures are referenced using keys, which can be non-numeric.

Answers for Hour 19

1. What is the primary limitation of cookies?

   Browsers cannot support or accept them.

2. *True or false*: Cookies are a good place to store passwords.

   False. Cookies are inherently insecure and should always be treated as such.

3. *True or false*: Client variables are a good place to store passwords.

   True. Although passwords should not be stored anywhere for too long, putting them in CLIENT variables for use while an application is being used makes sense.

4. Why are client variables safe to use if they rely on cookies?

   Because the cookies are only used to identify the browser, the data is actually on the server.

Answers for Hour 20

1. What is eavesdropping, and how is it prevented?

   Eavesdropping is listening in on a connection to try and steal the data being sent between hosts. Eavesdropping cannot truly be prevented, but the risk can be averted by encrypting transmitted data.

2. *True or false*: Access control is a ColdFusion developer's problem.

   True. Access control is the primary security concern for Web application developers (including ColdFusion Express developers).

3. *True or false*: Every directory in a ColdFusion application must have its own application.cfm.

   False. The application.cfm file is designed to be shared, and so ColdFusion automatically tries to locate it in higher directories if it is not present in the current directory.

4. Why are CLIENT variables used in an access control system?

   CLIENT variables persist across multiple requests and are thus ideally suited to store login information. (Without them, users would have to log in on every request.)

Answers for Hour 21

1. *True or false*: If ColdFusion Express is not running, a "Server not found" error will be displayed.

   False. "Server not found" usually means the Web server is not running.

2. What is the first thing to do if errors are generated when trying to use a data source?

   Verify that the data source is valid and working properly.

3. *True or false*: Debug output can be used to examine the execution time of each line of code.

   False. Debug output can be used to determine the execution time of queries and of an entire page. To determine the execution time of specific lines of code, look at the ColdFusion Express documentation for the GetTickCount() function.

4. What kind of information can you learn by examining the APPLICATION.LOG file?

   Application or syntax errors that occurred at runtime.

Answers for Hour 22

1. What is the number one culprit in poorly performing ColdFusion Express applications?

   The database.

2. How can unnecessary database retrieval be eliminated?

   By saving reusable queries in the APPLICATION scope, and by using cached queries.

3. *True or false*: Cached queries are best suited for dynamic queries.

   True. Because cached queries time out, and because they are dynamic SQL aware, they are very well suited for dynamic SQL statements.

4. What is nesting?

   Calling tags from within tags; for example, a <CFLOOP> within a <CFLOOP>.

Answers for Hour 23

1. Can ColdFusion Express process multiple requests at once?

   Yes, it can. Administrators can specify the exact number of concurrent requests.

2. *True or false*: Strict validation slows system performance.

   False. By being stricter when validating your code, ColdFusion Express can actually process pages far more efficiently.

3. *True or false*: The ColdFusion Administrator password can be changed or removed altogether.

   True. However, removing it altogether is generally not a good idea (unless you were developing on your own machine and no one else could connect to you).

4. Which option can you use to help track poorly performing pages?

   The Log Slow Pages option on the General Error Logging page.

Answers for Hour 24

1. Why is a permanent Internet connection needed to host ColdFusion applications?

   Applications are only accessible when connected to the Internet. If you do not have a permanent connection, your application will be inaccessible when you are not online.

2. *True or false*: HomeSite does not require the use of external FTP software.

   True. HomeSite features an integrated FTP client.

3. What HomeSite feature must you use to be able to deploy entire applications at once?

   Projects.

A

INDEX

ArraySet( ) function, 379
ArraySort( ) function, 380
ArraySum( ) function, 380
ArrayToList( ) function, 374
ASPs (Application Service
  Providers), 468
asterisk symbol (*), 178
attributes
  CACHEDWITHIN
    (queries), 444
  <CFOUTPUT> tag, 317
  <CFPARAM> tag, 114
  <CFQUERY> tag
    Datasource attribute,
      240
    DEBUG, 281
    Name attribute, 241
  CHECKED (radio but-
    tons), 182
  CLIENTMANAGEMENT,
    398
  <FORM> tag, 176
  FORMFIELDS (<CFIN-
    SERT> tag) 249
  NAME (<INPUT> tag),
    178
  TARGET (<A> tag), 312
  WRAP, 185
authenticate.cfm, 402
authentication
  access control, 408
  authentication pages,
    417-418
  implementing, 417-418
  users, 414-418
authoring tools (Web sites),
  21
Auto Indent (HomeSite),
  58-59
autonumber data type, 226
averages, arrays, 380

Avg Q Time counter, 448
AvgDB Time counter, 448
AvgReq Time counter, 448
avoiding bugs, 432

B

<B>/</B> tags, 17
backing up databases, 425
Basic Server Security
  screen, 42, 459
behavior of text fields,
  modifying, 178
BGCOLOR attribute, 17
blocked resources, freeing,
  457
<BODY> tag, 17
Bookmark button, 68
books.cfm code, 88
Boolean values, 149
brackets, square ([ ]), 378
Browse modes and Edit
  modes, toggling between,
  64
Browser Safety Palette,
  136-138
browsers, 14-15
  cookies, 393-394
    default, 397
    deleting, 397
    disabling, 396
    expiration, 396
    limitations, 396-397
    reading and writing,
      394-396
    resetting, 396
    supported, 396
  integrated, 62-64
  Web. See Web browsers
  windows, splitting, 309

bugs
  avoiding, 432
  searching, 427-428
buttons, 187
  Bookmark, 68
  creating, 187
  Deployment Wizard, 475
  Editor toolbar
    Indent, 59
    Show Line Numbers in
      Gutter, 57
    Tag Completion, 56
    Unindent, 59
  HomeSite
    Edit toolbar, 60-61
    Help tab, 67
    Standard toolbar,
      59-60, 69, 72
    Tag Inspector tab,
      68-69
    toolbar, 53-54
    Tools toolbar, 61-62
    View toolbar, 61
  New Project, 470
  Open Project, 473
  Password, 455
  Quick Bar Forms toolbar,
    181
  radio. See radio buttons
  Reset, 187-188
  Submit, 187-188
  syntax, 188
Bytes In / Sec counter, 448
Bytes Out / Sec counter, 448

C

CACHEDWITHIN attribute
  (queries), 444
caching results of queries,
  441-444

F

fallback decisions
  <CFDEFAULTCASE>
    tag, 129
  conditional processing
    (<CFELSE> tag),
    120-121
FALSE values, 125, 127
families, variables, 100-102
**features (HomeSite),
  accessing, 59**
fields
  check box, 181
  form, prefilling, 403
  hidden, form field valida-
    tions, 199-200
  identity fields (SQL
    Server), 226
  <INPUT>, 400
  on/off, 180
  text area, 185
    columns, 185
    creating, 186
    wrapping text, 185
File menu commands
  New, 70
  Save, 72
file servers. *See* **servers**
File Transfer Protocol. *See*
  FTP
files
  application framework,
    399
  application.cfm, 416-417
  APPLICATION.LOG, 431
  authenticate.cfm, 402
  CFM, 85, 476
  extensions for Web pages,
    82
  filtering, 471

HomeSite
  opening, 66, 71-72
  saved, 53
  switching between, 53
index.cfm, 157
linking
  with drag and drop
    method, 160
  manually, 157-159
  with Tag Editors
    (HomeSite), 159
log files, 431-432
  reading, 432
  storing, 462
  system log, 462
login.cfm (creating login
  screen), 399-400
server.log, 462
Files tab (HomeSite), 66
filtering
  data, 256, 285-287, 437
  files, 471
  SELECT statements, 290
filters
  compound logic, 285-287
  conditions, 285
  dummy clauses, 287
  SELECT statements, 256
fixing error 403, 83
flags, 180. *See also* **on/off
  fields**
floating point numbers
  CFML server-side
    validations, 200
  numeric validation, 203
floating toolbars, 62
folders
  application root, 79
  work, 80
footer.cfm code, 90-91
foreign keys, 227

form controls, 177
  naming, 323
  password fields, 178
  text fields, 178-180
  troubleshooting, 180
**form field validations,
  197-203**
  CFML custom validations,
    211, 213
  CFML server-side,
    199-200
    dates, 200
    European dates, 200
    floating point numbers,
      200
    hidden fields, 199-200
    integers, 200
    ranges, 200
    required, 200
    time, 200
  client-side validations
    JavaScript, 213-215
    validation types, com-
      paring, 215-216
  date calculation action
    pages, 209
  date calculation forms,
    207-209
  dates, 204, 206
  HTML hidden form
    controls, adding, 199
  numeric, 203-204
  ranges, 211
  required, 200-203
  time, 209-210
  types, 199
form fields
  creating action pages, 191
  prefilling, 403
form input, validating, 331
form letters, 110-113
<FORM> tag, 176

J-L

This CD-ROM uses long and mixed-case filenames requiring the use of a protected-mode CD-ROM Driver.

Windows 95, Windows 98, Windows NT 4, and Windows 2000 Installation Instructions

1. Insert the CD-ROM into your CD-ROM drive.
2. From the Windows desktop, double-click the "My Computer" icon.
3. Double-click the icon representing your CD-ROM drive.
4. Double-click the icon titled START.EXE to run the installation program.
5. Follow the onscreen instructions to finish the installation.

 If Windows 95, Windows 98, Windows NT 4.0, or Windows 2000 is installed on your computer, and you have the AutoPlay feature enabled, the start.exe program starts automatically whenever you insert the disc into your CD-ROM drive.